SCOTLAND'S SHAME?

Best wishes,

James MacMillan

Gerry P.T. Finn

David Aspinwall

Tom Gallagher

SCO†LAND'S SHAME?
Bigotry and Sectarianism in Modern Scotland

EDITED BY
T.M. DEVINE

MAINSTREAM
PUBLISHING

EDINBURGH AND LONDON

First published in Great Britain in 2000 by
MAINSTREAM PUBLISHING COMPANY (EDINBURGH) LTD
7 Albany Street
Edinburgh EH1 3UG

ISBN 1 84018 330 6   .

A catalogue record for this book is available from the British Library

Typeset in Stone Serif
Printed and bound in Great Britain by Creative Print Design Wales

CONTENTS

This book is concerned with prejudice in modern Scotland. Prejudice can take many forms, perhaps the most obvious of which is racism in today's world. But this collection of essays takes a much narrower focus. It seeks to examine in more detail than ever before considered in a single volume the specific and controversial issue of anti-Catholic bigotry and discrimination in present-day Scotland.

A few decades ago this subject would have caused little disagreement among Scottish commentators. The historical record demonstrates unambiguously that Catholics in Scotland, the vast majority of whom were descended from Irish immigrants, experienced routine discrimination in the labour market. Presbyterianism at that time was not only the religion of most Scots but also a defining element of the national identity of Scotland. Scottish Catholics, around 18 per cent of the population, could easily feel excluded. Their lowly position in the class structure of the nation compounded their sense of being marginalised. As late as the 1920s and 1930s, for instance, the General Assembly of the Church of Scotland waged a relentless campaign against the supposedly malign effects of Irish Catholic immigration which was judged a 'menace' to 'our Scottish nationality'. In the same period, a politicised anti-Catholic movement emerged in the cities of Edinburgh and Glasgow which for a time had considerable success in local elections. For many years afterwards discrimination in the job market was commonly practised against ordinary Catholics.

There has been a pervasive assumption that this was all a long time ago. Historians have argued that discrimination started to crumble in the 1960s and ended in the 1980s with the sudden death of the staple industries of shipbuilding and engineering, where sectarian controls endured longest. Scotland had become a more secular society where religious affiliation and tribal loyalties seemed to matter less and less. Thanks to an expanding higher education system, upward social mobility among Catholics became common and they began to make their mark at the highest level in the professions, the universities, the arts and politics. A formerly despised ethnic group had apparently become fully integrated into the mainstream of Scottish life in the space of two generations. The tribalism demonstrated at Rangers and Celtic football matches could be dismissed as unrepresentative, a nasty hangover from the past, like the Orange marches which now only attracted an underclass whose behaviour was treated with contempt by middle-class Scotland. Increasingly sectarianism became a subject which was not discussed in polite circles.

All that changed in August 1999 when James MacMillan, the country's foremost young composer, gave a lecture on 'Scotland's Shame' at the Edinburgh International Festival. MacMillan did not mince his words.

Scotland in his view was a land of 'sleep-walking bigotry', where 'visceral anti-Catholicism' disfigured the professions, academe, politics and the media. He warned that the latest threat was to Catholic schools, which in his view risked destruction in the wake of devolution and the establishment of a Scottish parliament. MacMillan insisted that the principal teaching union, the Educational Institute of Scotland, heard speeches at its conferences calling for an end to separate Catholic schools and the withdrawal of their state funding. In a chilling sentence he noted that 'The slavering of the mouth at the prospect of the new parliament being involved in this vandalism has become a frightening spectacle for many of us.'

In a sense, even more significant than MacMillan's passionate speech was the unprecedented reaction to it. For weeks Scotland's broadsheets were crammed with letters for and against his forceful opinions. Indeed, some of this correspondence merely served to confirm by its tone and its rhetoric that Scotland was indeed still disfigured by sectarian attitudes. Pandora's box had been opened in spectacular fashion. An issue which had long been swept under the carpet became an obsessive talking-point among the nation's chattering classes and beyond.

This book is a response to this *cause célèbre*. It aims to provide a more considered assessment of the subject than was possible in the media among the furious rhetoric, claims and counterclaims of summer 1999. Contributions have come from some of Scotland's most eminent writers, historians, sociologists and thinkers. Some pieces, particularly in parts one and two, are reflective. Others, especially in part five, provide much-needed academic evidence without which the debate cannot progress. For the first time, the text of James MacMillan's lecture is printed in full. At the end the editor gives his personal view of the controversy, as elucidated in the earlier chapters of the book. MacMillan also looks again at the issues in the light of these contributions.

I am grateful to Bill Campbell of Mainstream Publishing for his enthusiastic support for the project. Jean Fraser and Alexia Grosjean helped to process the material and Professors Steve Bruce and Lindsay Paterson of Aberdeen and Edinburgh Universities first suggested that I edit this book. My thanks for their encouragement and advice.

Tom Devine
Research Institute of Irish and Scottish Studies
King's College
University of Aberdeen

CONTRIBUTORS

Bernard Aspinwall	Senior Research Fellow in Scottish History, University of Strathclyde
Joseph M. Bradley	Lecturer in Sports Studies, University of Stirling
Steve Bruce	Professor of Sociology, University of Aberdeen
Robert Crawford	Professor of Modern Scottish Literature, University of St Andrews
Joseph Devine	Bishop of Motherwell
T.M. Devine, FRSE, FBA	University Research Professor and Director of the Research Institute of Irish and Scottish Studies (RIISS), University of Aberdeen
Gerry P.T. Finn	Reader in the Department of Educational Studies, University of Strathclyde
Tom Gallagher	Professor of European Peace Studies, University of Bradford
John Haldane, FRSE	Professor of Philosophy and Director of the Centre for Philosophy and Public Affairs, University of St Andrews
Peter Lynch	Lecturer in Politics, University of Stirling
David McCrone	Professor of Sociology, University of Edinburgh
James MacMillan	Composer and Visiting Professor, Faculty of Education, University of Strathclyde
Andrew O'Hagan	Author of *Our Fathers* and *The Missing*
Iain R. Paterson	Formerly Research Student, Department of Sociology, University of Aberdeen
Lindsay Paterson	Professor of Educational Policy, University of Edinburgh
Patrick Reilly	Professor Emeritus and formerly Head of the Department of English, University of Glasgow
Michael Rosie	Research Student, Department of Sociology, University of Edinburgh
David Sinclair	Secretary, Church and Nation Committee, General Assembly of the Church of Scotland

Scott C. Styles	Lecturer in Law, University of Aberdeen
Graham Walker	Reader in Politics, Queen's University of Belfast
Patricia Walls	Research Scientist, Religion and Health Programme, MRC Social and Public Health Sciences Unit, University of Glasgow
Rory Williams	Senior Research Scientist MRC Social and Public Health Sciences Unit, University of Glasgow

PART 1

'Scotland is a Divisive, Bigoted Society'

[Andrew O'Hagan]

1. SCOTLAND'S SHAME

James MacMillan

There is a palpable sense of optimism in Scotland at this time. Women and men of goodwill detect that the circumstances are ripe with opportunity and challenge. The arrival of our new devolved parliament, the latest step in the nation's desire to slake its thirst for democracy, seems providential in its timing on the eve of the new millennium. We are fired by a hitherto unparalleled potential to refresh and renew our society in its politics, in its culture and in its soul.

John Haldane, the professor of philosophy and director of the Centre for Philosophy and Public Affairs in the University of St Andrews, wrote an article for the *Catholic Herald* (an English Catholic paper) on the eve of the Scottish parliamentary elections in the spring. In this he expanded on the question of what specific ideals *Catholics* can offer the new Scotland:

> One is the concept of society as a moral community in which responsibilities stand alongside rights, in which material goods are produced with an eye to benefit as well as its quality being promoted. Intellectually and culturally the Catholic contribution should be to challenge materialism, instrumentalism, hedonism and short-term gratification, and to present in Scottish context the central ingredients of the Catholic philosophy of culture: abstract reflection, artistic endeavour and joyous good living.

As a composer I have become increasingly aware of the significance of this Catholic influence and inspiration behind my work – whether in its theology and philosophy, or in its liturgy, or simply in the encultured experience of my own localised upbringing in the west of Scotland. Since childhood I was brought up to deal with reflective and abstract concepts like the metaphorical, the metaphysical and the sacramental. In later life there was a thankfully smooth transition of these concepts from the purely religious sphere to the artistic sphere, although these two things are one and the same thing for me. And in my fruitful engagements with other artists, regardless of their own religious beliefs, I have found these to be common concepts. It is almost as if, on one hand, the adherent of a sacramental religion and, on the other, the artist, although they may speak different 'languages' and to different purposes, nevertheless share a common 'linguistic' root. The Catholic and The Artist, at a fundamental level, can understand each other because the origins of their most precious metaphorical concepts are the same.

For example, the idea of transubstantiation can seem remote, mysterious and irrelevant mumbo jumbo until one analyses a symphony by Beethoven or Maxwell Davies. There before your eyes and ears one can see and hear musical material transforming itself into something other than its original apparent substance. A musical theme metamorphoses from one shape into a heightened version of itself through time and development, or can even change its shape and essence into something completely different, while keeping its core recognisable significance.

And lovers of music claim that their lives are changed through music. Being openly receptive to the transforming power of music is analogous to the patient receptivity to the Divine that is necessary for the religious contemplation at the heart of sacramental religion.

I don't like being too self-analytical but preparing for a talk like this forces you to be. I am sometimes asked if I have an artistic mission as a Scottish composer. If I have a mission I think this must involve acts of remembrance, of recollection, of rediscovery of our past, or re-animation of our heritage, of a reawakening of our culture. There has been a forgetting of our past with the result that modern-day Scotland lacks proper cultural roots. In contrast to England, the received history of our nation seems to be one marked by discontinuities, by breaks with, repudiation, and ultimately denial of the past. The greatest such discontinuity within cultural memory is, of course, the Reformation. 1560 became year zero marking the beginning of a cultural revolution – and one could draw interesting parallels between Mao Tse-tung and John Knox, Pol Pot and Andrew Melville (well, perhaps not). This cultural revolution involved a violent repudiation of art and music from which it could be argued we have not fully recovered. So a Scottish composer like myself is left with only fragments from a broken past. All that we have left from distinctively Scottish music are the remnants of plainsong, such works of the Scottish renaissance as survived the 1560 cultural revolution, Gaelic psalm-singing from the Western Isles, and folksinging from the Lowland peasantry. So, if one is to pick up the pieces and maintain continuity with Scotland's past, contemporary Scottish music could be infused by those disparate fragments of Latin, Gaelic and Scots tradition. And given the history of the religiously inspired conscious destruction and abandonment of our musical heritage, contemporary music is channelled to reflect and express this in violence and turbulence rather than simply harmonic pastoral. As Catholics, we can serve an important cultural role. We are not afraid of pre-1560 Scottish history. We can embrace it because in its Catholicism it chimes in with our own continued cultural expression.

The fact that many in the arts recognise the importance of reconnecting with our past, and the analogies and parallels between sacrament and art that I mentioned earlier, could be why, of all the spheres of public life in Scotland, the world of the arts is one arena where I have never encountered anything approximating the visceral anti-Catholicism which so disfigures many other walks of life in our society.

On my trips abroad or to England I am often asked curious, probing questions about my country, and specifically about the extreme nature of our anti-Catholic past and rumours of a still-prevalent sour anti-Catholicism. This is mainly sparked by the activities of our referees and our sporting bodies, but sometimes it can be about much more. A foreign academic brought it to my attention that the *Collins Encyclopaedia of Scotland* has no entry for the Irish in Scotland or the Catholic Church. Foreign visitors to Edinburgh attended an exhibition a couple of years ago at the Scottish Record Office, recounting the history of immigration to Scotland. Large displays set out the history of the immigration of Flemish weavers, Jewish traders, Italian peasants, Asian shopkeepers, Chinese restaurant owners, black bus conductors, and rightly praised the contribution they had all made to Scottish society. The massive Irish immigration in the nineteenth and early twentieth centuries was dealt with in something like three sentences, as follows:

> In the mid-19th century an increasing number of seasonal Irish farm labourers who worked in the summers in lowland Scotland stayed over due to poor economic conditions in Ireland. Many of them became a burden on the local Parish Poor Laws.

Sometimes people I meet are surprised that there is such a thing as Scottish Catholic – it seems oxymoronic to many. I'm afraid our traditional anti-Catholic phobias and paranoias have gained us infamy abroad. These questions embarrass me and I try to say it's not like that anymore – we have moved on – we are putting sectarianism behind us in the dustbin of history – things have changed for the better. But, deep down, I know this is a response charged with ambiguity. Yes, it's true that for many Scots, religious bigotry does not impinge on their lives, but for a significant minority Catholics continue to be a source of puzzlement if not anxiety, and its concomitant bigotry.

Because of this most Scottish Catholics learn at an early age that the best self-defence mechanism is to keep one's head down. Try not to attract attention to the fact that you are a Catholic – it will only annoy them. In fact I know that most Catholics of an older generation would be appalled at me raising this subject at all at a public forum. I have already had a friendly and well-meaning warning shot across my bows from a journalist in *The Herald*. My grandfather, God rest him, used to become very nervous when he saw the words 'James MacMillan' and 'Catholic' in the same sentence. 'No good will come of it,' he cautioned. 'There's bound to be a backlash – you'll suffer the consequences in the end.' On dining out with my parents recently in Ayr, conversation eventually drifted to the topic of the Christmas mass which they had attended at the cathedral. I noticed that every time the waiter came close to our table they hushed their voices. They did not want to give themselves away as Catholics. I have found myself doing exactly the same thing even in the company of younger co-religionists, in public places. There is still, even today, a palpable sense of some threat and hostility to all things Catholic in this country. Some of these anxieties are a result of a lack of self-confidence among Catholics, some are because of vague and not so vague hints that Catholics are not really full citizens – possibly because some of them support a team associated with Irish rather than Scottish roots.

But the sense of threat and hostility is there and has huge implications for the so-called 'new era' and Scotland's potential to refresh and renew which I mentioned at the beginning. If Scotland is ever to establish a genuinely pluralistic democracy where differences are not just recognised and respected but celebrated, nurtured and absorbed for the greater good, we will first have to clear a seemingly insurmountable hurdle. In many walks of life – in the workplace, in the professions, in academia, in the media, in politics and in sport – anti-Catholicism, even when it is not particularly malign, is as endemic as it is second nature. Scotland is guilty of 'sleep-walking' bigotry, a writer recently claimed. The recent unofficial grassroots letter-writing campaign, organised at parish level within the Church of Scotland and some other churches, against the inter-faith aspect of prayers at the new Edinburgh parliament, is an indication of this. Although multiculturalism and the non-Christian faiths were the main targets of this campaign, *The Scotsman* reported that many of the letters make disparaging remarks about the Roman Catholic faith. I know that many of my friends in the Church of Scotland were as saddened by this development as I was, and it will take more than this to derail the powerful ecumenical activity in which many Protestants and Catholics are now engaged.

But, at the heart of this malaise is a very Scottish trait – a desire to narrow and to restrict the definition of what it means to be Scottish. One letter states 'this country's national religion is Protestant and Presbyterian, and the Scottish Parliament is duty bound to reflect this fact'. This tendency to restrict, to control and to enforce conformity and homogeneity is an obsessive and paranoid flaw in the Scottish character. It is not confined to the Presbyterian mind. It has eased effortlessly into the collective psyche of much secular discourse, so that even the humanist and liberal objections to religious belief (and to Catholicism in particular) are motivated by the same urge to restrict, control and enforce. They are motivated by something much more primal and tribal. Perhaps it is the case that Catholics can appear a little eccentric from a post-modern perspective – perhaps we are! But it is perfectly possible to believe in transubstantiation and be a good citizen simultaneously – High Anglicans and Episcopalians manage this all the time after all.

One point of this talk is to suggest that pluralism need not equate with a bland homogenisation, where differences are ironed out and we all do and think the same. Yes, Scotland is Presbyterian; yes, Scotland is secular. These are two aspects of the national character in which I rejoice wholeheartedly – but I want to celebrate much, much more about our country and I think we all can. The obsessive attempts, historically and contemporaneously, to periphalise and trivialise the Catholic experience in Scotland (and in particular the Irish Catholic experience) is a self-defeating tendency. It represents the very opposite of the enriching multicultural pluralism which I crave for this country. Another point of this talk is to suggest that we as a nation have to face up to the ignominy of our most prevalent if unspoken bigotry, if we are to move together into the next millennium with a sense of common purpose. Many of us are either happy to live with, or to deny completely the existence or the importance of, an anti-Catholicism which is still a significant element of Scottish culture.

I don't have supreme confidence in the ability of the Scottish media to tackle this topic fairly or seriously. Every time the issue is raised it is hijacked and sidelined into the ubiquitous, banal and knee-jerk injunction that everything would be hunky-dory if only we were to abolish Catholic schools. In fact, the Scottish media has become one of the main players in the anti-Catholic-schools industry which is now just as much part of the problem as anything else. Fear and alarm are spreading in the Catholic community over what is perceived as an ideologically motivated campaign against Catholic education which seeks to remove a Catholic voice and public presence from Scottish society. The slavering at the mouth, in some quarters, at the prospect of the new parliament being involved in this vandalism has become a depressing and frightening spectacle for many of us.

With the Glasgow-based press especially going into campaign mode for the abolition of Catholic schools, there is a widespread perception among Scottish Catholics that the media is prejudiced against them. *The Herald* has a number of feature writers who regularly and vociferously attack Catholic belief and practice in unguardedly visceral ways that would never see the light of day in a London quality newspaper, or tabloids for that matter. English visitors to Glasgow are regularly bewildered at the strength of feeling aimed against Catholicism in *The Herald*'s letters page. Can you imagine the English press working itself into such a lather over any religious belief and practice? Yet it is quite a common occurrence to find in *The Herald*'s pages the ridiculing and lampooning of the Catholic concept of transubstantiation, the deep pietistic fondness for the Blessed Virgin Mary, and a whole range of other aspects associated with the practice of the faith. One writer regularly and in passing refers to Catholicism and Islam as 'false and barbaric religions'. Another, with deliberate determination, uses 'Catholic schools' and 'sectarian schools' as interchangeable terms.

In the wake of the Donald Findlay saga the inevitable excuses for him finally arrived in the Glasgow press. There was a palpable anger with him anyway in some quarters for having given the game away. The sanctimonious Scottish myth that all bigots are uneducated loutish morons from the lowest level of society was undermined at a stroke. Although there is a very real resentment against him for having so foolishly squandered the alibi, it did not prevent this, in his defence in the *Sunday Herald* on 13 June:

> There was a time in living memory when Irish Catholics were discriminated against, *and with reason* [my emphasis] . . . by undercutting Scots workers, they were taking the bread out of the mouths of Scots children. The resentment was real at the turn of the century and it was justified . . . there is still a strong victim mentality among many of the descendants of those early immigrants, a terrible debilitating melancholy that they like to indulge . . . If you're not discriminated against, then you're not truly Irish, not a faithful Catholic. And the need to be a victim leaves them open to taking offence if a nice but tipsy man sings a folksong that doesn't quite reflect admiration for them and their kind.
>
> They are always alert, anticipating insults and bigotry . . . Donald Findlay was caught out, that's all that happened . . . at the end of the day he only sang a few rousing songs. [Donald Findlay] is a one-off, a man of huge character. He is not and never has been a bigot. Neither is he prejudiced against Catholics – only Celtic football club, and that is not quite the same thing.

The rousing but harmless folksongs that didn't 'quite reflect admiration for them and their kind' include the immortal lines 'Fuck your Pope and the Vatican' and 'We are up to our knees in Fenian blood/Surrender or you'll die/Because we are the Bridgeton Billy Boys'.

On the same page as the initial *Daily Record* exposé of Findlay there is another headline. ONE DEAD, ONE SHOT, referring to Thomas McFadden, a young Catholic teenager, wearing a Celtic top, who was butchered to death shortly after the Old Firm Cup final, and to Karl McGroarty, a Catholic student, again in a Celtic jersey, shot in the chest by a bolt fired from a crossbow as he returned from the same match. Anti-Catholic violence on the streets of Glasgow is not new. In 1996, Jason Campbell from Bridgeton, whose family had links with loyalist paramilitaries, was jailed for life after fatally slashing the throat of young Celtic fan Mark Scott at Bridgeton Cross. Last year, Campbell's friend, Thomas Longstaff, was jailed for ten years after another vicious attack on a Catholic. Both Campbell and Longstaff were defended at their trials by Donald Findlay, QC.

Donald Findlay is not a one-off. To believe this is self-delusion. Because our professions, our workplaces, our academic circles, our media and our sporting bodies are jam-packed with people like Donald Findlay. This from *The Sunday Times* Ecosse section (6 June 1999):

> You see a lot in the toilets of Bar Brel in Glasgow's salubrious west end: it must be one of the few gents to feature graffiti praising Scottish Ballet. But little could rival the spectacle witnessed there last Saturday night when members of the Scottish international rugby team turned up for a drink, as one unfortunate fellow in a Celtic top discovered on answering the call of nature.
>
> He was followed into the toilet by a star player; a man of high professional standing and wide renown. The Celtic fan readied himself to hear a lusty chorus on the charms of the landlord's daughter or a burst of 'Flower of Scotland'. Celtic, however, had just lost the Scottish Cup to arch-rivals Rangers. As I said, it isn't every day you hear a member of the Scottish sporting establishment belting out that loyalist chart topper 'The Sash' in a pub toilet.

The writer then tells us about David (not his real name) who played on a schoolboy form for Rangers. He recalls:

> His coaching in sectarianism was as rigorous as his coaching in the game and was heartily encouraged by some in the upper echelons of the club. 'A lot of boys I played with had dads who were well off, like doctors and lawyers, and far more into the sectarian thing than the players,' he says. 'In the dressing-room after the youth games it was the dads who were singing "The Sash", not so much the players.' David's father recently retired from a senior management position with one of the world's biggest corporations. He has never missed a Rangers game, excepting those at Parkhead which he will not attend. 'He refuses to give money to Catholics,' says David. As a boy, the player was told he could marry anyone he wished to, bar Catholics.

To fully appreciate the truest nature of anti-Catholic triumphalism and the hegemonic aspirations of those in our society who would happily see the disappearance of Scottish Catholicism, one has to understand the totemic significance of Glasgow Rangers at the heart of Scottish football. Donald Findlay's performance took place in a Rangers social club next to Ibrox Park. In his autobiography *My Life*, Andy Goram (until recently Rangers and Scotland's goalkeeper) boasts of his sympathies for the Ulster Protestant cause.

He has made more trips to Belfast than any other player. Along with Ally McCoist he was invited to the Shankill Road in 1995 to turn on the Christmas lights. At the Old Firm game on 2 January 1998, five days after the murder in the Maze Prison of the loyalist murderer Billy Wright, otherwise known as King Rat, Goram wore a black armband. His club, and most of the Scottish press, chose to believe his risible story that this gesture was an expression of delayed grief for an aunt who died the previous October. No great significance was placed on this by the Scottish press, who chose instead to concentrate on Goram's sexual misdemeanours. What would the English press reaction have been had David Seaman ever supported the BNP or Combat 18? Or could you imagine the Scottish press reaction if a Celtic player had dared to wear a black armband for a murdered IRA man? The Scottish tabloid press eventually published a photograph of Goram with a UVF terrorist flag – but this was after he had left Rangers and had moved to Motherwell.

My interest in football tends to lead to easy, animated and good-humoured discussion anywhere I go in the world. My fellow musicians seem to be as obsessed by it as I am. But because I'm Scottish, the gentle ridicule and barely repressed sniggers I generally encounter is not just due to the decreasing quality of our national game. Scotland, after all, is known as the only country in the footballing world where a player can be given the referee's red card for making the sign of the cross. I've just come back from Australia, where the only piece of Scottish news in three weeks to make it into TV, radio and newspaper coverage was the national team manager frantically defending himself against the charge of singing anti-Catholic songs. In the light of the precedent set by Donald Findlay none of the Australians I spoke to about it seemed the slightest bit surprised. In what other country do retired referees boast of having done their best to help one team against another? And in what other country is there a special kind of rage in the press reserved for those who cry foul in these matters?

Remember the sports press's fury at Fergus McCann in his terrier-like determination to face down Jim Farry in the court case to prove that the SFA had deliberately and unjustifiably delayed the registration of Jorge Cadete. The delay ensured that Cadete was unable to play in a crucial Old Firm game which Celtic narrowly lost. Remember that Mr Farry was completely exonerated by two internal SGA enquiries before being sacked for gross misconduct after independent counsel advised an out-of-court settlement in a case that could not, in counsel's view, be defended. The snarling jibes about Catholic paranoia were for once brought to a sudden gobsmacked silence.

What am I to say the next time I'm asked, as I was by some Italian journalists recently, why Scottish football is so corrupt? What am I to say when they next ask about the Scottish media's complicity in this? Knowing me, I'll probably just talk about metaphors again.

Football in Scotland is a prime metaphor for a deep malaise in our society as this letter to *The Herald*'s agony aunt Tessa Simpson (on 19 June) makes clear:

> Recently I applied for a job and managed to get an interview. On the application form there had been a box to fill in relating to religion. I did not fill this in as I believe it is completely irrelevant to being able to do a job or not.

At the interview I was asked about my religion, and I said I felt that was personal. This response was obviously not what they wanted to hear. The interview seemed to be going well and I thought I was in with a good chance. Later in the conversation they asked what football team I supported and when I said Celtic I could see the change in their expressions. It was as if they had made up their minds and it was not for the better.

I went downhill from there on and it made me very angry. I did not expect there to be such prejudice in the workplace today, although since moving to Glasgow from Inverness I have realised that things are different here.

I have since discovered on the grapevine that this firm is very sectarian in its views. They are willing to take on Catholics in the menial posts, but they only have Protestants in management posts – which is what I was going for. Are they breaking the law in taking this view?

With no further comment on this, I would like now to read from an article written for *The Observer* by a previous editor of *The Herald*, Arnold Kemp, which was illuminating and basically lets the cat out of the bag.

When I was appointed editor of the *Glasgow Herald* in 1981, the then managing editor of the publishing company came to me in great embarrassment. A board member, evidently confused by the fact that I was a Hibs supporter, had insisted on knowing whether I was a Catholic. When I answered in the negative, a cloud lifted from his brow . . . Some days later I was visited by a rather sinister member of the personnel department who wished to assure himself that I would observe the company's traditional recruiting policies. This meant that applicants' letters would be placed in three piles – probables, possibles and those you don't want to see. This last was a euphemism for those whose name or educational history betrayed their religious affiliation.

All through this time, the 1970s and 1980s, people at *The Herald* would argue themselves blue in the face that there was no anti-Catholic prejudice on the newspaper. That was a long time ago, and things may have changed. The present editor makes a similar claim that there is no anti-Catholic bias in the paper. However, the official editorial line of *The Herald* against Catholic schools must be scrutinised in the wider perspective of that journal's pervading culture.

Education, like football, has expanded out of all proportion to become a monstrous focus of sectarian discontent. The anti-Catholic schools lobby is at work with political figures and activists (such as members of the EIS). Their pleas will not exactly be met with deaf ears in certain political circles. John Maxton, the Labour MP, and Lord Mackay of Ardbrecknish, the Tory peer, have been up and running on this issue for a while. In spite of the friendly noises from nationalist luminaries such as Alex Salmond and Jim Sillars it is usually the SNP who have played the Orange card in local politics of central Scotland. Was it absolutely necessary for the nationalists in a recent West Lothian by-election to 'out' the Labour candidate's Catholic roots by revealing her middle name was Teresa? Was it absolutely necessary for the SNP activists in the 1994

Monklands East by-election, on the death of John Smith, to highlight the religious beliefs, Irish-sounding maiden name and Catholic school history of the labour candidate Helen Liddell? It undoubtedly played some part in the massive reduction to a 1,600 majority in one of Labour's safest seats, amid regular catcalls of 'Fenian bitch' aimed at Mrs Liddell at her public appearances.

Many in the press make much of the high Catholic involvement in the Labour Party in the West of Scotland. There is a constant implication that Catholics have plotted a take-over of political and government organs. This drip-drip propaganda only feeds the imaginations of those who want to believe Catholic conspiracy stories.

But it is not only in the murky world of local politics that these conspiracy stories prevail. It has cropped up in the comparatively enlightened academic world of Glasgow University which recently merged its Faculty of Education with St Andrew's College of Education, the Catholic teacher training college in Bearsden. There is nothing unusual about Catholic educational institutions having an integral association with larger mainstream universities in other countries. South of the border, for example, Trinity and All Saints College is a Catholic liberal arts college (which incorporates teacher training) and is also a university college of Leeds University. St Mary's College, Strawberry Hill, a similar Catholic institution, is now a college of the University of Surrey. Digby Stuart is a Catholic college and part of the ecumenical Roehampton Institute, also of the University of Surrey. Heythrop College is a Jesuit college which also provides degree courses at the University of London. St Benet's Hall and Blackfriars (the Dominican Priory) are well-respected colleges of the University of Oxford. St Edmund's, a Catholic foundation, is also a full university college of Cambridge University.

But the Glasgow merger did not proceed without some unpleasantness. There was resistance to it from within the university. In some quarters there was great resentment that the Catholic dimension of the new faculty was to be maintained. Professor Eric Wilkinson, the Director of Higher Degrees in the new Education Faculty, went to *The Herald* to voice his concerns. He said that he considered the Catholic Church's motives behind the merger were 'imperialistic to the extent of wishing to turn the clock back to before the Reformation' and was 'hoping to use its new-found position within Glasgow University to begin that process'.

Now, those of us with some intimate experience of the organisational and intellectual skills of the Scottish Catholic hierarchy have been rather bemused at how such a monumental conspiracy as the complete reversal of four centuries of cultural and theological history might be effected. We are intrigued as to how our beloved leaders, the princes of the Church, who are more normally taxed by the organisational complexities behind an altar boy's trip to Millport, might cope with a retrospective counter-Reformation of such epic proportions. But hey, the Holy Spirit moves in mysterious ways! In fact, some might say that the only reason the shambles that is the Scottish Catholic Church exists at all is solely and completely due to the Holy Spirit.

Seriously though, the mounting of such a huge conspiratorial plan would require a fiendishly well-organised and reactionary Catholic intelligentsia. The intelligentsia in Scotland is neither organised nor is it reactionary. The Catholic intellectuals in this country are theologically mainstream,

21

sociologically moderate and politically liberal, even left-wing in their general outlook. They are not a homogenous group but can be encapsulated in the character of certain individuals – John Haldane and his benign scholarly traditionalism, Richard Demarco in his intoxicating and effervescent artistic and spiritual idealism, Gilbert Markus in his liberation theology and Dominican orthodoxy, children's rights campaigner and academic Kathleen Marshall and the late Anthony Ross, nationalist, friend of the excluded, saintly and beloved of many different faiths and none. Any grand Catholic plan would have to have the input of these kind of people rather than that of Cardinal Winning and his pals. In that sense, the future of the Catholic Church in Scotland lies with the former type of Catholic rather than the latter, and the former are not interested in undermining institutions like universities. Whether this is likely to reassure Professor Wilkinson and others at Glasgow University, I am not so sure.

I did notice though that a few days after Wilkinson's outburst there was a letter published in *The Herald* from Sir Graeme Davies, Principal of the university (a New Zealander with a wide experience of education in the real world and its interface with faith communities), which publicly disassociated himself and the university from Professor Wilkinson's remarks. Another letter from the faculty's Head of Religious Education and the Director of Inservice Education delivered a rebuke to their colleague Wilkinson and put the whole thing into perspective, saying:

> A metropolitan university seeking to extend its reputation and influence in and beyond the new Scotland should surely be a place which rejects old myths and suspicions and celebrates difference and diversity, recognising the huge spectrum of possibilities for presenting the promise of higher education to all of the nation's communities.
>
> In such a spirit, but with notably less public controversy, the university recently opened a Centre for Islamic Studies, bravely affirming the multicultural and multi-faith dialogue which ought to mark educational development in a *mature democracy* . . . institutions which aspire to the intellectual excellence and academic credibility which Professor Wilkinson justifiably seeks have for the most part given up their attachment to conspiracy theories, whether these involve Jews, black people or Roman Catholics.
>
> We find ourselves left wondering if these insinuations would be acceptable if directed towards any other religious communities in the country.

These points should be a clarion call to all those who are willing to understand the true meaning of genuine pluralism in the mature democracy we are trying to create here.

Catholics have a lot to offer this society, although I am aware that many would prefer to regard Catholicism as just a lifestyle option to be pigeonholed under 'anachronistic reactionary tosh'. However, it is a faith that claims universality. Lindsay Paterson of Moray House Institute of Education (a self-confessed Protestant atheist) in his searching analysis 'Social Citizenship and Catholic Education' states that:

If the implications of that faith can be made relevant to a predominantly secular age, then there might indeed be a coherent basis for maintaining a distinctive and public system of Catholic education.

This is precisely what we want to do – to make our experience available for the greater good, beyond the Catholic constituency. He also states that:

Catholic schools did more to promote the attainment of working-class pupils than other schools did. The same is true of other outcomes: for example, among working-class pupils with two or more passes [at Higher grade] the proportion going to higher education was 52 per cent from Catholic schools, but only 42 per cent from other schools. What is more, the social gap in attainment was smaller in Catholic schools than in others; in other words, Catholic schools were more egalitarian.

Surely this must start bells ringing in Scotland where egalitarianism and inclusiveness are prized as the most important political, social and civic virtues.

In short [continues Professor Paterson] Catholic schools have been a classic instance of education's capacity to integrate socially excluded groups into the mainstream.

If this works for us, it will work for others too. On this evidence, far from abolishing them the most radical political initiative would be to extend the influence of Catholic schools in Scottish society, and even create more of them!

Why are Catholic schools such a stunning success story? Paterson cites the researches of J.S. Coleman in a paper for the *American Journal of Sociology*: 'Social Capital in the Creation of Human Capital':

[J.S. Coleman] found that Catholic schools were more effective than others, and he also found that a plausible explanation of that success lay in the social capital on which they could draw. Their communities were infused with norms that expected high achievement. These norms were enforced partly by what he called 'social closure'; pupils' parents tended to know each other, and to be known by officers of the church. So each individual pupil was surrounded outside school by a network of expectation and sanctions, encouraging achievement and discouraging disaffection.

Nowhere in his researches does Paterson find evidence that Catholic schools are socially divisive or foster bigotry. Rather:

. . . teachers in Catholic schools believed more than teachers in other schools that engaging with the democratic process was worth while. So teachers in Catholic schools, far from being agents of intolerance, would appear to have quite firm commitments to the ideas of social capital – to the principle that society works best if people respect and trust each other, and that it may work best of all if these values are embodied in enduring civic institutions such as a welfare state.

As I say, we have a lot to offer Scottish society, if only people would stop thinking the worst of us. Catholics welcome the interest which our media is showing in the future of Catholic education in Scotland – but the debate about its future should be a positive and enriching one, enabling us to develop a new and refreshed legitimacy. Professor Paterson states that the best defence of an autonomous system of Catholic education in a highly secular society is that it is a 'laboratory of experience, a source of experimental ideas on how to live together that might be of relevance to society as a whole'.

In all the positive examples I have cited in this talk I have deliberately drawn from those who see the opportunity and challenge of opening Scotland up to a benign Catholic contribution. In an age of depersonalisation mass market production and the empty despiritualisation of consumer society this is increasingly difficult to achieve. Perhaps the most destructive opposition to Catholicism is not to be found in Orange parades, sour editorials and EIS conference motions, but in the very nature of free market capitalism itself. In facing down this particular beast I believe Catholics can find common cause with countless others in Scotland. This is a real opportunity to turn Scotland's shame into Scotland's virtue.

2. INTO THE FERMENT

Andrew O'Hagan

Scotland is the world's best hypothetical nation. Its most vocal heroes are its dead ones. Many of its tragedies are tragedies of speech: the same men talking the same rubbish for too long. The country is lucky to have any artists really. It is no country for a man or a woman of letters. It is no place for a poet. It is a graveyard for any painter not interested in the weather. It's a sad valley for any willing singer of songs. For all the glories of its humane tradition, Scotland has no time now for the discomfiture of thinkers, no ready heart for the excoriation of myths, and no spirit, no confidence, no capacity for tolerance, in the face of unsettling truths.

Scotland is a divisive, bigoted society, and in August 1999 James MacMillan, the country's best composer, felt the need to come out and say so. Good on him. He deserves all the blessings of the God he believes in. He did what people in his position might well suppose themselves to do: speak difficult truth to power, and damn the ranters who shrink at the hearing of it. Those who think this was out of character – as much as out of order – should remain fearful of MacMillan's music, where the attempt to confront barbarity has been a hallmark since the beginning.

In *The Confession of Isobel Gowdie* a woman accused of witchcraft is burned after being forced to confess to fraternising with the devil. The text of *Busqueda* is from poems written by the Argentinian mothers of the disappeared, whose children were snatched and murdered by the state police. With a Scotsman's love of traditional ballads, a Catholic's memory of the Requiem Mass, a scholar's interest in Gregorian chant, a socialist's wish for the righting of wrongs, a modernist's mind for the fragmentation of forms, and a quite original manner with voices, string harmonies and woodwinds, MacMillan has made himself known. There is no mystery about where he stands; the only surprise is people's surprise. He said it in words. He said it out loud. He said there is something wrong with Scotland: institutional bigotry. And down, and down, with their customary blunt instruments, came the great and dispirited doctors of the Scottish media, filling the air with their oaths and denials, their idiot charts, their poxy prescriptions. In a matter of months the Scottish clergy were denouncing homosexuals.

Religion is everything in Scotland. The women in the wash-house could tell you that. The dominant culture, whether it means it or not, whether it chooses to see it or not, is washed and dried in Protestant values, and the depredations of Calvinism on Scottish art are evident to this very hour. Scottish cultural life is a kind of ongoing guerrilla warfare – a struggle to touch something real in a time of abstraction, to express truth, to give form to what you know or imagine, against an inclination of blood and bone, which serves to render you quiet. The local sites of religious zeal in everyday Scottish life – sport, marriage, education, architecture, the newspapers, the pubs – are pervaded with a notion of the Catholic underdog. A long-term resistance against this notion is also present, in Celtic Football Club, in the Scottish Labour Party, and in the troubled hearts of those in favour of Catholic schools.

This has been true for so long in Scotland that people have forgotten it. 'In a country whose culture is almost exclusively religious,' wrote Edwin Muir over 60 years ago, 'conscience finally becomes a matter concerned with only two spheres, the theological and the crudely material. There is no soil on which an artistic or imaginative conscience can grow, and no function for the artist except that of a public entertainer.'

And yet they do grow, but how sorely, how subtly, they are punished for the nuances of that growth. The Scottish middle classes love a bit of high culture, but they are not willing to pay too high a price for it, and neither, quite evidently, do they find themselves unprotesting when the intelligence of art pokes a finger at their society. In France or Ireland or Italy or Spain this would be expected to happen: people would look for it, and they would, even in anger, somehow consider themselves all the richer for the having of it.

The question of bigotry is the black backing on the Scottish mirror: it allows each of us to see our own face.

James MacMillan is about ten years older than me. I know from his music that he's someone of considerable sensitivity and grace. I also know that we have spent time in the same town in Ayrshire, a place with a good claim to having the first Masonic Lodge in Scotland, and his lecture sent my mind back to that place, of which I have fond memories, as well as memories not so fond. I was a Catholic too. I don't hold that candle any more, and in many another context I could see myself disagreeing with James MacMillan. But at the same time I can see that much of that west-of-Scotland history that formed him also formed me. I've no doubt about that; it was that kind of history.

The birds on the trees sang sectarian songs. The Catholics seemed out on their own somehow: a happy group for the most part, an irrational group sometimes, but a group nonetheless, and one that saw itself partaking in the traditions of their fathers' and mothers' fathers and mothers, in a country where things were inclined away from them. The Catholics came to Mass in a small church next to the old Caledonian railway station. One of the earliest things in my head is the sight of a blue hut right across the road. The blue hut had no windows. You hardly ever saw anyone around it. But on Sundays the hut would almost leap from its mooring as a band struck up inside. The band of the Orange Lodge. Right across from the chapel. And what a mad cacophony came out of that hut, the unforgettable sound of pure aggression.

Now don't misunderstand me. There was no shortage of Catholic head-bangers as well, but no way would a group of young Catholics have been allowed to keep a shed outside the local Kirk. That was obvious even to a six-year-old. That's all I want to say about being a Catholic child in a modern Scotland. After a number of years had passed they tore the hut down and repla-ced it with a new library. A lot of this is funnier than sad – at least to me – but I still remember my boffinish glee at the new library's usurpation of the blue hut. I didn't care about football. I didn't care for the priest. But I loved books, and I felt, even then, that if any small thing would help in changing the character of that place it would be a vertiginous increase in book-borrowing rights. I was young and stupid enough to imagine that people might read themselves into pluralism.

There were no novels in the new library written by Scottish Catholics. If the novel was thought to be the great social form, and Scotland was thought to be a progressive society, where then were the Catholic novelists? There were converts – Muriel Spark – but that wasn't the same. Where were the novels of those millions of people, or more likely the descendants of those people, who had travelled out of Ireland, who had played into an industrial revolution, who had drunk, and prayed, and talked, and loved, and died here? Where were they? The millions of lives.

They had James Joyce. They had Edna O'Brien. But was there really nothing – not even a short story – that cast imaginative light on the life of, say, one young girl on her First Communion day, or one old man at a football match? I read every other Scottish book I could lay my hands on. I read Stevenson and Scott and John Galt, and new novels too, as time passed, by people like Alasdair Gray, who gave a sense of a coming Scotland. I loved and was shaped by much of what I read there. But the truth is I never read a single scene in any of those books exactly like a scene from my own life. Never a sense of a room in the evening. Never the look on a Catholic mother's face; the talk of a father; the sense of a past rearing up in the present. Nothing like that. And though I knew it was not to do with discrimination – more like disadvantage – it added to my sense of Catholics being not altogether present in Scotland. It made me feel we were outsiders, even to ourselves.

The Protestant writers on those shelves made me aware of a gap, and not just a gap in Catholicism, but a gap in Scotland. And none of them seemed any more at home in the general culture than I did. They seemed exiled, even so close to home. Years later, after I'd become a writer myself and moved away, I still wondered at the strange case of Scottish society. Why was there no proper national feeling there? Why, in such an old place, was there no sense of gathered wisdom? Why did so many people define themselves according to their prejudices?

James MacMillan said his thing. He could have said more – or said less – but the stunning fact is not what he said, but the unwillingness of his own culture to allow him to say it. The face of Donald Findlay singing 'The Sash' – a sad melody from the blue hut – is a disturbing one, a disgusting one, but not at all unusual. I was once next to a Scottish poet at an Edinburgh dinner. A foreign author asked the poet about discrimination against Catholics in banking and insurance in Scotland, and asked about the Masonic influence in the police. And why no writers? The foreigner wondered if Scotland was now the only place in the world where to be a Catholic was to be at a distinct disadvantage. The poet was not enjoying himself. 'No,' he said eventually, 'it's just not like that. You're asking the wrong questions.'

There are no wrong questions in a civilised society. There are wrong conclusions – there are mistakes in facts or the judgements based upon them – but there are no wrong questions, except in a society that enjoys a traditional uniformity of stupidity on certain issues or, even worse, one which aims to supervise a totalitarianism of belief and custom. James MacMillan is not a branch of the tourist trade. He goes out there, as many of us do these days, and performs his tasks in a shrinking world. He represents Scotland with an optimistic face. But don't ask him to behave like a stranger in his own country. Don't ask him to play the docile part of the joy-addled entertainer. He is right: in this way or that way Scotland is a country disabled by local hatreds. His is a voice in opposition to that, a pluralist Scot, willing a brand new tune into existence.

3. KICKING WITH THE LEFT FOOT: BEING CATHOLIC IN SCOTLAND

Patrick Reilly

To ask if there is anti-Catholicism in Scotland is like asking if there are Frenchmen in Paris. But when James MacMillan gave his now notorious answer there were widely differing reactions north and south of the border, a fact in itself instructive and revealing. In its editorial the *Sunday Times* of 8 August 1999 referred to his criticisms as 'shocking but necessary and timely' – patients who deny they are ill seldom recover – and pointed out that a country which hosts Orange marches the year round while ceaselessly campaigning for the closure of Catholic schools has small cause to bridle indignantly at any suggestion of religious discrimination. In Scotland, by contrast, there was deep and widespread resentment at the imputation of intolerance towards Catholics within its borders. Commentators spoke in the accents of the injured Lear confronting the inexplicable ingratitude of his thankless daughters: how dare MacMillan say what he said after all that the true, native Scots had done for these, let's face it, unwanted interlopers? Blessed with any sense of fairness, Scottish Catholics would be gratefully acknowledging the unprecedented generosity shown them rather than whingeing over exaggerated or imaginary ills.

Yet the unpalatable truth, as recent evidence from our ethnic minorities confirms, is that Scotland is far from being the warm, welcoming, accommodating haven that it flatters itself on being. Professor T.G. Fraser of Ulster University tells us that Orangeism in Scotland is on the increase, an integral part of our culture, its multiplying marches an established feature of west-central Scotland; and Orangeism flourishes only where there is a strong perception of a Catholic threat and the sense of a need to resist it – even its closest admirers will not claim that Orangeism has been historically distinguished by the friendliness of its welcome to papist idolators.

The instances multiply to unmanageable degree. Bishop Devine is prevented by the threat of public disorder from visiting Catholic children preparing for the sacrament of Confirmation in a shared school in Harthill. No Pope here: it is not just a rhetorical flourish in Harthill. Football players are red-carded for the offence, unique to Scotland, of blessing themselves during games, a practice commonplace in the rest of the world without anyone batting an eyelid, but certain to provoke riot among us, hence demanding stern repression and draconian punishment. Michael Kelly tells us that it *is* a provocative and offensive act; but, then, so too is the flag which he allowed to fly over his stadium for so many years. Alan Massie declares that players bless themselves with the deliberate intention to offend. He doesn't divulge the source of this information, but he is certainly correct as to the riotous consequences – the Firhill referee gave this as his reason for acting as he did.

And there's more. Professor Eric Wilkinson, unperturbed at the establishment of a Centre for Islamic Studies within the University of Glasgow, descries in the institution's merger with St Andrew's College a papist plot to undo the Reformation in Scotland and restore the land to Roman tyranny. John MacLeod finds in the latest Kennedy tragedy yet another satisfactory instance of Jehovah smiting the contemporary worshippers of Baal. The Free Presbyterians in their journal consign the dead Cardinal Hume to hell, not out of any especial dislike, but simply because that's where all Catholics automatically go. Arnold Kemp tells a story, at once hair-raising and comic, of how his employers panicked on thinking, mistakenly, that they had appointed a Catholic. Every second week at Ibrox many thousands of voices raucously remind the watching Fenian scum that they, Scotland's Catholic-haters, are the people, born to walk the Glasgow equivalent of Garvaghy, and that, consequently, Catholics are merely imitation Scots, here on sufferance and lucky to be here at all. And so, depressingly, on.

These are all undeniable facts, but some will reply that they are so trifling as to need no denying: why should any sensible person fret over such inconsequentialities? But even allowing that these are mere straws, of no intrinsic significance, straws can be helpful in showing us the wind's direction – and many Catholics may conclude that it is still a chill blast rather than a balmy zephyr.

The allegation of Scotland's shame by MacMillan invites three routine responses. The first is to deny that there is or ever has been any significant discrimination, to insist that the only enemies Catholics have ever had exist within their own fevered skulls, figments of their own morbid creating – paranoia is a once clinical term that even football commentators now use with an easy familiarity. The second is to concede that once upon a time there was discrimination, although, as in all good fairy tales, the ending is a happy one, because discrimination no longer exists and need not concern us except as a historical curiosity. The third admits the continued existence of discrimination but warns against publicly discussing it, since this can do no good and may well do harm, worsening the very situation to which it calls such injudicious attention. Let sleeping dogs lie. The less talk about anti-Catholicism, the sooner it will die away altogether.

And yet there is a good deal of talk about religious prejudice within Scotland, even from those who dismiss it as anachronistic and irrelevant. We are not only allowed to talk about religious antagonism, we are encouraged to do so, provided we first identify separate Catholic schools as its prime fomenter and make it clear that, but for these, there would be unalloyed harmony throughout the land. In so perversely, unnecessarily clinging to their redundant schools, Catholics are the chief culprits, the instigators of that very discrimination against which they complain: they spread the disease and then protest at being its victims. How many times have we heard it said that the threat that justified the 1918 Act has long since gone, that for Catholics to fear an aggressive, proselytising Presbyterianism today is akin to posting lookouts on the Clyde for Viking raiders, that Catholic schools have served their purpose and outlived their need and should be boarded up for the sake of social harmony? It's a strange argument: there is no discrimination and Catholics are to blame for its persistence. On the one hand, we are told that there is no significant bigotry, hence no need for separate Catholic schools. It follows that these schools should be closed down. On the other, we are told that there still is considerable bigotry and that Catholic schools are responsible for perpetuating it. It follows that these schools should be closed down. The conclusion is the same, even if the routes towards it are incompatible and self-contradictory.

We are encouraged to talk about discrimination – we even set up official enquiries under distinguished jurists to investigate it – but only when the context is political, those suspected are Catholic, and the charge is one of favouring their co-religionists. Witness Monklands. What we are not encouraged to discuss is any possible discrimination *against* Catholics (other than as the regrettable but ineluctable consequence of their own intransigently perverse education policy), because to do that would be to risk souring relationships between our differing groups, thus endangering the delicate balance so laboriously, precariously achieved.

The irony is that, far from favouring their co-religionists, many Catholics who have commendably climbed to positions of influence within our society have clearly vowed never to expose themselves to such a charge. My father and two elder brothers worked all their lives as what were once called pipe-coverers, now more grandly referred to as insulation engineers. They told me that when times were hard and jobs scarce, the last person you would look to for help would be a Catholic foreman, for he would be too concerned with protecting his own back to take any risk for yours. We have all met such Catholics in every field of activity, people resolved not to compromise their own hard-won success by any act that might be construed as favouring their own; much safer to err in the opposite direction. It is from this category that the advocates of the policy of *quieta non movere* are mainly drawn.

As for anti-Catholic discrimination in employment, there is a Himalayas of anecdotal evidence from almost every Catholic family in the west of Scotland as to alleged injustices suffered. Cynics (from within and without the Catholic community) are unimpressed. What a marvellously convenient excuse for failure, to be able to ascribe it to religious prejudice rather than personal shortcomings. Every incompetent presents himself as a victim. No doubt this is often the case, but no sensible forger tries to pass £9 notes. No one says he lost a job because he was bald or blue-eyed, for the obvious reason that no one would believe it. If, by contrast, people try to persuade us that religion is the cause, it can only be because the claim is credible, given the circumstances in which we live. It is, of course, all too easy to claim that you lost the game because of a biased referee, but that in itself does not prove that every referee is fair. The fact that some people pretend to be victims doesn't mean that there are no real victims: there *have* to be real ones, otherwise why bother to pretend?

One understands all too well the concern of those, especially on the Catholic side, who urge against trumpeting stories of injustice and discrimination lest we provoke a backlash in which the very substantial gains of the last half-century may be put at hazard. Look at how far we have come, they say; do you really want to risk throwing all this away, and for the sake of what? Gains which will in any case surely if slowly arrive, provided we are patient, but which may be postponed indefinitely if we are too headstrong, demanding too much too soon. We already have so much; why jeopardise it by unreasonably demanding more? So curb your tongue, look small, go on tiptoe and perhaps nothing worse will happen – because, be sure, worse could happen. Things are not perfect, but they are improving. There is, admittedly, a sickness abroad, but it is diminishing and will pass away altogether if only we ignore it. This trepidation, nervousness, fear of giving offence is the result of many years of social conditioning in which we have been taught that the best way to prevail is to be self-effacing, not abrasive, to wait patiently for doors to open rather than attempt to break them down. Hasten slowly. Our unacknowledged culture-hero is Fabius Cunctator, the Roman general who finally overcame the enemy by *not* fighting him. We shall overcome, but not by forcing the issue.

It is a powerful argument and it can summon irrefutable facts in its support. No one will deny the great changes (mainly but not entirely for the good) that have occurred in the last 50 years, altering beyond recognition what Patrick McGill called 'the black country with the cold heart', the situation encountered by the Famine immigrants and their first descendants. At the time of the Famine, *The Times* rejoiced in a future when an Irishman in Connemara would be as rare as a Mohawk in Manhattan and recommended one vast diaspora to America or the valley of the Ganges, one massive bout of ethnic cleansing to solve the Catholic problem forever. When, instead, the scourge of wandering, famishing Irish landed in Scotland, there were fears that Glasgow would become a city of paupers, plague and popery.

The newcomers were regarded as improvident, intemperate and unreasonable, the mammoth task of civilising them intensified to despair by one insuperable obstacle: they were not just savages but Romanised savages, and in their coming the Scots (anticipating Professor Wilkinson today) descried a plot to annex Scotland as a papist colony. The dirge of eugenic and cultural disaster tolls like a bell from Carlyle onwards, and that the alien religion more than the alien race incited the bellringers was made crystal clear by the fact that they saw no problem in the Orange influx of the 1920s: the threat to Scots purity came from those immigrants loyal to Rome. (Even today one hears people deploring the Irish songs sung at Celtic Park, as though the Boyne were in Banffshire and Derry's walls hewn from Grampian granite.) Scot equals Protestant, Catholic equals alien: upon these equations Scotland conducted its business. In such a spirit a report to the General Assembly of the Church of Scotland in 1929 recommended the repatriation, by all means necessary, of these unassimilable aliens to their place of origin as the only way of preserving the purity of Presbyterian Scotland. The government in London pondered long and hard before rejecting pleas to stop all Irish Catholic immigration and to deport as many of the interlopers as possible. But no one denied that there was an Irish problem and comparisons were drawn between two parallel dilemmas: that of the Jews in Germany and that of Irish Catholics in Scotland.

Given this ideological climate, it is unsurprising that the inter-war years were marred by serious sectarian conflict, and the strain of policing the strife was one of the arguments urged at Westminster for sending the Irish home. But that was then and this is now. Today we inhabit a transformed landscape. The 'Irish' have been integrated and socially included; discrimination in housing and employment is of the past; we are all Jock Tamson's bairns and only paranoiacs think otherwise. True, even as late as 1957 in her novel *The Comforters*, Muriel Spark, born a Jew in 1918, educated at an all-girls Presbyterian school and a convert to Catholicism in 1955, was still exploring a shared experience of discrimination between Jew and Catholic and arguing that her new co-religionists were as doomed as her kinsfolk to be suspected and misunderstood by the modern world. But Muriel Spark belongs to another age and so, too, if we are to believe Donny O'Rourke, do the much younger James MacMillan and Andrew O'Hagan; like those Japanese soldiers on deserted Pacific islands, they are still fighting a war that ended many years ago.

So runs the argument, and there is much in it to celebrate. Only when we enquire into the causes of these changes do doubts linger and reservations resurface. Social scientists tell us that sectarianism in Scotland has been undermined, not by changes in mind and heart, but by the unintended, unforeseen consequences of large-scale structural upheaval. Not in the souls of men but in the world of business – here is where the transformation occurred. Discrimination flourished when industries were owned by local magnates who were kirk elders, Masons or Orangemen. Jobs were allocated on the basis of religious affinity: Protestants found work, unemployed Catholics were left to find comfort (if they could) in the fact that they were suffering for the faith. But steadily, remorselessly, economic control shifted to London, New York and Tokyo, where they are not nearly so obsessed with defending Derry's walls against the Whore of Babylon. Consider, for example, the breaking of the print unions by Rupert Murdoch, who, pursuing his own private agenda, coincidentally put an end to anti-Catholic discrimination within the industry. Catholics are doubtless grateful for the opportunity to work, regardless of the gift-horse that brings it and even if it means looking to such as Murdoch as their inadvertent liberators, the unconscious Lincolns who freed them from their chains. But, if the analysis is correct, they owe their manumission to the multi-nationals, but for whom they might still be standing destitute outside the factory doors where no Catholic need apply. A man, your sworn enemy from birth, attacks you every time you meet. One day you come across him wearing a straitjacket. It's a relief not to be attacked, but has he changed or do you owe it all to the straitjacket? All the above argument proves is that discrimination in employment has diminished because it can no longer be so extensively practised. Catholics will rejoice that the world has changed economically in their favour, but will look sceptically upon those who would claim credit for changes that could not be prevented and might otherwise not have occurred. Indeed, one of the arguments advanced for closing Catholic schools today is that it would make it more difficult for employers to discriminate against Catholics, that if only they merge, chameleon-like, with their surroundings, become as far as possible invisible people, they will improve their employment prospects. It's the same old contradiction: there is no employment discrimination in Scotland and if Catholics closed their schools there would be even less. It scarcely gives credence to the view that sectarianism is dead. Less potent, perhaps, but only because in certain areas the power has moved elsewhere.

'So what?' some will respond. All that matters is that in the labour market, where it counts, discrimination has much decreased. Who cares how it has come about just so long as it has? There are two answers. Crucially important though employment is, it is *not* the only thing that counts. And the trouble is that sectarianism does not disappear, but simply moves to other lodgings. That a cancer moves from lung to colon is not really a cause for celebration. It is pointless to look for discrimination where, by definition, it can no longer exist, and impertinent to claim credit for what is no longer within our control

– before we know it, we will be told that Catholics enjoy the sunshine in Scotland too.

The outside world can change and old attitudes remain entrenched. This is evidently true of our national sport, where the old anti-Catholic spirit was always less circumspect in concealing itself. In football a curtain is lifted upon certain attitudes and mindsets otherwise customarily kept discreetly hidden. For over a hundred years our most successful, most prominent, most wealthy team was allowed, without rebuke or reproach from the game's governing body, to pursue an openly anti-Catholic policy until they themselves decided, for their own opportunistic reasons, to change. There was never any official pressure or even persuasion from within Scotland to get them to change; they were in no sense penalised for being anti-Catholic – some, indeed, have muttered darkly that they were, if anything, rewarded for being the people's team, the team to defeat the unwelcome Irish intruders. For some years now they have been signing foreign Catholics and they recently extended this to include a native Catholic of Irish descent, a breakthrough by any yardstick.

We are invited to celebrate this as an ecumenical milestone, proof of the more genial, more tolerant times in which we live. But, as with the employment changes already discussed, this, too, is the child of necessity rather than choice, of pressure from without rather than enlightenment from within, something enforced rather than embraced. It is to Europe, not Scotland, that the credit is due. Rangers have become not more tolerant but more judicious, realistic and circumspect. To have gone on recklessly pursuing their traditional anti-Catholic policy might have led to expulsion from Europe; Scotland had always turned an obliging blind eye on the people's team, but Europe might not. But even had they escaped expulsion, the policy was clearly damaging their chances of European success. Invincible in Scotland, they were flops in Europe. They changed because it was necessary or expedient or both, not because they had belatedly come to see bigotry as a bad thing in itself. Success is the single spur. Could they have prevailed in Europe with an all-conquering, all-Protestant team as they have so consistently, so tediously, done in Scotland – and there's a mystery to muse on: why did their policy of excluding Catholics not harm them here as it so manifestly did abroad? – does anyone seriously believe that a single Catholic would have crossed their threshold?

Again it will be asked: why not just be grateful that the policy change has occurred without enquiring too closely into the motive? Because, as T.S. Eliot tells us in another context, it is possible to do the right thing for the wrong reason. In the light of recent events, it is legitimate to ask if the change is any more than a cosmetic convenience, a tactical rearrangement of the surface while the depths stay undisturbed. Herein lies the true significance of the Donald Findlay affair and the anger it provoked in non-Catholic circles. In so unforgivably, so publicly letting the orange cat out of the bag, Mr Findlay has irreprievably undermined that hoary, self-flattering Scottish myth that all bigots are morons, uneducated louts from the slums, the dregs of our society in whom prejudice and unintelligence are precisely matched. After Mr Findlay no one dare say this any more, and the resentment against him is great for having so foolishly thrown away the alibi. But, in his own perverse way, he has done us all a service by exploding the lie that only among the rabble are the bigots to be found. Mr Murray tells us that Findlay had to resign because 'a private meeting . . . unfortunately became public'. Don't get caught being a bigot and you can go on being vice-chairman of Rangers, seems to be the advice. What the episode reveals is that nothing has really changed, that deep down, where it truly matters, Rangers are still what they have always been: the team of those who so truculently bellow out that they are the people. It is still far from clear that bigotry is on the wane at Ibrox. Jocky Scott of Dundee thinks it would be a good thing for Scottish football if the Old Firm were to move into Europe. I think it would be a good thing for Scottish society, since it is being in Scotland that brings out the worst in them. Mr Murray would seem to agree when he begs his own supporters to refrain from singing certain songs that make him cringe and to think of Rangers as a truly European team, not a parochial Scottish one. What clearer admission could there be that the malaise is a Scottish one and that the cure is to move to a larger arena where our peculiar animosities will be blunted, attenuated and, in time, forgotten?

For it is not just one team, however important, that is the problem; it is a Scottish problem. Where else in the footballing world is a player's blessing himself an offence? What other national team manager is obliged to defend himself against the charge of singing sectarian songs? In what other country do retired referees boast in their cups of the part they played in helping one of our great teams defeat another? Ask any follower of Celtic if he would have preferred the transfer of Cadete to have been handled in Zurich or Glasgow and ponder the implications of the answer. We are, remarkably, still in the dark as to what actually happened – all we know is that Mr Farry was completely exonerated by *two* internal SFA enquiries before being sacked for gross misconduct after independent counsel advised an out-of-court settlement in a case that could not, in his view, be defended. But for Fergus McCann's tenacity, the old jibes about paranoia would still be being levelled at those who complained about the handling of the transfer. In the absence of a better explanation, those who suspect discrimination have every right to go on doing so. It is not a trifling matter. We are rightly concerned at the rise of racism among us, signalled by the murders of two young Asians within the past two years. But youths wearing green-and-white colours are even more at risk in west-central Scotland, with the casualty rate higher still. This, too, is a problem that should concern us, and it cannot be denied that anti-Catholicism is at its root.

Yet one need only contrast the killing of the black teenager Stephen Lawrence in London with the killing of Mark Scott at Bridgeton Cross to see our reluctance to admit that there is a problem, far less solve it. No serious commentator in England would dare to describe the Lawrence murder as an isolated, one-off event, *sui generis*, totally unrelated to certain sinister developments in English society – to do so would be to risk association with the noxious racism that destroyed him. Stephen Lawrence died for the colour of his skin and his death indicates intolerant forces in English society; he was not killed by a pack of psychopathic thugs representing no one but themselves. They simply carried what others think to a hideous enacted extreme.

Mark Scott just as surely died for the colour of his scarf, but in his case we are instructed against regarding his killer as in any way representative of dark forces within our society. No explanation is offered as to why the London murder is sociologically significant while the Glasgow one is simply individually aberrant. Jason Campbell butchered a boy at Bridgeton Cross, a complete stranger whom he identified as an enemy by the colours he wore, the team he supported and the faith he presumably professed. A standard science-fiction cliché is that of the changeling, when the soul of a demon is surreptitiously smuggled into the body of a human child and the substitution only becomes apparent when unspeakable depravities begin to be carried out. This is not what happened with Jason Campbell. He is not some weird creature from another galaxy, fallen from the sky while we slept. He is from Bridgeton, an entirely predictable if abhorrent product of our society, as Scottish in his own perverse way as Irn-Bru, much as it may chill us to say so. I belong to Glasgow: fearfully but undeniably, he is entitled to sing the words along with any one of us. He was taught, in his tribal heartland, to be a Catholic-hater: any Catholic, every Catholic. Mark Scott's tragedy was to be the chosen one.

How comforting it would be to dismiss Campbell as a freak, an individual psychopath, completely atypical – and how deluded and dangerous, for if we do not track these atrocities to their lair and kill them in the egg, we ensure their continuance. The kind of pathological hatred inculcated in Campbell from childhood on was an education for slaughter and we have a right to be shocked, but not surprised, that so it proved. He was driven – and there are many more of him than we care to admit – to homicidal frenzy by a certain colour of scarf, as Stephen Lawrence's killers were by a certain colour of face. They both killed what they had been taught to hate, but they would not have done so without the tuition of their mentors. They did not invent themselves, were not their own creators. Up to the knees in Fenian blood: Campbell made the song come true, but he did not write the words. It is not his song any more than it is Donald Findlay's, or any other individual's. He was taught to sing it as a child, he joined in with the rest on match days, he made it hideous reality on a Glasgow street, but he did not compose it, is not responsible for it. But something is. These young killers have been born into a tradition that has existed among us for over a century; they are, in a sense, as much victims as the victims they slay. When people are being maimed and slaughtered on our streets for being 'Fenians' or for wearing green, it is perhaps time to stop proclaiming our readiness to wade in their blood. Or is no one at all responsible?

Folk culture is fine but not when it's lethal, not when it turns anyone wearing green into a legitimate target of attack. The UVF actually requested that Campbell be 'repatriated' to Northern Ireland to serve his sentence there as one of their own, a political prisoner who had killed a political enemy. The chaplain to UVF prisoners in the Maze argued that it was 'an ethnic crime', part of the same war being waged in Bridgeton as in Belfast, and that Campbell should accordingly be able to benefit, along with other terrorists, from the Good Friday agreement. Incredibly, the Scottish Office seemed prepared, however briefly, to consider this argument and only the decisive intervention of the Northern Ireland Office put paid to the idea. But the very fact that some people in Northern Ireland and Scotland were of a mind to regard this murder as a political act is of itself enough to rebut the glib assurance that Campbell is a solitary psychopath whose actions tell us nothing about the society that produced him. 'This thing of darkness I acknowledge mine.' At the end of *The Tempest*, Prospero, mortified at his relationship to the monster Caliban, nevertheless manfully accepts responsibility. The Calibans are among us and will continue among us until we ask why this is so and how best we can prevent it. Until we do, it behoves Celtic Football Club to sell their merchandise with the unambiguous warning that wearing it may seriously damage your health.

Some who accept the preceding analysis will reply that Catholics already have the remedy in their grasp, that they need only close their by now unnecessary schools and the problem of bigotry will solve itself. This argument begins by assuming that something is wrong with our society and then identifies separate schools as the culprit. But this confuses cause with responsibility. Houses are not to blame for burglars, though without the first there could not be the second; nor should we fault the rope industry because people hang themselves. All over the world people smoke and get lung cancer and this universality allows us to postulate a causal link; but only in Scotland are Catholic schools perniciously divisive, which tells us more about the country than the schools. We are being persuaded that the only way to abolish bigotry is to eliminate, or at least make invisible, religious differences among us. It is a variant of the old axiom from the wars of religion that no land could be at peace till all attended the same church; substitute 'school' and it is the same mindset.

One feels grateful for seeing the argument so unequivocally put and for having done with the clutter of irrelevancies that has hitherto clouded the debate. Many Catholics will feel relief, even satisfaction, at being no longer summoned to defend their schools on educational grounds. That battle has been won. Never have these schools been stronger or their denigrators more discredited. From every objective observer, from every impartial witness comes the evidence testifying to their virtues. The educationist tells us that in terms of the number of Highers and Standard Grades passed or the number of pupils going on to tertiary education, Catholic schools, comparing like with like, are outperforming their non-denominational counterparts. The sociologist praises their superior discipline and points to a powerful underlying moral direction as the paramount cause. The philosopher, attacking the depressingly narrow idea of education as an assembly line producing spare parts for the social machine, finds the wider cultural and spiritual aims of education best fostered within the Catholic system. Educationally speaking, the real bigots would seem to be those who, for purely ideological ends, are bent on destroying such good schools – how otherwise explain such educational vandalism? For even were these schools bastions of the highest excellence, they must still be shut down: they are Catholic and this single offence cancels out every other merit. In England and America people want to know the secrets of their success; in Scotland all we want to know is the date of their closure. Alone among the nations, we are allergic to Catholic schools, and any serious attempt at understanding, let alone solving the problem should begin here. But that would mean having the courage and humility to admit that the fault might lie elsewhere than in the schools themselves, something that up to now Scotland has never been able to do.

Catholic schools cause bigotry: it is axiomatic. Yet the bigotry predates the establishment of the schools; historically, the schools did not produce the bigotry, so why should we believe that their abolition will end it? Was ever cart more egregiously placed before horse? If you dislike someone for being different, the dislike will persist so long as the difference endures. Close the schools or suffer the bigotry: many will find offensive what seems suspiciously like a precondition for extirpating an evil that no civilised society should tolerate.

If, however, the secret integrationist hope is to obliterate in time these obsolete, bothersome differences and so end bigotry – how could there be bigotry when we are all the same? – this is an altogether different argument that has nothing to do with tolerance, everything with homogenisation. In Lamb's essay the Chinese think the only way to get roast pork is to burn down the pigsty; it is no more absurd than to dream of achieving social harmony by closing Catholic schools. Bigotry is not taught in the schools, it is ingested with the mother's milk and the father's venom, and there are some differences never to be eliminated however long we sit in integrated classrooms. The Jews who died in the death camps and the black youths slain on our streets attended the same schools as their killers. It is, admittedly, much easier to stop being a Catholic than it is to stop being Jewish or black, to discard a coloured scarf than to discard a coloured face, but it is depressing to think that this desiderated abandonment of religion is our best, if not only, hope of social harmony.

Bob Crampsey, whom no one will accuse of being rash or alarmist, rightly remarks that the minority population no longer fears or has reason to fear orthodox Protestantism, but is, nevertheless, still understandably extremely wary of the dark current of anti-Catholicism which is never far below the surface of Scottish life. Nothing confirms this more than the never-ending harping on about separate schools, the interminably wearisome chevying that resembles being married to a scold. Scotland has ceased to be a Protestant country without ceasing to be an anti-Catholic one and it is a change that no Catholic will applaud. Catholics are still made to feel that their habit of kicking with the left foot is, at best, an inconvenience, at worst, a disaster. To do anything on or with the left, the sinister, side has long been a synonym for perverse, crooked, aberrant. Right is right and left is wrong: what could be plainer? From 1872 onwards there was pressure upon Catholics to stop kicking with the left foot and to switch to the right. Today the pressure is for them to kick with no foot at all, to purge their schools of religious education other than as a purely academic discipline sanitised of faith commitment. Once the wish was to make them Protestant; now it will suffice if they stop being Catholic. They were formerly criticised by Protestants for being Catholic; they are presently criticised for being religious by Protestant atheists (they do exist) and by those who have deserted Calvin for Marx. But whatever else changes, one thing abides: the animus against Catholics and their schools.

Norman Tebbitt once implied that the only way for an Asian to become fully British was to forswear being Asian. Catholics in Scotland are no strangers to this type of ultimatum. The national distrust of the alien creed continues to manifest itself in the Acts of Settlement and of Union, as though the Armada were still at sea and the fires of Smithfield burning. Yet the political and cultural situation in Britain and Europe alike is in vast, unforeseeable transformation. The United Kingdom, based upon the Protestant victory throughout these islands, is in danger of fragmentation and even dissolution. The Great Britain which emerged from the Glorious Revolution and the Act of Union to become the dominant European and world power is as past as the Empire of the Aztecs. Tony Blair claims that Britain has found a new role in the world to replace the old one which Dean Rusk once famously said it had lost. Whatever this new role may be, we can safely predict that it will be very different from the *pax britannica* that the great Protestant power once imposed upon the world. We are now irrevocably a multi-faith, multi-racial, multi-cultural society and we need a new mindset, a new psychology, to match this new reality.

In Scotland this entails, as a matter of urgency, a new and more inclusive definition of Scottishness if the nation is to be one and at peace with itself. The old, time-sanctioned identification of Scot and Presbyterian will no longer serve, unless we wish to marginalise increasing numbers of people from different races and religions born and domiciled within our borders; the Scotland of the future must contain no inner exiles. The old definition of Scot once employed to urge the repatriation of unassimilable Catholic 'Irish' is now completely unusable; to be a nation at peace with itself, we must all become Jock Tamson's bairns, regardless of creed or colour. It follows that there must be no pressure upon Scottish Catholics to surrender their identity in a devolved or possibly independent Scotland. Indeed, as the oldest, largest migrant group, Scottish Catholics could become a pattern for those who came after, lending a powerful voice to those other peoples who followed in the tracks of the Irish. But this means allowing them, without any hint of disapproval, to go on kicking with the left foot. After all, anyone conversant with the game will tell you that it should be encouraged, not forbidden. Who ever heard of a well-balanced team without good left-sided players? Ask Sir Alex Ferguson. Ask Dick Advocaat.

4. HOLDING A MIRROR TO SCOTIA'S FACE: RELIGIOUS ANXIETIES AND THEIR CAPACITY TO SHAKE A POST-UNIONIST SCOTLAND

Tom Gallagher

James MacMillan's lecture on 9 August 1999, at the start of the Edinburgh Festival, ignited the first major controversy about the condition of the Scottish nation seen in the post-unionist era, one which can be said to have begun with the inauguration of the Scottish parliament in May of that year.

He contended that religious bigotry with a specifically anti-Catholic focus remained alive and well in Scotland. It didn't just lurk at the margins of society but had exponents who held prestigious positions in Scottish life. He warned that the complacent response of those in authority towards anti-Catholicism was stifling Scotland's ability to evolve into a modern nation.[1]

The unsettling claims made by MacMillan about the position of the Catholic minority encompassing around 15 per cent of the Scottish population came at a time when Scotland appeared to be showing a united and self-confident face to the rest of the world. The economy continued to be in the doldrums, but an undeniable renaissance in the arts, and the successful acquisition of a parliament with tax-raising powers, suggested that the potential to change the face of Scotland from within had never been greater than it was at the end of the millennium.

This text will not try to determine the validity or otherwise of MacMillan's claims. The unwillingness of officialdom to gather statistical data on religious discrimination in employment or to contemplate acquiring legal powers to penalise it where it occurs means that the issue remains a hotly contested one (as, indeed, it was in Northern Ireland during the first half of the religious conflict there). Instead, I will assess the reaction of different sections of Scottish society to MacMillan's speech and the way they shaped the subsequent controversy.

MacMillan's lecture not only challenged the Scottish self-image of being an egalitarian, democratic and meritocratic society where achievers could rise irrespective of their social or religious background, it was also completely at variance with the way that MacMillan's own Catholic community had previously responded to the challenge of coming to terms with living in a Scotland where collective identity had, until recently, been shaped by Protestant symbols and public affirmations. So it is appropriate to begin with Scottish Catholics when examining the fall-out from the speech.

Its content directly challenged existing Catholic behaviour patterns. The design for living in a culture that could be hostile to the Catholic faith and its adherents had been to blend in, not to speak out or draw attention to oneself. MacMillan himself admitted that 'there are older Catholics who would be appalled at me raising the issue. That generation had survived through the avoidance of conflict, not putting their heads above the parapet.'[2]

This stoical endurance of injustice was very much the reaction of the Jews of central and Eastern Europe in the century of emancipation which they enjoyed following the lifting of anti-Jewish laws in post-1789 France and an increasing number of other countries. Religious solidarity and a belief in education enabled the Jews to survive and sometimes flourish in an often hostile secular environment. They lacked a national mission, at least before the emergence of Zionism at the turn of the century, and in times of national danger they were usually prepared to demonstrate loyalty to their country, as the patriotism of German Jews in the First World War clearly showed.

In Scotland, Catholics of Irish extraction also acquired much of their collective consciousness from a Church which was widely seen as a source that made hard and cramped lives bearable before offering the prospect of everlasting salvation. Catholic schools socialised young members of the community, at least in the west, following the granting of state aid under the 1918 Education (Scotland) Act. State-funded 'denominational' schools were equivalent to 'Rome on the Rates' for indignant Protestants. But their detractors overlooked the fact that Catholic schools were vitally important in encouraging ethnic minorities overwhelmingly located in the working class to largely accept their fate in an often unjust social system.[3] But a minority of alienated and radicalised Catholics rejected the path of acquiescence. They were prominent in the Communist Party just as the Jews were in east-central Europe.

The appeal of Marxism was the first indication that the Catholic enclave in Scotland was not immune to secular or even irreligious influences. It is Celtic Football Club, a secular institution overladen with religious and Irish symbolism, which provides an anchor of identity for many in the west of Scotland Catholic community as regular religious observance enters what may well prove an inexorable decline. For a not insignificant number of Catholics, identification with the Celtic cause has been combined with membership of a pro-Irish national sub-culture.[4] The management has discouraged the club from being viewed as a recreational substitute for Irish nationalism, and supporters' associations such as Bhoyzone, with its own magazine and Internet site, have promoted their own less embattled and often entertaining and witty forms of identification with the Celtic FC phenomenon.[5] But for a long time to come Old Firm games involving the Glasgow rivals Celtic and Rangers are likely to resemble international matches with rival national flags underlying the differences in loyalty. Not a few Celtic fans will urge on whatever team defeats Scotland, especially if it is from a Catholic country, as was the case with Costa Rica in the 1990 World Cup.[6]

It is not surprising in areas of social disadvantage where the decline of industry has put a halt to upward social mobility that pockets of Catholics have embraced a rebel Irish culture and opted out from identifying with anything Scottish or British. Institutions like Celtic and denominational schools, through their discouragement of Irish symbolism, may well have played a role in preventing this alienated group of Catholics (often attached to faith only in its tribal manifestation) from becoming a disruptive force in Scottish society. They are increasingly isolated in enclaves where high unemployment and premature death from a range of illnesses and high-risk lifestyles often prevail. MacMillan, with his commitment to radical Labour politics and his experience of growing up in a declining corner of industrial Scotland, cannot be unaware that many of those most affected by the sectarianism which he decries are found on the margins of society and that it is far from unusual for them to respond with a sectarianism of their own.

Simultaneously, a Catholic middle class has expanded beyond the professions traditionally servicing the Catholic community as shown by the 1992 survey on Scottish mobility, which revealed that the percentage of Catholics in non-manual employment had risen from 31 to 38 per cent in the space of 20 years.[7] An enlarged public sector and the arrival of multi-national firms to take over or supplant failing Scottish industrial companies meant that religious barriers preventing the emergence of a Catholic white-collar stratum slowly began to disappear.[8]

Catholic professionals from an underprivileged background who have enjoyed success in their chosen careers are unlikely, in many instances, to have warmed to MacMillan's speech. Like perhaps most members of the middle class, they are likely to be generally satisfied with the existing social system. It has afforded them success and to criticise it might only result in drawing attention to their own humble origins. Indeed, arguably the toughest criticism MacMillan received came from a prominent middle-class Catholic, Michael Tumelty, music critic of *The Herald*, who insisted that the composer's reputation had 'been damaged by the whole affair'.[9]

Middle-class Catholics are much more at ease with a Scottish identity than their mainly working-class forebearers. A 1998 compilation of opinion polls found that 58 per cent of Catholics would vote 'Yes' in a future referendum on Scottish independence, compared with 51 per cent of non-Catholics.[10] The fear that, in the absence of a British safety-net, a Scottish state might reproduce some of the ugly features of a self-governing Northern Ireland seems to have receded. Seven out of ten Catholics still backed Labour but the Scottish National Party (SNP) now received electoral recruits from Catholics that slightly exceeded their percentage in the population.

The swing to nationalism among Catholics is hardly surprising. It is the political equivalent of escaping from the ghetto and making one's way in mainstream society, a route taken by Jews, Poles and Irish in American cities as they shook off their Democratic Party affiliations to embrace the Republican Party as they moved from the inner city to the suburbs. Nationalism in Scotland, as in countless other places in the 200 years in which it has reshaped the world, is a political family offering acceptance and fellowship for people experiencing or desiring change in their lives. It has played this role for people moving to Scotland's new towns in the 1970s, for Asians, and even for some English incomers. So why should it be different for successful Catholics moving from the inner city or the housing scheme, perhaps allowing their attachment to regular church attendance to die away in the process, and thus becoming more receptive to membership of a new imagined community defined by Scottishness?

Thomas J. Winning, head of the Catholic Church in Scotland, has shown increasing empathy for nationalism. In 1998, at a conference of European bishops, he said that Scottish nationalism was 'mature, respectful of democracy, and international in outlook'.[11] In a statement from the bishops read out at every Catholic church in Scotland on the eve of the 1999 elections for the Scottish parliament, the church hierarchy pointedly re-affirmed its support for policies which the Labour Party had abandoned or diluted. It opposed Labour's introduction of university tuition fees and it demanded that nuclear weapons be scrapped, and resources re-allocated 'for our people's needs'. The document also called for legislators who were prepared to respect and support Catholic schools. Labour councils were closing Catholic schools in some areas for financial reasons at a time when the SNP backed their existence. In the 1990s, the SNP had done much to allay residual Catholic fears that they might be hostile to Catholic interests, by defending denominational schools as an integral part of the Scottish educational system that deserved to be funded from the public purse. The document read at Catholic Masses in Scotland on 2 May 1999 was careful to state that 'It is not our intention to tell electors which party or candidates they should favour', but it was clear that the policies which the bishops were championing were mainly ones now promoted by the SNP rather than Labour.[12]

An accommodation between the Catholic religious establishment and the SNP should not be seen as outlandish. The nature of their discourses is not dissimilar. Both institutions stress obedience and conformity to higher transcendental goals that require self-denial and sacrifice. The Church, in its constant search for relevance, is proud to emphasise its unbroken continuity with the past when Scotland was a state and Catholicism was one of its pillars. For its part, the SNP is content to enjoy closer links with an institution which promoted Scottish nationality despite the non-Scottish origins of most of its present adherents.

Alex Salmond, the SNP's leader, often uses radical rhetoric. But he will not be the first crusader to disguise what is essentially a conservative cause, that of creating a new state, by using radical language. The self-discipline and conformity that will be required by at least the first generation of citizens in an independent Scotland before it can hope to enjoy Scandinavian-style success will probably leave little room for the politics of radical redistribution. Thus, institutions like the Catholic Church, with a long track-record of persuading its adherents to endure hard times in this world before experiencing the miracle of salvation in the next, may find they have an important role to play in lowering expectations.[13]

For a conservative institution like Cardinal Winning's Church, the radical populism of Alex Salmond is an easier potion to swallow than James MacMillan's radical socialism. Both the leader of the SNP and Scotland's Cardinal are practised showmen whose use of the radical sound bite is designed to promote two conservative causes which have worked in tandem during this century to create new European nation-states from Ireland to Slovenia. MacMillan is a radical Catholic who has no time for unaccountable hierarchies and who thinks that it is the Church's duty to make sure that gospel values are the basis of life in today's Scotland. If his drive to eradicate religious bigotry from Scottish life got going, the Catholic Church could not afford to sit on the fence. It would be required to throw its weight behind sensible proposals to rectify abuses, and questions might be asked about why the Church had not spoken out during all those years when Catholics dominated the large underclass of underprivileged Scots.

It is hardly surprising that the reaction of Church spokesmen to MacMillan's speech was low-key and tight-lipped. That could also sum up the response of the SNP. Like all nationalist parties, it promotes a synthetic unity and prefers to turn its gaze away from awkward examples of division that dent the image of Scotland as a united community fit to walk into the everlasting sunset of national statehood. Mike Russell MSP was prompted by MacMillan's address to call for the revision of the 1701 Act of Settlement which prevents anyone who is a Catholic or married to a Catholic succeeding to the British throne.[14] But though clearly well meant, this initiative from the SNP was not likely to challenge the institutional discrimination which MacMillan claims still exists in Scotland.

Neither the SNP nor the Labour Party showed any enthusiasm for my proposal (expressed in a letter published in *The Guardian* on 11 August 1999) that the Scottish parliament authorise an official inquiry into MacMillan's charges and that, if they are found to have substance, consideration be given to introducing an anti-religious-discrimination law. The SNP's reticence about drawing attention to social and religious dissension in Scotland has already been discussed. Labour, a coalition of interests in a working class patently divided until recently along religious lines, has always been afraid of taking any step to promote one religious element over another. Socialism, or at least a commitment to policies of welfare rights and full employment, was the glue which enabled discordant religious interests to co-exist within the Labour Party. But following Labour's transformation into a non-socialist centre party, it no longer possesses a philosophy or a project able to contain religious differences. Its reluctance to appeal to patriotism or to urge the relegation of sectional rivalry in order to make Home Rule work attests to its own confusion about where to go now that it is the leading player in a devolved Scotland. It is unlikely to retain that position for many more elections if it doesn't use the institutions of a Scottish parliament to root out abuses which disfigure Scottish life. It is hardly good enough for John Reid MP to dismiss claims about bigotry still being in existence by saying that 'I don't think I would be standing here as Secretary of State for Scotland if it were'. MacMillan is likely to find that some of the biggest opponents of his call for openness and, if necessary, action on the question of religious discrimination comes from individuals of a Catholic background like Reid whose own personal success convinces him that little is wrong in this area.[15]

As for the Tories, Lord Forsyth, the former Secretary of State for Scotland, describes the 1701 Act of Settlement as the British Constitution's 'grisly secret'.[16] But the party's religious insensitivity was shown in 1997 when Donald Findlay QC was appointed to head its 'No' campaign in the referendum for a Scottish parliament. The revelation in the spring of 1999 that Findlay enjoyed singing sectarian songs which contained violently anti-Catholic lyrics strengthened MacMillan's claim that bigotry was not something that existed on the margins of Scottish society but had adherents in respectable walks of life.

The standard response to the charges contained in MacMillan's address from prominent Scots such as Tom Devine, Director of the Research Institute of Irish and Scottish Studies at Aberdeen University (and editor of this volume), and the nation's foremost novelist, Allan Massie, was that he was at least 20 years too late in articulating them.[17] Both of them emphasise that anti-Catholic prejudice was retreating in the face of secularism, the unprecedented number of religiously mixed marriages and the growth of a Catholic middle class as changes in the labour market, in terms of employment access and promotion, favoured religious minorities.

Editorials in the Scottish press also broadly emphasised these themes.

Unfavourable profiles of MacMillan, such as the one in *The Scotsman* of 14 August 1999 under the heading 'Bitter Melody', and headlines such as that in the *Sunday Herald* of 15 August, 'MacMillan calls for Catholic street marches', implying that 'the firebrand composer' was prepared to conjure up the sectarianism he decried, were not unusual. The editorial in that issue of the *Sunday Herald* insisted that 'a bloodless revolution' overcoming sectarianism had occurred. But its utter disapproval of MacMillan's call for an annual ecumenical procession in which Catholics would take the lead and its insistence that it would soon be seen as 'the Green walk' by 'the Orange enemy' suggests that it was not so sure after all that Scotland's religious divisions were disappearing into history.

The Scottish press has rarely shown an equivalent concern about Orange marches, regarding them as a quirky but familiar aspect of life in some of Scotland's major cities and towns. Nor has the press's search for a story that will generate controversy or lively debate extended to an interest in carrying out in-depth investigations into the extent of religious discrimination in Scottish life.

But in the 1990s the press did not shirk from publishing stories which suggested that bigotry in high places still enjoyed staying power. Arnold Kemp, editor of *The Herald* from 1981 to 1994, revealed on 11 August 1999 in a letter to the paper that the last question he was asked at the interview before his appointment was whether he was a Catholic. A few days later, it emerged that in 1994 Scotland's premier law officer Lord Hardie had 'faced apparent sectarian bias when standing for a senior post in the Bar'.[18] During the same week, leading Catholic professionals, the lawyer Joe Beltrami and the journalist Harry Conroy, described in some detail how bigotry had either held back their careers or had been rife in the professional arena which they were familiar with.[19] It is unlikely that such revelations would have been conveyed to print without the catalytic effect of MacMillan's high-voltage address, or that so many Catholics or ex-Catholics would have given accounts in the letters columns of *The Herald* and *The Guardian* of discrimination which they faced or observed on a regular basis. Joyce McMillan, the well-known columnist, recounted that for anyone travelling around central Scotland on public transport it was hard to avoid being confronted with sectarian hatred.[20] Andrew O'Hagan, the novelist, like James MacMillan brought up a Catholic in Ayrshire, related the strength of antagonism there in his younger days, and he had no doubt that Scotland remained 'a divisive bigoted society'.[21]

Doubtless spurred on by these claims and the life histories and experiences bolstering them, *The Herald* commissioned a poll to test Scottish perceptions about the staying power of religious divisions (to my knowledge, the first time such a poll had ever been commissioned by a Scottish newspaper). The findings were published in the 3 September 1999 edition of the paper. Nationally, 34 per cent of respondents felt that 'there is a deep-rooted anti-Catholic attitude through Scottish society'. A total of 13 per cent agreed strongly with the statement and 45 per cent disagreed with it.

Interestingly, it was in central Scotland, in the small communities and towns surrounding Glasgow and Edinburgh, that the highest incidence of those agreeing strongly with the statement (20 per cent) was to be found, compared with 14 per cent in Glasgow itself. A total of 43 per cent of Labour voters agreed with it, as did 37 per cent of Liberal Democrat supporters, but only 27 per cent of nationalists and 24 per cent of Tory supporters were prepared to say it was accurate. No significant variation emerged in terms of age, which suggests that a sizeable number of people aged between 18 and 34 still see bigotry as a noticeable feature of life.

The benign impact of the labour market and secularisation on institutional discrimination cannot be denied. But examples from countries with similar ethnic tensions suggest that the animosity can live on even when the objective basis for it disappears. Thus, in countries like Poland and Hungary, which largely lost their sizeable Jewish populations in the holocaust, anti-Semitism emerged as a noticeable trait in barometers of public opinion for the early 1990s. Politicians supposedly challenging traditional values were denounced for their Jewishness even though, in many cases, they were gentiles. Thus, in Scotland entities such as football clubs, bowling clubs, pubs and social clubs which were meant to mark a clear religious boundary in a divided society may still outlive the social and economic realities which brought them into being and even apparently thrive, like the Orange Order.[22] 'Anti-Semitism without Jews' is a distressing feature of life in parts of Eastern Europe. So why not 'Anti-Catholicism without Tims'? Might the Orange Order continue to be visible during the marching months even if the Catholic Church, under the weight of irrational policies emanating from the Vatican, loses its priests and finds its churches emptying?

Raw bigotry is also likely to survive in Ulster even as the Irish Republic becomes an emphatically secular society and attendance at Mass declines among young Catholics outside rural areas who already have a very attenuated relationship with the faith of their fathers.[23]

In Ireland – and, indeed, other societies such as Spain marked by heavy political conformity up to the 1970s – intellectuals play an important role in political life. Both the general public and elected representatives expect writers, musicians and performers to encourage debate, offer timely re-assessment of issues and generally act as a Fourth Estate along with the media, however discomfited the powerful may be at times with the results.

But the MacMillan episode strongly suggests that in Scotland there is a widespread feeling against intellectuals presuming to trespass into the political arena.[24] The composer claimed in his speech to detect a long-standing 'tendency to restrict, to control and to enforce conformity and homogeneity in Scottish life'. Scotland is certainly not a land which possesses the easy and rich oral culture so noticeable in its Celtic cousins. The dearth of summer schools debating multifarious aspects of the national condition which seem to proliferate behind every crevice and bush of Wales and Ireland may be an indication of that.

It is 'experts' who possess professional qualifications and respectable positions in the public services and academia who are expected to pronounce on awkward social questions and are listened to far more readily than a novelist, a poet or a composer. Maybe this is not altogether a retrograde thing. The diminished standing of intellectuals may have saved Scotland a lot of trouble when religious tensions were at a critical pitch in the inter-war years. George Malcolm Thomson, who could hardly conceal his hostility towards the Irish Catholic presence in Scotland, wielded a brilliant and dangerous pen, but he eventually found fulfilment working for the Beaverbrook press empire in less contentious areas.[25]

Twentieth-century intellectuals such as Hugh McDiarmid, Charles Rennie Mackintosh, Wendy Wood and Patrick Geddes have been prophets without an audience in their own country, and were not infrequently mocked when they made public pronouncements.

How far does a philistine attitude which regards it as the height of impertinence for a man of letters or music to comment on the condition of society in which his work is produced still resonate in Scottish society? If Michael Tumelty is to be believed, very widely indeed. Tumelty argued a week after MacMillan's address that the composer had forfeited a lot of his reputation by switching roles. He claimed that 'within the arts world a huge range of people, from orchestral managers and directors to the shop-floor workers – the musicians themselves – have expressed themselves shocked at what he has done, and dismayed by what they describe as his "loss of integrity".'

Tumelty claimed to 'have lost count of the number of folk – from commonplace to important – who have stated categorically . . . that . . . when they hear MacMillan's name, they know they will no longer think of the composer but of the controversialist and the bigot'. This sentence suggests two things: that controversy is beyond the pale in douce Scotland, and just what a divided society it must really be for a mere speech to elicit such a strong reaction from members of what I had always hitherto regarded as a rather open-minded profession. Perhaps it is too flimsy evidence from which to deduce that Scotland remains a deeply conformist society hardly at ease with itself or capable of self-examination when one of its brighter talents holds up a mirror to its face. But Tumelty's article, the views of the author himself and the ones he claimed were widespread in the profession he knows best, was one of the most dispiriting things I read about Scotland for many a month.[26]

Popular musicians like Sir Harry Lauder, Jimmy Shand and Andy Stewart celebrated the synthetic unity of a folksy and invented Scotland. Why shouldn't a composer who has already earned fame far from these shores as a pioneering and gifted exponent of his craft pause for a moment to reflect on the nature of the society in which he makes his music? Musicians have played a role in challenging injustice and promoting a range of reputable causes. The violinist Yehudi Menuhin, with his championing of Jewish rights, and the cause of nations like Romania, trampled under by communism, springs immediately to mind. So does Pablo Casals, the Catalan cellist who, in exile, was an inspiration to his people during the dark years of Francoism.

But at least the response in the press and in *The Herald*'s poll to the accusations made in MacMillan's address suggests that Scots are less willing than before to endure discrimination or public displays of sectarianism in silence. MacMillan himself suggested that the impetus behind publicising his thoughts on sectarianism lay in an incident which had occurred two years before, when his six-year-old daughter, Catherine, 'came face to face with sectarian abuse from some drunks' outside the church where she attended her first Easter vigil service. He stated, 'When I was a young man I thought this would disappear from Scotland but now I find myself having to explain to my children why there is resentment aimed at them.'

Significantly, the man who passed on to a Scottish newspaper the video that forced Donald Findlay QC to resign as vice-chairman of Rangers says he took the decision for not dissimilar reasons. This Protestant Scot said he acted because 'I don't want my daughter to be brought up as a bigot'.[27] This whistleblower deserves to be a hero but he lives in fear of his life after a Rangers fanzine published his name and address.[28] If bigotry truly was on its last legs, would someone who had pointed the finger at an example of the genre in high places really have to be so fearful in Scotland today? I very much doubt it.

The man's courage should be hailed by influential Scots who have the power to change attitudes and practices by recourse to legislation if necessary. But Scotland's First Minister Donald Dewar showed his distaste for becoming embroiled in the controversy about religious prejudice by issuing the platitudinous comment 'I don't believe the average Scot is a bigot'.[29] Was there a society, even Nazi Germany or Milosevic's Serbia, where a *majority* of the population ever held such views?

It might have been preferable if MacMillan had found space in his 9 August talk to acknowledge that no branch of Christianity in Scotland has a monopoly on bigoted or intolerant attitudes. At different times in their history, those monotheistic religions which claim to be the only true road to salvation have often behaved in appallingly similar ways in order for their righteousness to prevail.

A glimmer of such rigid orthodoxy was provided by Cardinal Winning at a ceremony in Glasgow's City Hall on 15 January 1999 to mark the 50th anniversary of his entry to the priesthood. According to the front-page report in the following day's *Scotsman*, the Cardinal argued that Catholicism would be Scotland's sole faith in the twenty-first century. He claimed that the papacy was prepared to cede control of Scottish Catholicism in the ecumenical cause but that a reunified Christian Church would be required to return to pre-Reformation doctrine and hierarchy. He told *The Scotsman*, 'The other Churches will have to accept bishops. There will be no movement on doctrine and no movement on the seven sacraments . . . When we speak to other Churches, we have the right to say to them, "Look right back to the beginning and ask yourselves, why did you abandon us?"'[30]

It is difficult to imagine that this speech was made at the beginning of Christian Unity week in Scotland, but it was. Nor would it be unusual if mainstream Protestant faiths were to see a hint of triumphalism and self-righteousness in Cardinal Winning's pronouncements, which are likely to hinder rather than promote progress in Christian understanding. Some who refuse to believe that the Catholic leopard can ever change its spots might see such public remarks as a throwback to the long cold war between Protestants and Catholics in which Scotland found itself one of the hot spots.

This article has offered backing for much that was in MacMillan's speech, but he may not have advanced his case for recognising injustice against Catholics past and present by drawing 'parallels between Mao Tse-tung, John Knox, Andrew Melville and Pol Pot'. He seemed to have realised that he may have been going too far, when he added the parenthesis 'well, perhaps not'. The effect of the Scottish Reformation on the arts was undoubtedly highly regressive, but Scotland was largely spared the brutal religious warfare which convulsed Ireland and even England in the seventeenth century; indeed, intra-Protestant violence was far more noticeable than active persecution of Catholics. Indeed, it has to be admitted by someone still attached to the Catholic faith, dismayed at the way that the reactionary papacy of John Paul II has hollowed out the Church nearly as effectively as Communist persecution might have done, that many of the Maos and Pol Pots were on the Catholic side during Europe's wars of religion. The evidence from Spain, France, Bohemia and Germany is compelling. Subjects who refused to bring their religion into line with that of the ruler were persecuted, killed or driven out in huge numbers.

The Church of Scotland responded with tact and restraint to this part of MacMillan's speech. Perhaps it feels, unlike its Catholic counterpart, that it is futile to be still engaging in the religious numbers game: which denomination will be the biggest one in the new millennium, which has the most blood on its hands, which suffered the greatest amount of persecution?

The religious intolerance which still prevails in an age of growing irreligion stems not just from inherited traditions which enjoy a stubborn afterlife when the objective conditions for them have diminished; it shouldn't be forgotten that Scotland remains a land of scarcity where the climate, the soil and finite natural resources make it difficult for a tolerable living to be had by many of its citizens. The struggle against natural adversity and also human injustice has given rise to institutions which stress co-operation and solidarity but others which promote exclusion and discrimination.

The heat is probably going out of religious discrimination but its decline has been a slower process than many expected, including commentators like myself who closely studied the phenomenon in the 1980s. The danger is that the spirit of narrow factionalism which acquired a life of its own beyond any specific religious message will prevail in a largely secular Scotland.

In politics, the trench warfare between activists in the SNP and the Labour Party will soon appear to be the bitterest in British politics if the unionist-nationalist compromise begins to work in Ulster. In communities stretching from Paisley to Dundee it is often impossible to tell the rivals apart because they look and sound so similar and their governing style is strikingly at one. Coalition politics has only made modest progress in the new Edinburgh parliament, perhaps because geography and a range of other factors have combined to make Scotland a land where factions easily form.

Scotland's shame is perhaps not bigotry's obstinate refusal to lie down and die but the fact that its metaphors and behaviour patterns have too easily reproduced themselves in other walks of life. Ironically, it is the Catholic Church establishment which, in the first weeks of the new millennium, has shown how easily that can be done. Cardinal Winning placed himself at the head of a campaign to prevent the Scottish parliament repealing Section 28 of the 1988 Local Government Act which outlaws the promotion of homosexuality in schools. He described homosexuality as a 'perversion', arguing that the mere teaching of homosexuality as an acceptable relationship could be interpreted as promotion of it. The playwright George Rosie was quick to see the irony when Cardinal Winning compared the 'threat' of homosexual lobby to the menace of German militarism: it was almost a carbon copy of what leading Presbyterian churchmen were saying in the 1920s . . . about the Cardinal's own flock. He cited the Rev Duncan Cameron who described Catholics as 'a menace more insidious by far, more formidable too, than the menace of the German Empire and its multifarious legions.'

Winning claims to abhor the sin while loving the sinner. But what this prelate says about homosexuals, other churchmen like the Reverend Ian Paisley are also careful to say about his Catholic quarry. There is plenty of evidence from Northern Ireland and Scotland that after Catholic-bashing or queer-bashing from the pulpit, there is no shortage of bigots willing to drive the point home with knives and fists.

Cardinal Winning has attracted the scorn of many within his own Church appalled at his readiness to give free play to the kind of intolerance visited upon Scottish Catholics right up to our own times. Winning's actions suggest that he sees the path to acceptance and influence in Scotland as being found in giving a lead to its most liberal instincts. Both James MacMillan and Alex Salmond who, in their different ways, have hoped to harness the Catholic Church behind ambitious projects of change, may well have been given plenty of food for thought by seeing the prejudices the Cardinal has been prepared to whip up.

The timorous reaction of the Scottish parliament to the controversy ignited by MacMillan suggests that it is not going to be a sounding-board able to reflect the unease felt in Scottish society about divisive issues that remain relevant in the post-unionist era and perhaps able to do something about them. This is a lost opportunity and it increases the likelihood that Home Rule will be superseded by the rhetorically radical but more conservative option of a separate Scotland. Concentration on state-building will be a long, arduous process that will probably leave little inclination to take remedial action to tackle social problems with a religious origin that still disfigure Scottish society.

MacMillan has held up a mirror to the face of Scotland. Forward-looking elements in Scottish society wish to put a divisive past behind them and contribute to creating a better world in which ethnic strife can no longer wreak such mayhem. But the prospect that sectarianism will completely die out in Scotland is a remote one as long as politicians avert their gaze from its ugly countenance.

Notes

[1] This paragraph summarises key passages of the speech which has been circulated to the contributors of this volume as well as drawing on Gerald Seenan's article about it on p.1 of *The Guardian* on 9 August 1999.

[2] Interview with Pat Kane, *Sunday Herald*, 15 August 1999.

[3] My researches suggest that James Breen, a Catholic headteacher in Coatbridge, was fairly exceptional when, in the early 1960s, he personally confronted bank managers in the town about their refusal to recruit new Catholic staff who possessed the same or superior qualifications to Protestant applicants who were being taken on. See T. Gallagher, *Glasgow, The Uneasy Peace: Religious Tension in Modern Scotland* (Manchester, 1987), p.251.

[4] See J.M. Bradley, *Ethnic and Religious Identity in Modern Scotland* (Aldershot, 1995), esp. chapter 6.

[5] Bhoyzone's address is www.bhoyzone.com. In November 1999 when I accessed its pages, the open forum facility had been temporarily discontinued owing to the extreme nature of some of the contributions which had resulted in the police being notified.

[6] This point is made by a Donegal Irishman resident in Glasgow, writing under the pseudonym 'Mick Derrig', in Sinn Fein's e-mail edition of 'Irish News' for 28–9 August 1999, the title of the article being 'Britain's Other Taigs'.

[7] Letter from Dr Rory Williams, University of Glasgow, in *The Herald*, 13 August 1999.

[8] Gallagher, *The Uneasy Peace*, p.307.

[9] Michael Tumelty, 'Knowing the score', *The Herald*, 19 August 1999.

[10] John Curtice, 'Support for independence takes a leap of faith among Scotland's Catholics', *The Scotsman*, 28 August 1998.

[11] Jack O'Sullivan, 'Bishops speak out for SNP policies', *The Independent*, 28 April 1999.

[12] Ibid.

[13] The limits of the SNP's radicalism are perhaps shown by the willingness of Scotland's most aggressively successful company, the Stagecoach group, to reportedly bankroll the party to the tune of several hundreds of thousands of pounds in 1999 alone. See Murray Ritchie, 'Souter speaks out in SNP funds row', *The Herald*, 13 July 1999.

[14] Iain Martin and Tom Peterkin, 'MSPs move to lift royal ban on Catholics', *Scotland on Sunday*, 15 August 1999.

[15] Murray Ritchie, 'Dewar claims the average Scot is not a bigot', *The Herald*, 11 August 1999.

[16] Iain Martin and Tom Peterkin, 'MSPs move to lift royal ban on Catholics', *Scotland on Sunday*, 15 August 1999.

[17] For Tom Devine, see Gavin Madeley, 'Backing for belief of anti-Catholic bigotry', *The Herald*, 3 September 1999; for Allan Massie, see his article, 'Cancer of bigotry in retreat', *The Scotsman*, 10 August 1999.

[18] Brian Donnelly, 'Bigotry claim in Bar poll', *The Herald*, 16 August 1999.

[19] Joe Beltrami and Harry Conroy, 'The barriers we had to overcome as Catholics', *Daily Record*, 10 August 1999.

[20] *The Guardian*, 9 August 1999.

[21] Andrew O'Hagan, 'A nation scarred by bigotry', *Sunday Herald*, 15 August 1999.

[22] See Jim McManus, 'Two contrasting comments from east and west', *Open House*, No 82, September 1999, p.3.

[23] For an insightful comparison of religious tensions on both sides of the Irish sea and the different ways in which they have been accommodated, see Graham Walker's *Intimate Strangers* (Edinburgh, 1995).

[24] I am quoting Dr Sarah M. Dunnigan, who wrote a letter defending MacMillan from criticism by *The Herald*'s music correspondent Michael Tumelty, which the newspaper published on 21 August 1999.

[25] For Thomson's anti-Irish Catholic writings, see his two books, *Caledonia, or the Future of the Scots* (London, 1927) and *The Re-discovery of Scotland* (London, 1928).

[26] Michael Tumelty, 'Knowing the score', *The Herald*, 19 August 1999.

[27] Deborah Orr, 'Dancing to the bigot's tune', *The Independent*, 16 August 1999.

[28] Ibid.

[29] Murray Ritchie, 'Dewar claims the average Scot is not a bigot', *The Herald*, 11 August 1999.

[30] John McCann and Ian Bell, 'Catholic faith will prevail – Winning', *The Scotsman*, 16 January 1999.

5. A CULTURE OF PREJUDICE: PROMOTING PLURALISM IN EDUCATION FOR A CHANGE

Gerry P.T. Finn

Introduction

James MacMillan's Edinburgh Festival lecture[1] was interpreted as an attempt to give voice to the prejudice experienced by Scotland's Catholic[2] community. The response to MacMillan's comments was inevitably dependent on how his talk was framed by the media. Media contributions from four leading Scottish academics formed an important element in the construction of this mediated reality of MacMillan's lecture. It is significant that not one of them had heard or read MacMillan's lecture before they commented.[3] Instant punditry raises ethical questions about the role of academics as commentators on Scottish social life.[4] However, the MacMillan episode is much more important for what it reveals about Scottish society's slow progress towards the development of a pluralist society, and that has profound consequences for all of Scotland's communities.

Speaking Out from Within

James MacMillan's Edinburgh Festival lecture was written in a spirit of optimism and excitement at the prospect of Scottish democratic renewal and with approval and support for the power of ecumenical activity in Scotland. MacMillan's main theme was the acceptance and image of Catholics in Scotland. Here he evidently did distinguish between the past and the present. However, the purpose of his lecture was to relate his experience of a culture of prejudice against Catholics, which he then illustrated. MacMillan described his own feelings of bemusement that although 'things have changed for the better', some prejudice remains. He illustrated some of the more dramatic forms by which that prejudice is expressed, but much of his own anxiety was to do with the more banal forms of anti-Catholic prejudice. He claimed that prejudice 'is not particularly malign' but a form of '"sleep-walking" bigotry'.

It requires considerable personal courage to describe so openly one's own responses to, and feelings about, this prejudice. MacMillan tried to communicate how it feels to be a Scottish Catholic and how Catholics experience this sense of anti-Catholicism. He successfully managed to convey something of the complexity of this response. He did not claim that his own personal experience was universal, although he clearly did judge much of it to be typical. He observed the existence of what could be termed a 'Catholic cringe' as one of the responses to anti-Catholic prejudices, and he owned up to it having had some influence on him. Nonetheless, he said he believed that 'keeping one's head down' is now more characteristic of past generations of

53

Catholics. And MacMillan's own decision to speak out gave substance to the power of this belief and to his belief that a Catholic voice should be allowed to speak and be heard on these matters. That is simply part of his overview that Catholics (and Catholicism) have much to contribute to Scottish civic society but are hindered from doing so, not necessarily as individuals, but as Catholics, because of anti-Catholic prejudice.

This distinction offers a subtle analysis and one that closely echoes the understanding of societal prejudices as being concerned with one's social identity, not one's individual being.[5] Some shrewd questions about the nature of Scottish society can be discerned in MacMillan's comments. The most important is what should pluralism in Scottish society really mean? Can Scotland be truly a pluralist society if it does not celebrate diversity and recognise the benefits of dialogue between different value-systems? On this issue, MacMillan worries that the 'tendency to restrict, to control and to enforce conformity and homogeneity is an obsessive paranoid flaw in the Scottish character'. That is what he perceives to underlie much of the response to Catholics, Catholicism and other Scottish minorities. But he does not perceive conformity to be a characteristic tied to any particular Scottish social group. The desire to control and enforce conformity is not bound up with any specific religion or set of beliefs; this desire is too widespread for that to be true. That is why diversity poses such a challenge for all Scots. Which is why, as many responses to MacMillan showed, this desire for conformity and homogeneity threatens to restrict recognition of the validity of the diversity of Scottish identities.

MacMillan, however, does appreciate the reality of diversity within social identities. He did not present a narrow view of Scottish Catholics, or of what it means to be a Catholic. His own opposition to some strands of Scottish Catholicism was clear. He described a heterogeneous Catholic community, containing a Catholic intelligentsia that is just as diverse. Although MacMillan's main focus was upon Scotland's Catholic community, it was apparent from his passing comments that he acknowledges heterogeneity to be a feature of all communities; indeed, the need to recognise and prize heterogeneity formed the leitmotiv throughout his composition. He believes these values to be an important concern for other Scots too; he said his piece in the expectation that, although some discordant notes would arise, there was much more potential for the development of further harmonies around his general theme. In his finale, he identified the potential power of an alliance which would unite 'countless' Scots in opposition to free-market capitalism and its threat to human individuality and precious Scottish civic and spiritual values. MacMillan proposed renewing Scotland through the realisation of the prized Scottish values of egalitarianism and inclusiveness.

A Land of Myth and Haver

Paradoxically, MacMillan, in addressing these core Scottish values, may have identified one of the problems faced by Scotland, and one reason for some of the responses to his lecture. Scotland can often be a land of myths and havers. Many Scots believe that egalitarianism and social inclusion are accomplishments that come with the territory. In an important study of

Scotland, David McCrone notes that the myth of egalitarianism has 'at root an asociological, an almost mystical element. It is as if Scots are judged to be egalitarian by dint of racial characteristics, of deep social values.'[6] McCrone's own position on Scottish myths is complicated, sometimes even unclear.[7] He recognises the complexity of this (and other) Scottish myths and outlines their use by both progressives and conservatives. Progressives can use this myth to support the need for change to overcome inequality;[8] conservatives can enlist it to argue that social inequality is unimportant because all Scots are recognised to be of equal value. This inter-relationship of myth with ideological visions of social reality leads McCrone to judge that the myth of Scottish egalitarianism is not open to scientific falsification.[9]

There can be little doubt that attempts to falsify myths will not follow the idealised model, or perhaps more accurately the mythology,[10] of the process of scientific falsification. Nonetheless, McCrone adopts an unduly pessimistic position,[11] one that would be unhelpful if the same logic were applied to other forms of mythology. Societal prejudices, for example, also rely on myths for their core content. Prejudicial beliefs are also inextricably interlinked to ideologies and their construction of social reality. That relationship cannot, and does not, excuse inaction in the face of prejudice. Indeed, this very myth of Scottish egalitarianism has been one of the obstacles that has hindered both the identification of racism in Scotland and recognition of the need to mobilise against it.

Instead, racism is often denied by the powerful chorus that there is 'No problem here'.[12] Or, if the problem of racism is accepted, the problem is localised and racism becomes equated with an identifiable presence of the racialised ethnic minority. Identification of racism with specific localities occurs because the presence of a target community makes the overt display of racism so much more probable there. However, this identification of racism with areas where the minority is to be found leads to the belief that the emergence of racism is itself the responsibility of the minority. So the target community whose presence becomes the rallying point for the racist 'cause' is now transformed into the cause of racism. That process also serves to deny majority ethnic responsibility for the racism. Mythologies of racism depend on underlying ideological beliefs,[13] but that simply underlines the importance of challenging the ideologies as well as the myths.

These comments very briefly outline some common mechanisms of racism that operate across a number of countries,[14] and Scotland is little different. Indeed, some parallels are obvious. Identification of a visible Catholic presence – whether that is defined geographically or in terms of social institutions, such as Catholic schools, or social or leisure activities, such as football clubs – has become associated with the belief that these displays of difference are the root causes of social division. And, strange though it may first appear, it is especially pertinent to present this important confusion of cause and effect in relation to the racism. One minor global difference in forms of racism concerns not the mechanisms of racism but the ethnic communities that are racialised. Throughout Britain[15] that process applied to the Irish and their descendants; in Scotland racialisation operated with greater intensity than in England.[16]

Some refuse to accept that the Irish or the Irish-Scots were racialised. A difficulty some have with this analysis is that they operate within a belief system that requires 'races' to be colour-coded. That is to compound the problem of racism. It is certainly untrue that the Irish or Irish-Scots constitute a 'race', but it is equally untrue to apply the notion of 'race' to other human social groups. Indeed, recognition and understanding of the process of racialisation of the Irish in Scotland provide one means to demonstrate the error (and injustice) of racialisation, regardless of the community to which it is applied.[17] Racialisation transforms insignificant human differences among members of the one human race into what are believed to be significant markers of racialised social division. An appreciation of this process teaches another important lesson: it is not human difference and variation, which are undeniable features of the global human population, that pose problems, it is the interpretation and assignment of meaning to these variations and differences that can be problematic. These are precisely the issues raised by MacMillan's talk.

MacMillan does not locate the problem of the treatment of religious difference in Scotland in its socio-historical context of beliefs in associated racial difference.[18] Nonetheless, this racial dimension was an especially important element in the cocktail of prejudices associated with the Catholic presence in Scotland. The Irish and their descendants were seen by many to be a race apart for much of the nineteenth century; their adherence to Catholicism was taken as proof of their racial degeneracy. In Scotland this form of racism grew worse over time and, fuelled by deteriorating socio-economic circumstances, reached its sad apogee in the inter-war years of the twentieth century.[19] In that period state funding for Catholic schools was turned to political advantage by those determined to heighten inter-group tension and stoke the fires of prejudice against the Catholic Irish.[20] Yet the provision of Catholic schools by the state was little more than the extension to Scotland's minority faith groups of the policy that had brought Presbyterian schools under state control.

The state schools formed as a result of the 1872 Education Act were non-denominational, but *de facto* non-denominational Presbyterian schools. Indeed, the 1872 Act was drafted to ensure a compromise between the different theological positions of the three main Presbyterian Churches on the relationship between Church and State, because that theological difference had direct practical consequences for the place of religious instruction within state-funded schools.[21] The Act deliberately fudged the status of religious instruction, but the provision of an exemption clause, which legitimised withdrawal from religious instruction, signalled what was expected to happen.[22] This fudge, however, did not please the more uncompromising Presbyterians. Consequently, Orangemen and Conservatives, including significant figures in the development of Glasgow Rangers FC,[23] became even closer allies in the successful campaign to prescribe Presbyterian religious instruction. Theological sensitivities required that some fudge remained, but the preamble to the bill was amended. Now it was explicitly stated that once Presbyterian Church schools became state schools they would continue on the basis of custom and practice to give religious instruction. As the 1914–18 'Great War' drew to a close, the British coalition government was eager to ensure a unified and modern educational system which would prepare British youth for the future. The intention was to guarantee that Britain could not only win on future battlefields but could also successfully compete in the arena of international economics. Proposed full state funding for Scottish denominational schools was a by-product of the government's desire to improve the quality of state education.[24]

Expressions of concern about the Presbyterian dominance of Scottish education were not based on antagonism between Catholics and Protestants. The Episcopal Church in Scotland, in communion with the established Church of England, could also make clear its fears about the treatment of Episcopal pupils in the state schools formed by the 1872 Act. Both minority faith communities had legitimate concerns about the operation of the non-denominational Presbyterian education system. As a result, denominational schools associated with both Churches remained in operation, outside the state system. Both Scottish Catholics and Episcopalians complained that full funding for what were generally recognised to be Presbyterian schools inflicted injustice on Catholic and Episcopalians alike.[25] They paid rates that supported these state schools but, though eligible for some state grants, they had to struggle to find funding for their own schools.[26] Government proposals for full state support for Scottish denominational schools were presented by leading politicians as a policy to remedy this injustice. When Scottish Secretary of State Robert Munro introduced the bill, he explained, 'I hope under the bill to retain for all classes of children in Scotland, whatever the religious belief of their parents may be, their natural birthright of equality of educational opportunity.'[27]

It is sad that Munro's invocation of justice and the need to counter inequality – perhaps one of the earliest examples of an appeal to equality of opportunity[28] – by providing full state funding to denominational schools has been forgotten. It is more than ironic that this neglect is the result of the rhetorically successful racial campaign of the inter-war years. Scotland then was viewed by some influential Protestants to be a nation 'swamped' by the Irish,[29] who were blamed for all manner of social ills, perceived to be gaining in political power and influence, and portrayed by some to be engaging in political plots to take over Scottish society. Provision of Catholic schools by the state, as a result of the 1918 Education (Scotland) Act, was fundamental to the construction of this framework of racist beliefs. The establishment of Catholic state schools, judged to be centres of paganism and biblical error, was presented as the result, and therefore also the evidence, of this supposed growth in Catholic power, influence and political intrigue. Opposition to Catholic schools then became central to the persistent political efforts to mobilise anti-Irish and anti-Catholic prejudices.[30] Unfortunately, not only do contemporary beliefs remain influenced by that history of misrepresentation, but that history itself is inadequately understood.[31]

As a result, debate on Catholic schools has even fallen victim to the usual rhetorical strategies mustered to buttress inequality. Catholic schools are presented as causes of inequality rather than as a remedy, which is to confound cause and effect. Moreover, the remedy has even become framed as a privilege rather than as the recognition of a right. There are those who do recognise something of this history of Catholic denominational schooling but now contend that there is no contemporary need for Catholic schools, because anti-Catholicism no longer exists. Perhaps this argument touches on the greatest irony: often criticism of Catholic schools (and Catholics for wishing their retention) is the most obvious and evident example of the hold of this sadly undeparted prejudice.[32]

Now the description of opposition to Catholic schools as a form of prejudice, derived from anti-Irish racism, causes some hackles to rise.[33] In part that is because the nature of prejudice is still embedded in a mire of misunderstandings.[34] Prejudice is seen by most people to be the property of others, best categorised as bigots, rather than themselves, and prejudice is believed to be easily detected as the self-evident expression of irrational and uninformed views. Yet prejudice is not some individual aberration. It is an intrinsically social phenomenon in which substantial numbers accept and share the same system of beliefs about another group; these beliefs can often appear in a sophisticated guise. Consequently, these strong societal prejudices are perceived to be, and treated as, unchallengeable forms of knowledge. Therefore, any challenge to these beliefs must be absurd. The denial of prejudice is itself assisted by another implication of this belief system. If the accusation of prejudice is taken to be absurd, then that perception of irrationality, itself a supposed characteristic of prejudice, provides a powerful means by which to dismiss and relocate the source of prejudice. Consideration of the nature of the accusation becomes unnecessary if it is to be dismissed as 'absurd'. Instead, it is the accusation of prejudice that becomes defined as the sign of the 'real' prejudice and the location of the supposed underlying cause of inter-group tension and friction. This patterning of social experience provides a very powerful denial of anti-Catholic prejudice.

Prejudice is usually accompanied by a range of rhetorical devices to deflect recognition of the legitimacy of the complaint of prejudice. Prejudice itself now takes subtle forms. For example, in the United States anti-black racism is now less often asserted in traditionally crude and obvious fashion. Instead this racism is increasingly coded in a more subtle manner and more often directed against the symbolic presence of the black community.[35] Again the parallels with prejudice directed against the symbolic legacy of the presence of the Catholic Irish-Scottish community are strong.

Psychologists have long recognised that prejudice is a complex social phenomenon which can be determined by evidence of involvement in a spectrum of prejudicial actions. Indeed, in his classic text, Allport distinguished five different forms of activity in the spectrum of prejudice.[36] First was 'antilocution', or prejudice in talk, which was followed by 'avoidance', in which the prejudiced simply avoid the disliked group. Then there was 'discrimination', by which Allport meant that some overtly detrimental distinction was made that was directly disadvantageous to members of the target community. For Allport, discrimination could be exhibited in any one of a number of ways, including employment, housing, education, politics and recreation. 'Physical attack', another form of prejudice, took the form of violence or semi-violence and produced feelings of threat and fear in the target population. Finally there was 'extermination', which for Allport entailed some systematic deployment of violence leading to death and which took its most horrific form in the Holocaust.

Allport did not identify these five different categories of prejudice with the intention of producing some exhaustive classificatory system. He certainly did not believe that he had provided some five-point scale that would allow precision in measuring the intensity of prejudice. He recognised that there could be important differences within each action; verbal expressions of prejudice could themselves range from the relatively mild to the intense expression of prejudice against a target group.[37] Instead Allport wished to emphasise the complexity, range and variability of actions that are characteristic of prejudice, and warn of the interconnections between these different expressions of prejudice. Although the mildest, 'polite prejudice' in private talk, could have no direct consequences, that did not mean that it could be ignored. Activity at lower levels made more intense activity at the higher levels much more probable; in fact, sustained and intense action at lower levels made prejudicial expression at higher levels almost inevitable. Therefore, the only course of action is to challenge all forms of prejudice.

Giving Voice to Opposition to Prejudice

MacMillan's talk may not offer some scholarly analysis of the complexity of prejudice, but it is clear that, unlike many who present a supposedly learned account, he does recognise the interconnectedness of its different forms of expression.[38] Nor does MacMillan labour under the illusion that prejudice and discrimination are equivalent. Discrimination against group members is dependent on prejudice but it is not a necessary consequence of prejudice.[39] Instead MacMillan gives voice to Catholic sorrow that there still exists a culture of prejudice which fails to recognise them equally as fellow Scots. His talk and his illustrations show that he is well aware that the most common expressions of anti-Catholic prejudice are now relatively mild. However, he is puzzled by the continued existence of this prejudice, and the persistence with which its existence is repeatedly denied. MacMillan is also troubled by the occasionally nasty manifestations, including physical attacks, that can result. He worries that the continued pattern of neglect, and denial, could make matters worse and believes that the present spirit of optimism in Scotland means that the time is now right for Scots to work together to eliminate this and other forms of societal prejudice.

Although MacMillan does not inter-relate anti-Catholic prejudice with anti-Irish racism, that is a substantial component of the history of the phenomenon. Nor is it the case that anti-Irish racism can safely be believed to have simply disappeared in Britain, let alone in Scotland.[40] The recent report for the Commission for Racial Equality[41] presented evidence that this manifestation of racism appeared on both sides of the Anglo-Scottish border; it noted that what was termed 'sectarianism' in Scotland was deeply embedded within this racist framework. One telling observation was that the very suggestion of the existence of anti-Irish racism, on either side of the border, produced hostility and denials of extremely high intensity. This process of denial was identified as adding to the exclusionary practices faced by the Irish and Irish-descended communities in Britain.

The denial of all forms of racism is common. In Scotland, the myth of egalitarianism has been extended to deny even obvious expressions of racism. As a result, everyday forms of banal racism continue unchecked in the face of little recognition, let alone opposition.[42] The mythology of egalitarianism may appear positive or irresistible to those Scots who do not suffer because of it, but it is strongly countered by voices from black and Asian-Scottish[43] communities.

MacMillan can be seen to be adding his voice to this broad concern. He has chosen to speak as a Scottish Catholic, which can be seen to be a more inclusive category than that of Catholic Irish-Scots.[44] MacMillan the composer is an internationally minded, forward-looking Catholic Scot,[45] and he derives much of his musical inspiration from this duality. Although anti-Catholicism has been so intertwined with anti-Irish racism, it is MacMillan's chosen accent for his own voice that should be addressed, and it is this voice that needs to be understood.

In both emancipatory research and teaching about social justice and inclusion,[46] the concept of voice has become an increasingly important one. It signals recognition that, without their active involvement and participation, minority communities cannot be defined, explained, instructed or, in some other sense, 'helped' by others. 'Voice' refers instead to the need for some recognisable form of reciprocity, which requires mutual respect, and an effort to collaborate and engage in dialogue. That means that a social reality is not imposed on the minority, nor is the minority voice silenced. Instead there is an awareness of the possible impact of power, position and authority in distorting the desired processes of social exchange, collaboration and dialogue. Silence is indeed one significant measure of the extent to which those factors have distorted the exchange. A more subtle sign is when minority voices feel obliged to echo the sounds of the majority, the dominant and more privileged account. Contributions to the development of the concept of voice have come from activists opposing prejudice in a variety of struggles against inequality, including civil-rights movements, disabled-people's movements and feminism and feminist pedagogy.[47] The concept of voice is still in the process of development, as are the associated notions of the authentic voice, representative voice or collective voice; the elaboration of how these images emerge in majority and minority communicative exchange is also still being explored.

Nonetheless, suggestions as to why some voices are given priority over others have emerged from a neo-Vygotskyan perspective. Wertsch has shown that the 'voice of decontextualised rationality' usually has power over others. This voice relies on a system of representation that is taken to be abstract and neutral and offers accounts in a manner that is independent of specific speech contexts. Normally this voice is contrasted with experientially based voices that are cast as 'contextualised forms of representation'. Their accounts are judged to be particularistic, leading to unsubstantiated generalisations, and influenced by emotions rather than detachment; this perspective draws on the individual's social identity and own experience.[48] However, the 'voice of decontextualised rationality' minimises, even denies, value in experience, and strives instead to present a contained and apparently independent narrative. Wertsch's analysis has some similarities with the supposed dichotomy between scientific and experiential modes in the interpretation of human experience; he recognises that this dichotomy is often a false one. There are occasions in which the voice of contextualised forms of representation is equally as good, or even better, in reporting social reality.

Wertsch ponders the precise circumstances that lead to one voice being privileged over another. He identifies the way that this outcome is related to power inequalities, which also explains why other voices can even be silenced. He provides some reasons why the dominant voice usually appears to be that of decontextualised rationality. Wertsch, however, also observes that this voice is traditionally dominant in the field of contemporary public policy, even though its role is questionable. In addition, this is the voice invoked to support or defend decisions in which it has played little or no part. Often this voice is appropriated by majorities for use in the social exchange with minorities. Wertsch concludes that understanding these types of issues is crucial 'for our understanding of some of the most pressing problems of our time'.[49] Responses to MacMillan's lecture underline the wisdom of that comment.

Mediating MacMillan

It is a salutary lesson to read James MacMillan's Edinburgh Festival lecture and then contrast it with its media representation. Media coverage of MacMillan's talk fulfilled in part his predictions about the media's inability to tackle adequately the issues he raised.[50] The talk did contain some errors, omissions and overstatements; then again it would be surprising if similar criticisms could not be made of any contributions to this debate. Yet the point of the talk was to give voice to the experience of anti-Catholic prejudice in Scotland. That does not mean that criticism of the content cannot be justified; some aspects were especially ill-advised in terms of the main message. The joking allusion to Pol Pot or Mao Tse-tung was bound to detract from an important observation about the neglect of the history of pre-Reformation Catholic Scotland.[51]

MacMillan is correct in his refusal to accept Donald Findlay's performance as unique. That is not how societal prejudice operates. Findlay's repertoire needs to be located as an element in that part of the spectrum of anti-Catholic prejudice that too many have accepted as relatively harmless fun, just like 'private prejudicial talk'.[52] It is not fun-filled to those identified as targets in these songs. It is a genuine tragedy to those with friends who were targets in reality.[53] Recognition of the interconnectedness of different expressions of prejudice is essential.

In his determination to deal with this specific issue, as in some others, MacMillan accepts that hyperbole accompanied his comments but, as such, he did not expect them to be taken literally. So it is perhaps with a sigh of some relief that the football chant 'There's only one Donald Findlay' can be reclaimed. Scottish society is not 'jam-packed with people like Donald Findlay'; he is, indeed, in many respects a 'one-off'. But MacMillan's point is that in terms of his expressions of prejudice, he is not. What has been missed in MacMillan's comments on Findlay is that they responded to, and deliberately used some of the phrases employed in, the defence of Findlay published in the *Sunday Herald*.[54] It was a serious mistake on MacMillan's part – as became evident in the rush to judgement by those with no need even to read his lecture – to expect this subtlety of comment to be detected, let alone to have his remark set in its proper context. However, this apologist had first excused Findlay, then, in case that project failed, explained him away as a 'one-off'. MacMillan's extract from the column is itself evidence of another who can display contempt for Scottish Catholics. Not only was discrimination against Catholics argued to be justified,[55] but the response to Findlay's 'folksongs' was simply the 'victim mentality' of *'them and their kind'* (emphasis added).

MacMillan's response gives the lie to this crass portrayal of a Scottish minority, but again this is a belief applied to minorities in other societies.[56] MacMillan speaks out to ensure that change will take place: to give voice to this demand is to underline the determination of minorities to resist prejudice and to refuse to accept the status of being victims.[57] However, minority resistance to prejudice (and thus to being victims) is often turned on its head and argued to be the cause of, or a justification for, the very same prejudice. And the failure to appreciate and understand the significance of minority resistance has unfortunate consequences. An attribution of victim status subtly defines minorities as weak and helpless, implying that the minority is incapable of self-help and irrevocably dependent on the goodwill and generosity of the majority. As a result, actions taken by the minority to address the issue of prejudice can lead to the judgement that the minority community is ungracious and ungrateful; the minority community is blamed for introducing friction, tension and division.[58] That rhetoric may be especially useful when there has been progress in the treatment of the minority.[59] The newspaper columnist presents a particularly offensive version in which the minority community, here Scotland's Catholics, persists with a supposed victim mentality. The writer conveys an image of a weak and unbalanced community which is castigated for its inability to face a predicament of its own making. This is truly denial with a vengeance, but denial in its various forms was a strong response to MacMillan too. There is a sadly satirical edge to the determined refusal to listen to MacMillan's claim that a Catholic Scottish voice fails to receive a hearing.

Perhaps this almost reflex denial explains why one serious omission in MacMillan's lecture was ignored: Scotland's shame must also be the United Kingdom's. It was only the arrival of a Scottish parliament that made it possible for Scotland to address the issue of anti-Catholic prejudice; indeed, this development occasioned MacMillan's identification of the issue. Despite popular mythology,[60] the problem of anti-Catholic bigotry is not a quintessentially Scottish one, but a prejudice that lies at the core of the United Kingdom of Great Britain and Northern Ireland.[61] Protestantism was the bond that united the kingdom; anti-Catholic sentiments were core characteristics of the UK state rather than defining features of Scottish life.[62] The location of anti-Catholic or anti-Irish prejudices in the Celtic periphery of Scotland and Northern Ireland deflects attention from the remaining manifestations to be found elsewhere.[63] Britain still remains only a partially reformed confessional state, with an established national Church in England, and in Scotland a national Church over which there is some uncertainty as to whether it remains established or not.[64] The sovereign not only cannot be a Catholic but must be a member of the Church of England and cannot marry a Catholic.[65] The interlacing of Church and State is evident in the sovereign's role as temporal head of the Church of England.

This neglected Protestant dimension to British public life determines that the Archbishop of Canterbury occupies the highest social rank after the royal family. Established Church Bishops are appointed by the sovereign, and the Church of England, as the state Church, takes precedence over all others in state-directed religious services. In the non-elected second chamber of government, the House of Lords, the Church of England commands an impressive bloc of votes. Both Church archbishops, plus the Bishops of

London, Winchester and Durham and 21 other senior diocesan bishops, are allocated seats in the House of Lords by right.[66] With the passage of time there has been growing acceptance of faiths outside the Protestant tradition. For example, some other Church representatives have been appointed to the Lords, but not as a statutory right. Catholic and Jewish faiths have received some forms of acceptance and recognition within the state; other faiths lag behind in their treatment by the state.

In the backwash to MacMillan's lecture there was a belated discovery[67] by some of the ban on Catholics marrying into the monarchy. Yet that is to ignore these much more complex and complicated socio-legal strands that have ensured that the United Kingdom was, and remains, a Protestant state. There was also a failure to recognise that this legislative framework underlines the way that societal prejudices are top-down social phenomena.[68] That was recognised by MacMillan; his lecture offered the possibility of a constructive and critical dialogue with the various analyses he offered. Some of that did take place. However, the immediate media response did not assist this form of engagement.

The initial media response falsely claimed that MacMillan had described Scotland as 'Ulster without guns'.[69] That misrepresentation caused many to prejudge the talk before MacMillan had uttered one single word. The same article also claimed, 'The composer will cite examples of careers being ruined by anti-Catholic discrimination and speak in detail of the problems caused by bigotry in employment.' The content of the lecture shows this prediction to be untrue. MacMillan's talk was about a culture of prejudice. Unfortunately the framework for the interpretation of the lecture was set, and the nature of the responses pre-set, by the way in which the media framed the talk. Other reports wrongly introduced the phrase 'institutional bigotry' as an important element in the talk. Another Scottish myth was well on the way to being established.[70]

Once the talk had been delivered, the immediate television coverage continued broadly within this same interpretative framework. However, as the lecture had now taken place, there was some engagement with elements of the real content of the talk. Television did present facets of the complexity of MacMillan's account. Nonetheless, the dominant theme was in tune with pre-talk reports. MacMillan's lecture was always going to be controversial; he himself expected that to be the case. However, it was not only the content of the talk that was dubbed controversial. Instead, MacMillan was presented as the voice of controversy and an unrepresentative Catholic voice. That perspective relieved many of the need to engage with MacMillan as a voice speaking for the Catholic community. Instead, there was the strong suggestion that it would have been so much better had MacMillan just remained silent.

Both Scottish evening television news programmes[71] showed MacMillan saying that Findlay was 'not a one-off': Scottish life was 'jam-packed' with Findlay followers. The STV news reported the talk as having met with near unanimous disapproval: 'James MacMillan says anti-Catholic attitudes are evident in every sphere of our society. But this evening, his high-profile speech at the Edinburgh Festival, which was titled "Scotland's Shame", has been attacked by churchmen and politicians alike.' One Presbyterian was shown strongly disagreeing with MacMillan. However, the comments of Kenny MacAskill of the Scottish National Party were much more equivocal.[72] He hailed progress and urged people to retain a sense of perspective, but he warned that there remained a need to remain vigilant. So two people, one offering somewhat ambiguous comments, were summarised by the phrase 'attacked by churchmen and politicians alike'. Two interviews with MacMillan's co-religionists were introduced with the comment that Catholics 'had mixed views on his decision to speak out'. A young male stated, 'I don't think he's doing it to cause offence or to stir. But I think he's doing it to make people think. There is bigotry. There is racism, and he raises some important points.' In the second interview an elderly woman reported, 'I'm Catholic, but I've never ever experienced it.'

These last interview comments perfectly fitted MacMillan's description of the different public perspective presented by different generations of Catholics. Moreover, different attitudes among minority members are, like those among majorities, to be expected. However, rather than being treated as a sign of diversity, it is common to find that minority differences are treated as evidence of disharmony and used to diminish the critical voice.[73] The BBC Scotland news was less harsh in how it framed the talk, but it played a stronger card in this representation of Catholic disagreement to dilute MacMillan's criticisms.

And Himself a Catholic

BBC Scotland introduced some supposed voices of decontextualised rationality. Professorial authority, albeit without knowledge of the content of MacMillan's lecture, now took centre stage. News presenter Sally Magnusson quoted a comment from Professor David McCrone in response to the notion of 'institutionalised bigotry', which had not been introduced by MacMillan. Academic authority and detachment were invoked despite McCrone's lack of knowledge of the precise question set by MacMillan.[74] It is significant that throughout the media frenzy, MacMillan was denied his own title of Professor (he is a visiting Professor at Strathclyde University); even the use of Doctor was avoided. Instead, he was fitted up with the image of the unworldy composer. By implication, MacMillan was here presented as the voice of 'emotion and anecdote'. Yet it was McCrone who was spellbound by yet another myth, the fable of MacMillan's lecture. Magnusson said:

> This is an area where emotion and anecdote rather than hard fact often rule, but there has been some research. Professor David McCrone, who carried out a study of sectarianism in Scotland, says the overwhelming evidence is that institutionalised bigotry is not rife, but street-level bigotry, as he called it, among some young males in the west of Scotland is alive and well. Now for another perspective, I am joined now by Professor Tom Devine of Aberdeen University. Professor Devine, James MacMillan does seem to have hit at least a nerve here. Is he right, in your experience?

Like McCrone, Professor Tom Devine also replied to the mediated image of MacMillan's talk. Devine tackled myth rather than substance. He commented on discrimination in the labour market and the institutionalisation of anti-

Catholic prejudice in Scottish society:

> He is certainly right to alert us to the fact that this is a subject that should
> be debated. I don't think he's right in his conclusions. I think there is
> clearly evidence of anti-Catholicism in Scottish society but it is certainly
> not institutionalised, and it doesn't, in my view, powerfully affect the
> labour market in anything like the way it did 40 to 50 years ago.

Magnusson clarified and expanded on Devine's theme of an ill-informed
MacMillan. MacMillan's was only a voice of personal experience, a voice of
singularly 'contextualised forms of representation'. So singular did this
experience appear to Magnusson that she presented MacMillan as talking
about what she now labelled a *'secret* shame' (emphasis added).[75] She
suggested:

> So do you think he's overstating the case because of his personal
> experience? I mean, secret shame is emotive and powerful stuff. Is he
> plain wrong?

Again Devine believed MacMillan's comments would act as a stimulus for
much-needed debate and research. Nonetheless, despite acknowledging this
need, and despite being privately[76] unaware of the details of MacMillan's
argument, Devine proceeded to dismiss MacMillan's case as academically
unsound and based on personal experience:

> I think it can only be on the basis of his personal experience and his own
> personal perception, because it's certainly not a soundly based academic
> argument. If some factual information could be provided to sustain some
> of his generalisations then I think undeniably they would have more
> impact, but my point is this: it is useful for Scottish society as it
> approaches the first few years of its new parliament to look at itself in a
> critical way. And if James MacMillan's comments allow us to do this in
> an important aspect of Scottish society, they have been positive. I don't
> agree, however, with the perspective of his conclusions.

The confusing contradiction between Devine's three themes was apparent. The
strong dismissal of MacMillan's argument was contradicted by his own
demand for 'factual information': what did this say about the basis for
Devine's own rebuttal?[77] And, if MacMillan was so wrong, then why was this
issue 'an important aspect of Scottish society' (and apparently for the Scottish
parliament) which would lead Scotland 'to look at itself in a critical way'.
These contradictions and inconsistencies had the saving grace of being a
gesture in the direction of opposition to societal complacency. Magnusson was
alert to this suggestion. She enquired:

> Where do you think, then, if we are not to be complacent as a society,
> where do you think we should be looking now as we address the future
> and look at our prejudices, if such they are?

Devine now stressed his own belief that there was an absence of academic knowledge that would allow critical evaluation of the issue. In doing so, he threw off the aura of academic authority that had cloaked his own remarks. Viewers would not have known that he was unaware of the actual content of MacMillan's talk, but the acute observer would have realised that, in the absence of 'sustained study', Devine's own comments could not be 'soundly based academic argument'. He pronounced:

> Well, one of the things is that this particular area that MacMillan has focused on has hardly really been debated at all, until the last couple of years, in the public media. And, therefore, the wraps are off it now and we can look at it critically. But also, even in the universities, although we know a lot about Irish immigration, and sectarianism in the first half of the twentieth century, to my knowledge there is no sustained study under way about current attitudes.

Devine's identification of his lack of knowledge of any relevant 'sustained study' meant that his 'academic argument', spoken by the voice of decontextualised rationality, was exposed: his comments must be based mainly on his own 'personal experience and . . . personal perception' too. Indeed, it was only in his brief allusion to the need to recognise historical change, in which he was doing no more than agree with MacMillan, that Devine presented a truly legitimate voice of academic authority. More often, this was a case of the voice of decontextualised rationality appearing to legitimise decisions which had to have been made on other grounds. Devine's reliance on his own experiences overtly dominated his next response.

As the interview closed, Magnusson wondered about MacMillan's worries over those campaigning to end state support for Catholic schools and asked:

> And is he right to see evidence of anti-Catholicism, for instance, in the moves to try and put an end to separate Catholic schools?

Devine now openly adopted the voice of 'contextualised forms of representation'. One implication was that the issue of Catholic schools was a singular case. When Devine spoke as a self-identified Catholic, his words were carefully chosen. He avoided any judgement as to the underlying motives, but struck a tone of balanced bemusement at these demands. He replied:

> I think this is an area that gives me personal concern because, like MacMillan, I am a Catholic. And I have some difficulty in trying to understand the continued focus on separate Catholic education, which is undeniably very successful academically and also has a certain spiritual power to convey to young people. Why is it that it is constantly being criticised from certain quarters, even including the Educational Institute of Scotland, or at least some of its members?

Given the pre-event framing of MacMillan's talk by the media, and not knowing what MacMillan had actually said, Devine had little option but to distance himself from MacMillan the myth: an emotional composer who equated Scotland to Northern Ireland without weapons and who took such an ahistorical view of Scotland as to judge anti-Catholic discrimination in employment still to be rampant in Scottish life. To have agreed with the mythological MacMillan would not simply have lost Devine his academic respectability, it would have identified him as another irrational Catholic. So it is to Devine's credit that an underlying disquiet was evident in his responses. His dominant theme was that MacMillan was wrong; the contrary theme was that anti-Catholic attitudes remained an issue of importance, which MacMillan had been right to raise but had mishandled.

On the issue of Catholic schools, it is striking that Devine sought the voice of a Catholic with personal concerns rather than the voice of academic authority. Orthodox views on this issue are so blinkered, a form of prejudice masquerading as everyday taken-for-granted knowledge, that the minority voice often cringes to avoid sounding like a whinge. So in bravely, but very politely, querying this dominant voice, Devine had little option but to adopt the voice of personal experience.

However, this Devine duality, academic and Catholic, was identified by others for quite different reasons. The front-page lead of *The Herald* stated:[78]

> Professor Tom Devine of Aberdeen University, one of Scotland's leading historians, and himself a Catholic, declared that: 'James MacMillan has gone slightly over the top. What he fails to realise is the enormous change of status of Roman Catholics in Scotland over the last 20 or 30 years.' As an academic, he said he dealt in evidence, adding that: 'All we have had is rhetoric. I await the evidence. If he has specific evidence to support these assertions then I would be interested in what he has to say.'
>
> Professor Devine added he had no experience of bigotry in universities – 'I have not come across any of this discrimination that he talks about.'

The substance of Devine's comments has the same failings and contradictions as his television testimony. An important nuance emerges in this particular framing of Devine's remarks. The appearance of academic authority remains important, but here, and reported in a harsher tone, he is clearly presented as admonishing a co-religionist. The more fundamental question now being asked was which was the authentic Catholic voice?[79] The implied answer was not MacMillan. A similar refrain was apparent in other newspapers too. Some implied it would have been much better had MacMillan not spoken. MacMillan was increasingly presented as the mad composer and, as such, his comments could, in the main, be disregarded.[80] However, it was the dismissal of MacMillan as an unrepresentative Catholic voice that was the unbalanced judgement.

An Authentic Catholic Voice

By the end of the week, there were songs of praise for MacMillan's lecture in the main Catholic Scottish newspaper.[81] An editorial used the phrase 'institutional bigotry', a phrase never used by MacMillan, to encapsulate all forms of bigotry, before stressing its own opposition to them. The horrific effects of racism were attacked, with the murder of Stephen Lawrence claimed to have shown the dangers of institutional racism.[82] The editorial went on to argue that there was no place for any form of bigotry in modern Scotland. Despite the writer accepting some of the MacMillan myth – and, like much of the Scottish media (and the academic authorities cited), revealing in passing its failure to understand the meaning of institutional racism – the editorial did identify that MacMillan had explored *prejudice*. It agreed that the problem of anti-Catholic bigotry was not that dramatised on the football terraces, nor was it 'the anachronistic spectacle' of Orange walks, but the more subtle forms of prejudice against Catholicism, 'and MacMillan has done us a service to highlight it'. The paper even took an ecumenical stance and claimed that there was not simply prejudice against Catholics but a wider prejudice against Christians and the radical message of Christianity, which led to attacks on its support for 'justice and peace'. Christianity, it continued, should be respected, rather than mocked, and praised for its opposition to 'blind consumerism and bloated capitalism'.

As an example of this threat to Christianity, the editorial offered a strange choice. This was the Edinburgh Festival Fringe play *Corpus Christi*, which 'demeans Christ to the level of gay sexual innuendo' and 'mocked Christianity'. In these comments, and in the mocking categorisation of this play as coming 'from such "liberated" parts of our society', there was a clear indication of the difficulty some Catholics (and some members of other faith communities and none) have in recognising the spirituality and humanity of gay people. Indeed, one interpretation of *Corpus Christi* was that it had, by the adoption of its Christological format, deliberately posed this very challenge to the Christian community.[83] Sadly, and all too predictably, that remains a challenge too far for too many supposedly inspired by religious messages of love.

Another columnist in the same newspaper gave considerable praise to MacMillan.[84] Successful Scottish Catholics who had been critical of the composer were gently scolded. Devine, who 'maintains that evidence of anti-Catholicism is only "anecdotal"', featured strongly in this small cast of sinners. Their stance was evaluated simply as an illustration of one of MacMillan's points. They were 'of a certain generation . . . who got on in life by keeping their heads down and "playing the game"'. However, younger Scottish Catholics no longer accepted those rules. They would now accept nothing less than the same respect and acceptance as other Scots. MacMillan, not Devine, despite being 'himself a Catholic', was the authentic Catholic voice on this issue.

An Authentic Academic Voice?

Another academic who became involved in the media adjudication of MacMillan's talk was Professor Lindsay Paterson. He was reported in the following way:

> It seems impossible to argue with MacMillan's phrase – that Glasgow is
> Belfast without the Kalashnikovs. Yet other observers, including some for
> whom MacMillan has respect, believes he is living in the past. Sociologist
> Lindsay Paterson of Edinburgh University, whom MacMillan consulted

before presenting his paper in Edinburgh last week as the artistic world gathered for the Festival, is among those who demur. They spoke together for an hour, but Paterson believes his advice was ignored. 'MacMillan is describing an old Scotland,' he says.[85]

Paterson also spoke without having heard or read MacMillan's lecture. Inevitably his response was based on how the media had framed the talk, but his own view is that good journalists do a good job in this respect and he was willing to accept the legitimacy of media reports.[86] However, this self-same *Observer* story identifies exactly some of the problems of relying on media reports; there is an even more exaggerated version of the equation of Scotland with Northern Ireland, a comparison that MacMillan did *not* make. MacMillan yet again becomes a ventriloquist's dummy, now apparently mouthing that the only difference between the two is that Glasgow lacks Belfast's Kalashnikovs! This claim, if it had ever been made, would have been to describe a non-existent (and, one hopes, and fully expects, a Scotland that will never exist) rather than even an old Scotland.

Paterson's claim that MacMillan failed to take his advice is an especially contentious one. MacMillan firmly states that he said very little about the precise content of his intended talk, and that it was a short telephone conversation. The call was made so that he could ask for a copy of a paper by Paterson,[87] and, as this request itself shows, the content of his talk was then far from being finalised. Paterson accepts that the phone call could have been shorter than an hour, but still he believes it to have been 'a lengthy discussion'. Both men agree that the requested paper was sent to MacMillan, and MacMillan did subsequently make considerable use of Paterson's paper in his Festival speech.[88] Now this difference in opinion may appear insignificant. However, the immediate impression conveyed by Paterson's remarks was again that of a headstrong MacMillan, who had simply disregarded Paterson's supposedly wiser academic counsel. As a result, Paterson is positioned as speaking with the voice of decontextualised rationality, whilst MacMillan initially appears to be located once more as the 'voice of contextualised rationalisation', or narrow personal experience. The implication of these reported remarks is that MacMillan's voice should have been much better schooled before it was heard.[89]

Yet the direction taken by this newspaper article demonstrates, as Wertsch had noted, that the privileging of one voice over another cannot simply be taken for granted. Sometimes that is because the voice of contextualised rationalisation is more potent, more relevant to the ongoing dialogue. On other occasions it is less obvious which account is the more comprehensive, the more systematic and analytical, and so it can be unclear which should be identified as the voice of decontextualised rationality. Indeed, in this very article, the positions of MacMillan and Paterson became reversed. Paterson's denial of discrimination against Catholics was treated as a form of 'contextualised rationalisation' that simply failed to address MacMillan's analysis. This article recognised that MacMillan was referring to something much wider, something close to a culture of prejudice against Catholics. As a result, the narrow focus taken by Paterson was presented as inadequate to explain the obvious manifestations of anti-Catholic prejudice. Consequently, it was Paterson's comments that were rendered particularistic; his reductionism was simply unable to cope with the interconnectedness of MacMillan's argument about prejudice. There is another irony here. When interviewed, Paterson was not asked to talk about MacMillan's lecture.[90] Instead he was invited specifically to discuss anti-Catholic discrimination in Scotland. Consequently, as was requested of him, he only dealt with that one form of the expression of prejudice. Paterson's position was one that did confuse prejudice with discrimination. Nonetheless, there was, given this background to his comments, still an injustice in his then being effectively criticised for disregarding other forms of the expression of prejudice.

In this article, it was MacMillan's broad theme that received full backing and more play-time. These journalists, despite an acceptance of much of the media spin and a recognition that MacMillan was talking from personal experience, hinted at a more important identification. That was that, although raw experience and hurt was evident in – indeed, sometimes even distracted from – MacMillan's talk, there was a serious reflection on his experiences that deserved praise, and which had led on to an erratic but sometimes detailed description of anti-Catholic prejudice. As a result, it was MacMillan, emotional warts and all, who could be presented as the sometimes decontextualised voice of rationality, for it was MacMillan who was attempting one of the tasks of early scientific development, the detailed description of the phenomenon. It was academics who persisted in the adoption of a narrow and inadequate perspective on anti-Catholic prejudice. The obsession with discrimination alone was a contextualised rationalisation of the issue. Moreover, in this article, MacMillan's perspective was supplemented by additional interview material in which he displayed a recognition of the interconnectedness of Scottish complacency about many forms of prejudice. He spoke of his concerns about sexism, racism and the denial of racism, and the growth in prejudice against the English, overt recognition of these acts acting as an antidote to the complacent belief in a Scotland free of prejudice. An important part of his Festival talk, his concerns about a narrowness in the vision of what it is to be a Scot, of a tendency towards control, conformity and restriction, was again identified, and his opposition to this desire for homogeneity became the dominant refrain. MacMillan was recognised to be an authentic Catholic voice and an authentic voice for social pluralism.

Bruce and the Media Web[91]

Professor Steve Bruce's knowledge of MacMillan's lecture was derived from what he had read in the Sunday newspaper stories that preceded the talk, which he then supplemented by the 'breaking news' stories posted on newspaper web sites. He was so irritated by the content of MacMillan's talk as relayed by these media sources that he faxed an unrequested article to *The Herald* early on the Monday morning. His column reached Glasgow before MacMillan had even given his talk in Edinburgh!

Bruce's article[92] confirms his irritation. Another Scots intellectual is ensnared by yet another myth, and mythological MacMillan strikes again. Bruce commences from the position that 'MacMillan believes Scotland to be a sectarian country: "Northern Ireland without the guns". If he is right, then the following facts need to be explained away.' So, having attributed a false position to MacMillan, Bruce then points to important differences between Scotland and Northern Ireland. Without his knowing it, Bruce agrees with MacMillan. They also agree that Scotland has changed much, and considerably for the better, with respect to religious harmony. In his ignorance, Bruce criticises MacMillan for failing to 'engage with that evidence', but in his anticipatory mood of emotional irritation, Bruce could not know that to be untrue.

So, there is an unknowing self-satire of some force at the end of Bruce's commentary. In passing he accepts that MacMillan might be brave to discuss such a controversial topic: 'However, it would be better if he were a well-informed man.' Irony is piled on irony; satire abounds. Bruce did not know what MacMillan was to talk about. Yet the much-irritated Bruce presents himself as the voice of decontextualised rationality, whilst music composer MacMillan is represented as not knowing what he is talking about. Bruce also invokes the cliché of artistic creativity when he implies that MacMillan's approach to 'sectarianism' is inadequate because he is trapped in the mindset of a composer:

> Some observations are clearly matters of taste. There are no factual grounds for determining whether or not MacMillan's compositions are good music. But the claim that Scotland is still a sectarian country is, like the deleterious effects of looking at the sun, a matter of fact that should be addressed with appropriate data.[93]

Bruce here confuses 'still' with 'the same'. He misinterprets MacMillan and misunderstands the nature of prejudice, which he reduces to anti-Catholic discrimination in the labour market. He uses the unhelpful and imprecise notion of 'sectarian'.[94] He displays the imprecision of this term when he uses it in another sense in his introduction of Catholic schools into the discussion of discrimination. Bruce claims:

> There is one labour market that is governed by a sectarian hiring policy: teaching. While members of every religio-ethnic group may be hired in the state's schools, only people acceptable to the Catholic Church can be hired for senior positions in the state-funded Catholic schools.

Bruce simply confirms MacMillan's belief that too many Scots cannot discuss this matter without making some attack on Catholic schools. He appears unable to comprehend that Catholic schools are also state schools. He is confused by the issue of Church approval. This requirement, which is in addition to those required by the state for employment in all state schools, strictly applies to all appointments but is not used in such an extensive manner. He appears forgetful of other denominational schools and neglectful of labour markets in which recruitment demands additional qualifications of a religious nature.

Throughout his commentary Bruce argues for assimilation. He writes:

> Inter-marriage is both a sign of change and the basis for further assimilation. Were it not for Catholic schools, little or nothing would now distinguish the descendants of the Irish from native Scots. One

71

might want to describe that assimilation as a bad thing, but it can hardly stand as evidence of sectarianism.

This extract contains too many gems of confusion for all to be mined here. But assimilation is usually a poor model of community relations, and it certainly is in the form outlined by Bruce.[95] Assimilation refers to the incorporation of the minority into the dominant group so that it conforms (or is made to conform) to the customs and practices of the majority. As a result, the minority would no longer constitute an identifiable community, because any distinguishing characteristics would have been eradicated. Tellingly, Bruce presents Catholic schools to be the last barrier to Catholics becoming 'native Scots'. He provides not a rejoinder to MacMillan, but a cartoon with which he illustrates MacMillan's themes.

And in an irony almost too far, MacMillan's experiences approximate to Bruce's 'assimilated' ideal. MacMillan attended the local 'non-denominational' but implicitly Protestant school, where he was soon dubbed 'Jim the Tim'.[96] There he met his future wife, made other excellent lifelong friends, but learned that some fellow pupils had best be avoided. He also discovered that with other pupils certain topics of conversation were to be shunned, and even teachers could espouse views that Catholics were more backward than Protestants. MacMillan's life has continued to be one in which he encounters and embraces social diversity, nationally and internationally. He does so openly as a proud Catholic who refuses to accept that all Scottish society cannot be transformed and become as harmonious, sympathetic and understanding as are his own most important social relationships. Bruce tried to address this issue of Scottish Catholic and Protestant inter-relationships. Perhaps 'it would be better if he were a well-informed man', for MacMillan is a voice speaking directly from the interface.

Engaging with the Evidence

The response to MacMillan produced a rich rhetoric about the need to take account of the evidence, and strong criticism of MacMillan's supposed failure to do so. Evidence is crucial to the development of meaningful understanding of any topic. However, for this to happen, the evidence must be relevant to the investigative question posed. That hints that evidence is not some neutral resource that can arbitrate on contentious questions. Instead, the issue of what constitutes relevant evidence is itself a matter of some weight. In this case supposed expert voices simply failed to answer the question MacMillan set them. In addition, they themselves failed to engage with the nature of the evidence presented by MacMillan and misunderstood how it related to his case.

There was another failure: not to see the relevant evidence of prejudice produced around MacMillan, the media show. Use of Wertsch's sense of voices has illuminated the different ways in which the media framed MacMillan's speech, incorporating a range of positioning devices, including the use of academic voices, to diminish MacMillan's critical Catholic voice.[97] MacMillan was presented as an atypical Catholic and, as an artist, to be an unschooled, emotional, irrational but creative deviant. This process of marginalisation surrendered a rich seam of subtle evidence about the place of the Catholic community in Scotland and how it is expected to behave – which is to be in tune with the siren song of majority orthodoxy. Denial of critical minority voices, even when carried out indirectly, is a form of prejudice. In terms of Allport's categories, denial involves operations dependent on avoidance and probably discrimination. The denial of voice, allied to the determination to insist on imposing an orthodox view of society, reflects the present inability of most majorities to understand the right of minorities to give voice to their concerns, to recognise the need to listen, and then, and only then, to engage in constructive dialogue.

Scots, their supposed egalitarianism notwithstanding, prove to be no different from other nationalities. Denial of voice simply mirrors the usual societal asymmetries of power: minorities are expected to conform to the views and values of the majority. Another aspect of the assimilationist model, in which minorities are expected eventually to become indistinguishable from the majority, becomes apparent. Minority deviation from this prescribed path to grace leads to prejudicial comment. That is accompanied by denial of the existence of this prejudice, and the determined effort to relocate the cause of conflict and prejudice within the minority community. As a significant section of MacMillan's audience responded in this way, the responses yielded evidence that confirmed the validity of much of his general case about the nature of anti-Catholic prejudice in Scotland.

This treatment of one of Scotland's oldest minority groups can scarcely be reassuring for other minority communities. Yet the response to MacMillan was not universally so negative; there were some reasons to be cheerful. There were those, such as the *Observer* journalists, who engaged, albeit imperfectly, with MacMillan and his evidence. It is possible to detect in some of these cross-currents of opinion a growing recognition that a truly multi-cultural Scotland, a pluralist Scotland that appreciated, even celebrated, social difference, would not only be a different Scotland but would also be a much better Scotland. So the MacMillan saga provided, in various shapes and forms, evidence that confirmed both the existence of this prejudice and that the time might indeed now be right to mount a campaign that would tackle this and other Scottish societal prejudices.

As a result, the persistent demand for specific forms of evidence in relation to the MacMillan lecture was sometimes naïve, if not simply misleading. MacMillan provided a description of anti-Catholic prejudice in Scotland, which he did well. His mapping exercise was an attempt to establish the boundaries and the contours of the phenomenon. His search for these perimeters too often became confused with a demand for the parameters of anti-Catholic prejudice.[98] That question, in turn, was reduced to the very important but narrow issue of discrimination in the labour market.

Yet there is no one issue to which prejudice can be reduced, just as there is no one standard against which it can be measured. Certainly there is no sovereign method that can rule on the nature and extent of prejudice. Indeed, the most subtle forms of prejudice require subtle approaches; some explorations depend on the examination of what those operating within a prejudicial framework do not accept *is* prejudice, which is to reiterate the earlier warning that prejudice is also intertwined with mythology and ideology. Prejudice is a truly complex social phenomenon and its study requires the adoption of a range of different methods and approaches which are adapted to answer the particular question about prejudice that has been asked.

Although prejudice cannot be reduced to the single issue of discrimination in employment, that does remain an important area for the potential display of one expression of prejudice. Bruce underestimates the nature and extent of prejudice, but he has provided a thought-provoking, if inevitably sometimes contentious analysis of the reasons to believe that widespread systematic discrimination is now much less probable.[99] Here he is in agreement with MacMillan, who also believes that progress has been made. Bruce outlines some considerable difficulties that would be encountered by any effort to reverse the social processes leading towards equality in Scotland. However, he is much too early in his declaration that this end-point has been practically achieved. Bruce relies on data from McCrone.[100] Interpretations quite different from those suggested by Bruce (or McCrone) can be made,[101] but the data are simply inadequate to settle this question with any certainty.[102] Intriguingly, both Bruce and McCrone and Rosie concede that there is evidence of prejudicial rhetoric,[103] but because of their faith that discrimination has now disappeared, they seriously underestimate the power and influence of prejudicial talk on minorities, and the treatment of minorities; they are unaware of the ratchet effect discussed by Allport, which means that more intense expressions of prejudice are made more probable by activity at the lower levels.

Bruce has suggested that 'sectarianism' is now merely a boys' game, mainly restricted to football. This thesis is taken up by McCrone and Rosie in their exploration of the 1992 Scottish Election Survey. (It was this research, and this argument, to which Sally Magnusson briefly referred on BBC Scotland's evening news, before she interviewed Tom Devine.) Now Bruce and McCrone are right to warn that sporting contests should not be mistaken for social reality; the relationship is especially complicated.[104] Moreover, sporting contests can exaggerate the nature of ethnic conflict.[105] But it is equally a mistake to believe that sporting contests and society are somehow unconnected. The attempt to confine anti-Catholic prejudice to the football arena was one of the common responses to MacMillan's lecture, in which he did put some effort into his survey of Scottish football. Most of MacMillan's focus was on the 'totemic' significance of football, but some distractions did appear, particularly when he referred to the murky issue of bias in refereeing. Only one point is truly worth making here: accusations of refereeing bias unite football fans the world over, but fans become crucially divided over which teams are favoured.[106] The social significance of Celtic and Rangers is to be found off the field of play, and in the way that popular narratives inter-relate with senses of social identity and accounts of majority and minority relations.[107] And, in this case as in many others, there has been a failure of critical academic analysis, with the result that élite voices support histories and sociologies that reproduce prejudicial analyses of the minority.[108]

In an attempt to explore the nature of religious conflict, Rosie and McCrone in a later chapter of this volume explore data from the Scottish Election Survey of 1992. Bruce relies on McCrone's data from 1992 and from the 1997 version of the survey for his own analysis. He reports the question asked to have been: 'Is religious conflict very serious/fairly serious/not very serious/none of the above?' This is a badly worded question. The use of both 'very serious' and its direct negative 'not very serious' is unhelpful. 'None of the above' is too imprecise: it could even mean 'extremely serious'. Yet, in interpreting the data, McCrone and Rosie decide that it means 'no conflict', and they treat 'not very serious' to be the same as the semantically distinct 'not serious'. For their analysis they then proceed to dichotomise the data. The last two categories are combined and described as being equivalent to statements that there was 'none or very little' religious conflict.[109]

The wording of the question means that it is unclear what these data do mean.[110] That problem is illustrated by the apparent increase in the perception of the seriousness of religious conflict which is reported, especially by Catholics, from 1992 to 1997. Even if the dubious proposition that 'none of the above' can be equated with 'none' is accepted, then in relation to MacMillan's descriptive map of prejudice, a response in any of the remaining three categories must support his case: each of these responses indicates agreement that some level of religious conflict is evident in Scotland. That means that, in the 1997 survey, at least 94 per cent of the Catholics, 87 per cent of those respondents identified with the Church of Scotland and 91 per cent of all involved in the study judged there to be some religious prejudice in Scotland. These results clearly do not contradict MacMillan's thesis, as was claimed. If this evidence does anything, it vindicates MacMillan's argument.[111]

However, there is a clue to one influence that contaminates many analyses of anti-Catholic prejudice in Scotland. Bruce, Walker[112] – who is also cited in support – and McCrone and Rosie all appear to rely on a scale that sets the conflict in Northern Ireland (incidentally, usually misnamed Ulster) as the real measure of serious religious prejudice. Bruce explicitly makes this point in his discussion of the Scottish responses to the question on religious conflict.[113] The existence of this baseline also explains the irritation when MacMillan the myth, falsely accused of equating Scotland with Northern Ireland, was presented as stepping over it. This Northern Ireland comparison seems to provide a comfort zone for Bruce, Walker, and McCrone and Rosie. On this basis, religious and ethnic conflict in Scotland can be minimised. Scotland does not compare to Ulster or, since partition, Northern Ireland. Undoubtedly Scotland has been, with very few exceptions – one of which was the anti-Catholic recruitment policy of Glasgow Rangers, a policy that was not matched by football clubs in Northern Ireland[114] – the much more harmonious society. That point is important, and worth making often. What must be stated much more often, but is consistently neglected, is that this offers small consolation to those who experience anti-Catholic prejudice in any of its forms in Scotland. That remains true, even when its most dominant expression now takes the form of symbolic prejudice around forms of visible Catholic activity.

McCrone and Rosie sadly misjudge the importance of this matter in their discussion of Catholic schools.[115] They accept that it has in the past been:

> a focus of sectarian conflict . . . [but] That is not to say that opposition to segregated education is necessarily a sectarian issue – indeed, it often manifests itself as an *anti*-sectarian issue. Many Scots object to segregated schooling because they believe that such a system inculcates and maintains *division*. There is evidence of a widespread belief across age and gender that Scottish schools should be integrated.[116]

This statement is clear evidence of their failure to appreciate the complexities of prejudice. It must only be the force of the cultural framing of this debate that could lead respected academics twice to refer so uncritically to 'segregated'[117] education and to offer the usual framework which confounds cause and effect, difference and division, and identifies Catholic schools as both a cause of division and a means of then sustaining it. It is a dramatic self-contradiction for McCrone and Rosie to hold that Catholic schools cause division in the middle of an account that argues that 'sectarianism' has now all but disappeared. Indeed, this accusation against Catholic schools cannot be sustained by anyone who does accept that religious conflict in Scotland has been much reduced. In addition, Paterson's investigation of Catholic schools leads him to conclude that 'there is no evidence at all' that Catholic schools lead to division or bigotry or create exclusive communities.[118] Instead, Catholic schools are staffed by teachers as liberal as those employed elsewhere in the state sector, but more committed to participation in liberal democracy and civic society.

McCrone and Rosie provide further evidence of their unsophisticated approach to prejudice when they explore views on whether Catholic schools should be retained or phased out. Only 15 per cent of those identified with the Church of Scotland were in favour of retention; 81 per cent argued that Catholic schools be phased out. For those with no religion, the equivalent figures were 12 per cent and 85 per cent. Among Catholics, however, 51 per cent favoured retention, and 47 per cent opted for the phasing out of Catholic schools. Rosie and McCrone write, 'Clearly *Catholic* opposition to Catholic education is a very interesting issue, and one that is by definition wholly free of any anti-Catholic sentiment that could be ascribed to non-Catholic opposition.' Catholic schools are, as Bruce suggested, the most striking and visible symbol of the Catholic presence in Scotland. In a society in which there is repeated and intense criticism of Catholic schools, this is exactly the issue on which one would expect to find the biggest cross-generation Catholic cringe.[119] That is a direct consequence of 'anti-Catholic sentiment'.

Bennie, Brand and Mitchell make this point not directly but obliquely when they caution care in the interpretation of these results. They advise against the too simple equation of 'phasing out' with opposition to Catholic schools: 'phasing out' could be seen to be a very 'long-term objective'. The potential elasticity of the imprecise timescale is argued to explain the proportion of Catholics who opt for phasing out. Another factor clouds matters some more. Removal of the responses of ex-Catholics makes an important difference: 'Among Catholic regular Church attenders . . . there is majority support [66 per cent] for the retention of separate schools.'[120]

Despite the popular prejudices about them, there has been increased recognition recently that Catholic schools have been one of the main reasons for the continuing advance towards Catholic socio-economic equality in Scotland. The schools have also had a powerfully beneficial influence on Scotland as a whole: 'As a means of offering an immigrant community a stake in society, acknowledging and accepting religious pluralism, minimising grievances and potential conflict, it is difficult to see the Act as anything other than a success.'[121] Moreover, the provision of Catholic schools reduced inter-group tensions and promoted inter-group reconciliation and harmony.[122]

Nonetheless, discussion of the place of Catholics in Scotland seems unable to escape an unhelpful, flawed and ill-informed debate on Catholic schools. The repetitive, near-obsessive nature of this debate must surely lead more to the diagnosis of the prejudicial framework on which it depends. MacMillan simply identified the alarm experienced by many Catholics (as well as others who support the cause of social pluralism) when this issue is returned to over and over again. Jim Sillars was right to state that the reversal of opinion on this matter will be an important sign of the emergence of a more mature Scotland.[123]

Given the nature of the debate, and the myth of segregation, there is one significant – if, to many, very surprising – sign of the genuine improvement in inter-group harmony between Protestants and Catholics in Scotland. It is provided by the attendance at Catholic schools of pupils of other faiths and none. Parents' decision to entrust their children to a Catholic state school is perhaps the best possible testament that some of the traditional prejudice directed against Catholics is truly disappearing.[124] For some Catholics, especially in the current climate of opposition to Catholic schools, this change in school populations can be seen as a threat; for others, it poses new opportunities and challenges. The meaning and mission of the Catholic school in the next century are topics of genuine debate for educationalists interested in the development of Scottish Catholic education.[125] Continued evolution of the nature of Catholic schools is guaranteed. It is unfortunate that so much popular discussion of Catholic schooling is not based on an accurate representation of the contemporary Catholic school, but instead on the mythology that surrounded Catholic schools in the past.

The inclusion of Catholic, Episcopalian and Jewish schools within a national education system should be celebrated as the creation of a model of inclusive education that recognises the value of pluralism. The establishment of the first Gaelic medium school to protect another form of Scottish identity is an important addition to this pluralist provision. There is no reason why, under the same guidelines, that opportunity should not be offered to Scotland's Islamic community, if that community desires the establishment of Islamic schools.[126] Minorities do usually worry about the effects of unsympathetic, let alone hostile schooling on young community members.[127] The establishment by the state of denominational schooling for minority communities is frequently seen to be an important sign of majority acceptance of the minority's right to be both different and simultaneously part of the society. Minorities rightly worry when that provision is threatened. These are global concerns; the provision of state-supported denominational schools is not simply a Scottish phenomenon. Nor are minority worries about the future of specific denominational schools restricted to Scotland's Catholics.

In another country, an archbishop publicly voiced his concerns. He asked his government to ensure that, as new legislation was considered, the religious ethos of the state-funded denominational schools under his care would be protected. This archbishop warned that the minority's communal identity 'should not be eroded in the cause of complacency, national acceptability, or lack of vision'. He explained, 'This is not a position derived from a siege mentality. Far from it. We have shown over the last few years just how willing we are to participate in the broad spectrum of education debate. We wish to see the current healthy diversity in education preserved into the future.'

This is a nation in which there has been no bar on members of this minority religion becoming head of state, and they have done so. This is a nation in which the socio-economic position of this particular minority has led to it being described as 'privileged'.[128] Nonetheless, this is a religious minority that fears erosion through assimilation,[129] and which is rightly concerned about its future position if its schools disappeared. This nation is the Republic of Ireland, in which 'the vast majority' of the 250 Protestant schools are Church of Ireland schools. Archbishop Dr Robin Eames, the Church of Ireland Primate, explained, 'The future of our schools, as Church of Ireland schools, must be guaranteed to allow parents the choice to send their children to schools which reflect this tradition and outlook.'[130] Minorities worry when there is insufficient dialogue, and insensitivity and neglect. They have cause for alarm when they are denied a voice. They are right to fear that these could be signs of worse to come.

However, discussions of majorities and minorities sometimes fail to make clear that these collectivities are not fixed, but normally situationally determined. On different issues and different concerns, they assemble and reassemble. For example, gender inequality rotates the discussion on to new terrain, but that also points to another myth – that dream of assembling a rainbow coalition, an alliance of sensitive minorities who have been able to generalise from their own social experiences to understand and empathise with the situation of other social minorities. Generalisation of that experience is possible, but far from probable and certainly not inevitable.The *Scottish Catholic Observer* editorial, with its identification with the black community but implied distaste for the gay community, illustrates that complexity. Minorities and majorities can be partially transposed on some issues and questions. And what is learnt in one condition need not be transferred to understand others in a comparable situation (the rhetoric of denial here rejects any sense of similarity and stresses dissimilarity).

Nonetheless, sometimes intriguing parallels emerge. The Church of Scotland, through the direction of the Board of Social Responsibility – effectively the Church's social-work division – operates around 80 units that provide sheltered housing. This work is seen to be part of the Kirk's mission. Staff recruitment is not now restricted only to Kirk members. But the ecumenical Christian approach adopted requires that all staff must have 'a shared Christian faith and ethic'. The Scottish Federation of Housing Associations, through which the government channels money to recognised housing agencies, threatened to withhold funding until this restrictive recruitment policy was changed. Yet this employment policy was legal and acceptable to the Commission for Racial Equality.

In an opinion piece in *The Herald*,[131] the convener of the Church of Scotland Board of Social Responsibility noted that, despite this additional qualification requirement, the quality of recruited staff was high. That was demonstrated by the reputation for excellence won by its housing projects. She asked:

> Why should the board then change its policy? Should all social care be based on a secular humanist policy? Is that what the people of Scotland want – a monochrome service where difference is disallowed? Is there in

the new Scotland, a multi-faith Scotland, no place for a Christian agency as a provider of social care? What implications does that hold for other faith groups?

Some similarities with the concerns and fears of minority communities in Scotland, particularly with respect to the educational care of their impressionable young, are not hard to find.[132] However, so far, in its public stance on denominational schools, the Church of Scotland has failed to recognise any of these similarities.

There are important lessons for *all* Scots to learn. Social-group differences cannot be disallowed, unless one wishes to advocate moving towards suppression. Instead, social difference should be celebrated, and identified as the antidote to MacMillan's warnings of the ills of homogeneity and conformity. Scotland must move towards becoming an open and proudly pluralist society, with a diversity of ways of being Scots and being accepted as Scottish. That requires recognition of the right to be different within an inclusive Scotland. Most societies and most people do have undoubted problems in working through what a pluralist society does really mean. The new Scotland could perhaps give a lead to the world in this field in the new millennium. After all, Scotland does have the advantage of the 1918 Education (Scotland) Act which can serve as a model of past and continuing success. That leads to the conclusion that true understanding and full appreciation of this genuine Scottish educational accomplishment are now both long overdue.

Notes

[1] I am very grateful to James MacMillan for allowing me to interview him about his talk, but I must take full responsibility for this representation of his lecture and its aftermath.
[2] There is a problem of nomenclature over the use of Catholic or Roman Catholic. Catholic will be used here; see G.P.T. Finn, '"Sectarianism" and Scottish Education', in T.G.K. Bryce and W.M. Humes (eds), *Scottish Education* (Edinburgh, 1999), p.871.
[3] I am indebted to Professors Steve Bruce, Tom Devine, David McCrone and Lindsay Paterson for their telephone (and, in one case, additional e-mail) discussions with me on the background to their interventions.
[4] However, the answer to this question is far from a simple one, and one that deserves further public discussion. Academics do have a responsibility to help inform and participate in public debate. That was the motivation for all four of these contributors. This episode, however, indicates some of the pitfalls and pratfalls that may be encountered when participation is dependent, as it usually is, on the media, and reflex rather than reflexive. Part of the problem is that the media do demand instant pundits. This phenomenon even led one noted broadcaster to imagine some prominent Scottish cultural figures who were commonly called on in this role to have formed 'an exclusive club with the acronym SIP (Scottish Instant Pundits)'. See K. Roy, *The Closing Headlines: Inside Scottish Broadcasting* (Irvine, 1993), pp.171–2.
[5] See, for example, H. Tajfel (ed.), *Social Identity and Intergroup Relations* (Cambridge/Paris, 1982), or R. Brown, *Prejudice – Its Social Psychology* (Oxford, 1995).
[6] D. McCrone, *Understanding Scotland: The Sociology of a Stateless Nation* (London, 1992), p.90.
[7] The argument that this myth is 'asociological' is particularly unclear, pessimistic and, in

part, contradicted by McCrone's own efforts at analysis. Moreover, McCrone's positioning of this myth as an ideological element very firmly locates it within the psycho-sociological domain; see note 11 below.

[8] McCrone is correct in this identification. However, the difficulty is that myths provide a dubious basis for progressive change, as conservative use indeed shows. Moreover, one myth can reinforce another so that the need for change is further obscured. One example is the interplay between the dominant interpretations of 'sectarianism' and racism in Scotland, which reinforce the misinterpretations of both; see P. Dimeo and G.P.T. Finn, 'Scottish Racism, Scottish Identities: The Case of Partick Thistle', in A. Brown (ed.), *Fanatics! Power, Identity and Fandom in Football* (London, 1998); P. Dimeo and G.P.T. Finn, 'Racism, National Identity and Scottish Football', in I. McDonald and B. Carrington (eds.), *Racism and British Sport* (London, 2000).

[9] McCrone, *Understanding Scotland*, pp.88–92.

[10] See the different positions on scientific practice espoused by, for example, Popper, Kuhn, Feyerabend and Bhaskar. Science is best seen as a social practice strongly under the influence of social processes and beliefs. Myths can accompany science, but are usually only detected when past practice is surveyed.

[11] See note 7 above. It is unclear what it means to categorise a myth as asociological, but to treat it as such is surely to locate it outside of society and societal processes? It is relevant, then, to note that this claim is more usually made by adherents of a faith community about elements of their belief system. Yet religion and religious beliefs can be studied psycho-sociologically.

[12] See, for example, G.P.T. Finn, 'Multicultural Antiracism and Scottish Education', *Scottish Educational Review*, 3, 1987, pp.89–101; B. Armstrong, *A People without Prejudice* (London, 1989); and especially R. Arshad and F.A. Diniz, 'Race Equality in Scottish Education', in Bryce and Humes' *Scottish Education*.

[13] See, for example, M. Billig, *Ideology and Opinions: Studies in Rhetorical Psychology* (London, 1991); T.A. van Dijk, *Ideology: A Multidisciplinary Approach* (London, 1998); G.P.T. Finn, 'Thinking Uncomfortable Thoughts about Prejudice: Is Educational Intervention Prejudiced by a Prejudice against Prejudice?', *Psychology of Education Review*, 24, 2000 (in press).

[14] See T.A. van Dijk, *Communicating Racism: Ethnic Prejudice in Thought and Talk* (Newbury Park, CA, 1987); T.A. van Dijk, *Elite Discourse and Racism* (Newbury Park, CA, 1993).

[15] See, for example, F. Neal, *Sectarian Violence: The Liverpool Experience 1819–1914: An Aspect of Anglo-Irish History* (Manchester, 1988); G. Davis, *The Irish in Britain, 1815–1914* (Dublin, 1991); S. Fielding, *Class and Ethnicity: Irish Catholics in England, 1880–1939* (Buckingham, 1993). See also M.J. Hickman and B. Walter, *Discrimination and the Irish Community in Britain: A Report of Research Undertaken for the Commission for Racial Equality* (London, 1997).

[16] See, for example, J.E. Handley, *The Irish in Scotland, 1798–1845* (Cork, 1943); J. Handley, *The Irish in Modern Scotland* (Cork, 1947); R. Miles, *Racism and Migrant Labour* (London, 1982).

[17] On this point see Finn, 'Multicultural Antiracism', pp.46–8; also Finn, "Sectarianism" and Scottish Education', and Dimeo and Finn, 'Racism, National Identity and Scottish Football' for further discussion.

[18] Perhaps that is just as well. The introduction of this factor might have added to the misunderstandings surrounding MacMillan's talk; see below.

[19] See, for example, S. Bruce, *No Pope of Rome: Anti-Catholicism in Modern Scotland* (Edinburgh, 1985); T. Gallagher, *Glasgow, The Uneasy Peace: Religious Tension in Modern Scotland* (Manchester, 1987); T. Gallagher, *Edinburgh Divided: John Cormack and No Popery*

in the 1930s (Edinburgh, 1987); C.G. Brown, *The Social History of Religion in Scotland since 1730* (London, 1987); C.G. Brown, *Religion and Society in Scotland since 1707* (Edinburgh, 1997).

[20] S.J. Brown, '"Outside the Covenant": The Scottish Presbyterian Churches and Irish Immigration', *Innes Review*, 42, 1991, pp.19–45; Finn, '"Sectarianism" and Scottish Education'.

[21] A small number of Scots advocated a genuinely secular educational system. There was an alliance of sorts between some Presbyterians opposed to any Church and State links and these secularists. However, voluntarist Presbyterians often stated that it was because Scotland was such an irreversibly Presbyterian country that the case for secular education could be advanced in safety.

[22] See R.D. Anderson, *Education and the Scottish People, 1750–1918* (Oxford, 1995), for discussion of the historical background to, and debates around, the 1872 Act.

[23] See G.P.T. Finn, 'Scottish Myopia and Global Prejudices', in G.P.T. Finn and R. Giulianotti (eds.), *Football Culture: Local Conflicts and Global Visions* (London, 1999). (This book is a special issue of the journal *Culture, Sport, Society*, 2 (3), 1999.)

[24] See Anderson, *Education and the Scottish People*, for the historical background to the 1918 Act.

[25] It can be no surprise, however, that Scottish Episcopalians, as another Protestant faith – and, indeed, as a very broad Church in terms of religious practice – were less united on this educational issue than were Scotland's Catholics.

[26] This debate was not necessarily about Presbyterians against non-Presbyterians either. Both non-Presbyterian Churches, especially the Catholic Church, identified anxieties that the non-denominational Presbyterian settlement offered potential for increased secularism within these schools. That position was also advanced by the Orange and Tory Presbyterian alliance.

[27] *The Scottish Chronicle*, 21 December 1917.

[28] This is an admittedly speculative comment, but Munro's appeal may have been one of the first to invoke equal opportunities in support of an educational innovation directed towards the inclusion, and recognition of the different educational needs, of minority communities within the state system.

[29] The term 'Irish' was used loosely and was applied to Catholics of Irish descent. In the inter-war years Irish immigration to Scotland was negligible. See T.M. Devine (ed.), *Irish Immigrants and Scottish Society in the Nineteenth and Twentieth Centuries* (Edinburgh, 1991).

[30] Brown, '"Outside the Covenant"'; Finn, '"Sectarianism" and Scottish Education' and 'Scottish Myopia'.

[31] Finn, '"Sectarianism" and Scottish Education' and 'Scottish Myopia'.

[32] Some opposition is derived not from this background but from secular humanism. That argument is quite different in its inspiration – or should be, if it is true to its premises – and is truly in opposition to all denominational schools. Nonetheless, even in this context, there remain pluralist arguments for the acceptance of a diversity of schools, including denominational schools, within an inclusive national educational system. Most secular humanist positions advocate the superiority of that belief system over the 'superstitious' religious beliefs of others. Intellectually I sympathise with that judgement, but it is a thoroughly inadequate socio-political stance to adopt with respect to the recognition of social difference and societal rights.

[33] See note 32 for opposition derived from secular humanism. However, the strong argument that equates religion with the teaching of error can easily be confused with the substance of past attacks. Moreover, this position again raises serious questions about the meaning and understanding of social pluralism in contemporary society.

[34] For further discussion see Finn, '"Sectarianism" and Scottish Education' and 'Thinking Uncomfortable Thoughts about Prejudice', and also, for example, Billig, *Ideology and Opinions*, and van Dijk, *Communicating Racism, Elite Discourse and Racism and Ideology*.

[35] See J.F. Dovidio and S.L. Gaertner (eds.), *Prejudice, Discrimination and Racism* (Orlando, Fla, 1986). Also see Brown, *Prejudice*, chapter 7.

[36] See G.W. Allport, *The Nature of Prejudice* (25th Anniversary Edition) (Reading, MA., 1979), pp.14–15. Allport's classic text on prejudice was first published in 1954 but has gone through many reprints. It is perhaps worth noting that his main purpose was the study of white Protestant American prejudice directed against blacks, Jews and Catholics. These three groups were the traditional targets for White Anglo-Saxon Protestant (WASP) prejudice in the USA.

[37] Allport, *Nature of Prejudice*, pp.49–51.

[38] See Finn, 'Scottish Myopia', for further dissection of this academic failure to understand prejudice.

[39] This result was demonstrated many years ago: R.T. LaPiere, 'Attitudes against Actions', *Social Forces*, 13, 1934, pp.230–7.

[40] See Finn, 'Scottish Myopia', and Dimeo and Finn, 'Racism, National Identity and Scottish Football', for further discussion in the specific context of football.

[41] See Hickman and Walter, *CRE*. They report the patchy nature of research carried out so far, and, as a result, the report is itself incomplete and speculative in analysis in places. It nonetheless remains an important contribution to this area.

[42] See, for example, Dimeo and Finn, 'Scottish Racism'.

[43] 'Asian' is a clumsy appellation to use with respect to fellow Scots. Yet so is 'Asian-Scot', and it is perhaps even less helpful than the term 'European-American' would be. Young Scots from the South-Asian diaspora in Scotland much prefer a more meaningful bi-cultural referent such as Scottish-Pakistani. See A. Saeed, N. Blain and D. Forbes, *Social Identities of Scottish Pakistani Teenagers*, Paper to the British Psychological Society Annual Social Psychology Conference, 1996. The retention of 'Asian-Scot' here is merely an attempt to identify the range of diasporic communities to which reference is intended; it is not meant to be an adequate or accurate reference to the diasporic social identities included within this usage.

[44] There can be little doubt that the recent history of Scottish Catholicism has been dominated by the Irish-Scottish experience. That has led to neglect of the diversity of Catholicism in Scotland. See R. Burnett, '"The Long Nineteenth Century": Scotland's Catholic Gaidhealtachd', in R. Boyle and P. Lynch (eds.), *Out of the Ghetto? The Catholic Community in Modern Scotland* (Edinburgh, 1998).

[45] This observation must not be taken to imply that an Irish-Scots identity is retrogressive. The complexity of that identity, and of the social processes that form it, are much misunderstood and misrepresented. See G.P.T. Finn, 'Sporting Symbols, Sporting Identities: Soccer and Intergroup Conflict in Scotland and Northern Ireland', in I.S. Wood (ed.), *Scotland and Ulster* (Edinburgh, 1994); Finn, 'Scottish Myopia'. Some of these issues are obliquely touched on in MacMillan's talk.

[46] See, for example, M. Adams, L.A. Bell and P. Griffin, *Teaching for Diversity and Social Justice: A Sourcebook* (New York/London, 1997).

[47] Ibid., pp.34–37.

[48] J.V. Wertsch, 'The Voice of Rationality in a Sociocultural Approach to Mind', in L.C. Moll (ed.), *Vygotsky and Education: Instructional Implications and Applications of Sociohistorical Psychology* (Cambridge, 1990), p.120. Wertsch's two contrasting voices are employed here as a heuristic device to aid analysis of the contrast in the representation of MacMillan with competing voices attributed with greater authority to speak.

[49] Ibid., p.123.

[50] A full study of the complexities of this response is merited.

[51] Television shows MacMillan to have changed the scripted talk here. He is less relaxed in making this comment than the written version indicates. An obviously nervous MacMillan actually said, '. . . although that may be stretching it a little far.' BBC2 *Newsnight*, 9 August 1999.

[52] For an elaboration on these points see Finn, 'Scottish Myopia'.

[53] Those who wish to dismiss this behaviour should read the letter from Cara Henderson, schoolfriend of Mark Scott, who was brutally murdered by someone living out these beliefs. See *The Herald*, 4 June 1999.

[54] *Sunday Herald*, 6 June 1999; see MacMillan's lecture in this collection.

[55] The belief that prejudice was justified because of wage-cutting is common, untrue and has been applied to most immigrant groups in Scotland; see G.P.T. Finn, *Prejudice in the History of Irish Catholics in Scotland*, History Workshop Conference (Glasgow, 1991). This myth lies at the core of racist beliefs throughout the world; see also van Dijk, *Elite Discourse and Racism*.

[56] See Dovidio and Gaertner, *Prejudice, passim*.

[57] That is why it is much more appropriate to describe minorities as the *targets* of prejudice.

[58] For example, in New Zealand, many in the majority white community accept a myth of a previously harmonious society between white and Maori until the Maori people complained; see M. Wetherell and J. Potter, *Mapping the Language of Racism: Discourse and the Legitimation of Exploitation* (Hemel Hempstead, 1992).

[59] Van Dijk, *Communicating Racism* and *Elite Discourse and Racism*, passim; Dovidio and Gaertner, *Prejudice, passim*.

[60] See Dimeo and Finn, 'Racism, National Identity and Scottish Football', for some additional comments on this belief.

[61] For ease of reference, UK or even Britain will be used hereafter.

[62] L. Colley, *Britons: Forging the Nation, 1707–1837* (New Haven Conn, 1992).

[63] It is tempting to conclude that these prejudices no longer have any purchase south of the Anglo-Scottish border. Sadly, especially in relation to anti-Irish racism, that judgement is too optimistic just yet; see Hickman and Walters, *CRE, passim*.

[64] See Brown, *Social History of Religion*, p.33 and p.206; L. Bennie, J. Brand and J. Mitchell, *How Scotland Votes: Scottish Parties and Elections* (Manchester, 1997), p.109. In neither Wales nor Northern Ireland is there now an established Church.

[65] There are those who present this merely to be an anachronism. Nonetheless, it still has symbolic significance and is central to the belief structure of the Orange Order, whose own rules of entry bear more than a passing similarity to this requirement. Candidates for entry must also uphold the Protestant succession to the throne. See K. Haddick-Flynn, *Orangeism: The Making of a Tradition* (Dublin, 1999), p.380. Removal of the series of relevant laws concerning religion and the throne is of symbolic significance for the state's Catholic community, and other faith communities too. The change could be of practical significance in Northern Ireland, and play a small but positive part in aiding inter-communal reconciliation by removing one justification for minority community alienation.

[66] K. Boyle and J. Sheen (eds.), *Freedom of Religion and Belief: A World Report* (London, 1997), pp.316–7. This is an optimistic interpretation of the position of religious minorities, especially with respect to non-Christian faiths, in Britain.

[67] The tragi-comic element associated with this discovery of formal state discrimination was most evident much earlier in 1999 when, following 18 years of Conservative Party

government, Michael Forsyth, a former government minister in some of those administrations, somewhat belatedly claimed to have discovered what he called Britain's 'grubby little secret'. See various media reports on 26/27 January 1999.

[68] See van Dijk, *Elite Discourse and Racism*. One excuse offered for this legislation is that it is merely an anachronism and not to be taken seriously. Usually that advice comes from those who are not allocated second-class status by this law. Once identified, a genuine archaism is usually speedily abandoned with equal measures of relief and embarrassment.

[69] See, for example, *Scotland on Sunday*, 8 August 1999. This supposed quote was included in the title of an article anticipating MacMillan's lecture. It is intriguing that this quote then became 'a Northern Ireland without the guns and bullets' in the text of the article. MacMillan did *not* compare Scotland with Northern Ireland. However, the phrase was then repeated elsewhere in the media before MacMillan spoke; see, for example, *The Guardian*, 9 August 1999.

[70] The power of this interpretative frame once it was established was evident in that Bruce, Devine, McCrone and Paterson, each of whom had by then read MacMillan's actual talk, still judged the issue of workplace discrimination to be central to the talk when I first discussed with them their responses to MacMillan.

[71] STV News and BBC Scotland News, 9 August 1999.

[72] Similar equivocal comments were made by others as they were presented as disagreeing with MacMillan. For example, representing the Church of Scotland, Dr Alison Elliot said, 'I think his view that anti-Catholic sentiment is endemic in Scottish society is an exaggeration. I think that the idea that sectarianism is still alive in parts of Scotland more than any of us would like to believe is probably true, unfortunately.' If MacMillan had been interpreted as talking about a culture of prejudice, now most evident in subtle forms, then the precise areas of disagreement would require much more careful delineation than does this statement, which overlaps with some of his sentiments. There was clear disagreement. Graham Blount used 'sectarianism' to assert a model of equal culpability; see Finn, '"Sectarianism" and Scottish Education', for further discussion. Paul H. Scott seemed to miss the point that MacMillan was talking about anti-Catholic prejudices when he denied having had any personal experience of it himself.

[73] See Dimeo and Finn, 'Scottish Racism', pp.127–33.

[74] I am grateful to Professor McCrone for confirming that he had then neither read nor heard MacMillan's lecture. McCrone was ill and would have been unable to attend the lecture, had he desired to do so.

[75] This slip was made twice by Magnusson. The extracts do not adequately reflect the non-verbal features of the exchanges in terms of hesitations, pauses, etc. Both, however, gave sufficient signs of an unease that recognised that this was an interview on emotive matters. Indeed, it was true that 'James MacMillan does seem to have hit at least a nerve here'.

[76] I am grateful to Tom Devine for confirming that he had not then read MacMillan's talk. In his dealings with the media he is confident that he prefaced all of his comments with this very acknowledgement, though it is hardly a surprise that these comments were never published. This acknowledgement was not made on-air in this seemingly live BBC Scotland interview. Recently Devine has, as his contribution to this book shows, re-evaluated some aspects of his perspective.

[77] A true absence of evidence does mean that the thesis cannot be sustained. That does not logically lend support to another interpretation. However, genuine negative evidence would do that and, if there really were only two options, that would mean that the other position must be true. However, prejudice cannot be reduced in scope so that it accommodates some crude model of binary opposition.

[78] *The Herald*, 10 August 1999.

84

[79] That question became more evident as *The Herald* sought to defend itself against MacMillan's attack on the newspaper's own stance. An evaluation of this specific issue is beyond the scope of this present paper.

[80] All of these currents converge in the Graham Speirs feature 'A composer out of tune' in which Devine's comments are made as a professor 'and a Catholic'. See the 'Analysis' (*sic*) section of *Scotland on Sunday*, 15 August 1999. Speirs provides numerous references to MacMillan as an unbalanced composer, despite this association of madness with creativity being an extremely tedious and hackneyed image. One typical example is when Speirs writes, 'The intemperate rabble of MacMillan's mind, it struck me, might work well in music, but not when it comes to preaching.'

[81] See *Scottish Catholic Observer*, Editorial, 13 August 1999: 'Christianity under attack'.

[82] Institutional racism refers to the intended and unintended policies and practices that operate against racialised minorities. Institutional racism and overt racism are inter-related, but it was institutional racism that led to the overtly racist murder of Lawrence being so badly handled by the police. See Sir W. Macpherson, The Stephen Lawrence Inquiry (London, 1999). Despite media comments on the Macpherson report, institutional racism has been recognised for many years. See, for example, A. Sivanadan, 'Challenging Racism: Strategies for the '80s', *Race and Class*, 25, 1983, 1–11.

[83] This interpretation of the play was made by one of its actors, himself a Christian, in one of the television programmes on Festival and Fringe events. Terrence McNally's much-acclaimed *Corpus Christi* made its European debut in Edinburgh.

[84] See B. Glancey, 'Bigotry . . . the point that had to be made', *Scottish Catholic Observer*, 13 August 1999.

[85] See A. Bell, M. Bradley and A. Kemp, 'New nation, old bigotry', *The Observer*, 15 August 1999.

[86] I am indebted to Lindsay Paterson for his careful exposition of his views on this matter. He is committed to the view that academics are duty-bound to try to explain events to the world beyond the university. Our main disagreement here is the relationship of media representation to human action.

Academic responses to MacMillan's lecture, however, highlight the underlying problem of communicating through the media evaluations of an analysis, of which one has no direct knowledge but only that image projected by the media. Here media mediation is central to the message, and perhaps that should caution academics as to how they can more usefully intervene. Paterson is correct to identify the role that academics should play in social life; the question that must be asked here is if that was achieved by these interventions. Perhaps a debate on just how academics are to interact with the Scottish media and its demands would be another positive outcome from MacMillan's talk.

[87] The original paper was given by Paterson to the annual gathering of Scotland's Catholic headteachers. See L. Paterson, 'Catholic Education and Scottish Democracy', *Journal of Education and Christian Belief*, 2000 (in press).

[88] I am grateful to both MacMillan and Paterson for taking the time to outline their different positions on this issue.

[89] Nonetheless, Paterson genuinely welcomes MacMillan's talk because it has promoted debate on the issue of religious difference in Scotland. He would, as his contribution to this collection makes clear, deplore any suggestion that MacMillan should not have spoken out.

[90] I am indebted to Lindsay Paterson for taking the time to report to me his own notes of this press interview.

[91] I am very grateful to Steve Bruce for providing me, in a long and informative phone

call, with a very honest account of his response to the MacMillan lecture. His *Herald* article, evaluated below, does not do justice to the complexity of his views or position.

[92] S. Bruce, 'Inspection of the facts points to a ready assimiliation', *The Herald*, 10 August 1999.

[93] Ibid.

[94] See Finn, *Prejudice in the History of Irish Catholics* and '"Sectarianism" and Scottish Education'.

[95] See Finn, 'Multicultural Antiracism'; for an introduction to some of the varying interpretations made of assimilation, see M. Banton, 'Assimilation', in E.E. Cashmore (ed.), *A Dictionary of Race and Ethnic Relations* (London, 1984), pp.25–6.

[96] 'Tim' denotes Catholics, but especially Scottish Catholics of Irish ancestry.

[97] See R. Harré and L. van Langenhove (eds.), *Positioning Theory* (Oxford, 1999). The employment of elements of the approaches encapsulated under this title might have supplemented the heuristic use of voice, and in some areas provided more subtle results.

[98] MacMillan did sometimes venture in this direction, but these were the weakest elements in his talk, although sometimes this was a deliberate use of hyperbole.

[99] S. Bruce, *Conservative Protestant Politics* (Oxford, 1998). Nonetheless, in this more reflective, much calmer and more authoritative piece than his *Herald* article, Bruce does still tend towards an assimilationist model of society and the decrease in prejudice is overstated.

[100] Ibid., pp.116–8. See also D. McCrone and M. Rosie, 'Left and Liberal: Catholics in Modern Scotland', in R. Boyle and P. Lynch (eds.), *Out of the Ghetto? The Catholic Community in Modern Scotland* (Edinburgh, 1998), pp.83–4.

[101] For example, Bruce's 1997 figures for the parental occupations of both Catholic and Church of Scotland respondents are the same, with both being 27 per cent middle class and 73 per cent working class. The occupations of Catholic respondents was 42 per cent middle class to 56 per cent working class. These figures are almost reversed for the Church of Scotland respondents, whose equivalent figures are 56 per cent to 44 per cent. Both show social mobility, but clearly this is much more apparent for those identified with the Church of Scotland than for the Catholic group. Variations between the 1992 figures and the 1997 figures could indicate that these variations are the result of sampling errors resulting from the small number of subjects studied.

[102] See Rory Williams and Patricia Walls, below.

[103] See, for example, McCrone and Rosie, 'Left and Liberal', pp.70–4.

[104] G.P.T. Finn, 'Football Violence: A Societal Psychological Perspective', in R. Giulianotti, N. Bonney and M. Hepworth (eds.), *Football, Violence and Social Identity* (London, 1994).

[105] G.P.T. Finn, 'Communal Contacts and Soccer: Conflict and Conciliation', Paper to the International Symposium on Youth, Soccer, Violence, Society, University of California at Santa Barbara (1994).

[106] See R. Giulianotti, *Football. A Sociology of the Global Game* (Oxford, 1999), pp.101–2.

[107] See G.P.T. Finn, 'Faith, Hope and Bigotry: Case-Studies in Anti-Catholic Prejudice in Scottish Soccer and Society', in G. Walker and G. Jarvie (eds.), *Sport, Leisure and Scottish Culture* (Leicester, 1994); Finn, 'Sporting Symbols, Sporting Identities'.

[108] See Finn, 'Scottish Myopia'.

[109] McCrone and Rosie, 'Left and Liberal', pp.77–9; Bruce, *Conservative Protestant Politics*, pp.127–8.

[110] I have problems in knowing how I could respond to this survey. Different interpretations and comparisons could lead to acceptance of almost any of these categories. However, 'none of the above' would be the most appropriate choice. None of the first three adequately describes my evaluation. The choice is much too crude and

does no justice to the complexity of prejudice.

[111] The status of these data does not justify the other manipulations and analyses done on them by McCrone and Rosie. However, it should still be pointed out that this association of estimates of greater seriousness with youth is not such an obvious sign of 'boys' games' being an appropriate term. In 'normal' football hooligans, there is usually some recognition of the ludic quality to the various exchanges. See Giulianotti et al., *Football, Violence and Social Identity*; Finn and Giulianotti, *Football Culture*.

[112] G. Walker, *Intimate Strangers: Political and Cultural Interaction between Scotland and Ulster in Modern Times* (Edinburgh, 1995).

[113] Bruce, *Conservative Protestant Politics*, p.128.

[114] Finn, 'Sporting Symbols, Sporting Identities'.

[115] Catholic and denominational are presented as being interchangeable, which suggests the authors are unaware that other religious denominations also have denominational schools.

[116] McCrone and Rosie, 'Left and Liberal', p.79. Subsequent references are from this page too.

[117] The 1918 Act determined that denominational schools are open to all children, regardless of religion. The use of 'segregated' is not only erroneous but highly value-laden.

[118] Paterson, 'Catholic Education and Scottish Democracy'.

[119] Various interacting historical and sociological influences would be expected to influence responses.

[120] Bennie et al., *How Scotland Votes*, p.111.

[121] Ibid.

[122] Ibid. Also see F. Wright, 'Integrated Education and Political Identity', in C. Moffat (ed.), *Education Together for a Change: Integrated Education and Community Relations in Northern Ireland* (Belfast, 1993), and Finn, "Sectarianism" and Scottish Education'.

[123] See *Flourish*, May 1991.

[124] As in much of the discussion of religious difference in Scotland, precise figures cannot be obtained. These are illustrative estimates provided by some past and present Catholic headteachers. One reason is that, at least at secondary level, religious affiliation is not necessarily obvious. Any determination of denominational numbers is also exaggerated by the attendance of nominal Catholics. Around 1990, one Catholic secondary school had an intake in which the percentage of all categories of Catholic pupils appeared to be no more than 55 per cent. It is not uncommon to have school populations with a maximum of 70–80 per cent Catholics. These figures can, however, show the operation of other prejudices, especially those based on social class. Some care has to be taken in interpreting them as signs of prejudice reduction.

[125] See the excellent collection by J.C. Conroy (ed.), *Catholic Education: Inside Out, Outside In* (Dublin, 1999).

[126] See Finn, "Sectarianism" and Scottish Education', pp.878–9.

[127] See, for example, Wright, 'Integrated Education and Political Identity'.

[128] K. Bowen, *Protestants in a Catholic State: Ireland's Privileged Minority* (Kingston/Montreal/Dublin, 1983).

[129] Ibid. Bowen discusses the various ways in which assimilation threatens the continued existence of this community. He instead advocates integration. However, as with most of these terms, including pluralism, it is open to misinterpretation; see Finn, 'Multicultural Antiracism'.

[130] *News Letter*, 18 May 1994. The Republic also contains two Jewish and one Islamic state-funded schools. Comparison of different national systems is difficult because there are

always important differences. Nonetheless, the issues identified here are clearly relevant to Scotland.

[131] *The Herald*, 2 March 1998.

[132] In this respect, the content of secular humanist criticism of denominational schooling increases the fears of the religiously devout.

6. GROWING UP

John Haldane

Introduction

Early in the course of the lecture from which this collection takes its title, viz. 'Scotland's Shame', James MacMillan quoted from an article I had published on the eve of the elections for a Scottish parliament. Having considered the general standing of the main Christian denominations and commented on the issue of sectarianism, I claimed that Catholics could hope to make a significant contribution to the development of politics and culture in Scotland; but I added that if they are to do so then they need to enter more fully into the nation's higher institutions and to establish new forums of their own for the discussion of values and policies. Towards the end of the article I returned to this theme:

> . . . entering existing institutions and creating new forums is not an end in itself. The question is what ideals Catholics can offer the new Scotland. One is the concept of society as a moral community in which responsibilities stand alongside rights, in which material goods are produced with an eye to benefit as well as to profit, and in which the value of life is respected as well as its quality being promoted. Intellectually and culturally the Catholic contribution should be to challenge materialism, instrumentalism, hedonism and short-term gratification, and to present in a Scottish context the central ingredients of the Catholic philosophy of culture: abstract reflection, artistic endeavour and joyous good living . . .[1]

Quoting most of this, MacMillan observed that he had become increasingly aware of the significance of the Catholic influence and inspiration behind his own work as a composer. He mentioned various traditional embodiments of Catholicism (philosophy, theology and liturgy) and added to these 'the encultured experience of [his] own localised upbringing in the west of Scotland':

> Since childhood I was brought up to deal with reflective abstract concepts like the metaphorical, the metaphysical and the sacramental. In later life there was a thankfully smooth transition of these concepts from the purely religious sphere to the artistic sphere, although these two things are one and the same thing for me . . . The Catholic and the artist, at a fundamental level, can understand each other because the origins of their most precious metaphorical concepts are the same.[2]

Since the press reports and general reaction to MacMillan's lecture focused on his charges of anti-Catholic bigotry in Scottish society, it is important to note the positive suggestion that the arts might provide a basis on which to establish a dialogue between Catholicism and the wider Scottish culture. MacMillan himself returns to the point, remarking that the arts is the one area of public life in Scotland in which he has not encountered anti-Catholic sentiment, and he suggests that this may be due to the fact that there is a sense among those working in this area of a need to reconnect with Scotland's artistic (pre-Reformation) past.

These ideas set me thinking about the connection between growing up a Catholic in Scotland and becoming disposed to the aesthetic and to the arts. This has been my own experience and in the following section I relate something of it, highlighting points at which it bore upon my impressions of aspects of non-Catholic Scottish culture. I am aware that these will seem unflattering and perhaps even offensive, so I must emphasise that they are certainly partial and are offered in the spirit of cultural phenomenology, not that of social science. In conclusion, I will return to James MacMillan's own thoughts about the effect of the Reformation on art, and to remarks made by Andrew O'Hagan, whom MacMillan quotes with approval in the programme notes of his Symphony No. 2.

Encultured Experiences

As a child growing up in the west of Scotland in the 1960s, I felt no threat of anti-Catholic sentiment. Of course, I was aware of Celtic–Rangers rivalry and of the sectarian violence associated with this, but I had no interest in football, never once attended a football match and rarely saw fans on their way to and from games, at least not at close quarter. Occasionally I witnessed an Orange parade, generally through the windows of my father's car as we were held back with the other traffic to let the marchers pass. The impression, I think, was one of physicality and roughness: bodies scrawny or fat, faces pale or flushed, ungainly swaggers, cheap, ill-fitting clothes and crudely coloured designs. These reactions seemed to confirm something that I picked up at home, namely the idea that for the most part Protestants were in certain ways unaesthetic, without sensitivity or cultural sensibility, particularly with regard to the expressive and the visual.

This aesthetic judgement now seems to me revealing about my own background and relevant to the question of the place of religion in Scottish culture. At home the sort of sectarianism that characterised inner-city divisions was almost never discussed, even though religion – Catholic *and* Protestant – was a significant formative influence.

I was an only child in a quiet and well-ordered home near to the Botanical Gardens in the West End of Glasgow. My mother's abiding preoccupations were me, my father and religious piety and Christian charity. She was and remains the most intensely prayerful person I have ever known outside of a religious community. She came from an interesting and gifted Irish family, but not one of those that had emigrated to Scotland or left for reasons of economic necessity. We had no Irish connections and until recently it never occurred to me to think of Ireland as a place that might have a special interest for me (indeed, I only visited Eire for the first time in 1999). My maternal grandfather had served in the Royal Navy and then in HM Coast Guard, settling in Cork in the south-west of Ireland. The 1916 uprising and then the establishment of the Irish Free State made life difficult for those who had served under the Crown, however, and this, plus a desire to provide his family with an untroubled life, led my grandfather to move to Kent.

Growing up there, my mother and her sisters found themselves attracted to the theatre and began to travel and work in Europe, where they enjoyed considerable success. Finding herself in Italy at the time of the declaration of war, my mother, who had dual British/Irish nationality, elected to stand by her British identity and paid the price for this by being interred, thereafter remaining in more and less restrictive forms of confinement until the liberation. It was there and then that she met my father, who was serving in the RAF, and they were married in Kent at the end of the war.

My father had come from a fairly dour background. An only child of older parents, he was raised in the Kirk, his father being a Master of the Masonic Lodge. Living within sight of the Ochil Hills, he spent much of his youth walking the glens and ridges. (Interestingly, given the popular tendency to associate the south of Ireland with Catholicism, there were Dublin family connections, and photographs show my father and grandparents holidaying in the Irish Free State.) Evidently a solitary and sensitive boy, he took to drawing and photography, producing work of some quality in each medium. He would have liked to study at art school, but my grandfather would have none of it, thinking such an education to be a waste of time. In retrospect this seems both sad and ironic, for my grandfather was no Philistine: an accomplished keyboard player, he served as organist in the local Presbyterian Church. As was typical, his interest focused on religious music, in particular the choral work of church composers, and I think he cared for little beyond this. My father had been encouraged to learn the piano and in due course this would be a point of shared interest with my mother, who also played. By her account, and in my memory, he was the better of the two and could carry off the likes of Gershwin's *Rhapsody in Blue*. But he remained largely unpraised by my grandfather, who may have resented his son's broader talents and the fact that they were applied more widely than his own.

Employment brought my parents to Glasgow. On arriving in Scotland my mother found the gloom very dispiriting. She had thrown herself into parish life and did so again in Glasgow while beginning to build a home there, decorating it far more brightly and with much greater imagination than was common even in middle-class circles at the time. No doubt she was attempting to recreate something of what she had known in Ireland, the south of England and Italy.

After the death of his wife my grandfather moved in with us for some while and so began an interesting time of our lives. A few years previously my father had converted to Catholicism, being received into the Church by a Franciscan, Fr Bonaventure. However, my grandfather never knew of this conversion and I believe he may have died in ignorance of it. What he did know, however, was that his son had married a papist and that I was being educated at Catholic schools. Like many other Glaswegians of my age and background, that education took place first at Hamilton Park in the west of the city, then at John Ogilvie Hall on the southside and finally at St Aloysius in the centre of town. The second and third of these were Jesuit schools and the Society of Jesus –

along with the office of Pope (the 'whore of Babylon') – was then, and for some still is, an object of deep Protestant abhorrence and contempt. Even so I never remember domestic rows over the issue of my schooling, though my grandfather once went to St Aloysius to speak to the then headmaster (the late Fr John Tracy, SJ), and I do recall Granddad telling me that the reason the Pope wore 'long dresses' was to cover his cloven hooves. Beyond that he used to say that if I didn't behave I should be given the 'nippy cane', an expression and a recommendation I otherwise never heard and which annoyed my mother, but he never actually shouted at me, let alone struck me. In fact he used to take me for long walks. I am not sure what we talked about on our outings but I became fond of him, no doubt picked up something from him, was sad when he died and now occasionally visit his grave in Clackmannanshire.

The combination of home and school formed me quite deeply and gave direction to my life. I suspect my mother had hopes that I might take up a religious calling, perhaps by joining the Jesuits, though I don't remember her proposing this. The only career she suggested was that of a 'poor man's lawyer'. This idea of serving others was also illustrated by example. For many years she was a member of the Legion of Mary, serving as a branch secretary and also helping in a hostel for 'homeless girls and women'. I would often go to the hostel, sometimes to serve at Mass (I was also an altar boy at St Charles, Kelvinside), and was made a fuss of by these ladies.

At school I was not particularly academically gifted and chose to pursue art. Sometime in my teens I formed the idea of going to art college. The fact that Charles Rennie Mackintosh's famous Glasgow Art School building was across the street from St Aloysius College may have been a factor, but more memorable and significant was the sight of stylishly dressed female art students around the Botanic Gardens area. I don't know whether any other pupil from my year had such ambitions but certainly at school-leaving time none was destined for art school. My impression then – and now – was that such an option was not likely to have approval from their parents, though my own were entirely supportive. There were probably concerns about what this would lead to as a career but there was never a single word of discouragement, and I think my father was happy to see me pursue what he had once hoped for himself.

By that point chronic ill-health had led my father to consider early retirement and my school-leaving was agreed to be the moment for him to quit work. We moved to Kent, where for many years I had spent my summer holidays, and I began my art-school education. The year I completed this my father died. Employment became necessary. I took up school teaching and part-time study in philosophy, a subject that had long interested me. Philosophy went well and I was then to return to full-time study. In the last year of this a post became available at St Andrews. I applied, was appointed and with my wife (a Glaswegian whom I had first met while at school) returned to Scotland, where we have lived ever since.

The town being closely associated with the Reformation, and the university being thought of as socially élitist and mostly English (or, where Scottish, overwhelmingly 'east coast'), there were very few Catholics on the academic staff when I arrived – perhaps three or four (all of them English). But I cannot say that I ever encountered anti-Catholic bigotry. It was only some years later when I began writing for the press and appearing on the radio that I began to receive pointedly anti-papist insults – and for the most part these came from correspondents in the west of Scotland!

In 1999 the Donald Findlay affair created a major difficulty for the university. On the one hand, as rector he had by all accounts served the student body very well, and there was every reason to maintain the recent tradition of according outgoing rectors honorary degrees. On the other hand, his loutish behaviour following a Rangers victory over Celtic, singing insulting anti-Catholic songs at a time when Rangers was trying to put its bad sectarian reputation behind it, caused general embarrassment. My own initial reaction was one of anger. Very quickly, however, I came to believe that whilst Findlay may have been irresponsible, foolish and vulgar, the university ought not to revoke the decision to award the degree, at least not without seeing whether Findlay might embark upon a course of social reparation.

As my thinking became more definite I decided to write a piece in *The Herald* to be published on the day that the university senate was due to discuss the affair. Entitled 'A matter of honour'[3], the article produced a significant amount of mail both to the paper and to me personally. Among the latter was a particularly abusive letter – from a Catholic in the west of Scotland. Though stylishly expressed, his accusations were extreme and bordered on the deranged, including the suggestion that I might owe my position at St Andrews to a willingness to serve the Protestant cause.

One defence of 'Findlay's songs of hate', as one paper headlined the story, is that they belong to a tribal ritual now far removed from its anti-Catholic origins and all but empty of its sectarian meaning. Likewise, a defence of my spluttering Catholic correspondent is that I had triggered a folk-memory of bigoted oppression. Each might then be excused on grounds of passion. But this is not an adequate response. Middle-aged men do behave like overwrought juveniles, and not just when they are tired and emotional; but actions occur in contexts and have consequences. The night Findlay misbehaved, a boy wearing a Celtic shirt had his throat cut and another was shot in the chest by a crossbow. Meanwhile, blinded by his own prejudices, my Catholic correspondent evidently failed to register the content of my article, grossly misrepresenting it and no doubt relaying his twisted account to others.

The Findlay affair, James MacMillan's lecture and other events have exposed several broad veins of deeply rooted sectarianism in Scottish society, particularly in the central belt and principally – but not exclusively – in the west. In Scotland we cannot afford immaturity with regard to such matters. There is a good deal of arrested development and cultural retardation on both sides of the divide. Growing up is not an inevitable process; it is an imperative that some may find difficult to follow but which is all the more necessary for just that reason. Learning good manners is an important part of that process.

Recovering Lost Ground

And so I return to the aesthetic. Generalising grossly, but hopefully in the direction of *a* truth, I suggest that whereas the Scots of Catholic backgrounds tend to uncritical sentimentalism and are fiery in reaction to perceived or imagined prejudices and slights, those of Protestant backgrounds tend to insensitivity and are unyielding in their self-assurance. The first is a defect of superfluity of feeling, the second one of the lack of it. The former is something I recognise in myself, the latter is what was conveyed to me by the sight of the Orange parades and by my grandfather's lack of response to his son's artistic talents.

There has been much talk in Scotland in recent years of the importance of the arts. Too often, though, this is perceived in terms of its contribution to the tourism industry, and when art is considered in its own right, the art in question is usually literary. There is no doubting Scotland's interest in the written word but this is a medium whose appeal is to the intellect and to the discursive imagination. What is underdeveloped in Scottish culture is a properly *aesthetic* sensitivity (from the Greek *aisthetikos*: concerning sense perception), the openness to beauty and transcendence, especially as these are present in music and the visual arts. Our backwardness in this regard is due, I think, to the Reformation and to what followed it.

In the late medieval and renaissance periods, St Andrews was to Scotland what Oxford and Canterbury were to England: home of its oldest university and ecclesiastical capital of the nation. Being poorer and more remote from the sources of European artistic and architectural innovation, St Andrews compared less favourably with its southern counterparts even then, but today the historical contrast is marked. Whereas Canterbury Cathedral stands as a proud and enduring witness to the achievements of the Gothic, the cathedral at St Andrews is a ruin only hinting at its glorious past. The medieval and renaissance university buildings have fared better but by comparison they are fewer and less grand than their Oxford contemporaries.

Relative wealth apart, a further factor serves to explain the difference: the Reformation. Prior to 1560 Scotland had a rich tradition of ecclesiastical art and music. Something of the latter has been rediscovered in recent years, but almost nothing remains of church and college art. Among the few exceptions, all the more remarkable for the fact that they are without parallel, are the three medieval maces of St Andrews University, the finest of which is that of St Salvator's College (1461).

Though rich in detail, the true accomplishment of this work is that it gives concise expression to a philosophical-cum-theological world view. The Gothic in architecture is based upon the plan as against the elevation-design of classicism. That difference may reflect a subsequent loss of conviction in the orderliness of nature and the proper place of humankind within it, for whereas Gothic forms grow out of the ground like trees and plants, classicism elevates a façade behind which may stand anything, and nothing.

No doubts about the orderliness of the world troubled the designer of the mace for whom architectural, botanical and human forms are combined in celebration of religion, science and art. The fact that it was made in Paris hardly detracts from the claim of a rich pre-Reformation artistic heritage since its very commission testifies to discerning patronage. Also, human, intellectual and cultural traffic then moved to and fro and the artisan may have been a Scot. Certainly the greatest contemporary philosopher-theologian in Paris was a graduate of St Andrews and later Provost of St Salvator's, viz. *Johannes Maioris Scotus* – John Major.

Five hundred years later there is renewed interest in Scotland in imaginative design. In 1999, the year of the new parliament as well as of MacMillan and of Findlay, Glasgow was UK City of Architecture and Design and celebrated with exhibitions of modern masters and of the earlier figure Alexander 'Greek' Thomson, who along with Mackintosh was the city's greatest architect. Architecture and design, however, are in general non-representational arts, thus escaping the biblical prohibition of graven images reaffirmed by the Protestant reformers. There is little doubt, though, that the revolutionary shift from a theology that embodied religious ideas in visual representations to one that accorded exclusivity to scripture had a damaging effect on art in Scotland. On the other hand, it may be that the substitution of the verbal for the visual laid the foundations for the Scottish Enlightenment and for the strong literary tradition that continues to the present day. Likewise, the Calvinist preoccupation with duty may have been a major factor in shaping the laudable Scottish concern for politics and public service.

Yet the repressed will return. Slowly and in stages the visual arts have recovered. Significantly, though, the subject matter has rarely been chosen for its intellectual interest. From portraiture in the seventeenth and eighteenth centuries, Scots stepped gingerly out of doors to paint the landscape and then returned to a domesticated version of this, the flower-based still life. More radical spirits moved beyond these themes and began to depict charged human situations, but thereby only confirmed the deep influence of Calvinistic moralism. One pronounced feature of Scottish art in the twentieth century was the interest in colour, though as John McEwen recently pointed out, the Scottish palette has always carried a good deal of black.[4] And when colour has been used unmournfully it has often been in the service of decoration rather than of profound ideas. With its crucifixion scenes, the work of Craigie Aitchison may seem to represent a return to pre-Reformation art, but the religious imagery in his paintings is in fact theologically idle.

In the programme notes to which I referred earlier, MacMillan recalls composing a piano sonata during a bitter Ayrshire winter and reflects on the way in which poets use the wintry Scottish landscape as a metaphor for the country's spiritual desolation. He then goes on to quote from his fellow Ayrshireman Andrew O'Hagan, writing of the 'tragedy of Scotland':

> . . . The country is lucky to have any artists really. It is no country for a man or a woman of letters. It is no place for a poet. It is a graveyard for any painter not interested in the weather. It's a sad valley for any willing singer of songs. For all the glories of its humane tradition, Scotland has no time now for the discomfiture of thinkers, no ready heart for the excoriation of myths, and no spirit, no confidence, no capacity for tolerance, in the face of unsettling truths.

This is too bleak a view, I think, and one hard to sustain save from afar. Nonetheless there is a need to overcome the legacy of Calvinistic hostility to the aesthetic sensibility and the creative spirit. To take just the case of the visual arts, if Scotland is to return to the European artistic fold it needs to find ways of combining its long-standing talent for design and its more modern interest in colour with its strong appetite for ideas – not substituting the latter for the former but synthesising them as has been the great achievement of Italian art, from the avowedly sacred art of Cimabue to the apparently secular spirituality of Morandi. The renaissance never had a chance to influence Scotland's visual culture, but that should be an additional incentive to help effect a rebirth of art and spirituality in Scotland.

In certain crucial respects our development was arrested. The situation is recoverable but it will take great effort and more than this generation to close the gap. What has not been commented upon thus far, however, is that Catholic and Protestant in Scotland now face a common threat: that posed by egotistic, hedonistic materialism, particularly as this grips the souls of younger generations, including the souls of artists. Growing up is hard enough without the temptation of infantile regression.

Notes

[1] John Haldane, 'A nation under God', *Catholic Herald*, 30 April 1999.
[2] James MacMillan, 'Scotland's Shame'. For the text, see chapter one in this volume.
[3] John Haldane, 'A matter of honour', *The Herald*, 16 June 1999.
[4] John McEwen, 'The Powers of Light and Dark: Colour in Scottish Painting', *Modern Painters*, vol.XII, no.4, winter 1999, pp.86–8. The previous paragraphs draw on my editorial introduction ('Return of the Repressed') to the *Modern Painters* Scottish Feature in which McEwen's essay is contained.

PART 2

'The Waning of Social Exclusion'

[Joseph Devine]

7. A LANARKSHIRE PERSPECTIVE ON BIGOTRY IN SCOTTISH SOCIETY

Joseph Devine

Introduction

Like many others, I was intrigued by the reaction to the speech by James MacMillan, made in August 1999, on the topic of a deep-seated religious bigotry against Catholics at the heart of Scottish society. It generated a huge response in the letters columns of the press at the time. In many ways it was a strange speech, and many people suggested it would have been more relevant if it had been aired 20 to 30 years ago. Personally, I thought that it would have been even more relevant if it had been made 40 years ago when I was a teenager, in the late 1940s and early 1950s.

I well remember the 1940s and the immediate post-war years, with the rationing of the time in the light of the immense expenditure incurred by Great Britain in defeating National Socialism in Germany. But it was a price that we were willing to pay to win the freedom of both Europe and the wider world from a perverse creed.

But other things also come to my mind from that time, such as my father having to forego a day's wages by taking a holiday on Christmas Day. The majority of Scots workers at that time worked on Christmas Day, as it was not a public holiday. Christmas Day was the 'Catholic thing', whilst New Year's Day was the 'Protestant thing', the real winter break for the dominant community in Scotland. This is the first form of 'proof' that I offer in support of my thesis that the speech of James MacMillan concerns a bygone age, though I admire him for making it, even if years too late in so doing. That was not his fault, as no other voice was raised in that era to make the point that he made about the dominant force in Scottish society at the time.

A change was to take place, largely in the past 30 years. Prior to that era there were several factors contributing to the kind of Scotland that James MacMillan alleges is still Scotland today. The first of these, in my judgement, is in relation to the locations in which the immigrant Irish community found itself in the latter part of the nineteenth century and the early part of the twentieth century.

'Ghettoisation' of Irish Immigrants to Scotland in the Second Half of the Nineteenth Century, as well as in the Early Years of the Twentieth Century

The vast majority of the immigrant Irish Catholics arriving in Scotland over that period came from Ulster. Ulster is broader than Northern Ireland. Ulster includes the counties of Donegal, Cavan and Monaghan, excluded from the Northern Ireland State created by Great Britain in 1922, in a treaty that resulted in 26 out of the 32 of the counties of Ireland becoming what we now know as the Republic of Ireland. It also had to meet the demands of the Protestant community in the other six counties to produce a dominant Protestant ethos in Northern Ireland, even if that community tended to see itself as Ulster rather than Northern Ireland.

The vast majority of the Irish immigrants to Scotland in the latter half of the nineteenth century came from the counties of Ulster, as the easiest links to Scotland were from the ports of Larne and Derry. In Catholic terms, the greatest number came from Donegal, while significant numbers in Protestant terms were to come to Scotland a few decades later from the Belfast area, to boost the production of shipbuilding on the Clyde at the time of the First World War. While this is true in general terms, there was one major exception. In the latter part of the nineteenth century, the Duke of Hamilton recruited a workforce, Protestant and Catholic alike, from around the town of Larne to work his mines, flax fields and orchards. Most of these settled in Larkhall. To this day, Larkhall is seen as one of the most sectarian towns in Scotland, with religious bigotry in evidence until recent times. When a church for the Catholic community was built there in 1872, it was on the condition that it had to be over half a mile from the town centre, effectively placing it outside the town at that time. Larkhall remains the exception to my proposition of the segregation of the Protestant and Catholic immigrant communities from Ireland.

The vast majority of the immigrants from Ireland in the nineteenth century, especially in Catholic terms, had little intention of finding a permanent home in Scotland. Most of them wanted to go much further afield, in most instances to America. However, a problem awaited them in Scotland: they had to find very quickly the economic means to achieve their dream. Given the circumstances of the time, it was a dream that would not be achieved by the great majority. So they remained in Scotland, mostly in Glasgow and major towns in the central belt such as Greenock, Paisley, Dumbarton, Coatbridge, Airdrie, Hamilton, Carluke, Stirling, Lennoxtown, Falkirk and Bathgate. Others settled in Edinburgh, Dundee, Ayr and Kilmarnock.

All of this is substantiated by an examination of the Catholic parish communities established in the nineteenth century. Prior to 1820, only two Catholic parishes were to be found across Scotland's central belt, in Glasgow and Edinburgh. These were established for a different purpose: to meet the needs of Highland Catholics moved from their homes in the north in the dreadful aftermath of the failed Jacobite revolution of 1745 and the quite savage Clearance of the Highlands in subsequent years.

Those two parishes in Edinburgh and Glasgow were to serve the small resident Catholic population quite adequately for the next 20 years or so. However, a steady trickle of Irish immigrants began to arrive in Scotland from around 1817, when the Catholic churches in Glasgow and Edinburgh were built, until 1849, the year of the disastrous famine due to the failure of the potato crop. The people who came were initially in the farming industry and were seen as cheap labour for the vegetable and orchard trades. Some stayed to find a better future. They were the first wave of an immigration from Ireland that was to increase massively in the years after 1850.

A second wave was connected to the industrial revolution, in its infancy in Great Britain around the year 1840. The term 'the Irish navvy' was born in that era, referring to a navigator, a builder of roads and railways. At that point Scotland had need of many of these workers to build the channels of that revolution by connecting its cities, Glasgow and Edinburgh, to the south, both by road and by rail. The Irish navigator was to play a significant part in making those connections.

A new phenomenon took place in Ireland soon thereafter: the potato famine of 1849. Immigrants from Ireland, both north and south, were located in 'segregated villages' across much of the area described earlier. Nowhere is this more true than Lanarkshire, the area for which I have pastoral responsibility as Bishop of Motherwell. Prior to 1850, there were but four Catholic parish communities in Lanarkshire: Airdrie, Hamilton, Coatbridge and Carluke. The last was wholly due to the presence of Irish navvies.

It is easy to trace where in Lanarkshire the immigrants came to reside in significant numbers over the second half of the nineteenth century; all one needs to do is look at the parishes founded in that period. They were: Rutherglen (1851), Wishaw (1859), Chapelhall (1859), Lanark (1859), Carfin (1862), Mossend (1868), Shotts (1868), Newmains (1871), Cleland (1874), Whifflet (1874), Motherwell (1875), Blantyre (1877), Longriggend (1878), Cambuslang (1878), Baillieston (1880), Glenboig (1880), Uddingston (1883), Cadzow (1883), Shieldmuir (1891), Langloan (1892) and Newton (1894). Those 21 parishes met the needs of the Catholic community in what is now the diocese of Motherwell. Today 74 parishes serve that same area, but more important is the fact that many of those parish communities had a nearby town or village in which the resident majority was Protestant. This is evident in such places as Rutherglen/Burnside, Chapelhall/Calderbank, Carfin/ Newarthill, Mossend/Bellshill, Newmains/Bonkle, Longriggend/Caldercruix, Glenboig/Gartcosh, Cardowan/Stepps, Newton/Hallside, Craigneuk/ Shieldmuir and Wishaw/Cleland.

Traditionally, many Catholics were coal miners while those who worked in the better-paid steel industry were almost exclusively Protestant. While places such as Chapelhall, Carfin, Mossend, Newmains, Longriggend, Glenboig, Cardowan, Newton and Cleland had coal mining as the chief local industry, the ironworks and steelworks of that era were to be found in Burnside/Cambuslang, Bellshill, Gartcosh, Hallside, Craigneuk and Wishaw. In effect, it meant that although the two faith traditions lived cheek by jowl, they were socially separated as well as religiously divided. No wonder, then, that historical, social and economic reasons contributed to the fact that even to this day Lanarkshire is not very fertile ground for ecumenical relationships.

Adding to the difficulty was the Education Act of 1872, the Act which made attendance at school compulsory for all children. But it was a by-product of that same Act that caused a huge difficulty for the Catholic community, as it required that all religious education given within public schools was according to the reformed faith. This was insisted upon by the national Church, although not for any sectarian reason. Quite the reverse. It was to avoid schools being deprived of all religious education and being overrun by the French rationalism of the time. This had a huge effect upon the Catholic community. Although impoverished, it made huge sacrifices in building its own schools, usually prior to the building of churches, and there came into being a network of Catholic schools that did not become a part of the state's educational provision until after the 1918 Education Act.

101

In all of this, two of Lanarkshire's major towns, Airdrie and Coatbridge, present a special challenge to the general thesis that I am attempting to substantiate. It is my impression that the great majority of people living in the central belt of Scotland see Coatbridge as the 'Catholic town', with Airdrie being the 'Protestant town'. There is some truth in that verdict, but not a great deal. The percentage of Catholics in Coatbridge is little over 50 per cent, while the percentage of Protestants in Airdrie is not quite 60 per cent.

Historically, both of these communities relied less on coal mining than on finding employment in the numerous iron foundries then located in what is today the town centre of Coatbridge, although there were also many miners in the area. The workforces of the foundries were drawn from both communities. Finding a job was never a serious problem there in the century from 1860 to 1960 except for during the 1920s and 1930s, even if the work was arduous and poorly rewarded in terms of pay. But what is unique to that area, particularly Coatbridge, is that the owners of those iron foundries, all of them members of the national Church, built churches for their own co-religionists to keep them in the area, lest the foundries be wholly populated by the incoming Irish workers.

Perhaps the most spectacular example of all is to be found in Craigneuk and Shieldmuir, where exactly the same geographical area was defined differently in the light of the faith traditions of the two co-existing communities. For Catholics, the name of the town was Shieldmuir; for Protestants it was Craigneuk. I stress this point for another reason. The old motto of Motherwell, in what was to become the centre of Lanarkshire, at least geographically, was 'Industria'. That Latin term is not to be translated as simply 'industry'. It really means a place where industry flourishes. For a century or more, industry did flourish in Lanarkshire, in coal mining, ironworks and steelmaking. But it is no less true that a great many of those who serviced all those industries came from separated backgrounds, socially and economically.

Therefore, when I look at the facts, some of which I have outlined, it is easy to see why a great deal of the social history of Lanarkshire over the century from 1860 to 1960 would have provided rich ground for the kind of address given by James MacMillan in 1999. Where I take issue with him is in relation to the impact of some significant events of the past 30 years or so.

Some Significant Events of the Past 30 Years Marking an End to the Social and Economic Exclusion of Catholics within the Wider Context of the Scottish Community at All Levels

In this final part of the chapter, I will settle for two such significant events in the emergence of the Catholic community at virtually every level in Scottish society today. The first of these was the introduction of comprehensive education by the Labour government of 1964. In my opinion, this was more beneficial to the Catholic community than anything since the Catholic Emancipation Act of 1829 and the repeal of the penal laws. That may seem an extraordinary thing for me to claim. Bear with me.

In 1964, only three Catholic secondary schools were in a position to offer their pupils a way into tertiary education: one in Motherwell, a second in Bothwell and a third in Coatbridge. Within 15 years, that number had risen to

13, with new schools or upgraded junior secondaries being able to do the same: a further two in Coatbridge and one in Airdrie, as well as others in Wishaw, Carfin, Bellshill, Burnbank, Hamilton, Rutherglen, Cambuslang, Easterhouse and two in East Kilbride. I clearly recall the effect of this. I became chaplain to the Catholic community at Glasgow University in 1974. The previous chaplain had been there since 1967, when the total number of Catholic undergraduates was no more than 700. By 1974, that total had risen to around 2,000, due to the effect of comprehensive education and better salaries for workers which made possible a university education for their children. I recall carrying out a survey of the Catholic entrants for that year, 1974. Over 90 per cent were the first members of their families ever to enter tertiary education.

For the rest of the '70s, the Catholic undergraduate numbers remained around the 2,000 mark. As a result, when Margaret Thatcher became prime minister in 1979, there were thousands of young Catholic graduates. Many of these had intended becoming teachers, but at that point in the mid-1970s school rolls began to drop at an alarming rate, only a short time after the school-leaving age had been raised from 15 to 16. The net effect was that many hundreds of recent graduates who had intended entering the teaching profession had to cast their net a lot wider.

Much worse was soon to follow for them and millions of others. When Margaret Thatcher came to power, the unemployment total was around one million, a figure that had been deemed just about acceptable for the previous 30 years. But two years later that figure had swollen to over three million. Market forces, profitability and the era of privatisation were the culture of the time. Profit margins were very tight and survival was the name of the game for thousands of businesses. Almost at a stroke, the 'old school tie' disappeared as an automatic entrance to a whole range of businesses in which Catholics had been greatly under-represented for decades. The traditional question of so many job interviews prior to that point, namely 'Which school did you attend?', became a secondary consideration to a much more pertinent question: 'What kind of degree or qualification do you have?' It's many years since I last saw the sign 'Vacancy; no Catholics need apply'.

Over the past 20 to 30 years, Catholics have found employment in all sorts of areas previously either denied them or unattainable for them, mostly in the fields of banking, commerce, corporate management and the upper echelons of the legal system. Of course, there was always a way up for the bright young Catholic graduate in law, medicine and the teaching profession, but there was not a lot more going for them outside those professions.

By the '80s, there was another force at work: the inward investment from other countries to Scotland, in the new forms of employment to be found in the fields of computing and information technology. Here the senior management were not of Scottish origin and had no interest in the faith tradition of their workforces. Their one concern was the skills and competence of their workers, irrespective of all other considerations.

Finally, of course James MacMillan is correct in his allegation that there is a lot of bigotry and sectarianism alive and well in Scottish society. This can easily be seen by the fact that Glasgow's two giant football clubs have a policy against bigotry and sectarianism. Why would they have adopted such a policy in recent years if no such problem existed? But a great deal of the social exclusion practised against Catholics in former times has waned, if not totally disappeared. Hopefully, that trend will continue in the years to come.

8. FAITH OF OUR FATHERS LIVING STILL . . . THE TIME WARP OR WOOF! WOOF!

Bernard Aspinwall

The Problem

The public huffing and puffing over James MacMillan's Edinburgh lecture and Patrick Reilly's persistent reflections in the *Scottish Catholic Observer* and *Flourish* are interesting comments on our contemporary predicament. The self-appointed guardians of Catholicism are stuck in their Tardis around 1939, crying wolf or barking up the wrong tree at some imaginary threat. They highlight 'The Lanarkshire Question'. That, far more than any Lothian question, has bedevilled our history and will continue to do so until we Catholics face our past with honesty and hard evidence.

In the Catholic magazine *Open House* in the immediate aftermath of the MacMillan lecture, Jim McManus wrote of past bitterness and the later 'revenge' of Catholic personnel officers in the area, while Denis Rice from the east recalled a very different picture. All these writers, with varying emphasis, suggest bigotry or tribalism within Catholicism in Scotland. Some examination of the assumptions of our writers and their historical evidence for an informed judgement is in order.

Some Perspective

First and foremost, the suggestion that Catholicism in Scotland is an Irish phenomenon needs to be challenged. Too many popular writers and even some scholars who should know better present the history of religion in Scotland as a permanent Rangers–Celtic match. No one could live like that and lead any kind of 'normal' life. Even white racists in the American South whom I often encountered in the '60s talked about many things with the very blacks they publicly despised. Reality is always a little more complex.

The Basic Facts of the Past

The Church in Scotland has never had a majority of Irish clergy. She has only had two Irish-born bishops in her modern history: the short-term bishop Lynch, who was briefly coadjutor vicar-apostolic of the Western District 1866–69 before Rome removed him to Ireland, and the more recent archbishop Keith O'Brien. The Irish Christian Brothers failed to establish themselves or their influence in Scotland during the decisive formative years; their shortage of manpower and Scottish Catholic misgivings meant they arrived belatedly to man an approved school after the Second World War.

These may be inconvenient facts but they show the fatuous nature and much of the nonsense of Catholic mythology. This mythology has sometimes been perpetrated by Catholics themselves, anxious to whip up folk loyalty among faltering flocks, and sometimes by critics eager to exploit the 'alien' nature of Catholicism in Scottish society. Irish equals Catholic is a useful tool for interested parties on both sides. Unfortunately it was not always true in Scotland. Reality is somewhat more complex.

Complexity or Blurred Lines

To assume that all Irish migrants came with a ready set of Irish nationalist assumptions, attitudes and solidarity is a distortion. To assume that all Protestants were virulently opposed to Catholicism is wide of the mark. Revd Dr Thomas Chalmers, the leading Scottish churchman of his day and later founder of the Free Church, preached to raise funds for Catholic schools. Free Churchmen attended Midnight Mass at Christmas in Carstairs House in 1850. The first Catholic chapel since the Reformation, begun in the old Mitchell Street tennis court in Glasgow, was established through Protestant businessmen. The redoubtable Father Theobald Mathew, the Irish temperance apostle, was rapturously welcomed by thousands of Scottish Protestants on his visit in 1842; on that occasion he administered the total abstinence pledge to the influential American Protestant minister Revd Theodore Cuyler. Many Catholic clergy received cash, school or church sites or even handsome presentations from prominent Protestants for their distinguished service. Protestant ministers, often in the most surprising places – contrary to the stereotype – paid tribute to the outstanding service performed in their localities by Catholic clergy. One could go on. Yes, others were virulent bigots. Reality is complex.

Drawing Wavy Lines

Bigoted sentiments usually flourished amid high political and social tension around St Patrick's Day and 12 July or around election time, especially in the Home Rule crisis, prior to the First World War. Even well-heeled bigots need employees or servants. Once these classes become voters, the equation has to change whatever the prejudiced may feel: permanent settlement slowly brought property, the vote, a stake in the social order or, at the very least, self-interest and self-defence, as with more recent immigrants. Class, ethnic consciousness or the need to pull rank in a democracy may aid discrimination but social democracy demands solidarity; even somewhat repulsive elements have to be won over. As Revd Gerard Manley Hopkins SJ saw, cleanliness and morality were understood by the Glasgow Irish Catholic poor even though they did not always practise them. At best, snobbery over poor benighted Catholics and inflated self-perception proved your own respectability. Even bigots have to get elected in a democracy. That adjustment takes differing times in different areas and the Catholic experiences of Galloway, the Highlands and Islands and the east differ from each other and from the west. Charges that Irish folk always worked for lower wages need to be proved conclusively; one suspects that some agitators used that as a mask for other motives. Liberal intellectuals and Labour leaders often attacked the (Catholic) Lithuanian presence. Working-class leaders like Keir Hardie could be as xenophobic as the next Scot. Many early Irish migrants worked in declining industries like handloom weaving or in work that locals found less than appealing, in a similar way to West Indians in London in the 1940s to 1960s, Pakistani or Indian restaurateurs and shopkeepers generally working in jobs abandoned by increasingly affluent whites.

Emerging 'Scottishness'

Irish-born Catholics in Scotland have been less and less a part of the Church throughout the twentieth century. They had fewer reasons to come as a result of the Depression, declining Scottish heavy industries and, more recently, the growth of the Irish economy. Nowadays we do not recruit Irish priests. (Would any be available?) To use the expression of the Irish in Scotland today is to talk of a tiny minority. Yes, there is a cultural baggage, but at what point do they become Scots or does Scotland absorb their positive values? It is like the misplaced descriptions of those descended from the Indian subcontinent as 'Pakistanis' or 'Punjabis'. The vast majority are Scottish-born Scots. The identity of Scotland has changed whether some Neanderthal Scots like it or not. The identity of the incomer and their descendants has similarly adjusted, often with some pain. If some elements still refer to Catholics in the same uninformed way, it reveals their inability to accept modernity. Some might call that ignorance or prejudice. Reality is complex.

Perceived as Alien – to What?

The worst burden of Scottish Catholicism through the last century was an identification with despotic government and poverty. And not without good reason. It was not perceived as 'progressive'. It was seen as the faith of the reactionary and often persecuting governments of Europe: Pius IX, Austria, France and Spain. The Church of the Syllabus of Errors and the extravagant publicists in the wake of Vatican I is a far cry from the Church of the oppressed, the marginalised and the social encyclicals. The Church was associated with poverty: the squalid Catholics of Ireland, the Highlands and southern Italy. It was also the aristocratic landowners' faith in many instances – again, an inconvenient fact. Reality is complex.

Integrating Into What?

As in Blair's Britain, its adherents are not seen as patrons of divisive private schools, upward mobility and leadership. Strange, as Ampleforth, Stonyhurst, Downside and the like still stand comparison with the best. But then of course we know Catholic schools are necessarily divisive. Strange how *private* education is never seen in those terms in spite of considerable evidence to the contrary. *The Scotsman* and *The Herald* regularly carry letters extolling educational integration. Hurrah! Your '60s mindset responds at the prospect of an end to the heavily state-subsidised, private fee-paying schools in Scotland – including some prominent Catholic institutions. But no, it only applies to those 'public schools for the poor' Catholic schools. The selective mindset is staggering. It is redolent of old Stalinist-style socialists or Scots unsure of their own identity. Catholic schools, as MacMillan rightly insists, like in Andrew Greeley's America, are often the only escape route for disadvantaged, ambitious folk from the bottom rungs of society. Ask Glasgow Muslims.

Diversity of Catholicism

In recent times we have begun to recognise the remarkable contribution of Italians, Lithuanians, Poles, Ukrainians and others to the development of Catholicism in this country. The work of Italian and Low Countries priests almost 150 years ago and Lithuanian clergy a century ago need to be better known. Strangely, we still need a serious scholarly assessment of the Highland contribution and of the English dimension. These gaps in our understanding reflect on Catholic inertia which may partly explain our present inadequate knowledge of the Catholic past.

Inadequate Structures

The way lazy, sloppy historians of the Scottish Catholic experience resort to the description 'the Catholic ghetto' is disgraceful. To portray Scottish Catholics as living in such a context is a disservice to scholarship, grossly inaccurate and an outrageous insult to Jews. To pretend Scottish Catholics ever lived in such a way is dishonest. It is an excuse for a slipshod approach to the issue.

We were never a tribe. To apply that description smacks of snobbery. And condescension at best, and racism at worst. To suggest soccer Neanderthals have any similarity with African or North American peoples is another insulting lazy approach. Why not use Klans? Oops, sorry, clans: at least that expression has the benefit of being Scottish. But then the respectable do not wish to admit that xenophobia, racism or antipathy to 'difference' is a very strong local *Scottish* characteristic. It has a longer historical tradition from vicious antipathy to Quakers, Mormons or more recent 'aliens' and is a far bigger problem they refuse to face. Reality is always complex.

All Glorious Within – Cohesion?

Catholics were always diverse. Aristocrats, middle class, however tiny – even in the earliest days Archbishop Scanlan's grandfather managed to become a doctor in the 1840s – and working class of varying conditions. For many reasons, pastoral and political, the myth of happy Scottish Catholic unity grew from 1840. That fiction of cohesion prevailed until the 1880s. Interestingly, as the Land League emerged to challenge 'property', so Celtic FC was founded to aid the Glasgow poor. It united Archbishop Eyre and Michael Davitt, that remarkable man, as patrons of a club linking temperance and publican interests. Celtic FC showed many of the tensions and strains within. It coincided with growing democratic aspirations. Sport was a great leveller: any man could be as good as the aristocrat, the businessman or the Orangeman on the field of play.

As working men were enfranchised from 1884, so they were less inclined to defer to aristocratic patrons or priests of somewhat more comfortable backgrounds – especially in politics. John Wheatley and his friends were symptomatic of larger shifts within the community. A clear indication comes when you look at the new stained-glass windows in many Scottish Catholic churches of the time. They were given by 'self-made' Catholics who had made it within the status quo. The church was now *their* home in a very real sense, to be beautified and upgraded. Theirs were as comfortable, fashionably well-decorated and beautified as the increasingly ornate Protestant temples, rapidly abandoning their ascetic heritage. Catholics were hardly temporary guests, sojourners, but a settled *Scottish* element.

Canon O'Flaherty's Fodder?

Catholics may have shared a common faith but on almost every conceivable issue they had differing outlooks. To pretend otherwise, as some historians have done, is to underwrite a less than subtle view of lay Catholics as forelock-tugging automatons or clerical slaves. That has never been the case. It is a useful device to excuse the failure of the left or liberal views to win that group. The fact that the propagandists might be wildly wrong never occurs to these people. Various works about Red Clydesiders invariably bring that notion out; the fact that faith might mean something to the believers is glossed over. A similar outlook affected evangelical zealots, colporteurs and lay missionaries working among poor Irish surrounded by statues, pictures and rosary beads in horrendous hovels. Their inability to secure mass conversions was a shock. Faith had to be dismissed as outmoded superstition – unlike their own naïve superstition, a belief in 'progress'.

The suggestion that the Irish always worked for lower wages than the native-born begs a large number of questions. That sort of argument was regularly deployed against immigrants to Britain and the United States. While that may have been true on occasion in the short term, as in the immediate wake of the famines of 1846–49 or *circa* 1879–80, immigrants quickly developed know-how. They often improved their lot. They acquired basic religious knowledge and education, better skills or funds to leave Scotland for lands of better opportunity. Some moved from Scotland, served in the British Army, worked in American industry, then moved to Australia before finally returning to Scotland, leaving their children settled elsewhere throughout the English-speaking world. The Catholic faithful were hardly permanent residents. They changed jobs, their rented housing and their parish repeatedly and so hardly formed a settled community in any real sense. Some parts of Scotland had a boom-and-bust American West feel at times in the last century. Little wonder canny Scottish-born Banffshire bishops and clergy were reluctant to invest heavily in churches, schools or other expensive aspects of infrastructure. The debts were enormous at the best of times.

The Aristocratic and Convert Dimension

They were saved by the conversion of numerous well-heeled converts like Robert Montieth of Carstairs, the Marquess of Bute, the Hunter-Blairs, the Lothians and many others. They joined with old Catholic families, the Constable Maxwells and substantial Highlanders to bankroll religious orders of men and women, churches, schools, teachers, choirmasters and the rest. The churches they scattered across the land are astonishing in number – an inconvenient fact for those believers in 'the pennies of the [Irish] poor only' version of Scottish Catholicism. These families, largely from British-minded-Tory backgrounds, and the religious orders they introduced transformed Scottish Catholicism. Socially conservative and invariably hostile to Irish nationalism, they injected stability, order and ultramontane zeal. Loyalty to the Pope abroad meant unity of differing strands at home, for the vicious internecine struggles between Irish- and Scottish-born Catholic clergy and laity alike reached depths that make contemporary anti-Catholic virulence seem tame by comparison. As a result Rome appointed an Englishman, Mgr Charles Eyre of Newcastle, to bring peace, order and financial stability to the west of Scotland. Glasgow henceforth would be the oak and upas-tree of Scottish Catholicism.

The Religious Orders

The introduction into Scotland of well-heeled and well-connected religious orders – Jesuits and Benedictines, for example – makes nonsense of the Irish identity of Scottish Catholicism. From Oxford and Cambridge backgrounds, they were English gentlemen transmitting values that would civilise the 'barbaric' colonials. The first Catholic professor in Scotland since the Reformation, John Phillimore of Glasgow, and renowned headmasters of St Aloysius, Glasgow, Revd Edward Bacon SJ and Eric Hanson SJ were English Oxbridge converts. The convert son of a prime minister and a distant relative of Princess Diana, Ignatius Spencer, the renowned Passionist, was typical. His praying crusade for the conversion of England contributed to the uplift of the Irish masses in Scotland, though education, self-improvement and discipline within the existing order made wild radicalism irrelevant. A non-voting mass of despised, poor Catholics would have been fools to espouse violent radical solutions to their predicament. At that time an Irish opt-out of the United Kingdom with their Catholic MPs would have left Scottish and English Catholics defenceless before a Protestant parliament, with much of the Irish property of the well-heeled Catholics at risk. After all, the Duke of Norfolk, premier peer of the realm and *the* leading British Catholic layman, presented a sword to the unionist Edward Carson at Blenheim at the height of the Home Rule crisis before the First World War. Political and pastoral interest demanded the status quo. Yes – reality is complex.

Upbuilding

Pastoral concern encouraged the parish missions from 1850. The various religious orders and some secular clergy revived parishes through intense periods of prayers, confessions, Mass and Holy Communion, and distribution of religious objects and literature to enable the Church's limited manpower to reach the parts of sociey traditional religion could not easily reach. Temperance campaigns were commonplace. Canon Edward J. Hannan (1836–91), the CYMS and temperance zealot, was the force behind the foundation of Hibernian FC. Temperance and social networks aided uplift, parish identity and fundraising. Improved self-perception meant individuals had passed beyond mere survival. In that way a parish community grew among those who persisted with residence, jobs and family in particular areas, and the physical building of the church was proof of that 'success'. Catholic roots were established and the phenomenon of the faith became a permanent feature of Scottish society. The Church represented change in that sense. That is why the virulent inter-war demagogues and the Church of Scotland Church and Nation Committee in 1920s could not cope: they did not like change. Like football fanatics, they had to live in a fantasy world of their endless dominance whatever the changing facts. Reality is complex.

Tradition?

Catholics have a long tradition of finding excuses for failure. After 50 years of the British welfare state I fear I sound a little like Shelby Steele[1] on the Afro-American condition after a generation of positive discrimination. 'Is there, I would ask, any place in the British dominions where you find so vast a number of Catholics with so few among them possessed of means or position or influence or any sort of distinctive pre-eminence as you find in this great city and its neighbourhood?' And lamenting the low achievements of Catholics in Scottish business, industry and intellectual life, the speaker continued, 'You will be near the mark if you admit the absence of Catholic apprentices is due not to poverty, not to the machinations of Jews and Freemasons, nor to the bigotry of Protestants but to the deplorable fact that only a small proportion of our boys and young men . . . have little ambition to rise high in their profession or knowledge how to do it.' A modern critic? No, Revd Fr Eric Hanson, the brilliant Oxford graduate, convert and distinguished Jesuit headmaster of St Aloysius, Glasgow, as reported in 1906.

The Church has always suffered from unimaginative bishops, a shortage of priests, apathetic laity, 'leakage', financial problems and restructuring. Apathy has been flayed so often in the Catholic press that one hungers for the old apocryphal Catholic Observer headline 'Priest dies at Lourdes: vows he won't go again'! And yet it moves. Or does it? In spite of all our Catholic graduates, brilliant careers and secular success, the predominant Church mindset had remained mired in ethnic loyalty: the foreign-born social and religious order which sustained their faith has long gone. To appeal to that fiction is easier than developing an intelligent approach to faith since Vatican II. Catholics as a whole have been reluctant in modern times to put their money and minds where their mouths are. Yes, like the present, the past is rather complex.

Talking of pastoral interest and concerns, it is time to set some records straight. The nonsensical traditional image of happy Catholic families with two Catholic parents leading exemplary lives needs to be addressed. In my considerable researches into Scottish parochial records, Catholics have never been insulated from the larger community. In the early nineteenth century clergy worried about inter-marriage with Protestants; it was not unusual to find 80 per cent were mixed marriages. Even after 1878 the numbers of mixed marriages and infants baptised from mixed-faith marriages ran from one in six to four out of five; that continued even after *Ne Temere* (1908). After 1920 the shift to mixed marriage, aided by better education, upward mobility, mass popular entertainment and increased lay assertiveness, is marked. From 1945 it grew further still, and by the early 1950s it was irresistible. We hear much of deathbed conversions, but marriage-bed conversions were far more common. Eve-of-marriage baptisms, however genuine, conceal much. Over the piece, whatever the 'leakage', both traditions slowly and unwittingly absorbed ideas from each other, and both were changed in the process.

Social change, the introduction of the welfare state and greater access to higher education further changed Catholicism long before Vatican II. In 1954 a parish priest friend lamented revealingly that access to university had cost the Church unimaginable numbers of vocations. Whatever dreamy Catholics may think, the Church was never the happy, stable regime of their fevered imagination. The evidence says otherwise. In recent times, several parishes I have examined had 100 per cent mixed-marriage rates. As the joke at a recent marriage I attended goes, the priestly celebrant said, 'We are so pleased that Jim and Judith are at last getting married today. In fact, the only person I know who wants to get married at all these days is Fr John, my curate here.'

The number of Catholic marriages is now much the same as a century ago but, according to 1995 Scottish Office figures, the proportion of Catholic marriages has declined 274 per cent since the highest average of 6,852 in 1961–70. To some unreconstructed Catholics, the rate of Catholic divorces will come as a surprise: from 1971 to the present, they have more than doubled in number. Catholics have maintained a steady annual rate of between 13 and 15 per cent of all divorces. Yet we forget that broken families were common during the nineteenth century, through disease, war, industry or childbirth; multiple marriage was not unusual. Equally, abortion or contraception were hardly on the agenda, with one in four Glasgow children likely to die before the age of five. Today single parents are hardly a negligible feature of Catholic life.

Clerical Continuity?

Priests were not any different then from now. There are now more priests per head of Catholic population than there were a hundred years ago. They may be more aged but they have less time consumed in confessions, devotional organisations and the rest. They have more time for angst amid the general crisis of the modern male. The number of priests in previous generations with drink, sexual or intellectual problems was considerable, whatever we may like to think. They may have been hidden, less obvious or more discreet, but desertions still happened. One Scottish priest abandoned his faith, became an Anglican priest, married and had four children – and then asked to be readmitted to his previous calling. His confessor encouraged him to do so! What happened to the poor woman and her children is unclear. *Plus ça change* . . . The Church has always been troubled by financial problems, inadequate bishops, restive priests, vocations crises and outspoken laity. So what else is new?

Active uppity women?

The Other (Hidden) Half

The history of Scottish Catholic women has still to be written, their role in history uncharted territory. The lives of women of religious orders is unknown. The influential convert artist Mother Xavier Traill, for example, was the first Scottish-born nun in modern times at St Margaret's, Edinburgh, the first post-Reformation convent founded in Scotland. It was founded by a Canadian-born priest and supported by wealthy Scottish-born men for a French religious order. Not much Irish there, then. The immense influence of numerous women's religious organisations is forgotten in male-dominated Scottish history. But then they were not rolling around drunk, shouting and fighting about the glories of Ibrox and Parkhead like men. Thank God. They made and ran the Church as nuns, teachers, mothers, faithful attenders to housekeepers and cleaners. They, like the rest of Scots today, have better things to do with their time. We do not waste our hard-earned money on increasing the wealth of rich entrepreneurs to bring overpaid hirelings carrying irrelevant banners of yesteryear like some nineteenth-century tradition. Only failures have to boost their own fading self-esteem by identifying with success; bigotry is the ultimate confession of inadequacy. As these football teams have become more cosmopolitan in their personnel, many of their followers seem to have retreated into even narrower mentalities. Sometimes I feel the fanatical Old Firm folk should have to watch endless videos showing their team winning 25–0 against the other side. It might enable active Scottish Christians to understand what their faith was; that Satan or evil was something more subtle than 'the mason in the black'. It would be cheaper on life and limb, police and casualty times, and would make for happier folk in their fantasies. Reality is more complex.

The Pilgrim Road To . . . ?

That is the failure of Christianity in Scotland. How does it enable us to deal with failure? None of us is likely to win the Lottery, so how do we cope with that fact of life? Become couch potatoes consuming evermore dreary televised football while the world goes to hell, as in East Timor, Kosovo or the immediate vicinity? Trot around in parades advertising our faith, as suggested recently by James MacMillan? [Editor's note: James MacMillan considers this to be a distortion of his view.] God help us if that is our future agenda. It is reminiscent of that Ayrshire neo-medieval fiasco the Eglinton Tournament

(1839), ruined by torrential rains. In my father's Lancashire recusant parish, their old banners were auctioned off some 25 years ago to some gullible American dealer. The proceeds went to the Third World and the banners went to the museum. Perhaps Scottish Catholics should have a similar emphasis. Better still, Scottish Catholics should learn the facts of their own history. Then we might have some substantial, intelligent debate rather than the 15-second wisdom of the sound-bite. Reality is more complex. Like a Philip Glass piece, that is the recurring theme of the symphony of life.

Notes

[1] Shelby Steele, *The Content of our Character: A New Vision of Race in America* (New York, 1990), and, for example, among Thomas Sowell's many books, his *The Economics and Politics of Race: An International Perspective* (New York, 1983), *Ethnic Americans* (New York, 1981) and *Market and Minorities* (Oxford, 1987).

9. THE NON-SECTARIAN CULTURE OF NORTH-EAST SCOTLAND

Scott C. Styles

When James MacMillan stated in August 1999 that religious sectarianism remained a major problem in Scotland he was exhibiting a Glasgow centricity all too typical of the inhabitants of west-central Scotland. Scotland was, and remains, an astonishingly diverse country, and this diversity extends beyond the obvious geographical differences to embrace religious and cultural attitudes. Whilst sectarianism certainly was and arguably remains a major feature of west-central Scotland, it is not and never has been a feature of the culture of north-east Scotland, and James MacMillan from Ayrshire would do well to remember that 'Scottish culture' is not just that of Glasgow or of west-central Scotland 'writ large'. I grew up in a working-class council scheme[1] in Aberdeen and was educated in the city and I can honestly say that in all my years at school or elsewhere I never heard or saw any anti-Catholic or anti-Protestant sentiments anywhere. At primary school we were entirely unaware of any religious divide, and even at secondary school we were barely aware of each other's denominations. The fact someone was a Catholic would excite no more interest than if they were Episcopalian or Baptist: in all cases it was a non-issue, of no more interest than the colour of someone's eyes.

The simple fact of the matter is the religious issue did not arise. I was vaguely aware of the religious preferences of the supporters of the Old Firm and dismayed to watch the unfolding tragedy of 1970s Northern Ireland. My first encounter with sectarian prejudice was when I paid a visit to a student friend in Airdrie. To my astonishment and dismay, everyone there seemed to be obsessed with the religious divide. Practically the first, and certainly the most important, question asked of me, namely the name of my school, was designed to establish my religion. I felt I was being unwillingly conscripted into a war I'd never heard of. To this day I, like everyone from the north-east, find the west-coast obsession with religion as incomprehensible as it is offensive.

Historical Background

Not so long ago in every Western nation political identity was, to a greater or lesser extent, associated with religion. Throughout mainland[2] Britain Protestantism was important to the national identity, and this was particularly so in large parts of Scotland, where, as Walker has remarked:

> . . . Protestantism – in effect Presbyterianism – was a driving force behind an imperial identity which viewed the Empire as a means of showcasing and enhancing Scottish national talents and virtues.[3]

In the west and central belt of Scotland a large part of this pride was focused on the zeal with which the 1560 Reformation had been supported and, more especially, on the Covenanting movement of the seventeenth century. The Reformation and the Wars of the Three Kingdoms,[4] the Covenant, and the 'Glorious Revolution' of 1689 became important historical reference points for many central lowland Scots, a position well expressed by one prominent Kirk minister in 1929:

> Our country was not a nation, in any strict sense of the word, before the Reformation, and the most efficient instrument in the making of lowland Scotland was the reformed religion.

Accordingly, when large numbers of Irish immigrants arrived in central Scotland in the first half of the nineteenth century, attracted there by the burgeoning Industrial Revolution and forced out by the Great Famine, this post-Covenanting mindset allowed the Protestant Scots to conflate their anti-Irish-immigrant sentiments with their anti-Catholic sentiments, a trend which was greatly strengthened by the Protestant Irish immigrants who imported Orangeism and a hatred of all things Catholic.[5] Thus was created a sectarian divide which lasted in west-central Scotland well into the twentieth century.

The historical experience of the north-east was quite different.[6] Whilst the majority of people in lowland Scotland supported the Reformation, the Covenant and the 1689 Revolution, the north-east was the heartland of religious and political conservatism and actively opposed or, at best, reluctantly acquiesced to each of those developments:

> No historian has failed to notice, for instance, the fact that the strongest opposition to the National Covenant was concentrated in and around Aberdeen.[7]

Politically the area tended to support the King, and religiously the area contained large numbers of Catholics, whilst many of the Protestants were Episcopalians or moderate Presbyterians. Accordingly the great Protestant triumphs of the sixteenth and seventeenth centuries inspired, and continue to inspire, considerably less enthusiasm in the north-east than in the rest of Scotland. The lasting legacy of this religious conservatism was the survival of large numbers of Scots Catholics in the area. By the beginning of the nineteenth century, therefore, the north-east was, along with a few parts of the Highlands and Islands, the stronghold of recusant Scots Catholicism, especially in Banffshire and Strathbogie, where approximately a third of the population was Catholic. This population was well integrated into the local community and suffered little or no discrimination. The Catholics were a minority, but a well-established and integrated minority.

This integration is unsurprising because ethnically the Catholics were indistinguishable from the Protestants and, as mentioned above, the ideological-theological basis for strife was also largely lacking. Contrawise, because of the lack of heavy industry and coal mining, the region attracted few Irish immigrants in the nineteenth century. The outcome of these developments is that in the north-east, unlike in west-central Scotland, Catholicism never became a badge of Irishness, nor Protestantism of

Scottishness. To this day, if one looks at a Catholic baptismal register or a church noticeboard in the north-east, the names are predominantly Scots, such as Grant or Forbes, and the absence of Irish-derived surnames such as Devine, O'Donnell or Maguire is striking compared to the surnames which would be found in equivalent lists in a west of Scotland Catholic church. This sizeable Catholic minority lived in amity with its neighbours and seems to have been as prosperous as the rest of the neighbouring community. Lasting testimony to this prosperity can be found in the many handsome Victorian Catholic churches which were erected in the north-east, many of which, unlike Catholic churches further south, are graced by spires.[8] To give but two examples, in the mid-nineteenth century, one of the Aberdeen priests was described thus:

> . . . there was no more prominent personality in the city in his day.
> Everyone knew him as Priest Gordon, and he was universally esteemed.[9]

When he died in 1855 Priest Gordon was mourned in a funeral attended by the Lord Provost, the city magistrates and 'many ministers of all denominations'[10], whilst the streets were 'lined with thousands of citizens'[11] – and this at a time when Catholics in Glasgow would have experienced hostility and prejudice on a daily basis. Secondly, at the end of the century a Catholic layman, John Craigen, held the chair of the local school board, a striking example of inter-denominational goodwill.[12]

These harmonious community relationships continued throughout the twentieth century. Thus, for example, it was said in 1951 about Tomintoul that 'The district is blessed in the very happy relationship existing between the Protestants and Catholics, who wholeheartedly patronise each other's social functions and live as one community, unmindful of religious difference'.[13] And of religious relations in Aberdeen in 1953 it was stated that 'Roman Catholicism has not been subjected here to the antagonisms found in some other parts of Scotland'.[14]

So little does sectarianism feature in the life and culture of the north-east that it is hard to find topics to write about – how does one write about an absence? Nevertheless, there are five areas where the absence of sectarianism in the north-east may be usefully explored: social geography, crime, professional football, education and the Orange Order marches of the 1980s. The first two topics will be considered very briefly, the last three in more depth.

No Ghettos: The Social Geography of the North-East

If you ask an Aberdonian where the Catholic parts of town are, he will look at you blankly. There quite simply are no specifically Catholic or Protestant parts of town, and there never have been. The city naturally has its prosperous and less prosperous districts, ranging from the granite mansions of Rubislaw Den to areas of social deprivation such as Sandilands, but nowhere is there segregation on grounds of religion. Nor was there indirect segregation, because the Catholic community was no poorer or richer than the rest of the community. Naturally, there has never been such a thing as a Catholic or

Protestant bar in Aberdeen.[15] In the countryside there was, and remains, rather more of a concentration of Catholics in certain districts, particularly in the villages of Strathspey, from Tomintoul in the hills down to Buckie by the sea, but this has never led to any tension and the communities have always been well integrated. For example, in Tomintoul early in the twentieth century, the building of a convent was a project which was supported by Protestant and Catholic alike.[16]

Absence of Sectarian Crime

There is no doubt that in west-central Scotland crimes of violence, such as assault and even murder, are often provoked by sectarian feelings, especially in the wake of Old Firm games. The Scottish Office does not keep statistics on the sectarian dimension of crime and one must therefore rely on anecdotal evidence rather than government statistics. I consulted someone who has a high degree of experience of the Scots criminal justice system in both west-central Scotland and the north-east, Sheriff Alexander Jessop. Sheriff Jessop is extremely well placed to comment on the respective sectarian climates of these two regions of Scotland because previously he was the procurator fiscal for Glasgow and now he sits as a sheriff in Aberdeen. He confirmed[17] the general impression that, whilst there is often a sectarian dimension to various breaches of the peace and crimes against the person in the west, such sectarianism as a criminal motive is almost unknown in the north-east.

Football

The importance of professional football in the sectarian history of Scotland is hard to overstate. Whether as cause or effect, the rivalry between Celtic and Rangers is undoubtedly in large part an expression of the tensions between Catholic and Protestant. The sectarian divisions in Scotland may originally have been based on the prejudice of Presbyterian Scots against immigrant Catholic Irish, but it is the existence of rival football teams which has done much to preserve these antagonisms. This bifurcation of Scottish football teams on religious lines began in the late nineteenth century and eventually afflicted three out of the four major cities of Scotland. Edinburgh has Heart of Midlothian and Hibernian, the latter's name standing as testimony to the club's Irish Catholic origins, and the city of Dundee has Dundee and Dundee United, the latter known as Dundee Hibernian until 1923. It must be noted, however, that the sectarian dimension to football in Edinburgh and, especially, Dundee has always been much milder than that existing within the Old Firm. Aberdeen, in contrast to the other three cities, has only ever had one professional football team. A city without a sectarian divide never saw any need to have separate Catholic and Protestant football teams and has always drawn its support on the basis of geography, not religion. Equally, the composition of the team was always non-sectarian, and from the club's creation in 1903 Irish Catholics played for the Dons. In 1906 they signed Irish international Charlie O'Hagan, and in the inter-war period the Irish link was especially strong.[18]

There was a strong connection between Aberdeen and the Irish Free State. In a good relationship, the Dons freely released their players for international duty and the gratitude of the football authorities in Eire can be witnessed to this day in the shape of a presentational harp.[19]

Just as Aberdeen has always had Catholic players, so in the north-east Catholics and Protestants alike support the Dons. With regard to the Old Firm, there has traditionally been a grudging respect for Celtic from Aberdeen fans, which, at least in the past, was reciprocated. The 1939 book *The Story of Celtic* states, 'Celtic and Aberdeen have always been very good friends.'[20] By contrast, despite the predominantly Protestant population of the north-east, Rangers has long been the team Dons fans love to hate. Over the last 20 years the rivalry has increased, and this enmity is returned in full measure by the Rangers fans. One of the more surreal aspects of contemporary Scottish culture is the songs sung by the two teams' fans when they play against each other. Unable to mock the Aberdeen fans with their usual repertoire of anti-Catholic songs, the Rangers fans instead taunt the 'Scottish' Dons fans with an assertion of English/Britishness by singing 'Rule Britannia' or the English rugby song 'Swing Low Sweet Chariot' – to which the Dons fans reply, if they sing at all, with 'Flower of Scotland'!

Sectarian sentiment has never played any part in the culture of Aberdeen supporters and fans sing for neither 'King Billy' nor the Pope. The advantage of this is obvious. Support for Aberdeen FC acts as a uniting element in the life of the city, whereas in Glasgow football supporting acts as a dividing element in the life of the city, perpetuating the sectarian divide. Indeed, given the increasing secularism of both communities, it is arguably the Celtic–Rangers rivalry that has done most to prolong the sectarian divide to the end of the twentieth century. Perhaps the high point of peacetime civic unity in Aberdeen occurred when the Dons won the European Cup-Winners' Cup in 1983, an occasion which had the normally rather inhibited Aberdeen supporters literally dancing on the streets.[21] By contrast, in Glasgow the victory of one of the Old Firm teams will inevitably entail sullen or even violent resentment from the other side's supporters, so much so that it is impossible for either team to parade through the city in the wake of winning a trophy.

Education

One very significant difference between present-day Aberdeen and the north-east and the rest of Scotland is that there is no separate Catholic secondary-school system. Given that the existence of separate secondary schooling in the rest of Scotland is a very hotly contested issue, it is worth considering how this situation came about. Up until the mid-1970s there was one Catholic secondary school in Aberdeen, St Peter's. This school was faced with falling numbers even in that era of large school rolls because it did not enjoy a particularly high academic reputation and Catholic parents had increasingly chosen to send their children to the appropriate local comprehensive or, if they were wealthy enough, one of the local private schools. The decision was therefore taken by the City Council[22] to close St Peter's. In its place, three secondary schools were designated as making special provision for Catholic pupils. The response from the Catholic community was muted, although there was a protest by a few of the St Peter's school parents. Likewise, the local Catholic church seems to have been remarkably relaxed about this development and made no real attempt to prevent the changes, seemingly content as long as the separate primary schools were maintained.

Given the fierce passions which separate Catholic schooling arouses in west-central Scotland, and the vigour with which Cardinal Winning and the west-central Scottish Catholic hierarchy defend separate schooling, the low-key way in which integrated schooling was attained in Aberdeen seems scarcely believable. The lesson of the Aberdeen experience is not, however, the familiar one that separate schooling promoted sectarianism; rather, it is the reverse. In Aberdeen, Catholics felt completely at home and experienced no discrimination in their everyday life. They knew their children would face no discrimination or hostility from the pupils or staff of the non-denominational schools, and in these circumstances they naturally had no fear of integrated schools. Even before the closure of St Peter's, many had already voted with their feet and sent their children to non-denominational schools. The decision to end seperate Catholic secondary education was the natural conclusion of this process.

Aberdeen Grammar School[23] was one of the schools designated to make special provision for Catholic education in the wake of the closure of St Peter's, and I was a pupil at the Grammar at the time when the former pupils from the Catholic school arrived. It caused no difficulties whatsoever, and certainly no one saw the issue in terms of Catholic versus Protestant, not least because there were already Catholics at the school. In a sense, even to view the issue in these terms is to place too much emphasis on it. The simple fact of the matter is that at my school, like in the rest of the north-east, sectarianism did not exist and therefore there was no 'religious problem' to be solved. Since that time, Aberdeen has enjoyed a fully integrated educational system and there has never been any request from the local Catholic Church for the restoration of separate secondary schooling.

The Orange Marches of the 1980s

In modern times there has only been one organisation which can be said to have tried to play the 'sectarian card' in the north-east and that is the Orange Order. Although the Order denies that it is a sectarian organisation, there is no denying that it is generally perceived, both by members and by outsiders, as a Protestant triumphalist organisation. Whilst in west-central Scotland, and even as far north as Dundee, Orange Lodges are a long-established feature of the scene, in the north-east they are a recent development. The Orange Order is an alien plant in the north-east with neither historical roots nor popular support in the region. The first, and only, Orange Lodge, 'Bon Accord' LOL 701, was established in 1978. The members were mostly individuals from west-central Scotland with existing Orange connections, along with one or two individuals whose parents had migrated to Aberdeen from Orange areas of west-central Scotland. The Lodge has never thrived in Aberdeen and its attempts to establish a 'tradition' of Orange parades down Aberdeen's Union Street ended in failure. The first parade in 1979 was a low-key affair attended by only a hundred or so individuals and it passed by almost unnoticed in the local media. Paradoxically, this local disinterest is in itself one of the strongest pieces of evidence of the non-sectarian climate of the north-east: no one, Catholic or Protestant, could be bothered to object. The only significant press coverage was one article in the *Evening Express* supporting the right to peaceful protest, but even it began by stating, 'Today, the city of Aberdeen plays host to its first Orange march. But it's a fairly safe bet that the minuscule local contingent, and the allies shipped in from outside, will be the only ones celebrating.'[24]

Two years later the Aberdeen District Council banned another attempt by the Order to hold a parade. In 1985 the Orange Order obtained permission from Grampian Regional Council, and the most the District Council could do was to ban the holding of a rally at the end of the parade. The parade nevertheless provoked widespread disquiet in the city, having attracted around 900 members 'from all over Scotland', as the *Evening Express* put it – which was a polite way of saying they were not from Aberdeen. Again the local media coverage was surprisingly muted, but one letter of protest noted, 'It was obvious from the banners that the vast majority of those marching were from the central lowlands and west of Scotland – not surprising, really, as religious intolerance is not a disease common to the Grampian region.'[25]

Matters came to a head in 1987. Once again the Regional Council, despite opposition from the District Council, granted permission for a march to be held on 30 March. This time there was widespread opposition to the parade from all sectors of society in the weeks leading up to the event. In the District Council the march was opposed by all political parties, including the Conservatives. Councillor Neil Cooney spoke for many in the city when he said, commenting on the 1985 march, 'I have never in my life been so ashamed to be Aberdonian. I followed the course of the march and there were several ugly incidents. It is totally shameful to see this kind of sectarian behaviour in the city.'[26]

Tapping into the local mood, the *Evening Express* gave the 1987 march much more coverage than it had events in previous years, adopted a strongly anti-Orange editorial line and ran several stories hostile to the parade. The editorial for 14 May 1987 was headed 'Unwelcome Marchers' and included the remark: 'Nothing could be more alien to Aberdeen than an Orange walk; for no matter how the organisers may seek to justify them, the events are nothing more than a sectarian display of sectarianism.' After going on to comment that the Townswoman's Guild could muster more members in Aberdeen than the Orange Order, it concluded, 'There is no tradition of Orange walks in Aberdeen, a city where religious tradition has been a feature for centuries. Councillors, regional and district, have a responsibility to ensure that outside influences are not allowed to alter this.'

Likewise, the *Evening Express* editorial for 29 May 1987, the eve of the march, was headed 'Walk Not Welcome'. Unsurprisingly, all this hostility angered the Orange Order, and their spokesman, David Bruce, Grand Secretary of the Grand Orange Lodge of Scotland, was provoked to remark, 'Aberdeen is beginning to get itself a bit of a reputation for being a bit odd and peculiar about this.'[27]

Much of the opposition to the Orange march was organised by the Aberdeen Trades Council. The Trades Council successfully solicited opposition from the local unions and also organised a highly successful petition against the march and a counter-demonstration, urging all citizens to turn their backs to the marchers when they paraded down Union Street. I was on Union Street that day and can testify that the vast majority of pedestrians present did indeed turn their backs on the marchers, and not a few shouted hostile remarks at the Orangemen, the vast majority of whom hailed from west-central Scotland. The following year Grampian Region bowed to public pressure and refused the Orange Order permission to march, and up to the time of writing, no further parades have been authorised in Aberdeen.

The Orange marches of the 1980s, far from promoting the Protestant and unionist cause in the north-east, as the organisers no doubt intended, provoked a near-universal backlash from the citizens who saw it as an unwelcome attempt to import an alien religious sectarianism from west-central Scotland into the region. Local people made it clear that they wanted nothing to do with a movement which they perceived as undesirable in itself and which is a major part of the problems in both Northern Ireland and west-central Scotland. People were proud of the non-sectarian nature of north-east culture and mobilised to ensure the region remained free of the sectarian prejudice. The anti-sectarian tradition of the north-east had been successfully defended and maintained. Sectarianism may be the shame of certain parts of Scotland but it is not the shame of *all* Scotland, and it has never been the shame of the north-east.

Notes

[1] Garthdee, in the south-west of the city.

[2] i.e. excluding largely Catholic Ireland.

[3] G. Walker, 'Varieties of Scottish Protestant Identity', in T.M. Devine and R.J. Finlay (eds.), *Scotland in the Twentieth Century* (Edinburgh, 1996), p.250.

[4] i.e. the Wars of the Covenanting period.

[5] For a discussion of the role of the Irish Protestants in exporting Orangeism and sectarian sentiments, see G. Walker, 'The Protestant Irish in Scotland', in T.M. Devine (ed.), *Irish Immigrants and Scottish Society in the Nineteenth and Twentieth Centuries* (Edinburgh, 1991). The size of the Protestant Irish immigration is larger than is generally realised. Walker, at pp.49–50, quotes an 1831 estimate which placed the percentage of Catholic and Protestant Irish in Glasgow at roughly 55 and 45 respectively.

[6] For a concise account see G. Donaldson, 'Scotland's Conservative North in the Sixteenth and Seventeeth Centuries', in Donaldson's *Scottish Church History* (Edinburgh, 1985), pp.191–203. By 'north' in this context Donaldson primarily means the north-east; see p.199.

[7] Ibid.

[8] St Mary's Cathedral, Aberdeen, has the tallest church spire in the city at over 200 feet. St Peter's, Buckie, boasts twin spires at the west end of the church.

[9] A. Gammie, *The Churches of Aberdeen* (Aberdeen, 1906), p.320.

[10] Ibid.

[11] Ibid.

[12] Ibid., p.317.

[13] V. Gaffney, 'The Parish of Kirkmichael', *County of Banff* volume (1951) of *The Third Statistical Account of Scotland*, p.404.

[14] H. MacKenzie, *City of Aberdeen* volume (1951) of *The Third Statistical Account of Scotland*, p.522.

[15] In recent years a couple of ersatz Irish themed pubs have been established by the brewery chains as part of the Europe-wide fashion for Irish pubs. These are about as authentic as the Frankenstein and Dracula themed bars which have been established in Aberdeen over the last few years.

[16] Gaffney, 'The Parish of Kirkmichael'.

[17] In a private interview.

[18] Several Irishmen played for the team, including the two Free State internationalists Paddy More and Joseph O'Reilly.

[19] J. Webster, *The Dons* (London, 1990), p.73.

[20] W. Maley, *The Celtic Story* (Westcliffe-on-sea 1939, reprinted 1996), p.44.

[21] And equally when the team is in the doldrums, as it is at the time of writing in November 1999, the gloom 'in the toun' among football fans is near universal.

[22] The initial decision to close the school was taken by the city's Education Committee on 14 May 1973, confirmed by the Schools Sub-Committee on 18 September and ratified by the full Council on 15 October 1973. It was done in 1973, i.e. before the 'regionalisation' caused by the Civic Government Scotland Act 1974. The secondary school was gradually run down over the next three years.

[23] Which was in the process of becoming a comprehensive at the time. In the mid-1970s the official name of the school was 'Rubislaw Academy (Aberdeen Grammar School)', but one of the first results of education becoming a regional function was the decision by Grampian to allow reversion to the older name.

[24] W. Raynor, 'The politics of protest', *Evening Express*, 19 May 1979.

[25] B. Cuthbert, letter published in the *Evening Express*, 10 May 1985, p.6.

[26] Quoted in the *Evening Express*, 13 May 1987, p.1.

[27] Quoted in the *Evening Express*, 28 May 1987, p.1.

10. SECTARIAN TENSIONS IN SCOTLAND: SOCIAL AND CULTURAL DYNAMICS AND THE POLITICS OF PERCEPTION

Graham Walker

Part One

In a recent discussion of nationalism and ethnic identity in the British Isles, the distinguished historian Hugh Kearney remarked of Scotland that 'the issues raised by Rangers and Celtic are not moribund'.[1] The impact made by James MacMillan's Edinburgh Festival speech of August 1999 has certainly borne this out. Perhaps, too, the Monklands by-election of 1994 should have prevented the rather facile optimism about community relations which accompanied the upbeat mood around the arrival of the Scottish parliament.

Academic work in this subject area has increased since the mid-1980s and there now exists a substantial corpus of studies across disciplines.[2] However, MacMillan has pushed the issue into the public domain with results that academics can only envy, even if many of them might have reservations over how this was accomplished. For, aside from the fact of MacMillan's celebrity, he made people sit up and take notice by couching his argument in arresting terms. The extreme nature of the claims made and the language employed have been the cause of both the vigour of the subsequent debate and, it might be said, the frustrating circularity of it. MacMillan's critics have in the main focused on his use of terms such as 'endemic', while his supporters have chosen to stress the general point about anti-Catholicism in Scotland. One side has formed the impression of a victim mentality founded upon relatively little in the contemporary as opposed to the historical context, while the other has tended to view any criticism of MacMillan as confirmation of his case. The long-standing difficulties of debating this issue – of penetrating the fog of anecdote, grievance, claim and counterclaim in the absence of much hard evidence – have been compounded by a sterile stand-off between demands for acknowledgement of guilt, and irritation about being invited to feel guilty.

This chapter will be critical of MacMillan's thesis, but in a way which hopefully will indicate the real complexities of the issue when so much flows from respective perceptions. Moreover, it will also attempt to situate the controversy in a context broader than that adopted by MacMillan or by most of those who have so far responded to him. In relation to context, a brief historical background sketch may be helpful.

Part Two

Catholics from an Irish background settled in Scotland in large numbers at different points in the nineteenth century. The Irish Famine in the 1846–49 period in particular brought waves of hungry and impoverished immigrants.

In contrast to many Protestant Irish immigrants to Scotland, Irish Catholics brought few skills and were thus at a disadvantage with regard to the better-paid and more valued manual occupations. That they also suffered from anti-Catholic and anti-Irish prejudice seems clear, although much anti-Irish Catholic feeling was the result of the Irish Protestant immigration referred to, and antagonism was mutual. Irish political quarrels were transplanted to Scotland along with respective secret societies like the Orange Order and the Ancient Order of Hibernians. Disturbances often followed 12 July Orange parades or St Patrick's Day and Daniel O'Connell celebrations. Immigrants who sought work in the coalfields of Lanarkshire or Ayrshire were sometimes divided into different locations by the owners to avoid conflict.[3] The larger Catholic immigrant community found it more difficult to achieve social mobility, but both Catholic and Protestant Irish were forced to seek poor relief in areas such as the East End of Glasgow[4], a hub of sectarian tensions to the present day. The Church became the focal point for the Catholic immigrant community in a social, educational, charitable and recreational sense; a Marist brother founded Celtic Football Club in 1888. However, Catholicism was viewed with suspicion by Protestant Scotland and the perhaps inevitable development of Catholic community introspection under the Church's care helped prevent the degree of acceptance accorded to the Protestant immigrants by the twentieth century, although even in this case the price may have been the virtual disappearance of their separate identity as a group.

Irish Home Rule controversies were played out in Scotland in the late nineteenth and early twentieth centuries and undoubtedly helped to popularise unionism politically, especially among Protestant workers. On the other hand, the Liberals remained the strongest political force and the amount of Scottish sympathy for Ulster's anti-Home Rule stand was decidedly limited.[5] The greatest impact of religious sectarianism on Scottish politics was to come after the First World War, in part a reaction to the entry of significant numbers of Catholics (either Irish or of Irish descent) into job sectors such as shipbuilding and engineering under conditions of 'dilution' and wartime changes. This influx gave rise to panic about 'Bolshevik Sinn Feiners' and, along with Irish Republican Army (IRA) activity in Scotland in 1920-22, did much to shape the post-war sectarian colouring of west of Scotland politics. The Orange Order expanded markedly and became less of a Protestant Irish immigrant society. Anti-Irish Catholic sentiment was expressed stridently in the Scottish Presbyterian Churches.[6] Against a backdrop of economic stringency, the rising emigration rate of Scots and trauma over the impact of the war, Irish Catholics were viewed as 'penetrating' the nerve centres of Scottish industrial life and undermining native Scottish values and achievements. This was the Scottish variant of the racial and ethnic 'scapegoating' which was a feature of the era internationally.[7] Jobs and houses were demanded for Scottish Protestants first, as reward for 'loyalty', and criticism was made of the 1918 Education Act's provision of full state support for Catholic schools. More than any other period, the inter-war years witnessed the 'politicising' of Orange versus Green issues in Scotland along similar lines to those in contemporary Northern Ireland.

Nevertheless, there were important differences. There was devolved government in Northern Ireland and the unionists there had the opportunity to use the resources and patronage at their disposal to reward supporters and keep them loyal. They also had the perennial vote-winning appeal of the cross-border nationalist danger and its allies within the Northern Ireland state. In Scotland sectarianism could only be pushed for political advantage so far; ultimately, Scotland was part of the wider British political context in which complaints about Catholic schools or Catholic numbers were irrelevant. The Scottish Unionists in particular were confined by the priorities of the Conservative Party in Britain as a whole. When Secretary of State for Scotland in the Unionist/Conservative government between 1924 and 1929, the Orangeman Sir John Gilmour did nothing in response to the calls from many of his own supporters to curb Irish Catholic immigration and to disqualify such immigrants from receiving state benefits. Moreover, Scotland's position within the Union, unlike that of Northern Ireland, was not seen to be under threat.[8]

The post-Second World War era saw a thaw in relations between the Churches, an increase in inter-marriage and a greater measure of social progress for Catholics. Discrimination in employment persisted but opportunities arose in local government, and the Labour Party was often a vehicle of social and economic mobility for its Catholic supporters. The Unionists, on the other hand, seemed to lose touch with many of their working-class Protestant voters by the 1960s, something symbolised by the official adoption of the name 'Conservative' in 1965. With the disappearance of the Empire and a rise in secular attitudes and practices, many of the old certainties underpinning Protestant Scotland began to fade. Football – the Rangers versus Celtic rivalry – provided a ritual setting for sectarian passions to be discharged and, arguably, contained. The rise of Scottish nationalism in the 1960s and 1970s was identified as a Protestant phenomenon by Catholics who largely steered clear, fearful of a Stormont-style parliament in Edinburgh. In the 1979 devolution referendum this was one factor in the substantial 'No' vote. Twenty years on, however, the Scottish National Party (SNP) have apparently been relatively successful in appealing to a new generation of Catholics, and the equation of Scottish national identity with Presbyterianism is greatly attenuated, notwithstanding the new Scottish parliament's temporary home in the Church of Scotland buildings in Edinburgh.

Part Three

In his speech James MacMillan went well beyond observations about anti-Catholic feeling in Scottish society; indeed, he painted a picture of a persecuted and down-trodden minority afraid to raise its head for fear of attack. It is my contention that this portrait of the Catholic experience in Scotland sits very oddly with a number of salient issues and with the hard evidence which is available to us.

Take first the issue of education. While it cannot be denied that there has been opposition to state-funded Catholic schooling since the 1918 Act, the more significant fact is surely that no amendment has been made to the legislation which in effect privileges Catholics in a number of respects. Only Catholics enjoy a legal right to religious instruction, as opposed to education, in schools; the Catholic Church enjoys power over teaching appointments and promotions; and Catholic schools have avoided closure in cases where there have been clear grounds for it.[9] The anti-Catholic agitation of the inter-war years referred to above should be put in the context of the Protestant Churches' reaction to the advantages enjoyed by the Catholic Church in contrast to their own loss of educational influence. Education has been an issue of immense symbolic import in Scotland and has been central to the nation's self-image. What seems to many Catholics to be bigoted prejudice against the fact of their schools' existence is to many non-Catholic Scots a question connected to wider notions of equality and national identity. Non-Catholic suspicions about Catholic schools being geared solely to Catholic Church and community purposes may be motivated by Protestant bigotry; they may also be motivated by an ideal of a broader national good. Moreover, although the arguments about the benefits of integrating schools may be facile in many respects, it is unfair of MacMillan and his supporters to suggest that they are underpinned by anti-Catholic prejudice. This is a travesty of the views of many people who have entered this debate, and smacks of an attempt to close it down by raising the bogey of 'bigotry'.

Questions about Catholic schools in respect of matters such as appointments ('only Catholics need apply' job advertisements), promotions, closures and the presence of non-Catholic pupils need to be addressed. This is particularly so in the context of the new ethnically diverse Scotland and the rights of other groups such as Scottish Asians and Chinese. Questions of educational policy and provision with reference to resource and financial implications will have to be considered by the Scottish parliament, and it will be necessary for such debate and decision-making to transcend the fetters around the issue put in place by the sensitivities of Protestant–Catholic relations. The defensiveness of the strand of Catholic opinion spoken for by MacMillan makes this very difficult. A culture of sectarian sensitivities in which Catholic perceptions of engrained Protestant hostility are particularly notable inhibits the development of the multi-ethnic discourse now required.

Catholic defensiveness might also be said to highlight the need to address non-Catholic perceptions of Catholics behaving in an exclusivist and intransigent fashion and exerting undue political pressure on parties and candidates over educational questions and moral ones such as abortion.[10] Some of Cardinal Winning's interventions of late have raised the spectre of moral authoritarianism attaining new political forms in a devolved Scotland[11], while Winning's prediction that Catholicism would be Scotland's sole faith at some point in the next century[12] arguably smacked of tribal triumphalism and was hardly sensitive to the current realities of a multi-faith Scotland. If James MacMillan is so concerned about pluralism, and if he is not always at one with the traditionalist Cardinal as he claims, then it is fair to ask why there was no critical reference in his Edinburgh speech to Winning's comments. What MacMillan seems to regard as 'anti-Catholic bigotry' would be defined by many non-Catholics as reasonable objections to the power wielded by a figure like Winning, to aspects of the Catholic faith and to proposals such as the recent one to extend the 1918 Act to include nursery schools. Some, indeed, might be inclined to regard MacMillan's remarks about John Knox and the impact of the Reformation in Scotland as clearer evidence of 'bigotry'.

To sum up, the 1918 Education Act's survival and the benefits and advantages it has through time secured for Catholics in Scotland ought to have weighed more heavily on MacMillan's thoughts than the criticisms directed at

Catholic schools, by no means all of which have been motivated by bigotry.

Another matter in relation to which the portrait painted by MacMillan is flawed is that of inter-marriage. The level of 'mixed marriages' between Protestants and Catholics has increased dramatically over the last 50 years or so[13], to the point where it is more difficult to identify Catholics as a distinct minority in the manner of the newer ethnic communities. In the light of the prevalence of inter-marriage, complex family realities have surely acted as a counterweight to the social and cultural separatism suggested by MacMillan's claims about Catholic community sufferings. If it is assumed that many Protestants are concerned to see the families into which they have married prosper and live contentedly, then it is difficult to imagine that the number of them anxious to 'keep Catholics in their place' is as large as MacMillan's rhetoric implies. Again, his use of terms like 'endemic' and 'jam-packed' is revealed as highly inappropriate and highly injurious to his case.

A second and perhaps more important point in relation to inter-marriage concerns the influence exerted by the Catholic Church over time to have the children of such unions brought up as Catholics, in accordance with the strictures of the *Ne Temere* decree of 1908. I would submit that MacMillan and his supporters are unaware of how much suffering and social damage the insistence on this has caused. In the Republic of Ireland it has been one factor in the drastic reduction of Protestant numbers, and in recent years Protestant feelings on the subject have elicited a formal apology from a Roman Catholic bishop. In Scotland there is little sign of appreciation in the Catholic community that many Protestants have resented the inflexibility of the Catholic Church on the issue, and that a perception has been engendered among Protestants of constantly 'losing out' in relation to it. They perceive there to have been precious little 'give and take' or sensitivity towards their faith, beliefs or wishes.

Further evidence at odds with MacMillan's depiction of a disadvantaged Catholic community concerns the most recent studies of Protestants and Catholics in relation to employment opportunities, social mobility and access to wealth, and numbers in higher education.[14] These show Catholics to be more than holding their own. As former *Glasgow Herald* editor Arnold Kemp has observed, the presence of those of the Catholic faith and Irish descent is substantial in most professions, and in politics, the law and the arts in particular their contribution has been enormous.[15] Moreover, MacMillan is surely obliged to explain the recent evidence of a positive Catholic view of Scottish identity and greater political autonomy for Scotland.[16] MacMillan's claims about Catholics feeling unaccepted in Scotland do not tally with the shift from scepticism and fear of devolution *circa* 1979 to the enthusiastic embrace of it 20 years on, sketched by recent voters' surveys. It is more plausible to conclude that most Catholics, against a background of such a better social and economic story, have come to the position where scare stories no longer sway them.

Part Four

Passages in MacMillan's address indicate that he entertains a stereotype about Protestant Scotland derived from Irish Catholic folklore regarding Orangeism:

that of a bigoted, triumphalist foe desperate to keep Catholics down. Remarks about 'anti-Catholic triumphalism' and 'the hegemonic aspirations of those in our society who would happily see the disappearance of Scottish Catholicism' were not widely reported in Scotland but, perhaps significantly, were highlighted in the newspaper of the Catholic and nationalist community of Northern Ireland, the *Irish News*.[17]

Two points might be made about this: first, as in Northern Ireland today, Catholics mistake for triumphalism what is a deeply defensive mentality shaped by a variety of fears and misconceptions; and second, that the Orange Order in Scotland is overwhelmingly proletarian, carries no significant political weight and is scorned by the Scottish Establishment. Aggressive and offensive as Orange parades may appear to Catholics, the marchers are motivated by concern over what they see to be threatened or by resentment over what they perceive to have lost rather than any notion of triumphalism. MacMillan's speech is as much a failure to understand Protestant Scotland – and in particular working-class Protestants of the west-central belt – as a defence of what he perceives to be his own beleaguered people.

Many working-class Protestants feel politically marginalised when they watch the Labour Party and the SNP compete for the Catholic vote of west-central Scotland.[18] They perceive the Labour Party in this region to have looked after with particular care the Catholic community for many years, and their resentment found voluble expression during the Monklands by-election in 1994, when accusations of pro-Catholic bias on the part of Monklands District Council over a period of years resulted in an inquiry. No firm evidence of religious discrimination materialised, but the perception of biased practices by Catholic-dominated Labour councils persists among disaffected Protestants. In the controversy over MacMillan's speech, the issue was raised of a long unbroken line of Catholic Lord Provosts in the city of Glasgow stretching back over 20 years. The 'West of Scotland Labour Question' has illustrated the links between unchecked local power, patronage and sectarian tension (all very reminiscent of Northern Ireland), and it may require the modernisation of the Labour Party in Scotland and proportional representation at local elections – as advocated by Hassan – to remove the conditions for further Monklands-style trouble.[19]

If MacMillan is so convinced of the operation of an Orange Order agenda more widely in Scottish society then he is obliged to explain the relentlessly hostile press the Order receives. It is true that media opinion in Scotland has stopped short of calling for parades to be banned, but their condemnation of 'Orange Order bigotry' has nonetheless been emphatic, particularly in the newspaper MacMillan bewilderingly finds so critical of Catholics, their Church and their schools.[20] A columnist in this newspaper described Orangemen as 'inbred lumpen scum'[21], and reporters in the same organ referred to Drumcree Orangemen in 1997 as 'white trash'.[22] Such insults would be unlikely to have been permitted in respect of any other set of people. That other expression of upfront Protestant identity, 'wee free' fundamentalism, fares no better in the secular atmosphere of contemporary Scotland, and the anti-Catholic stance of fundamentalists – as revealed, for instance, in the case of Lord MacKay in 1990 – is widely disowned. Anti-Catholic sentiment may lurk in the mainstream of non-Catholic Scotland beyond militant Protestantism, but on the evidence of public discourse it does not amount to the threat imagined by MacMillan and certainly finds no serious political platform – unlike, it may be said, the Catholic Church's lobby. Already, the Catholic Church in Scotland has organised a lobbying campaign over issues like education in the new Scottish parliament.[23]

Overall, the terms of MacMillan's address demonstrate a clear tendency to reduce the diversity and heterogeneity of Protestant Scotland to stereotypes about Orange 'triumphalism' or fundamentalist intolerance, neither of which is given the indulgence in the Scottish media which he appears to believe. Neither is he cognisant of the perceptions of Protestants who care about their identity as Protestants – as he cares about his as a Catholic – concerning the relative coherence and purposefulness of the Catholic community, and the decline symbolically and materially of Presbyterianism in Scotland. Perhaps, as he recoils from the bitterness of the populist Protestantism still on display in Scotland, he might ponder on the extent to which this reflects a sense of loss – of confidence, of pride, of the salience of certain ideas of Scottishness. A genuinely pluralist Scotland in which religious identities can be affirmed proudly but not triumphantly will require sensitivity towards the impact of social, cultural and political changes on different groups. Maybe as a professed socialist MacMillan ought also to be more aware of how adherence to the kind of sectarian subculture to be found in west-central Scotland can be a means of maintaining the kind of communal or collectivist values of a working-class outlook. 'Tribal' and class identities have long been interwoven in Scotland and often mutually re-informing. For better or worse, the 'Orange or Green' subculture has supplied for many a vital sense of belonging which in turn is a condition for this subculture's reproduction. MacMillan would have been better advised to address his remarks to the complexities of these social and cultural dynamics.

Part Five

Then there is football. MacMillan's speech was delivered in August 1999, three months after the vice-chairman of Rangers, Donald Findlay, was caught singing sectarian songs at a club party. Without the Findlay affair, it is doubtful if MacMillan's claims would have been so widely discussed. It lent a ring of plausibility to them, given Findlay's professional eminence and his prominence in Scottish life. It was a short – if specious – step from Findlay's antics to conclusions about Rangers' status as a 'totem' in Scottish society.

This latter assertion has never been as simple a matter as MacMillan implies. It may be true that complacent assumptions of Protestant cultural dominance in Scotland in the past prevented the kind of criticism of Rangers' Protestant exclusivism which should have been forthcoming. However, such criticism has been in regular supply since the 1960s and has, indeed, come from parts of the Church of Scotland itself as well as the media.[24] Rangers for many years found their most enthusiastic support among the rougher working-class elements whose behaviour on the terracings, and on Orange marches, provoked middle-class Presbyterian abhorrence. To suggest, as MacMillan does, that the club enjoys a kind of national blessing on account of its Protestant identity is to fly in the face of the volume of hostility currently directed towards it from all parts of Scotland; moreover, it is to overlook the momentous changes in player selection policy which have turned the team into a multi-national, multi-denominational outfit over the last decade.[25]

What is striking about Findlay's sing-song is the extent to which it is out of sync with the new Rangers, as guided by David Murray, and the sense of it being an exercise in nostalgia. Findlay, a maverick figure always on the lookout for ways to polish his populist credentials, identified himself in an intoxicated moment with supporters who feel that their loyalty and dedication is no longer valued in the hyper-commercial age which football now inhabits.[26] Again, MacMillan arguably sees a threat of persecution in what is a rather well-worn communal ritual. It needs hardly be added that media condemnation of Findlay was absolute; in the furore he was obliged to resign and he has since been fined and censured by his profession and snubbed by St Andrews University, of which he was once rector. All of this may be just deserts, but what is surely beyond dispute is that it does not conform to MacMillan's image of a society rife with bigotry and an Establishment which connives at it.

Moreover, the sectarian sentiments still spouted by Rangers fans have been highlighted and lambasted regularly by Scotland's most prominent sports journalists such as Ian Archer, James Traynor and Graham Speirs.[27] Has MacMillan simply not noticed any of this? Did he also not notice that his team – Celtic – were the subject of a congratulatory parliamentary motion at Westminster in 1998 after they had won the championship, a motion put forward by a clutch of Scottish Labour MPs?[28] This was the first such motion to be put for ten years – since, in fact, Celtic's last championship success. In between, no motions were tabled concerning Rangers' remarkable run of domestic success, and, indeed, no Scottish politician has rhapsodised about the club in the manner of, for example, George Galloway about Celtic.[29] For a club which is supposed to be a microcosm of what MacMillan identifies as 'endemic' in Scottish society, this comparative lack of praise in public life is somewhat incongruous. It might be added that Scottish celebrities who are Celtic fans are more apt to proclaim their loyalties, including MacMillan himself, who rarely wastes a chance to do so in media interviews![30]

The contention that Celtic are disparaged in the mainstream of Scottish life on account of their Irish Catholic identity – a position also taken by certain academics[31] – ignores the aforementioned critical press given to the sectarian subculture around Rangers, ignores the respectful, on occasion lyrical appreciation accorded by the same journalists to Celtic's Irish roots and influences[32], and ignores the generally more admiring and positive attitudes expressed in Scottish public discourse on matters Irish and on the achievements of the Republic of Ireland. The global fashionableness of an Irish identity which is *de facto* an Irish Catholic identity has affected Scotland as well as countless other countries. The sociable and artistic nature of Irish culture has been appreciated as much in Scotland as elsewhere, in spite of the propensity of many Celtic supporters to sing about Irish republican militarism and to convey in some of their songs the same hatred, intolerance and contempt which characterises certain songs sung by Rangers' followers.[33] MacMillan's failure to acknowledge that Protestants in Scotland do not have a monopoly on sectarianism and bigotry was a serious omission in his address.

Part Six

As possibilities emerge for a reconfiguration of relationships on these islands – particularly perhaps between Scotland and both parts of Ireland – it is appropriate that matters of religion and ethnic and national identity be debated openly. Sectarian attitudes are traceable to many sources, and we need to distinguish those which are formed out of perceptions of a threat to certain forms of identity from those which are set against any fair and equal treatment of people on account of their religion. We have to be aware that the habitual and ritualistic nature of much sectarian behaviour does not always carry with it the maliciousness which James MacMillan sees all around him. It may be the case that MacMillan's arguments about Catholic alienation require urgent attention. However, I would submit in conclusion that they are only part of a much louder percussion in Scottish society, and that the extent to which that society has changed over the last 20 to 30 years has complicated perceptions crucially about cultural hegemony and victimhood. This classical composer's ear seems to hear only the threnody of 'The Fields of Athenry' as lustily sung at his favourite recreational amphitheatre.

Notes

[1] Hugh Kearney, 'Contested Ideas of Nationhood 1800–1995', *Irish Review*, no.20, 1997, pp.1–22.

[2] Recent significant works include: S. Bruce, *No Pope of Rome: Anti-Catholicism in Modern Scotland* (Edinburgh, 1985); T. Gallagher, *Glasgow, The Uneasy Peace: Religious Tension in Modern Scotland* (Manchester, 1987); G. Walker and T. Gallagher (eds.), *Sermons and Battle Hymns: Protestant Popular Culture in Modern Scotland* (Edinburgh, 1990); T.M. Devine (ed.), *Irish Immigrants and Scottish Society* (Edinburgh, 1991); G. Jarvie and G. Walker (eds.), *Scottish Sport in the Making of the Nation* (Leicester, 1994); I.S. Wood (ed.), *Scotland and Ulster* (Edinburgh, 1994); J.M. Bradley, *Ethnic and Religious Identity in Modern Scotland* (Aldershot, 1995); G. Walker, *Intimate Strangers: Political and Cultural Interaction between Scotland and Ulster in Modern Times* (Edinburgh, 1995); C.G. Brown, *A Social History of Religion in Scotland* (2nd edn., Edinburgh, 1997); R. Boyle and P. Lynch (eds.), *Out of the Ghetto? The Catholic Community in Modern Scotland* (Edinburgh, 1998); B. Murray, *The Old Firm in the New Age* (Edinburgh, 1998).

[3] A. Campbell, *The Lanarkshire Miners* (Edinburgh, 1979), pp.179–201.

[4] See G. Walker, 'The Protestant Irish', in Devine (ed.), *Irish Immigrants*.

[5] See G. Walker and D. Officer, 'Scottish Unionism and the Ulster Question', in C.M.M. MacDonald (ed.), *Unionist Scotland 1800–1997* (Edinburgh, 1998).

[6] See S.J. Brown, '"Outside the Covenant": The Scottish Presbyterian Churches and Irish Immigration', *Innes Review*, 42, 1991, pp.19–45.

[7] Including Ireland: see D. Keogh, *Jews in 20th Century Ireland: Refugees, Anti-Semitism and the Holocaust* (Cork, 1998).

[8] See the comparative treatment of popular Protestant and Unionist politics in Walker, *Intimate Strangers*, chapter 3.

[9] See Boyle and Lynch (eds.), *Out of the Ghetto?*, especially the chapters by editors; E. Kelly, '"Stands Scotland Where It Did?" An Essay in Ethnicity and Internationalism', *Scottish Affairs*, no.26, 1999, pp.83–99; and comment in *New Statesman (Scotland)*, 6 September 1999.

[10] There is much evidence on the Catholic Church's political pressuring of MPs in the papers of former Glasgow Labour MP Hugh Brown in Strathclyde Regional Archives TD 1252.

[11] See 'In defence of family values', *The Herald*, 18 January 1999; also commentary in Niall Ferguson, 'Scotland the Disunited', *Daily Telegraph*, 21 July 1999; and controversy over Cardinal Winning's views on the suitability of gays working with young people, *The Herald*, 8 November 1999.

[12] *The Scotsman*, 16 January 1999.

[13] S. Bruce, *Conservative Protestant Politics* (Oxford, 1998), p.119.

[14] Ibid., pp.116–36; also comments of Professor Lindsay Paterson in *The Observer* (Scotland), 15 August 1999, and Professor Tom Devine in *Times Higher Educational Supplement*, 10 September 1999.

[15] See letter from Kemp in *The Herald*, 11 August 1999.

[16] D. McCrone and M. Rosie, 'Left and Liberal: Catholics in Modern Scotland', in Boyle and Lynch (eds.), *Out of the Ghetto?*.

[17] *Irish News*, 10 August 1999.

[18] See, for example, 'SNP bids to woo Labour's Catholic voters', *Scotland on Sunday*, 20 September 1998.

[19] G. Hassan, 'Caledonian Dreaming: The Challenge to Scottish Labour', in A. Coddington and M. Perryman (eds.), *The Moderniser's Dilemma: Radical Politics in the Age of Blair* (London, 1998).

[20] See *Herald* editorials, 30 September 1998 and 15 October 1998.

[21] Jack McLean, *Glasgow Herald*, 5 July 1991.

[22] *The Herald*, 13 and 17 July 1998.

[23] Ibid., 16 September 1998.

[24] See B. Murray, *The Old Firm* (Edinburgh, 1984), pp.235–40.

[25] Ibid.

[26] See Findlay's comments on the affair reported in *The Herald*, 16 October 1999.

[27] See Speirs's critical comments on MacMillan in *Scotland on Sunday*, 15 August 1999.

[28] House of Commons motion, 19 May 1998.

[29] See his comments in the Catholic journal *Flourish*, June 1998.

[30] See range of pop stars including Eddi Reader, Jim Kerr and the rest of Simple Minds, Bobby Gillespie, as well as film-makers Peter Broughan and Michael Caton-Jones and entertainers such as Elaine C. Smith.

[31] For example, Joseph Bradley, Patrick Reilly and Gerry Finn. It should be pointed out, in the light of Professor Reilly's comments (*The Herald*, 7 June 1999) regarding the recent murders of Celtic fans, that a Rangers fan died after being beaten up in West Lothian following the Old Firm game of 2 May 1999, and that another Rangers fan was killed in Pollok, Glasgow, in what was apparently a retaliatory attack after the murder of Thomas McFadden following the Scottish Cup final on 29 May 1999. Murderous attacks by both sets of fans on one another have a long history. See, for example, 'Thrown from a bridge – because he wore a Rangers scarf', *Daily Record*, 1 September 1975.

[32] In the souvenir programme of the North American Federation of Celtic Supporters Clubs in 1996, Speirs wrote, 'The character of Celtic was indelibly written in the blood of Ireland, in the poetry of Catholicism, and in people who had a shared sense of who they were and to whom they belonged.' This echoes the sentiments of George Galloway MP (see endnote 29 above) and surely strikes a chord with James MacMillan himself.

[33] A version of the Irish national anthem favoured by some Celtic supporters includes the lines: 'North men, South men, comrades all / Soon there'll be no Protestants at all'.

11. COMPARING SCOTLAND AND NORTHERN IRELAND

Steve Bruce

Introduction

Other chapters in this collection present data which suggest that the Irish in Scotland have been successfully assimilated and that sectarianism is no longer a major social problem. I have previously argued this case a number of times[1] and been criticised for taking too sanguine a view of religio-ethnic relations.[2] I do not want to repeat the evidence that leads me to a conclusion utterly at odds with the view of James MacMillan. I plan to take the data for granted and explain the change.[3] Although it may seem perverse to take for granted what is, for some, still at issue, this method has two advantages. First, for those who accept my conclusion that sectarianism is no longer an important social force, the explanation may be interesting. Second, the explanation of change, if it is plausible, poses a major challenge to those who would insist that nothing has really changed. If I am largely right in what follows, then those who insist that Catholics in Scotland are still the victims of discrimination and disadvantage have to explain how that can be the case given the considerations that I will shortly describe.

My central theme is that beneficial change came not from personal virtue but from necessity. A number of very significant structural differences between Scotland and Northern Ireland eroded animosity in the former while institutionalising it and stabilising it in the latter. I do not believe this outcome is to be explained by the idea, not surprisingly popular with Scots, that Scotland's egalitarian Presbyterian background makes it a particularly tolerant place. Though one should never deny that the well-meaning can do good, I want to stress the inadvertent and ironic nature of the crucial changes. I am less concerned with the well-meaning than with those who meant otherwise. Let us assume that bigots remain bigots so long as they find satisfying outlets for, and rewards from, their bigotry, and that what we need to examine are the structures which provide, or fail to provide, opportunities for sectarian actions. My approach is to suggest that changes in the social, political and economic structure of modern Scotland undermined the conditions for the reproduction of sectarianism. People inadvertently became good because the environment gave them increasingly little reward for behaving badly. That sectarian actions in Scotland were not as effective as they were in Northern Ireland removed most of the forms of social pressure that would have forced Catholics to maintain a tight, coherent social identity. Hence instead of what one has in Ulster, where each side had the power to structure life as a battle between the two peoples, in Scotland sectarian identity gradually diminished in importance.

The key elements of the decline in religio-ethnic conflict are: (1) the initial lack of cohesion among the native Scots; (2) the degree of secularisation at the time when ethnic competition started in earnest; (3) the desire of the Irish to be integrated; (4) the political and economic impotence of those who would have it otherwise. In all these, we can draw a very clear contrast with the situation in the north-east of Ireland.

Scottish Fragmentation and Secularisation

One of the greatest obstacles to sustained Scottish hostility to the Irish was the lack of a strong and shared Scottish identity. There was no one unified, conservative Protestant culture which could serve as a basis of sustained hostility to the Irish Catholics. The internal fragmentation of Scottish Protestantism undermined the ability of militant Protestants successfully to construct Catholics as a major threat to any shared way of life. The Scottish Highlanders spoke the same language as the Irish; Lowlanders spoke English. The Highlands were evangelical; the Lowlands moderate and liberal in their religion. Even within those broad areas, Scottish Protestants were divided into competing Churches, which made it difficult for many to argue for religious exclusion. This did not prevent some Presbyterian dissenters from arguing that they and only they should be tolerated, but such claims were unconvincing. Though most of those responsible for it did not welcome this consequence, the diversity within Scottish Protestantism forced the state to become increasingly neutral on religious affiliation. Furthermore, their disputes with each other distracted many conservative Protestants from the less pressing contest with the Irish.

That many could see Irish Catholics as less of a concern than their separated Presbyterian brethren was made possible by the distribution of the migrants and their descendants. In 1878 Catholics formed under 10 per cent of the Scottish population, a number which rose to 14 per cent in 1931 and 16 per cent in 1977.[4] They were heavily concentrated in Ayrshire, Lanarkshire, Glasgow, the Vale of Leven, the Lothians and Edinburgh. Organisations such as the Church of Scotland and the Free Church, which could have done far more to demonise the Irish, had national parish structures which had been slow to adapt to movements of population. Thus in the councils of the main Protestant Churches, relations with Catholics were an issue for only some representatives, while relations with competing Presbyterian organisations were a major interest for all. It is significant that attempts in the second half of the nineteenth century to create non-denominational anti-Catholic organisations regularly failed. The Scottish Protestant Alliance, for example, was overwhelmingly Free Church because that body was more theologically conservative than the Kirk, but also because the disputes over property that followed the Disruption of 1843 created a huge amount of bad blood between the two largest bodies of Presbyterians.

Both in class and in region, cultural and material interests failed to match up. The working-class Protestants who most resented the presence of the Irish and who most keenly felt the competition for work and for space were rarely evangelical Christians. The Calvinists in the Highlands thought the Pope was the anti-Christ but they were not competing with the Irish. Those agitators who strongly objected to the Irish on the grounds of them having the wrong religion were hampered in their campaigns by the fact that most of those who were willing to support public protests were very obviously not total-abstaining born-again Christians. From Jacob Primmer in the 1890s to Jack Glass in the 1990s, the legitimacy of those who were spiritually and theologically anti-Catholic was undermined by the irreligious behaviour of those who supported them. Although Ulster Protestants such as Ian Paisley are faced with something of the same problem, it is nowhere near as severe because in Northern Ireland a far larger proportion of groups such as the Orange Order is actually born-again evangelical.

Furthermore, the internal fragmentation of the Scottish Churches itself hastened secularisation. It did so in the very practical sense that the Kirk was no longer capable of providing social control, social welfare or education and hence the state had to increasingly intervene to provide national services. But the fragmentation of Protestantism also had the effect of weakening the certainty with which Protestants held their convictions.

However, it must be stressed that there is seldom anything fixed or immutable about social identities and divisions. It was always possible that the internal fragmentation of Scottish culture and society could have been reversed if enough Scots Protestants had felt that something which they valued very highly was under enough of a threat. The Ulster case offers a good example of increased cohesion among Protestants. In 1840, the two main Presbyterian Churches united (and did so without major dissent). By itself this is not important. After all, the major Scottish Presbyterian Churches reversed two centuries of fission and by 1929 all the main bodies were reunited in a national Church. What is important is that the Irish Presbyterians came together on the basis of increased doctrinal orthodoxy and cohesion while the Scots Presbyterians united on the basis of increased liberalism and doctrinal tolerance. In Ulster Protestants were made more alike by external pressure; in Scotland the reorganisation of Presbyterianism was an agreement not to bother about differences. If the Ulster case demonstrates that increased cohesion is possible, then its absence in the Scottish case requires explanation – and the explanation rests on the absence of any strong sense of threat from the Irish Catholics in Scotland.

The same point can be made about secularisation. Ethnic conflict frequently inhibits secularisation by giving a special importance both to religious ideas as a legitimation of conflict and to religious identity as a mark of belonging; Catholicism remained strong in Communist Poland and Calvinism remained strong among the Afrikaners because in both settings religion was an important part of what identified a people against their enemies. But what I have termed the 'cultural defence' function of religion only *inhibits* secularisation; it does not reverse it. We can think of many cases where conflict appears to explain why one country has become less secular than another apparently similar, but I cannot think of one where crisis has created a sweeping religious revival in a thoroughly secular culture. But places are neither entirely religious nor secular; we are talking about degrees. The important point of contrast between Ulster and Scotland is that in the former the ethnic conflict began in the seventeenth century, when religion was much more part of an all-pervasive world view. The Protestant settlers adopted religious interpretations of their situation and their strong attachment to their religion inhibited inter-marriage. In Scotland the conflict between Catholics and Protestants did not begin in earnest until the middle of the nineteenth century, a fortunate accident of timing. By then it was too late for religion to matter enough to enough people for the internal divisions of Scottish Protestantism to be overcome.

Political Aspirations

The third key consideration for understanding the decline of sectarianism concerns the political actions of the Catholic migrants. Not surprisingly, they remained active in Irish politics. After all, until the formation of the Irish Free State, Ireland was a 'British' political issue. But once the Irish problem was (albeit temporarily) solved, interest in the politics of the old world faded into nostalgia. Once most migrants came to see themselves as permanent residents in Scotland rather than sojourners, they could have developed a distinctive Catholic politics, but, apart from the education issue, they did not. Nor did they follow the Dutch example of trying to create a series of autonomous Catholic institutions. Influenced by European developments, Hugh Murnin, the Catholic miners' leader who was later MP for Stirling and Falkirk Burghs, in 1912 suggested the formation of a centrist Catholic party, but he only had to do his sums and remember the elections he fought were of the winner-takes-all variety to appreciate that such a party would be trivial. And, though their opponents often described Scots Catholics in the labour movement as operating a well-oiled machine, unlike their counterparts in Australia, they did not systematically pursue sectional interests. There was no equivalent of Santamaria's 'Movement' to be expelled from the Labour Party.

The crucial difference between Scottish Protestant and Ulster Protestant perceptions of Catholics is that the Catholics in Scotland did not have a political agenda that, if successful, would have radically changed the political structure of Scotland. The Catholics in Scotland were not trying to win independence or trying to take Scotland into another country (after all, it had already been taken into another state when James VI took the English throne in 1603 and the position was consolidated with the Act of Union in 1707). Though some Scots Protestants felt their material interests were threatened and some (but, as I have just argued, too few) felt their cultural interests were endangered, the political desires of Scottish Catholics were not incompatible with the interests of Scottish Protestants generally. To put it another way, once Ireland and education were resolved, there was nothing about the interests of Protestants and Catholics in Scotland (unlike their neighbours in Ireland) which need polarise them, which need set them in competing political parties, and hence which need encourage competition. To illustrate the point biographically, it was possible for Glasgow socialist William Reid to support the Ulster Volunteer Force in 1912 and the cause of the Union all his life and yet work closely with Catholic socialists in the Labour movement in the 1930s and 1940s. His contemporary Harry Midgeley, the leader of the Northern Ireland Labour Party, had to choose between class politics and the constitutional issue and chose the latter.

Political and Economic Impotence

The fourth key consideration is impotence. It does not seem too cynical to suppose that the decline of anti-Catholicism owed much to the inability of militant Protestants to act on their beliefs. We only have to think again of the way in which Ulster Unionists ran Northern Ireland or the National Party ran South Africa to appreciate the part which being able to reward supporters and disadvantage opponents plays in maintaining divisions.

One can quite well imagine that the relationship between religion and politics in Scotland would have been radically different had Scotland been an autonomous and democratic political unit. That second adjective is important. In many ways, Scotland, despite its formal position in the Union, had enjoyed considerable autonomy, but it was a corporatist autonomy managed by a small ruling élite which was quite happy in pursuit of Scottish interests to ignore the baser instincts of some of its subjects. Sir John Gilmour was a leading Unionist and Orangeman but as Secretary of State for Scotland he refused to give any support to those who wanted to prohibit Irish immigration. Sir Charles Cleland was a Unionist and Orangeman but as chairman of the Glasgow Education Authority he pointedly refused to give any encouragement to his fellow Orangemen who campaigned against the 1918 Education Act (which they saw as 'Rome on the rates').

The way that the centralised structure of British politics militated against Scottish anti-Catholics can be seen very clearly in the fate of Alexander Ratcliffe, the leader of the Scottish Protestant League (SPL), and John Cormack, leader of Protestant Action (PA). In the 1930s the SPL and PA, in Glasgow and Edinburgh respectively, rose rapidly and then died away just as quickly. Both Ratcliffe and Cormack had grand ambitions. In 1929, Ratcliffe stood for Westminster in the Stirling and Falkirk Burghs constituency and won a respectable 25 per cent of the vote. He never again thought it worth standing. When Cormack offered himself to the electors of the Leith constituency in 1945, he won only 2,493 votes (less than 7 per cent). A few months later he stood for his council seat, which was entirely subsumed within the Westminster constituency, and gained over 4,000 votes. Electing Ratcliffe or Cormack to the local council made some sense but sending two militant Protestants to Westminster was obviously pointless and their electors knew it. Conflict with Catholics was only important in parts of Scotland. In Britain as a whole it was irrelevant, and the heavily centralised nature of the British state forced the major political parties to concentrate on UK-wide considerations.

Imagine Scotland of the 1930s being like Northern Ireland in having its own parliament with considerable power over education, housing, policing, social services and local economic development – precisely the areas in which it is possible to reward one's own people and alienate 'them'. Imagine that the SPL and PA had each won five seats. Like the small religious parties in Israel's Knesset, they could have held the balance of power between right and left and might have persuaded the Conservative and Unionist Party to pursue anti-Catholic policies (such as restrictions on immigration and the end of state funding for Catholic schools). Actually, the actions of Gilmour, Cleland and other members of the ruling élite suggest that even in those circumstances they would have put social harmony before religio-ethnic interest. But by imagining the space that would have been created for militant Protestants in a democratically accountable autonomous Scotland, we can see very clearly the inadvertently benign consequences of Britain's unusually centralised polity.

Not only did the SPL and PA fail to win any influence on the national stage but their rapid collapse as local parties showed their impotence. They were not helped by the erratic and demagogic leadership of Ratcliffe and Cormack, but they were destroyed by their members' inability to agree on anything other than their anti-Catholicism and their inability to shape the political agenda so as to keep the sectarian issues on which they could agree to the fore. SPL councillors voted against each other more often than they voted together.

Within their own councils, militant Protestants were powerless. Within Scotland, they were trivial. Scotland itself was relatively powerless within the highly centralised structure of the United Kingdom. As David Seawright has documented in great detail, the Conservatives became far more interested in appealing to the right-wing vote throughout Britain than in courting the Orange vote in the west coast of Scotland or Liverpool.[5]

A similar lack of autonomy effected Scottish capital. Sectarianism was most successfully reproduced where, as in the once strongly Orange Vale of Leven, factory owners lived locally, were elders of the Kirk, patronised local football teams, held high office in the Orange Order and the Masons, funded the Sunday School picnic and took the constituency seat at Westminster as a matter of right. We do not have to assert that such local magnates were deliberately anti-Catholic in employment practices. We do not even need to suppose that the foremen who controlled entry to apprenticeships were consciously excluding Catholics. More often they were simply promoting the interests of family, friends and neighbours. But the close-knit nature of that world and the close integration of workplace, community groups and neighbourhood ensured that Catholics found it hard to move up the occupational ladder. In the second half of the nineteenth century four firms in the Vale of Leven, all in the printing, dyeing and bleaching business, employed 6,000 workers.[6] By 1952 only 1,700 people (two-thirds of them women) worked in the textile industry. About 2,000 out of a local working population of around 12,000 worked on the Strathleven industrial estate, three-quarters of them employed by just two American firms. And this pattern was repeated all over central and lowland Scotland. As small companies became absorbed by increasingly distant companies, the communal ties which linked masters and men broke down. Economic power moved to London, to the United States, and then to Japan. Scottish industry became increasingly subject to the universalistic values of multi-national corporate capitalism. An English manager answerable to an American or Japanese board was not interested in the religion of his workforce.

At the same time as the control of capital shifted out of local hands, the old manufacturing industries which Protestants dominated declined and were replaced by new enterprises, requiring new skills, built on greenfield sites in new towns.

The above is a clear example of what Bryan Wilson meant by 'societalisation': the shift of attention and power from the local community to the larger society.[7] We see another crucial part of the same process in the rise of the welfare state. As local (and often voluntary) welfare services were gradually rationalised into mandatory national provision, so the opportunity for any group to act in a discriminatory manner was reduced. Especially in its improved provision of education and social security, the welfare state enhanced living standards for everyone, irrespective of religio-ethnic identity. More than that, it provided a whole range of white-collar professional middle-class jobs which were staffed by people who were geographically, as well as socially, mobile, and who took as their reference groups not their family and friends and co-religionists but their fellow professionals. The local-government civil servant may have been schooled in Bridgeton but he might have gone to university in Edinburgh and served in a variety of London boroughs before moving to the Midlands and then returning to Glasgow in a senior position with the City Council. He might have kept his father's Orange sash. He might even know the words of 'The Sash my Father Wore'. If keen on football, he might attend Old Firm games and shout sectarian abuse at Celtic players, but his involvement in that world will no longer be deep or natural. Rather it will be a very limited performance, played with ironic detachment; a bit of slumming at the weekend before returning to the detached house in East Kilbride and the wife who has not even a passing interest in sectarian animosities.

Though made frivolously, this is not a trivial point. One of the greatest social changes of the second half of the twentieth century was the decline of the public and communal in favour of the private and domestic. With increased affluence, the decline in the length of the working day, the decline in average family size and the improvement in the quality of housing, the role of the public space in people's sense of identity has drastically shrunk. The street, the public house, the football ground, the Orange or the Masonic Lodge, the church, the trade union meeting – all of these have declined in popularity and importance as the home has become the place where we find ourselves.

Conclusion

Shared identities and animosities do not free-float. To be sustained over generations and over large numbers of people they must be rooted in economic, political and social structures. If not, they become – like British fascism or British Israelism – the arcane preferences of very small numbers. The thrust of my argument is this: though the migration to Scotland of large numbers of Irish Catholics created the potential for enduring religio-ethnic conflict, features of the Scottish environment prevented that conflict from becoming embedded and enduring. To suppose Scotland to be like Northern Ireland is to exaggerate the superficial similarities and to overlook the much more important structural differences.

Notes

[1] See S. Bruce, *No Pope of Rome: Anti-Catholicism in Modern Scotland* (Edinburgh, 1985); S. Bruce, 'Sectarianism in Scotland: A Contemporary Assessment and Explanation', *Scottish Government Yearbook* (1988), pp.150–65.
[2] J.M. Bradley, *Ethnic and Religious Identity in Scotland: Culture, Politics and Football* (Aldershot, 1995).

[3] The ideas in this brief essay are explored at length and in a wider comparative context in Bruce 1998. I would like to acknowledge the financial assistance of the Economic and Social Research Council, the British Academy and the Irish-American Partnership for a number of specific research projects over the years that have contributed to my understanding of conservative Protestant politics.

[4] J. Darragh, 'The Catholic Population of Scotland, 1878–1977', in D. McRoberts (ed.), *Modern Scottish Catholicism, 1878–1978* (Glasgow, 1979).

[5] D. Seawright, *An Important Matter of Principle: The Decline of the Scottish Conservative and Unionist Party* (Aldershot, 1998).

[6] R. Gallacher, 'The Vale of Leven, 1914–75', in T. Dickson (ed.), *Capital and Class* (Edinburgh, 1982), pp.186–211.

[7] B. Wilson, *Religion in Sociological Perspective* (Oxford, 1982), p.154.

PART 3

The Schools' Question

12. SALVATION THROUGH EDUCATION? THE CHANGING SOCIAL STATUS OF SCOTTISH CATHOLICS

Lindsay Paterson

Introduction

There is a contradiction running through many of the claims about the distinctive social experience of Scottish Catholics. On the one hand, the very existence of Catholic schools is celebrated. In particular, they have enabled working-class Catholics to gain credentials that are recognised by the whole of Scottish society. That much seems to be agreed by all sides, especially because the academic effectiveness of Catholic schools has been demonstrated repeatedly by non-partisan researchers. It is a view found in the interviews reported in a 1997 investigation for the Commission for Racial Equality.[1] And it is a point agreed by James MacMillan in the speech in August 1999 that provoked the current debate; he described Catholic schools as 'a stunning success story'.

And yet, on the other hand, the corollary is frequently denied by the same people who praise the schools: it is denied that decades of relative educational success have made any real difference to Catholics' chances in the labour market. The CRE study reported 'a belief that religious discrimination still operates in the field of employment'.[2] And James MacMillan draws a general lesson about 'a deep malaise in our society' from a story told by a columnist in *The Herald* newspaper on 19 June 1999 about a firm which would 'take on Catholics in the menial posts, but . . . only have Protestants in management posts'.

If this were the case – if better credentials were not yielding better job prospects – then Scottish Catholics would indeed be uniquely discriminated against in the Western world, where the link between credentials and the labour market has become ever tighter since the middle of the twentieth century.[3] Occupational success has depended increasingly on merit selection or meritocracy, as it is more commonly called: the rewarding of ability and effort.

The debate provoked by James MacMillan's speech has been helpful in allowing a much more public airing of issues that were previously discussed mainly in the pages of academic books and journals. But a lot of this debate has been based much more on rhetoric and personal impressions than on verifiable facts. The purpose of this chapter is to attempt to offer some reliable evidence about two aspects of the position of Catholics in Scotland: what has happened to Catholics' chances of getting good jobs, and what – if any – has the role of education been in that respect?

Catholic Schools

The system of Catholic schooling was started in the nineteenth century by the Church to serve the needs of mainly Irish immigrant labourers.[4] It was believed that neither the spiritual nor the secular needs of Catholics would be met within the state system that was set up in Scotland after 1872, even though, it should be noted, the Scottish parish school system did in fact teach very large numbers of Catholic children and did allow them religious instruction by their own Church.[5]

But that wholly independent Catholic system was not ultimately tenable for a community that was so poor. The result was the Education (Scotland) Act of 1918, which integrated the Catholic schools into the public system while retaining the Church's role in managing the schools and in approving staff appointments. This compromise was, on the whole, welcomed by all sides. The Catholic schools, and most of the Church, accepted that only state funding could allow a distinctive education to survive. Social reformers – notably in the Labour Party – believed that public finance would promote the social mobility of individual Catholics, and so would gradually overcome the isolation and poverty of Catholic communities. And most segments even of firmly Presbyterian opinion preferred some state regulation of what went on in Catholic schools to the development of a wholly autonomous system, which they feared – sometimes on more or less racist grounds – would threaten the coherence of Scottish education as a whole.

The state finance then allowed the system to flourish. By giving Catholics access to publicly recognised certificates, the schools allowed them to compete on much more equal terms for jobs. By the mid-1960s, this process of enabling social mobility had advanced significantly[6] in the sense that many individual Catholics had gained access to middle-class jobs. But the Catholic community still lived in much greater relative poverty than the majority, and the opportunities were available only to a selected few within it. Comprehensive secondary education had a substantial impact on that, a potential which had already been appreciated by the Church: in Glasgow, comprehensive Catholic schools were being built from the 1950s onwards. Probably the most important feature of comprehensive schooling in this respect was simply the ending of selection. Up to 1965, just 5 per cent of senior secondaries were Catholic, even though about 19 per cent of secondary pupils were Catholic.[7] After 1965, all Catholic schools could offer their pupils the full range of academic courses up to age 18, and so could encourage them to use educational qualifications to get better jobs than their parents had had. This opening up of opportunity through educational credentials was aided by profound changes in the labour market in west-central Scotland, where most Scottish Catholics lived. The discriminatory recruitment practices had been exercised mainly by locally owned firms, many of them small. As the old economy based on shipbuilding and heavy engineering collapsed between the 1960s and 1980s, the main employers came to be firms owned in England or overseas who operated much more meritocratic forms of selection.[8]

Catholic schools now make up a substantial minority of the public provision, receiving full state support for both their running costs and their capital costs. Their teachers take part in the same systems of training and development available to teachers in non-Catholic public schools, although

146

they also have their own networks. In 1994 (the most recent year for which full information is available) there were 355 Catholic primary schools, 15 per cent of the total of 2,336 public primary schools in Scotland, catering for 18 per cent of primary pupils. There were 65 Catholic secondary schools, 16 per cent of the total of 405 public secondary schools, catering for 17 per cent of secondary pupils. There were two independent Catholic secondary schools. This is by far the largest denominational sector in Scottish education; the only other religious schools are a few Episcopalian primaries and one Jewish primary. There is also one Catholic teacher-education institution, St Andrew's College in Glasgow, which in 1999 was absorbed into the new Faculty of Education of the University of Glasgow.[9]

The Effectiveness of Catholic Schools

The relative academic effectiveness of Scottish Catholic schools has been shown by many researchers[10], who have reached conclusions similar to those found for Catholic schools in other countries.[11] In terms of crude averages of educational attainment, Scottish Catholic schools appear in such studies to be slightly behind non-denominational schools, but in most cases that is entirely explicable in terms of the relative social deprivation of the communities which Catholic schools serve. Indeed, when researchers have compared the effects of Catholic and non-denominational schools on pupils from given social circumstances, the Catholic schools appear to do better. Put differently, working-class children do better in Catholic schools than in non-denominational schools.

That research used data from the 1980s and earlier. In this section we update it by using the Scottish School Leavers' Survey to examine whether the relative effectiveness of Catholic schools persisted into the 1990s. The tables below use the surveys of people who left school in 1980 (conducted in spring 1981) and 1994 (spring 1995); they thus relate to the experience of Catholic secondary schooling from the mid-1970s (when the 1980s leavers entered secondary school) to the mid-1990s.[12] There were 5,550 people in the 1980 survey and 3,223 in the 1994 survey; these are large numbers by the standard of social surveys, and so allow us to draw conclusions that are quite reliable. Nevertheless, despite these large sample sizes, our conclusions are still subject to sampling error; small differences may well be due to the chance mechanisms of the sampling rather than to any changes in real life. Only differences for which there is firm evidence are commented on below.[13]

The surveys report attainment among leavers from Catholic schools, which is not the same as attainment by Catholics; no information on the religion of respondents was collected by these surveys. (We return to this point in the next section, where we look at data that does relate to Catholics as individuals.)

Five measures are shown in the tables:
- the proportion of leavers with no qualifications at all;
- the proportion gaining three or more passes in the Higher Grade examination (roughly the minimum needed for entering higher education);
- the proportion gaining five or more passes in their Highers (a very good level of attainment);

147

- among people who did not go on to any post-school education, the proportion who succeeded in getting a full-time job or a place on a training scheme (as opposed to remaining unemployed);
- the proportion of people with three or more Highers who actually did enter higher education.

For each of these, we look at the difference between Catholic and non-denominational schools, at whether that changed between 1980 and 1994, and at whether any differences varied according to the social class of the school leaver. There was no evidence that any of the conclusions differed between male and female leavers, and so gender is not shown as a variable in the tables in this section.

Table 1 shows that in 1994 the average examination performance in Catholic schools continued to be below that for non-denominational schools. Compared to non-denominational schools, Catholic schools had rather more leavers with no qualifications, and slightly fewer with either three or more Highers passes or five or more Highers passes. Nevertheless, the improvement in attainment in Catholic schools in the 14-year period was just as great as the improvement in non-denominational schools. For example, the proportion with three or more passes rose from 14 per cent to 27 per cent in Catholic schools, and from 20 per cent to 31 per cent in non-denominational schools, and the difference between these two rises is small enough to be attributable to chance.

Table 1: Attainment and Progression amongst Leavers from Catholic and Non-denominational Schools, 1980 and 1994

	1980				1994			
	CATHOLIC		NON-DENOMINATIONAL		CATHOLIC		NON-DENOMINATIONAL	
	%	sample size	%	sample size	%	sample size	%	sample size
No qualifications	36	1029	29	4519	13	335	7	2888
3 or more Highers	14	1029	20	4519	27	335	31	2888
5 or more Highers	6	1029	10	4519	14	335	18	2888
Entering a job or training scheme, among people not in full-time post-school education	77	795	82	3306	65	188	75	1440
Entering higher education, among people with 3 or more Highers	23	186	25	1096	23	115	25	1081

Percentages are weighted; sample sizes are unweighted.
2 cases are omitted from 1980 because of missing data.
Source: Scottish Schools Leavers' Survey.

The same is true of the first of our two measures of progression beyond school. Leavers from Catholic schools who did not enter a full-time educational course were rather less likely to get a job or a place on a training scheme than leavers from non-denominational schools. For entry to higher education among leavers who had three or more Highers, there was no reliable evidence of any difference between the school sectors.

However, all of these differences can be explained by the relative social standing of the fathers of leavers in the two sectors. We define social class as the dichotomy between manual and non-manual;[14] we refer to these as working class and middle class respectively. People who could not be assigned to a class are omitted from this part of the analysis (15 per cent of the whole sample in 1980 and 24 per cent in 1994). The legacies of labour-market disadvantage earlier in the twentieth century were still evident in 1994. For example, in 1980, 32 per cent of leavers from non-denominational schools had fathers who were in non-manual jobs, while the proportion for leavers from Catholic schools was just 16 per cent. The gap had narrowed somewhat by 1994 – it was 37 per cent and 29 per cent respectively – but it was still undoubtedly there.

When attainment and progression are examined separately for people from different social classes, the Catholic schools come off better than in the raw averages. The two parts of table 2 are essentially repeats of table 1 but for people with fathers in non-manual and manual occupations separately. For proportions gaining no qualifications at all, there is now no reliable evidence that leavers from Catholic schools are disadvantaged; the small differences in table 2 could well have occurred by chance. For example, among working-class leavers in 1994, 12 per cent from Catholic schools did not gain any qualifications compared to 8 per cent from non-denominational schools, but this difference is of the size we would expect simply from random fluctuations associated with the sampling. The same is true of the other two measures of attainment: by 1994 the Catholic schools were at least as good as the non-denominational schools for each social class. For example, 21 per cent of working-class leavers from Catholic schools in 1994 passed three or more Highers, compared to 19 per cent of working-class leavers from non-denominational schools (a difference that is small enough to be due to chance). For passing five or more Highers, the proportions for working-class leavers were each 9 per cent.

The results for getting a job by leavers who did not go on to any further education show a persisting but small disadvantage in Catholic schools.[15] For example, the proportions in 1994 were 71 per cent for working-class leavers from Catholic schools, but 81 per cent for working-class leavers from non-denominational schools. But for progression to higher education among people with at least three Highers passes, working-class leavers had a clear advantage in Catholic schools: in 1994, 65 per cent of them went on to higher education, compared to 56 per cent of such leavers from non-denominational schools.

The conclusion of this analysis of the survey data is that Catholic schools have continued to be effective, long after the initial move to establish comprehensive secondary education took place. Above all, they are the means by which working-class pupils have gained enough qualifications to enter

Table 2: Attainment and Progression amongst Leavers from Catholic and Non-denominational Schools, 1980 and 1994, by Occupational Class of Father

(1) non-manual

	1980				1994			
	CATHOLIC		NON-DENOMINATIONAL		CATHOLIC		NON-DENOMINATIONAL	
	%	sample size	%	sample size	%	sample size	%	sample size
No qualifications	12	187	9	1616	5	112	3	1171
3 or more Highers	38	187	40	1616	50	112	51	1171
5 or more Highers	18	187	21	1616	31	112	32	1171
Entering a job or training scheme, among people not in full-time post-school education	90	105	87	889	77	50	77	411
Entering higher education, among people with 3 or more Highers	66	82	59	723	56	63	60	658

(2) manual

	1980				1994			
	CATHOLIC		NON-DENOMINATIONAL		CATHOLIC		NON-DENOMINATIONAL	
	%	sample size	%	sample size	%	sample size	%	sample size
No qualifications	38	666	35	2302	12	129	8	1086
3 or more Highers	9	666	10	2302	21	129	19	1086
5 or more Highers	3	666	4	2302	9	129	9	1086
Entering a job or training scheme, among people not in full-time post-school education	77	551	82	1920	71	78	81	670
Entering higher education, among people with 3 or more Highers	60	75	48	298	65	35	56	263

Percentages are weighted; sample sizes are unweighted.
Non-manual is Registrar General's classes I, II and III non-manual; manual is classes III manual, IV and V. Cases which could not be assigned to a class are omitted (15 per cent of the whole sample in 1980 and 24 per cent in 1994).
Source: Scottish Schools Leavers' Survey.

higher education. As in earlier studies (for example, by Willms[16]), there appears to remain some disadvantage in the labour market for people leaving Catholic schools to enter jobs directly; in that sense, leavers from Catholic schools are even more dependent on gaining qualifications than are leavers from other schools. So this updating of the survey evidence to the mid-1990s shows that Catholic schools are effective to the extent that they use the system of credentials that is accepted as currency for employment throughout Scottish society. They have succeeded because they have taken part in the burgeoning Scottish system of meritocracy.

The Occupational Status of Catholics

So what happened to these people who benefited from the effectiveness of Catholic schools, not just during the couple of decades reflected in our tables but also during the last half-century, as measured by the earlier research? Did they manage to translate their educational success into success in the labour market? We look at this question by means of a different source of data: the Scottish Election Survey of 1997. As its title implies, the purpose of this was to study the attitudes and behaviour of Scottish voters in the UK general election of that year. These political matters do not concern us here (for that, see the chapter by Rosie and McCrone in this book). The survey is relevant to present purposes because it also asked questions about religion, occupational status and educational qualifications. There were 882 respondents.[17]

With this survey, we do have information on the religion of the respondent, but there is no information on the type of school which the respondent attended. So the question we are assessing here is whether access to educational credentials, by whatever means, has been a route by which recent generations of Scottish Catholics have gained better jobs than their predecessors could find earlier in the century. We approach the topic by dividing the sample into two cohorts: those aged 51 or over in 1997, and those aged between 18 and 50; the younger cohort can be thought of as the generation of the welfare-state era, because they were born in 1947 or later. If Catholics have been overcoming discrimination in the labour market, then we would expect the younger cohort to have obtained better jobs than the older one, and we would expect any improvement to be greater among Catholics than among people with other religious affiliation.

Table 3 shows that that is exactly what we do find.[18] Among older Catholics, only 22 per cent were in non-manual jobs, compared to 52 per cent of other Christians and 38 per cent of people with no religion. Among the younger cohort, there was no reliable evidence of any difference among the religious groups: the proportions in non-manual jobs were 57 per cent of Catholics, 59 per cent of other Christians and 51 per cent of people with no religion. Thus the difference between cohorts for Catholics was 35 per cent, whereas it was only 7 per cent for other Christians and 13 per cent for people with no religion.

Unlike the analysis of Catholic schools, however, there is an important gender difference here, as shown in table 4. The cohort difference in occupational status was greater for Catholic men than for Catholic women: the proportions of men in non-manual jobs were 11 per cent in the older

Table 3: Occupational Status by Religion and Cohort: Proportion in Non-manual Occupations

	AGES 51–96		AGES 18–50	
	NON–MANUAL OCCUPATIONS (%)	*sample size*	NON–MANUAL OCCUPATIONS (%)	*sample size*
Catholic	22	47	57	79
Other Christian	52	265	59	201
No religion	38	50	51	219

Percentages are weighted; sample sizes are unweighted.
'Non-manual' is defined to be the first three class categories in the Goldthorpe scheme.
There were too few people with a religion other than Christianity (eight in total) to be included in this table.
Thirteen cases with missing data are omitted.
Source: Scottish Election Survey 1997.

cohort and 61 per cent in the younger; the corresponding proportions for women were 32 per cent and 54 per cent. This is because, in the older cohort, the difference in occupational status between Catholic and non-Catholic men was much greater than the difference between Catholic and non-Catholic women (37 per cent compared to 20 per cent). That, in turn, is probably because Catholic men used to be much more discriminated against in the labour market than Catholic women: employment in the small manufacturing firms of west-central Scotland was overwhelmingly male.

Table 4: Occupational Status by Sex, Religion and Cohort: Proportion in Non-manual Occupations

	AGES 51–96		AGES 18–50	
	NON–MANUAL OCCUPATIONS (%)	*sample size*	NON–MANUAL OCCUPATIONS (%)	*sample size*
Men				
Catholic	11	18	61	34
Non-Catholic	48	133	45	189
Women				
Catholic	32	29	54	45
Non-Catholic	52	187	64	238

Percentages are weighted; sample sizes are unweighted.
'Non-manual' is defined to be the first three class categories in the Goldthorpe scheme.
'Non-Catholic' is made up of non-Catholic Christians, other religions and no religion.
Thirteen cases with missing data are omitted.
Source: Scottish Election Survey 1997.

These results are technically robust, insofar as they did not seem to depend on how we defined occupational status, religion or cohort. Broadly the same patterns were obtained if, instead of non-manual versus manual occupations, we compared professionals with non-professionals, or working class with non-working class. It also did not seem to matter what we did with people who were not currently in any paid job: assigning them to the occupational status of their spouse's occupation led to the same results as simply omitting them from the analysis altogether. The same conclusions were reached if religion of upbringing was used instead of current religion. Similar effects were evident if the cohorts were defined as under and over age 34 instead of under and over 50. And, to check if differential migration could have been distorting the results, the analysis was repeated on the Scottish Referendum Survey of 1997, where information was available on where the respondent was born; again, the same conclusions were reached.[19]

What is more, this apparent rise in occupational status among younger Catholics was found for all classes of origin. In other words, the relative social standing of Catholics differs between the cohorts even for people who started life in the same social class, and – as before – this is especially true of men. So the change in occupational status seems to represent a change in the status of an entire religious group.

But can this be attributed to education? One reason to suspect that it can was the result of a comparison with the experience of Catholics in England,[20] where there was no difference between Catholics and other Christians in the apparent rise in occupational status between the cohorts. Indeed, any difference was between Christians as a whole and non-Christians, with all types of Christian faring much better than people with other religions or with no religion. So the experience of Scottish Catholics in this regard seems to have been distinctive. The most obviously relevant feature of their history is the school system. Finally, then, we examine whether the apparently disproportionate rise in Catholics' occupational status (compared to non-Catholics') can be explained by their doing particularly well in the educational system.

Table 5 suggests that there is certainly scope for this. The cohort differences in educational levels for Catholics are greater than for non-Catholics. For example, between cohorts, the proportion with a higher-education qualification rose from 9 per cent to 21 per cent among Catholics, but by the smaller 19 per cent to 27 per cent among non-Catholics. The effects of these qualifications are then illustrated in table 6, which shows the proportions in non-manual jobs according to qualification level, grouped broadly into those with at least a pass in a Higher Grade examination and those with no such passes. For the older cohort, there is weak evidence that their educational qualifications were not being fully rewarded in the labour market (although we must be cautious about this inference because the sample numbers are small).[21] But for the younger cohort, there are no religious differences whatsoever: Catholics aged under 50 seem to have been able to make use of their educational credentials in exactly the same way as non-Catholics.

Table 5: Educational Qualifications by Cohort and Religion

	AGES 51–96		AGES 18–50	
	CATHOLIC	NON-CATHOLIC	CATHOLIC	NON-CATHOLIC
No qualifications	64	49	18	18
Ordinary Grade etc	17	21	33	30
Higher Grade etc	10	11	22	24
Higher education	9	19	21	27
Don't know	0	1	1	1
unweighted sample size (=100 per cent)	47	320	79	427

Percentages are weighted.
'Non-Catholic' is made up of non-Catholic Christians, other religions and no religion.
'Ordinary Grade etc' consists of Ordinary Grade, Standard Grade, O level, GCSE and CSE; 'Higher Grade etc' consists of Higher Grade, Scottish and Irish school-leaving certificate and A level.
Nine cases with missing data are omitted.
Source: Scottish Election Survey.

Table 6: Occupational Status by Qualifications, Religion and Cohort: Proportion in Non-manual Occupations

	AGES: 18–50				AGES: 51–96			
	CATHOLIC		NON-CATHOLIC		CATHOLIC		NON-CATHOLIC	
	%	sample size	%	sample size	%	sample size	%	sample size
No Higher Grade passes or better	44	44	42	221	16	38	41	228
At least a Higher Grade pass	70	35	67	206	51	9	71	92

Percentages are weighted; sample sizes are unweighted.
Nine cases with missing data are omitted.
'Non-manual' is defined to be the first three class categories in the Goldthorpe scheme.
Source: Scottish Election Survey 1997.

Conclusions

Education was of enormous benefit to Scottish Catholics in the twentieth century, especially in the last three or four decades. The Catholic schools have been consistently more effective than non-denominational schools in enabling their working-class pupils to gain good qualifications. In a classic instance of education's role in fostering social mobility, these formerly working-class young people have been able to use their credentials to compete successfully for good jobs. Over time, this has benefited men more than women, because Catholic men used to be even more discriminated against in the labour market than Catholic women. The result is that the occupational status of both younger Catholic men and younger Catholic women is now close to that of non-Catholics.

Catholic schools have not been the only reason for this, but they have almost certainly been a very important one. We do not have reliable information on the proportion of Scottish Catholics who have attended Catholic schools, but it would be very surprising if it was not the vast majority, simply because encouraging Catholics to attend Catholic schools was official Church policy throughout the twentieth century. In any case, even if some of the occupational success of younger Catholics is due to their attending non-denominational schools, that serves merely to reinforce the main conclusion of this analysis. Education has secularised the Catholic community, in the sense that it has made them more like the rest of the population in their educational and occupational careers.

None of this should be taken, in itself, as an argument against the continued separate existence of Catholic schools. As in the USA and many other countries, there are justifications for a distinctive Catholic education which rest on the special ethos that Catholic philosophy encourages.[22] For example, it has been claimed frequently that Catholic social teaching is a basis for social capital, fostering the norms, values and trust that can be the basis of a renewed democracy.[23] It could be that only an autonomous system of Catholic schools can allow that social ethos to flourish.

But the present analysis does address the claim that Catholic schools are still needed to defend a beleaguered community against discrimination. The community is not beleaguered. Its younger members are not systematically discriminated against in the labour market. And, for this achievement, Catholics can thank their own successful use of education and the pluralism of Scottish policy that encouraged that.

Acknowledgements

The chapter has benefited from discussions with David McCrone, Michael Rosie, Steve Bruce and Jim Conroy, and from an airing of some of the arguments at the annual conference of the Catholic Head Teachers' Association of Scotland in Crieff in April 1999; the responsibility for the conclusions, however, is mine alone. The 1980 Scottish School Leavers' Survey was funded by the Social Science Research Council and the Scottish Education Department and was carried out by the Centre for Educational Sociology at Edinburgh University. The 1994 survey was funded by the Scottish Office and was carried out by SCPR, London. I am grateful to Karen Brannen of the CES for access to the data from both these surveys and for advice on how to interpret it. The 1997 Election Survey was funded by the Economic and Social Research Council (grant number H552255004), as was the 1997 Referendum Survey (grant number M543/285/001). Full details of the grant holders and of the management of the election surveys is provided on the CREST website: http://www.strath.ac.uk/Other/CREST. I am grateful to the grant holders and survey managers – especially Katarina Thomson and

Alison Park – for access to the data and for advice on its interpretation.

Notes

[1] M.J. Hickman and B. Walter, *Discrimination and the Irish Community in Britain*, Commission for Racial Equality, p.140.

[2] Ibid., pp.140 and 142.

[3] J. Gray, A. McPherson and D. Raffe, *Reconstructions of Secondary Education* (London, 1983).

[4] T.A. Fitzpatrick, *Catholic Education in South-West Scotland before 1972* (Aberdeen, 1986); J.H. Treble, 'The Development of Roman Catholic Education in Scotland, 1878–1978', *Innes Review*, 31, pp.111–39.

[5] Education Commission (Scotland), *Second Report by Her Majesty's Commissioners*, PP XXV (London, 1867).

[6] G. Payne and G. Ford, 'Religion, Class and Educational Effects', *Scottish Educational Studies*, 9, pp.83–9.

[7] A. McPherson and J.D. Willms, 'Certification, Class Conflict, Religion and Community: A Socio-historical Explanation of the Effectiveness of Contemporary Schools', in A.C. Kerkhoff (ed.), *Research in Sociology of Education and Socialisation*, 6 (Greenwich, CT, 1986), pp. 227–302.

[8] T. Gallagher, *Glasgow, The Uneasy Peace: Religious Tension in Modern Scotland* (Manchester, 1987); D. McCrone, *Understanding Scotland* (London, 1992); see also chapter by S. Bruce in this book.

[9] The Scottish Education Department intermittently publishes statistics on Catholic education, the most recent being in *Summary Results of the 1994 School Census*, Statistical Bulletin Edn/B1/1995/17, Table 1, Edinburgh.

[10] McPherson and Willms, 'Certification, Class Conflict, Religion and Community'; L. Paterson, 'Trends in Attainment in Scottish Secondary Schools', in S.W. Raudenbush and J.D. Willms (eds.), *Schools, Classrooms, and Pupils* (New York, 1991), pp.85–100; J.D. Willms, 'Pride or Prejudice? Opportunity Structure and the Effects of Catholic Schools in Scotland', *International Perspectives on Education and Society*, 2, 1992, pp.189–213.

[11] A.S. Bryk, V.E. Lee and P.B. Holland, *Catholic Schools and the Common Good* (Cambridge, Mass., 1993); J.S. Coleman, 'Social Capital in the Creation of Human Capital', *American Journal of Sociology*, 94, 1988, S95–S120; J.C. Conroy (ed.), *Catholic Education: Inside Out, Outside In* (Dublin, 1999); T. Hoffer, A.M. Greeley and J.S. Coleman, 'Achievement Growth in Public and Catholic Schools', *Sociology of Education*, 58, 1985, pp.74–97; T.H. McLaughlin, J. O'Keefe and B. O'Keefe (eds.), *The Contemporary Catholic School: Context, Identity and Diversity* (London, 1996).

[12] This survey has been running in some form since the late 1970s, and is based on an approximately 10 per cent sample of school leavers from Scottish public and independent schools. The questionnaire was sent by post to the respondents' home addresses; the response rates were 80 per cent in 1980 and 66 per cent in 1994. To allow for any unrepresentativeness of the samples, the data are weighted so that the distribution of attainment in the samples matches that reported nationally for Scottish school leavers as a whole. Further details can be found in P. Lynn, *The 1994 Leavers* (Edinburgh, 1996), and Gray et al., *Reconstructions of Secondary Education* (London, 1983).

[13] In technical terms, differences are inferred to be real if they are statistically significant at the 5 per cent level or lower. The evidence is assessed by multi-level logistic regression, since all the criterion variables are dichotomous – for example, passing or not passing

three or more Highers; see M. Aitkin, D. Anderson, B. Francis and J. Hinde, *Statistical Modelling in Glim* (Oxford, 1989). It is necessary to do this in a multi-level framework because the leavers were grouped into schools; see H. Goldstein, *Multilevel Statistical Models* (London, 1995, 2nd edn). Multi-level regression has been the main way in which the effectiveness of Catholic schools has been assessed by other researchers in the last decade; see, for example, Paterson, 'Trends in Attainment in Scottish Secondary Schools'; Willms, 'Pride or Prejudice?'.

[14] Non-manual is classes I, II and III non-manual in the Registrar-General's scheme; manual is classes III manual, IV and V.

[15] Similar results were obtained from an analysis of the proportion entering jobs among people who had no qualifications.

[16] Willms, 'Pride or prejudice?'.

[17] The sample was chosen using random selection from the Postcode Address File, stratified by political and demographic data at the level of constituency. The main questionnaire was administered by face-to-face interviews in respondents' homes. The survey was conducted by SCPR, funded by the UK Economic and Social Research Council and directed by the Centre for Research on Elections and Social Trends. The response rate was 62 per cent. The data are weighted to take account of the sampling mechanism. Further information on the survey can be found at the CREST website: http://www.strath.ac.uk/Other/CREST.

[18] Further details of the analysis are reported in L. Paterson, 'The Social Status of Catholics in Scotland', submitted for publication and available from the author. The class scheme used in this part of the chapter is that devised by Goldthorpe; see G. Marshall, D. Rose, H. Newby and C. Vogler, *Social Class in Modern Britain* (London, 1988).

[19] Information on the Referendum Survey can also be found on the web at http://www.strath.ac.uk/Other/CREST.

[20] This used the British Election Survey, which ran in parallel with the Scottish Election Survey.

[21] In a logistic regression of non-manual proportion on cohort, qualification and religion, the qualification variable in fact explained most of the cohort change in the statistical association of religion and occupational status; see Paterson, 'The Social Status of Catholics in Scotland'.

[22] This argument is developed further in L. Paterson, 'Catholic Education and Scottish Democracy', *Journal of Education and Christian Belief*, 4, 2000.

[23] See, for example, Conroy (ed.), *Catholic Education: Inside Out, Outside In*.

13. CATHOLIC DISTINCTIVENESS: A NEED TO BE DIFFERENT?

Joseph M. Bradley

> Jesus said: I came to set the earth on fire, and how I wish it were already kindled. Do you suppose that I came to bring peace to the world? No, not peace, but division. From now on a family of five will be divided, three against two and two against three. Fathers will be against their sons, and sons against their fathers; mothers will be against their daughters, and daughters against their mothers; mothers in law will be against their daughters in law, and daughters in law against their mothers in law (Luke 12:49–53)

Introduction

According to Luke's Gospel, although Christ's intention was to show humanity how to live as one, at peace and with love, He was also aware that His message would cause a great deal of division. His peace was not to be based on ideas invented by man which for Christians invite the possibility of falsity and superficiality. God's plan for mankind was to be fulfilled through the work of Christ. Christ recognised that His work and message would be accepted or rejected by people. In rejection was to be found the seeds of conflict. Christ came to engage people to make a choice between right and wrong, a choice that as well as bringing people together would invariably also create distinctions between them and others. For Christians, such conflict manifests itself in the form of materialistic economic ideologies, political doctrines that dehumanise, social policies that deprive and ignore, and the many cultural attitudes and beliefs that focus on the self rather than on concern and love for the other.

For most supporters of Catholic schools, the idea of taking sides, of opting for a body of beliefs contrary to these manifestations and of promoting the teachings of Christ through attitude and action, is to be found at the heart of the rationale for their continued existence. In Scotland, Catholic schools have long been a subject of controversy. Although the vast majority of people within the practising Catholic community support these schools,[1] their existence also causes wider divisions. In his 1999 Edinburgh Festival lecture, James MacMillan referred to Catholic schools as being under constant threat by many elements in Scottish society.

Much, if not most, of the argument concerning Catholic schools has long been conducted within a cultural, political, social and ethnic discourse. Although Christianity generally and Catholicism specifically can be considered in these contexts, most Catholic discourse supporting the existence and retention of these schools is in the form of a spiritual thesis. James MacMillan's lecture explicitly implied a range of positive attributes possessed by Catholic schools, a view at odds with many of the opinions expressed by their antagonists. Indeed, MacMillan stated that Catholic experiences and views should be made available for the greater good, beyond even the Catholic constituency.

This work will review the essence of the differing accounts of Catholic schools in Scotland. The first section focuses on some of the arguments used against the schools, both in an historical and in a contemporary sense. The second part of this essay reflects on the Catholic perspective and the spiritual testimony that for Catholics is at the heart of the issue. Despite its seemingly minority status, this view endeavours to invoke the life and teachings of Christ in the school's rationale as well as in the social, cultural, economic and political life of the individual and community thereafter.

The Constant Threat: Perceptions of Catholic Education

The Education Act (Scotland) of 1918 was passed while the country was preoccupied with the outcome of the First World War, and this may have prevented an immediate backlash occurring. It is also relevant that the Act was introduced by Robert Munro of the then declining Liberal Party and passed into law by a coalition government. This meant that although Labour supported the Act, and thus increased its support among Catholics, militant Protestants did not see the Party as being oversupportive of the Catholic community.

Nonetheless, with Catholics frequently becoming scapegoats for the harsh social and economic times occurring in Scotland, for one commentator, 'the schools question breathed life into the No Popery movement to an alarming degree in the two subsequent decades'.[2] The schools question was to become symptomatic of the hostility towards Irish Catholics. In 1935, the *Glasgow Herald* reported a Church of Scotland minister as saying:

> The indignant opposition to the provision of Section 18 of the Education (Scotland) Act, 1918, is that public money is being expanded in educating an increasing section of the population, in the main Free Staters or their offspring, in a faith and a loyalty hostile to the tradition and religion accepted by the vast majority of the Scottish nation . . . Why should we feed, clothe and educate these people who everywhere plot and plan for the downfall of Great Britain?[3]

Tom Gallagher believes that this minister 'was only expressing what a large number of ministers and their congregations elsewhere shared, if in a somewhat modified form'.[4] Certainly, the almost non-existent hostility towards the Episcopalian Church (a comparatively small Church) whose voluntary schools were also transferred under the 1918 Act seems to bear out the argument that it was Catholics who remained the target.

One of the most prominent manifestations of general anti-Catholicism but primarily of the feelings against Catholic schools was to be found in Alexander Ratcliffe's 'Scottish Protestant League' of the 1920s and 1930s. The popular

Ratcliffe and his thousands of supporters saw Catholic schools as sectarian and his party gained much political success at the time.[5]

In Edinburgh, anti-Catholic demonstrations and violence reached a high point during the mid to late 1930s. Although not specifically concentrating on Catholic schooling, such ideas were inevitably included in John Cormack's Protestant Action programme, given that it was to call for the expulsion of Catholics from Scotland. The political successes gained by Cormack's party were based upon both working- and middle-class support.[6] In addition, the 1930s also witnessed some of the founders of the Scottish National Party expressing similar antagonism towards the 1918 Act.[7]

According to the Revd Andrew Douglas, a member of the Church of Scotland's General Assembly Education Committee in the 1970s:

> With the passage of time, and the graver concerns of World War Two, controversy died down. It became an almost annual habit for the highest court of the Kirk to agree that 'the time was not opportune' to raise the question of the separation of children of school age simply on the grounds of the religious preferences of their parents.

Nonetheless, Douglas had the matter reopened. He:

> proposed that the Kirk declare itself opposed to segregation in schools, and in favour of a national integrated system without respect to denominational interests. The motion, accepted by the Committee, was submitted to the General Assembly and approved.[8]

For Douglas, and presumably for many of his adherents, 'only educational factors ought to determine the nature of the provision to be made'.[9] Ironically nonetheless, Douglas argued that 'sectarianism in schools is not the cause of division. Religious bigotry has a longer history in Scotland than the situation created by the Education Act of 1918.'[10]

In contemporary Scotland, the Free Church of Scotland is against Catholic schooling, though its members also fear secularisation,[11] which has diminished Christian (i.e. Protestant) teaching in schools in general.[12] The Free Presbyterian Church can be seen to take a similar line, whilst the Orange Order in Scotland has opposition to Catholic schools at the top of its social and political agenda.

Like other protagonists engaged in the argument, the Orange Institution, which views Catholic schools as sectarian and divisive, favours 'integrated education'. A recent Grand Secretary of the Institution in Scotland believes that in the wake of such a religious amalgamation, the number of Catholics in Scotland would steadily fall.[13] The Orange Institution argues that it wishes to end Catholic schooling for the 'benefit' of Scottish society, so that young people would come together in toleration and togetherness. 'Rome on the Rates' and 'Religious Apartheid' have become amongst the most penetrating of cries for this community. Nevertheless, organisations like the Orange Institution in Scotland can do little but argue against Catholic schools. The views of the Scottish political parties are more significant for their future.

The contentiousness of the schools issue was brought to the fore in 1970 when the Glasgow City Labour Party passed a resolution that 'segregation of schools on religious grounds be terminated but that provision for religious instruction be continued in accordance with individual belief'.[14] In as much as there is continued support for Catholic schools, and despite official Labour policy to phase them out, Scottish Labour accepts the 1918 Act. Tony Worthington, until 1992 Labour Party spokesman on education, states that Labour's position is purely 'an acceptance of the facts as they stand'. Although not religious himself, and supporting the eventual amalgamation of schools, he believes that there is value in Catholic schooling to society.[15] Essentially, the views of Worthington reflect those officially stated by Scottish Labour, that:

> Religious education should include a genuine introduction to major religious beliefs and children will be encouraged to be aware of the influence of religion throughout the world.

Similarly, Labour says of denominational schools that it:

> understands and appreciates the circumstances which gave rise to the present situation of separate schools. We do not believe a further extension of separate schooling would be helpful in the Scottish context. Indeed, we hope that changing circumstances will eventually encourage gradual integration through the growth of understanding and mutual respect.[16]

The Scottish Conservative Party's position on Catholic schools in Scotland is similar to that of Labour and again their presence is accepted. It too stresses that it is more concerned with education generally, proposing nothing to upset the present state of affairs. So long as Catholics in Scotland want a Catholic dimension within the state system, the Conservatives are 'happy to accept them'.[17] In 1993, the Scottish Liberal Democratic Party conference voted against Catholic schooling, though it agreed that it could only end after the widest public debate.[18]

In the context of a traditional though probably diminishing antipathy towards the party on the part of many Catholics, the SNP has clearly trodden a cautious line with regard to policies and statements lest it alienate Catholics further. This has been especially so with regard to that community's strength in the vital west-central belt area. Compared to other parties in Scotland, during the 1990s SNP recognition of the need to maintain Catholic schools was the most conspicuous.

Catholic defensiveness is increased by the generally held beliefs of the Educational Institute of Scotland (EIS), the schoolteachers' main trade union. A motion passed at a conference in 1979 displaying opposition to Catholic schooling resulted in a large proportion of its Catholic membership threatening to leave the union. In a speech in 1985, the retiring president of the EIS also criticised Catholic schools, stating:

> The segregation of children only five years old on religious grounds is wrong, grossly so . . . In this matter the law is not merely an ass but an assassin . . . the tribalism of broken heads at Hampden and the broken hearts of couples whose plans to marry in good faith have been defeated by prejudice are unacceptable to the majority of the Scottish people.[19]

During June 1999, the EIS decided to carry out a review of the place of denominational schooling within the education system in Scotland. This occurred after an attempt to set up an immediate campaign through the new Scottish parliament for the abolition of denominational schools was narrowly defeated (164 votes to 153) and the motion amended. The EIS resolved to 'formulate a policy on campaigning for denominational schools' abolition – subject to the consent of churches and parents'.[20]

The media are opinion-formers but they also reflect attitudes and identities. Throughout the 1990s the (Glasgow) Herald's letters column reflected the heated nature of the schools debate with correspondence on a regular basis. The letters originate from people from a wide range of social and political backgrounds in Scottish society. Many repeat those arguments of the past that remonstrated against Catholic schools. These arguments are evidence of how the schools issue is connected to many matters in contemporary society, which may otherwise seem unrelated.

> Why should there be such antagonism to our inter-denominational system of education having as its aim integration rather than separation, combined with a purposeful unification of all factions? In perpetuating the ghastly system of apartheid it is obvious what is feared most by the Roman Catholic hierarchy is losing the tenacious grip that is invaluable for indoctrination during the child's tender years. Such a loss would spell a major blow to Roman Catholicism.[21]

> I do believe that the religious prejudice which still exists in some quarters, and in many ways is peculiar to the west of Scotland, will disappear altogether within a generation if separate schools are removed from our educational system.[22]

> Religion should be left to parents and the Church . . . it is certainly not the business of teachers.[23]

> Why can't those who advocate the retention of the dual education system admit that they are both bigoted and hypocritical? They want to maintain their segregationist policies while living under a façade of Christianity. The only contribution the system makes to the Scottish nation, and to the west of Scotland in particular, is to provide us with a breeding ground of superstition and mistrust. The sooner the children come together, the sooner they will stop growing up to perpetuate their parents' hatred.[24]

> The answer is simple. The Roman Catholic Church should be given two options: their schools remain within the state system and appointments are made by the education authority; or Roman Catholic schools opt out of the system and are funded by the Church . . . The situation as it stands is unacceptable.[25]

163

> . . . Scotland's very own 'apartheid' – separate schools with children divided by religion . . . In an increasingly secular society, why should religion, any form of religion, be taught in state schools? Religion is divisive.[26]

> . . . referring to the last Old Firm match at Ibrox, and the continuation of segregated schools . . . If we are serious about eradicating the hatred which is vented in the name of sport, let's not try to ease our conscience by arresting a few overpaid footballers. The only solution is for a full integration of our schools.[27]

Perhaps one of the greatest pressures exerted upon the Catholic school identity originates within the popular press in Scotland. Again, popular Scottish media reporting on the subject reflects many of the elements used in previous decades. Such reporting in Scotland's most popular regular, the *Daily Record*, periodically proclaims, 'Barred: kids caught in the storm over Catholic schools', 'We are united' (a headline repeated on occasion), and 'It's pupil power: walkout kids in schools protest'. One article stated:

> They swim together . . . they play football together . . . and last night David became old enough to join his pal in the Beavers. But there is an Act of Parliament that says Douglas, six, and five-year-old David could be kept apart during the day – because one is a Protestant and the other is a Catholic.[28]

In 1998, the *Daily Record*, promoted as 'the Voice of Scotland', described two schools in Lanarkshire as 'side by side, but the children who play together outside are kept apart when they go through the gates'.[29] The terminology and arguments used by antagonists of Catholic schools – letter writers, some Churches, newspapers and TV presenters, as well as many members of the wider public – have been thematically similar over the period of time since these schools were accepted into the state system.

James MacMillan referred to *The Herald* newspaper and some of its feature writers as providing a dimension of the hostility towards Catholic schools. Other Catholics share this perception.[30] During June 1999, a *Sunday Herald* editorial stated:

> . . . some might conclude that it is time we moved on towards ending separate state-funded education based on religious selection . . . We have to ask if we want our children to be educated to be 'separate' and to grow up feeling alienated from their neighbours in twenty-first-century Scotland.[31]

The Herald's use of 'it is time we moved on', 'separate' and 'feeling alienated' reflected some of the terminology used in many of the letters and comments from other groups and individuals. An implication of *The Herald's* comment is that Scotland is backward in relation to this matter, conjuring images of a time when, some writers believe, Catholic Irish immigrants lived in self-imposed religious and ethnic ghettos. Catholics like MacMillan oppose this view, believing that schools can be socially and morally beneficial to the rest of Scottish society.

Catholic Differentiation

Lost amidst the cultural and political arguments are the religious dimensions of the rationale for Catholic schools. Most of these rest on ideals based on spiritual perceptions of the purpose of human existence. This in itself is interesting, especially in a largely secular society where Christianity has diminished in social, cultural and political relevance in recent decades.

In his 1999 Edinburgh lecture, James MacMillan asserted his belief that Catholics in Scotland have something to offer the rest of Scottish society. Where the faith is practised with humility, honesty and holiness, role models and examples are created for others. He implied that the ultimate role model is Christ, whom Catholics and other Christians aim to follow. For MacMillan and others like him, the Catholic school is an essential social avenue to shaping the kind of people he views as offering stability in an unstable and often morally ambivalent society. This setting also helps provide an alternative set of ideas in the face of challenges from an accelerating secular and materialistic age.

In a letter to a broadsheet newspaper in late 1999, a minister of the United Free Church of Scotland asserted that this alternative set of beliefs, considered to be 'in step with Jesus Christ', as opposed to the ways and beliefs of modern Scotland, was the most fertile set of ideas to draw upon. The minister concluded:

> It is certainly the case that Jesus was often out of step with the political correctness of his own day. I suppose he was something of a revolutionary. He insisted that God's will always took precedence over man's will. Never a popular notion when God's will doesn't coincide with our own. Which is why he warned that in this world his disciples would face tribulation, i.e. they would be under pressure from the society in which they lived. Society and Christians have frequently been at odds.[32]

Another commentator opined that in contrast to an education system that exists merely to serve society by equipping it with an appropriately trained workforce oriented to the values and practices of contemporary Western capitalist cultures, Catholic education has a different rationale, one rooted in a philosophy of human nature and society.[33] In these views, Catholic schools become a positive force in society – an idea fundamentally different from those promoted by people hostile to the schools' existence.

Many faiths believe that everyday living cannot be divorced from religion. In this context, for practising and conscientious Catholics, faith has a role in every thought and deed governing human life. It provides and sustains the motivation for what is good while helping to provide a counter to that viewed negatively. Here we can also find the rationale for Catholics seeing faith as something that cannot be compartmentalised. It is intrinsic in a way which conflicts with the idea that faith can be taught in school at a particular time of day. Faith is intended to be a resource used on a regular if not constant basis. It is a referral for all thought and action. It goes beyond overt and simple religious observance. For Catholics who see their faith in this way, a secular society and a secular school system have little to offer. The Catholic vision is one characterised by an ennobling conception of the human condition, a conception which recognises that humans are created in the image and likeness of God. This philosophy is intended to determine Catholic ideas concerning matters economic, political, social and cultural. For Catholics, such a philosophy is best shaped by reference to Christ and a Christian lifestyle.

Nonetheless, the 'real world', so called in popular parlance, often means that such ideals hold little apparent influence. Therefore, does this mean that Catholic schools are failing and are to be judged redundant via the criteria set by Catholics themselves?

Part of the assessment of a Catholic school arises from a reflection of how its current and former members live up to these ideals. It would not surprise anyone that Catholics continually compromise these ideals. In religious terms, they sin. In relation to this sinfulness, sensational stories during the 1980s and 1990s about wrong-doing, even among some high-ranking members of the Church, invariably reflect negatively on the failures of Catholics to live up to their professed ideals. Assuming that many, if not most, sinful Catholics attended Catholic schools, this might also be used to argue that the schools are failing even in relation to their own aims. They are, indeed, redundant?

Although criticism might be warranted, such an approach can also miss the essential focus for Catholics. For commentators like MacMillan, arguments which negate the social and spiritual value of Catholic education in Scotland also embody a mindset of a society that is failing to deliberate its own misdemeanours and which simultaneously lacks spiritual appreciation or direction. Indeed, in an increasingly secular society, it might be argued that the context for such reflection is shrinking.

Robbery, murder, sexual abuse and exploitation, lies, cheating and selfishness are part of the make-up of the Catholic faith community as well as other religious or non-religious sections of the population. From a Catholic perspective, these are sins and sin demeans all individuals and societies. Most conscientious Catholics strive by their daily thoughts and actions to distance themselves from sin, to continually reorient their personal lives away from sinfulness. However, when reported in the popular press, it seems to many Catholics that distinct from a genuine shame visited upon their community by these deeds, the society that by its own actions contributes to the creation of sin seems to gloat over Catholic sinfulness. For some Catholics this constitutes a type of recycled bigotry and sectarianism. This process also means that society absolves itself of its own contribution to and responsibility for those sins. Catholic sin is highlighted in such a way as to demean aspects of the faith beyond the actual instance of sin. Thus, when standards which Catholics set themselves, via their interpretation of the teachings of Christ, are transgressed, this can serve the satisfaction and righteousness of parts of a society which may have a contrasting notion of what constitutes sin and the damage it does to individuals and communities. Indeed, sin as understood by Catholics, and many Christians generally, has little meaning for secularists, human law and order constituting a basis of any understanding of wrongfulness. It might be argued that since the 1960s, in many Western societies there has at least been a blurring of the lines between dominant or common notions and Christian perceptions of right and wrong.

For some Catholics, the highlighting of Catholic misdemeanours in social and moral isolation is akin to people condemning teenage promiscuity, street violence and rampant materialism while accepting the constant promotion of these same practices and attitudes through the mass media. For many Christians, such images have become culturally dominating influences as the media and computer technology gain an all-pervading influence in modern life, acquiring the status of both surrogate teacher and moral arbiter. In other words, as integral parts of human society, like everyone else Catholics are also influenced by these human experiences. They are issues affecting society *per se* rather than Catholics alone. In this context, despite their failings, Catholics believe that Catholic schools are required even more now than at any time during the twentieth century.

An aspect of the belief in the need for Catholic schools is a perception that sin has become highly acceptable or even popularised in the wider society. This is evidenced by the contemporary practice of admitting to what many Christians would perceive as sin on popular chat shows or in magazines and sensationalised tabloid articles. This usually bears no relevance to a consciousness of Christian sin, sorrow and subsequent forgiveness, and appears to be seen as right or wrong in a way privatised and solely interpreted via a secular mindset. Indeed, so distant are these instances from ideas of Christian sinfulness that they are often characterised more by humour, voyeurism and revenge. In this way, they may even become accepted and inadvertently promoted. Sin and the idea of human betterment become lost or at least clouded in such experiences, and introspection, if it takes place at all, acquires a framework absent of any Christian moral value.

If robbery, murder, sexual abuse and exploitation, lies, cheating and selfishness are recognised as being aspects of the Catholic community, Catholics reason that they should also be recognised as part of the 'sinfulness' of the general community. Religious and non-religious peoples share these wrongs. Catholics might argue that such sinfulness is not a consequence of Catholic schooling. Likewise, it is not the product of non-denominational schooling. It is the consequence of a range of internal and external experiences gained through living in a particular society at a particular time amidst particular circumstances.

A more accurate assessment of Catholic schools might emerge by also looking at other sections of society, including other schools, and assessing them on the same Catholic/Christian criteria. After all, for Catholics and many other Christians, these are the only criteria that shape the human relationship with God and are therefore primary over all other considerations. Such an assessment may in fact be impossible, and would certainly be highly subjective. Nevertheless, this approach does help us to understand how Catholics view Catholic schools. It reflects how their supporters determine to engender and formulate an ethical and moral mindset as well as a behavioural and attitudinal framework that can often conflict with other more dominant aspects and features of society. For Christians, this is often perceived as the way of Christ against the way of man.

So, do Catholics believe that they are uniquely good and everyone else is wrong or sinful? Where do Catholic schools fit into conceptions of sin? In what ways do Catholic schools make a difference? What has this to do with education?

In answer to these questions, Catholic educationalists believe that human conduct and endeavour emerge as part of the rationale for Catholic schooling in Scotland as elsewhere. In Scotland, an intention of Catholic schooling is to assist in the creation of a different version of what the human experience should be in a way that is integrative in spite of the negativity perceived beyond the faith. It aims to assist in the formation of individuals and a community set apart by its actions, beliefs and attitudes. In other words, although fully integrated, distinctiveness becomes a goal, desirable in relation to the human social experience as determined by little or no reflection on the Gospels.

In a practical sense, if it is found that a majority in society support abortion, it should also be found that Catholics are against it; if a majority in society practise or believe in pre-marital or extra-marital sex, then Catholics should oppose this; if a majority in society are materialistic, then Catholics should confront this; if a majority in society appear prepared to lie and deceive in their daily lives, then Catholics should face up to this; if a majority in society believe in the self rather than the common good, then Catholics should lead lives which are anathema to this way of thinking. If a majority in society appear to have no regard for Christ, nor experience any reference to Christ in their lives, then Catholics should demonstrate difference. With this they are compelled by their faith to show that there is an alternative set of beliefs and lifestyles. For many Catholics, this alternative is assisted in its formation by the work of the Catholic family, Catholic parish and Catholic school. Such an alternative may also be viewed as striving to create difference and distinctiveness, to shape individuals and society in a fundamentally different way from that governed by other cultural, social and economic forces.

For Christians, negative human experiences are inevitable in a world 'divided' between good and evil. Christ's intention is to convert people from being inhuman to being more human and holy. For Christians, sin represents a life less than human, a life less likely to be full. Becoming Christ-like is thus interpreted as the true path in life. For many Catholics in Scotland, a Catholic school can make a significant contribution to the formation of a follower of Christ.

For Catholics, if people are infused with the teachings of Christ, society is morally improved. Matthew says in 16:23 that the ways of man are not the ways of Christ. The implication here is that although problems are produced in Catholic schools as in any school, these problems are the result of people turning their backs on the ways of Christ. The best way to change society is not by advancing materially, or simply by looking at the world in a politically right- or left-wing fashion, although these will also be important. The principal way for Catholics and for Christians is to be Christ-like in thought and deed. Catholics believe this helps them formulate a plan for life which is advanced and promoted in the setting of a Catholic school. The Christian calling is not an easy one. For Timothy, in the face of the temptations around us we cannot sit still: 'You must aim to be saintly and religious' (1 Timothy 6:11).[34]

Catholic education, which contributes to the building of a faith community, strives to offer a different vision of life's purpose from that manifest in a secular and non-Christian society. The intention is to build a community that, although distinctive, also integrates through example and love while rejecting ways that are not Christ's. Paul explains this in his letter to the Ephesians (4:13–16):

> And so we shall all come together to that oneness in our faith and in our knowledge of the Son of God; we shall become mature people, reaching to the very height of Christ's full stature. Then we shall no longer be children, carried by the waves and blown about by every shifting wind of the teaching of deceitful men, who lead others into error by the tricks they invent. Instead, by speaking the truth in a spirit of love, we must grow up in every way in Christ . . . the whole body grows and builds itself up through love.

The Catholic educational idea is that Christ's community is built up as the journey of life proceeds. This idea provokes the image of a 'pilgrim people' which is continually growing and developing. In this thinking can also be discerned the Catholic argument that the three important institutional dimensions to this growth and development are expressed in the family, in the parish and in the Catholic school.

A perception of the dehumanising and depersonalising aspects of contemporary life is taken to task by reference to Christ and his teachings. In their broadest sense, Christ's teachings are viewed as anti-racist, anti-poverty, anti-capitalist, anti-discriminatory, anti-bigotry, anti-abortion and anti-war, pro-people, pro-family, pro-tolerance and pro-equality. Also, in a way which strikes at misconceptions about freedom and of what it consists, pro-freedom is also at the heart of Christ's teachings. True freedom for Christians is discovered through the enlightening path of Christ. Many of these themes lie at the core of the Catholic rationale for Catholic schools.

> So Jesus said to those who believed in him, 'If you obey my teaching, you are really my disciples; you will know the truth and the truth will set you free . . . everyone who sins is a slave of sin . . . If the Son sets you free then you will be really free.' (John 8:31–36)

Such themes also reflect why many Catholics in Scotland believe it important that certain subjects in school are taught by conscientious Catholics. Where subjects like modern studies can continually engage not only politics, sociology and history but morality too, a Catholic and Christian dimension is viewed as important to the content, style and method of teaching. If a teacher in a Catholic school states that cosmology, Darwinism or science has proved the improbability of the existence of God, then the Catholic school comes into conflict with the teachings and examples of both the home and the parish. The contribution teachers can make to a young person's life is emphasised by a Department of Education leaflet of the 1990s. Advertising the general teaching profession, the document stated:

> You can't overestimate a teacher's contribution to a child's development. School helps to shape future adults. Not simply in terms of careers but in less obvious ways too. Attitudes, outlook and self-confidence, for example, are all affected by a teacher's skills.

Catholic educationalists believe it is important to have Catholics guiding a school in a direction commensurate with the values that link with Christ's teachings. They are also of the opinion that the atmosphere and ethos of a school is governed and shaped by those same teachings. This is viewed as essential to the Catholic school as a distinctive setting. Indeed, although being a community that integrates with the rest of society, it is the intention of thinking Catholics, including the leaders of the Church, to be distinct, a people set apart. This is not intended to be a permanent state but one in which society becomes more Christ-like, thus bringing about a more Christian society and, ultimately, a people at one. In other words, for Catholics the Catholic school is but one step in the creation of the Kingdom of God. How large the step will be depends on the individuals who comprise a particular school.

Although formal religious observance is viewed as part of the life of the Catholic community, it is an important aspect of the faith formation of pupils and an important adjunct to religious education; as with every school, the formal educational dimension of Catholic schools is always to the fore. The school's role remains specifically 'educational'. Nevertheless, Christian and Catholic examples, role models, precepts and ideas are expected to be integral aspects of the Catholic school. The idea is propounded that it is better to be a disciple of Christ than to have all the knowledge, power, wealth, fame and success that man creates. If these are not used in the interests of building God's Kingdom, then it becomes like the work described by John when discussing Christ as the 'Bread of Life', as well as Matthew in reference to wrong-doing:

> Do not work for food that goes bad; instead, work for the food that lasts
> for eternal life. (John, 6:27)

> 'Satan! You are an obstacle in my way, because these thoughts of yours
> don't come from God, but from man.' (Matthew, 16:23)

Mark's gospel (16:15) states; 'Go out to the whole world: proclaim the Good News to all creation.' The 'Good News' leads to faith, and for Catholics, as well as those of other religions, faith needs nurturing. Although parents are expected to be the first teachers in all instances, especially in matters of faith, Catholics also rely on the support and co-operation of the school and the parish environments. The school undertakes the task of teaching and in a religious sense makes all aware of the nature of their faith. The integration of faith and the values of daily living are expected to symbolise the idea of a community at one.

In addition, and in a less insular fashion than in the past, Catholic schools also teach an appreciation of other world faiths through an appropriate knowledge of their principal beliefs, spiritual values and traditions. Supporters of Catholic schools believe that Catholic religious education has the capacity to help pupils to develop not only an understanding of their own faith but an understanding of and respect for those who adhere to other Christian traditions and other world religions as well as those of a secular identity. Likewise, a Catholic school is expected to be sensitive to and help to promulgate appeals for peace, justice, freedom, progress for all peoples and assistance for countries in need.

In a Catholic school, pupils ought to be encountering an environment illuminated by the light of Christ. The spirit of the Gospel should be evident in a Christian way of thought as well as the life that permeates all facets of the educational climate. Daily witness is important to those Catholics conscious of where their children learn and who teaches them. If this is not present, there is little which distinguishes the school as being Catholic apart from the routine, ceremonial and ritual. For conscientious Catholics, Catholic schools have a significant role in a secular society. Catholic schools are intended to assist in the development of young people with attitudes, opinions and lifestyles that challenge those which often seem to dominate throughout much of society. This does not equate with exclusion or isolation, but on the whole is seen as a contributory influence among many in society and, for Catholics and Christians generally, an influence for the better. As with other Christian denominations, this is considered a belief born of faith and the need to bear witness to that faith.

The idea of a Christian lifestyle means that morals are crucial to the formation of people. Religious education necessarily entails the imparting of a basic knowledge as well as the skills to make a reasonable moral decision and to act on it. In a Catholic school, moral education is not solely the remit of formal religious educators, but the concept of a moral community or of being a moral person is transmitted through example and precept and through the relationships which exist within the whole school. Although many Catholics may fail to live up to their Church's teachings, lifestyles are viewed as more indecisive, varied and equivocal in the greater society, and are therefore viewed as a greater danger to the moral self. For Catholics, there are invariably fewer expectations as well as practices with regard to the examples and teachings of Christ in the wider society. If Christianity is to be a determining factor in life choices, supporters of Catholic schools say it must therefore be integrated into everyday life, in terms of community and lifestyle. Indeed, Catholic educationalists argue that despite their schools' failings, this helps Catholics make a positive contribution to Scottish society.

In 1999, a lecturer at St Andrews University argued that by copying a model taken from the USA, children in Scottish schools could engage in 'marriage lessons' to equip partners 'with well-developed relationship skills'.[35] Although this argument was opposed by some teaching unions and politicians, the idea that schooling in Scotland should be partly about future wider life experiences rather than solely concerned with formal education links with the rationale for Catholic schools. Formal education is recognised as important, but a universal education grounded in Gospel values is viewed as having the capacity to equip children to deal better with many of their life experiences.

Although a Catholic school is in many ways like any other school, its distinguishing feature is expected to be the inspiration and strength drawn from the Gospels. God is found in the everyday experiences of human relationships and work. Therefore, for supporting Catholics, Catholic schools are important aspects of the Christian journey. They are seen as essential in equipping children and young people with the capacity to cope with the vicissitudes of life. From a Catholic perspective, these cannot be adequately dealt with without faith formation. Ultimately, Catholics will and do choose their 'lifestyle'. Where the example of Christ is missing, is viewed as an historical or educational nicety or is seen as an intrusion in the formation of personality and character, many practising Catholics (and, indeed, many practising Christians) perceive life itself as losing meaning and value.

Like other members of the wider population, many Catholics clearly value formal education, recognising its general advantages, its requirement for rewarding employments and its capacity for creating a better society. However, supporters of Catholic schools believe that a Christian lifestyle and the nature of a person and the community have a fundamentally more significant role to play in creating a better society than that which is based purely on educational attainment. Theoretically, a Catholic school teaches that God sees everyone equally, as we should all see each other. If it does not matter to God whether we are black, brown or white, fat, thin or tall, blind or deaf, He is also not interested in how many school passes, degrees or postgraduate qualifications we have. Indeed, if this were not the case, such restrictions would diminish a God who is concerned about how we use what we have, rather than what we have. Luke's Gospel supports the view that a list of worldly virtues, though important in context, does not provide guidance for a spiritual life which is the essential requirement above and beyond that which man finds important. Luke's Gospel states that 'Man cannot live on bread alone' (4:4). In other words, lifestyle and faith are crucial. Christ's apostle Paul reaffirmed his belief in his letter to the Corinthians:

> I may be able to speak the languages of men and even of angels, but if I have no love, my speech is no more than a noisy gong or a clanging bell. I may have the gift of inspired preaching; I may have all knowledge and understand all secrets; I may have all the faith needed to move mountains – but if I have no love, I am nothing. (1:13)

This is similar to that explained in Paul's first letter to the Corinthians (15:1–4), in which he stresses that 'believing anything else will not lead to anything'.

For those who advocate Catholic schools and a Catholic/Christian lifestyle, the way to live is to go beyond oneself, to consider the other as much as if not more than the self, to be less selfish and more giving, 'to love your neighbour as you love yourself' (Matthew 22:39). A lay commentator has given voice to this line of thinking: 'Our neighbour is more than our immediate circle. Who is my neighbour? My neighbour is all mankind.' This author believes this to be one of the most revolutionary, radical, subversive sentiments in the entire history of mankind. 'It means no stereotyping, no categorisation of Jew and Gentile, Irish and English, Catholic and Protestant, man and woman, old age and youth.'[36] In these sentiments also lie moral lessons against secular values. In the context of accepting the continued presence of human frailties and imperfections, for Catholic educationalists this also means that ideas of equality, toleration, understanding and generosity of spirit are at the heart of Catholic education.

Catholic educationalists, as well as non-Catholics, believe that concepts of truth and goodness have become indelibly vague throughout modern societies, whilst young people (as well as their seniors) are faced with role models and patterns of living which are human-created opposites to the teachings of the Gospels. Gospel values are largely ignored and alternatives, which stress 'fashionable' and 'popular', dominate. All this is not to say that human happiness has been enhanced. Many social commentators stress that the contrary is the case. Some argue that human relationships are in flux. The evidence for this might be seen in increasing drug and alcohol abuse, society's preoccupation with sexual matters, and the frequency of breakdown in family relationships, as well as rampant capitalism with all its concomitant hedonistic attitudes. Some Catholic writers say that society is burdened, crippled and caged by what is frequently considered fashionable and popular.[37] For such advocates, Christianity has the potential to give more freedom than is often perceived.

Nonetheless, the ideal remains. Hope is an aspect of faith and this also exists in abundance amid the negativity. Like the Church itself, as well as the people who consciously comprise it, for adhering Catholics, a Catholic school aims to retain its mission to show the real face of Christ. Therefore, it aims to be different from the un-Christ-like nature of much of society. It aims to equip its pupils with the make-up and character that enables them to live lives fully human and fully holy.

The reality is that, like all of humanity, the Church and Catholics are touched by 'sin'. Nonetheless, amidst considered social confusion, moral ambiguity and 'inhuman' ideologies, for Catholic supporters of Catholic schools, their educational institutions remain conduits for the advancement of Christian lifestyles. Whether this is important or has any real meaning for the wider population seems certain to remain a matter of continuing debate.

Notes

[1] See J.M. Bradley in T.M. Devine (ed.), *St Mary's Hamilton: A Social History, 1846–1996* (Edinburgh, 1995), pp.95–121.

[2] T. Gallagher, *Glasgow, The Uneasy Peace: Religious Tension in Modern Scotland* (Manchester, 1987), p.104.

[3] *Glasgow Herald*, 8 May 1935.

[4] Gallagher, *Uneasy Peace*, pp.138–9.

[5] For Ratcliffe, see ibid., chapter 4.

[6] For Cormack, see T. Gallagher, *Edinburgh Divided* (Edinburgh, 1987).

[7] R.J. Finley, 'Nationalism, Race, Religion and the Irish Question in Inter-War Scotland', *Innes Review*, 42, no.1, 1991, pp.46–67.

[8] A.M. Douglas, *Church and School in Scotland* (Edinburgh, 1985), pp.94–5.

[9] Ibid., p.95.

[10] Ibid., pp.95–7.

[11] In 1967, the Free Church's General Assembly stated that education cannot be utterly secular.

[12] *Free Church Monthly Record*, Editorial, March 1986.

[13] Interview with David Bryce, 15 January 1990.

[14] *Glasgow Herald*, 10 March 1970.

[15] Interview with Tony Worthington while Labour Party spokesperson on education in Scotland, 18 June 1991.

[16] Quoted from a Scottish Labour Party document of the early 1990s.

[17] Interview with Craig Stevenson of Conservative Party headquarters, Edinburgh, 14 June 1991.

[18] *The Herald*, 27 March 1993.

[19] *Times Higher Education Supplement for Scotland*, 14 June 1985.

[20] *The Herald*, 12 June 1999.

[21] Ibid., 10 May 1991.

[22] Ibid., 24 April 1991.

[23] Ibid., 14 December 1990.

[24] Ibid.

[25] Ibid., 5 November 1990.

[26] Ibid., 14 September 1990.

[27] Ibid., 18 November 1987.

[28] *Daily Record*, 17 May 1988, 18 May 1988 and 13 January 1989.

[29] Ibid., 13 February 1998.

[30] See Devine (ed.), *St Mary's Hamilton*, pp.83–121.

[31] *Sunday Herald*, 6 June 1999.

[32] *The Herald*, Saturday Essay, Professor J. Haldane, 6 November 1999.

[33] Revd David Cartledge, letter to *The Herald*, 12 November 1999.

[34] Catholic Church/Mass literature 1999, undated.

[35] *Sunday Herald*, Seven Days, 15 August 1999.

[36] Professor Joe Lee, University of Cork, quoted in Michael Commins, 'Don't let traditions get left behind', *Irish Post*, 29 August 1999.

[37] For examples, see articles of Professor Patrick Reilly during 1999 in Monday's editions of *The Herald* newspaper.

PART 4

Perspectives from the Presbyterian Tradition

14. THE IDENTITY OF A NATION

David Sinclair

Towards the end of the First World War the Church of Scotland embarked on a wide-ranging inquiry into the whole life of the Church, including what its members thought it could be doing better. The answers, for those who choose to read them now, can bring a kind of perverse satisfaction because they could, with some allowances for changes in the use of language, be quoted as the views from the pews of today. If the members of the Church in its heyday could speak in this way, perhaps we should not be too surprised that the same things are still being said. What might concern us, however, would be anything which suggested that not only is the membership of the Church saying the same critical things today as 80 years ago but its attitudes to those in other countries or other Churches has also not changed.

Part One

One of the reports prepared by the Special Commission in those days was entitled *The Life and Efficiency of the Church*. This was submitted to the General Assembly of 1919 and contained many recommendations. One of them, coming right at the end, was the proposal that the Assembly 'appoint a permanent Committee of Assembly to deal with matters affecting The Church and the National Life as they may from time to time arise'.

This was justified on the following grounds:

> The Church is facing a new era, and among the readjustments to which she is called is that of the creation of a strong Committee, to be her handmaid and her voice, when National Interests emerge which concern the Kingdom of Christ. In coming days, both at home and abroad, such emergences will be far more frequent than they ever have been in the past. In the decade lying immediately ahead they will of necessity be exceptionally numerous, as a consequence of the many questions in connection with home developments which are already rushing upon us, and in which moral and spiritual considerations are vital to a right settlement. Abroad too it is the same. Imperial relations to the backward races in our own Dominions, and to other Powers in backward areas, can only be rightly adjusted by a steadfast regard to the principles for which Christianity stands. On all such national developments the Church's voice ought to be heard, and regarding them therefore the General Assembly ought to be kept well and timeously informed.

The tasks of being handmaid and voice of the General Assembly and of keeping the General Assembly well and timeously informed have been in the job description of the Committee on Church and Nation ever since.

Two phrases from the report of 1919, however, can be seen to betray a mindset which was to blight the Committee's early years: 'the decade lying immediately ahead' and 'backward races in our own Dominions'. Here we find a belief about history and a view of humanity which were typical of much that was soon to come. The idea that the coming period was particularly important in the life of church and nation was, on one level, a reasonable assumption to make following a war of such upheaval and human catastrophe; it also brought with it, however, ideas of destiny and *kairos* which were to lead the Committee down one or two blind alleys before many years had passed. The same can be said of the reference to backward races; contained there are ideas, planted and cultivated by an imperial history, not only of societal and technological development but also of human possibility and natural place. This combination was to prove conducive to an acceptance of ideas which were soon to flow around Europe of racial superiority and inferiority, and of God-given national and 'racial' endowments which were to be kept pure and unsullied.

The period which followed was dominated in the Church of Scotland and particularly in its Church and Nation Committee by the Revd John White, whose influence has been well documented by Stewart J. Brown.[1] White's great project was Presbyterian unity. The schisms which historically have proved Presbyterianism's greatest temptation were to be put into the past with the union of the established Church of Scotland with the United Free Church. Part of this project was the reassertion of the identity of Scotland with Presbyterianism, a reaction in part to the Education Act of 1918. The identification of a common enemy has always been one of the greatest encouragements to unity and Presbyterian Scotland discovered just that during the 1920s. The target was Irish Catholic immigration.

Stewart Brown relates how the General Assembly of 1922 received two overtures from the west of Scotland bewailing the effect of the immigration of the Irish Catholics, people who were providing unfair competition for jobs as well as being drains on parish and philanthropic resources – twin accusations which have been placed at the doors of immigrant groups for centuries and which are not always absent even today. Combined with this economic attack, however, was an ideological one which was voiced at that 1922 Assembly and which reappeared in later reports from the Church and Nation Committee, such as this from 1925:

> While immigration continues unregulated and unrestricted, emigration affords no remedy for unemployment. The outlook is extremely grave for our Scottish nationality, and it is rendered no less serious by the immigration regulations of the United States of America for 1927. In that year the total number of immigrants will be 150,000. Of this number the British and North of Ireland quota will be 83,000, and that of the Irish Free State only 8000. At present the British quota is 34,000 and the Irish quota 28,567. There is no doubt that a very large population of the 83,000 assigned to Great Britain and the North of Ireland will be Scottish, and the United States will receive with open arms a virile and competent people, while Scotland must be content with the redundant population of Ireland, which the United States refuses to receive. The

178

outlook for Scottish nationality is such as to fill the minds of all thoughtful people with grave anxiety and alarm. The Committee expect to confer with the Secretary for Scotland at an early date on the racial problem in Scotland . . .

One year later the broader racial ideology which lay behind these reports became even more clear:

> If it were the case of an inferior race being supplanted by a superior race, however unpalatable it might be, we would be compelled to resign ourselves to it. But we are convinced that the very opposite is the case; that a law-abiding, thrifty and industrious race is being supplanted by immigrants whose presence tends to lower the social conditions, and to undermine that spirit of independence which has so long been a characteristic of the Scottish people, and we are of the opinion that, in justice to our own people, steps should be taken to prevent the situation becoming any worse.

At the time the *Glasgow Herald* published evidence that the 'problem' of immigration was being wildly exaggerated and grossly overestimated, but in a sense that is not important. What is relevant here is what people thought and said, the mindset which provided the framework for their analysis and their action. The Church of Scotland was setting itself up as the defender not only of Presbyterianism but of 'Scottishness', defined in terms of both nationality and race. It was espousing a hierarchical idea of race which bestows on 'superior' races rights and privileges which 'inferior' races have simply to thole, 'however unpalatable it might be'. This was 1926, not many years before such an ideology took hold in a way which not all Christians were able to recognise as evil – and perhaps we can begin to understand why.

The union of the Presbyterian Churches took place amid great rejoicing in 1929, with John White as the first moderator of the united Church. His time, however, was beginning to draw to a close. Other voices were beginning to be heard, voices which had never been absent but which had often been drowned. When another world war came along, another Commission was called for under a very different convener, John Baillie. When Baillie produced his report, White accused it of being 'full of naïveties', but perhaps by then even he had seen where ideas of racial superiority could lead. Two damaging decades had passed; they had filled the time between wars, time that could have been much better used, time in which the Churches all lost ground in the affection of the population, time in which the Church of Scotland in particular had signally failed to read the signs of the times and to cope with the real menace to Scottish nationality – unemployment.

Part Two

David McCrone in 1997, while acknowledging this history, wanted to move swiftly on from it. In a paper given to a conference of the Centre for Theology and Public Issues of the University of Edinburgh, he argued that:

War, welfare, affluence and secularism in the intervening 60 years have managed to relegate these events to a bad historical memory, but the debate continues as to how alive 'sectarianism' is in modern Scotland . . . By the late twentieth century, we can argue that there has been a convergence in the socio-political identities of Protestants and Catholics in Scotland. The mainstream Churches have espoused a similar identity which is mainly civic, social democratic, pluralist and 'Scottish'. Indeed, it is hard to distinguish the mainstream denominations in these terms, as sectarian identities have declined, especially in their political manifestations . . . in key respects, Scottish Catholics, who represent about one in six of the population, are much more similar to other Scots than they are like their co-religionists elsewhere in Britain.[2]

Compare this analysis, then, with that of James MacMillan:

It's true that for many Scots, religious bigotry does not impinge on their lives, but for a significant minority Catholics continue to be a source of puzzlement if not anxiety, and its concomitant bigotry. Because of this most Scottish Catholics learn at an early age that the best self-defence mechanism is to keep one's head down. Try not to attract attention to the fact that you are a Catholic – it will only annoy them.

He accuses Scotland of a sleep-walking bigotry, what Macpherson in his report on the Stephen Lawrence case called 'institutionalised racism'. It is the kind of deep-seated prejudice which becomes as natural as the air we breathe, neither noticed nor in need of justification, just the way things are. MacMillan wants us to wake up and look around, to see with whom we are walking and in whose footsteps. Part of this wake-up call is a call to pluralism and toleration, even to a rejoicing in difference and variety. He accurately diagnoses the disease which afflicted the Church and Nation Committee in the '20s and '30s and which can still be the cause of suffering and pain:

At the heart of this malaise is a very Scottish trait – a desire to narrow and to restrict the definition of what it means to be Scottish . . . this tendency to restrict, to control and to enforce conformity and homogeneity is an obsessive and paranoid flaw in the Scottish character.

Perhaps, however, the disease is rather more endemic than is allowed for in MacMillan's description. Perhaps it is more human than Scottish, infecting not only the Presbyterian mind and the secular mind (the two locations he identifies). Perhaps the controlling tendency is shared by all of us, part of the sin which killed Christ.

Part Three

When Professor Philip Esler, vice-principal of the University of St Andrews, addressed the Church of Scotland's Co-ordinating Forum in September 1999, he challenged the Church to look at its categorisation of in-groups. He used the parable of the Good Samaritan to examine the human (and ecclesiastical) tendency to work in enclaves, to identify with them and to exclude others from significance. He suggested that a non-hierarchical, decentralised Church had within it the danger of fragmentation into ever smaller such enclaves. There are, Esler said, two possible answers: *re*-categorisation and *de*-categorisation; the first draws boundary lines around a larger group, the second refuses to draw lines at all, preferring to see people simply as individuals rather than in terms of any group loyalty whatsoever.

Esler recommended the second, de-categorising route. We might pause to consider, however, if that is indeed the best route to take. The Good Samaritan, Esler says, saw not a member of a group of human beings but a human being in trouble; he was able to help because the situation was defined by need rather than by status or belonging. But the point about the story is not that there were no categories being employed, rather that there were different categories. Esler's advice to the Church of Scotland was not to forget its identity as the Church, but to re-examine the categories in use: did they see themselves operating *as a Church* or as separate and discrete units?

Similarly, James MacMillan does not seem to want to go down the individualist road of forgetting altogether about group identity; rather we get the distinct impression that his group identity is vitally important to him. Perhaps, then, it is re-categorisation to which we are called.

Norman Hogg, writing in appreciation of John Smith's identity as a Scottish Presbyterian, spoke of the Scottish Labour movement in their opposition to the segregation of the working class by coal owners or iron masters:

> To the lasting credit of the movement its members were treated simply as members, whether Catholic or Protestant. This gave Catholic Irish immigrants their best opportunity for emancipation in local communities. They took it and throughout this century . . . Catholics have played . . . leading roles in equal partnership with Protestants, Jews, Moslems and non-believers. The Labour movement practised its egalitarian principles while organised religion fostered sectarianism or at best failed to address it. They denied St Paul's edict that in Christ Jesus there is neither Jew nor Greek. Today in industrial Scotland the churches of all denominations are declining.[3]

In that account there are a couple of clues about the re-categorisation towards which Philip Esler points us and which might take forward the debate which James MacMillan initiated. The first clue is that 'members were treated simply as members'; in other words, it is the identity for which they are gathered which is important – no other identity is important *in that context*. That is not, however, to deny the importance of those other identities to the individuals involved when in another context. The second is that 'in Christ Jesus there is neither Jew nor Greek'; but there *is* Christ Jesus. We do not abandon identity at baptism, but rather take on a new one. It is, however, an *in*clusive rather than an *ex*clusive identity. Perhaps all of us would do well to look at the overlapping identities which define us and thus be enabled to re-categorise not only others but also ourselves. For the Church and Nation Committee of today, the question of identities is central; from this comes our concern for true social inclusion, for social and racial justice, for equality, for human rights. It will therefore be worth devoting the next section to this very matter.

Part Four

There was a great enthusiasm among the Reformers, echoed today more often in the thinking of the Eastern Orthodox Churches, for what is known as 'territoriality'. It is both a tidy and a dangerous system. (It may be that tidy systems are inherently dangerous.) The world view of territoriality is all-inclusive, for it brings together nationality, culture and religion into one identity, fusing geography with a total belonging. In this way of thinking, for example, Scotland was to be Presbyterian and Ireland Roman Catholic. Terms became for many interchangeable, hence the tendency for many even today to refer to the Scottish Episcopal Church as 'the English Church'. Today the break-up of the former Yugoslavia has exhibited all the worst traits of this way of thinking, where to be Croat is for many to be Roman Catholic, to be Serbian is to be Orthodox, to be Bosnian is to be Muslim. Kosovo or Kosova (the spelling is significant) was meant to be saved from this mono-ethnic fate by a NATO bombing campaign, but as Alison Elliot, convener of the Church and Nation Committee, has discovered through the process of international and ecumenical consultation conducted since the war by the Churches of Europe, it now appears that all that has resulted from that widespread destruction is a change in the mono-ethnic victors.

Territoriality is what lay behind what the Church and Nation Committee had to say in the 1920s and '30s. To be Scottish was to be Presbyterian. It is a way of thinking which ties too many things together to be reliable. Whenever our national, cultural and religious identities become intertwined we become a danger to ourselves and to others, for it is then that we begin to set tests of belonging which pretend to promote unity but in fact foster division and bigotry. Norman Tebbit famously wanted to define Englishness by those who supported England at cricket (rather than, of course, India, Pakistan, Sri Lanka or the West Indies). Belonging had to be examined by whatever loyalty test came to hand. We are, however – or ought to be – rather more complicated beings than that. We are called to render to Caesar and to God but not to confuse the two.

When I was interviewed for the post of secretary to the Church and Nation Committee, I was asked what I thought were the big issues facing us in the years ahead. My first answer was that the biggest question was what kind of nation Scotland wanted to be. I do not think my answer would be different now. The big question for any nation today is what its relationship is, if any, to culture, to ethnicity, to religion, to identity. Must we 'belong' to a close-knit group of identities, or might it not be that our post-modern tendency to have several overlapping but non-identical identities is in fact a liberation from the straitjacket of territoriality? Michael Jacobs, in a talk given in March 1995 to the Scottish Association for Pastoral Care and Counselling in Stirling, spoke of the same kind of phenomenon on an individual level:

> Clients can present different aspects or sides of themselves . . . There is a psychological defence . . . which is known as splitting: a phenomenon where clients need to keep parts of themselves separate from each other within themselves, as much as they separate their symptoms in speaking to different people. They may therefore only present part of the picture to one person.[4]

In Jacobs' terms, we attach different *labels* to different parts of our lives or of ourselves and it is possible to see this as either negative or positive. It is negative if thereby we are left dis-integrated, unable to function as a whole person. It is positive, however, if we are able to recognise the labels and wear each of them with pride without confusing any of them with our own selfhood. Jacobs' term for this true selfhood, our proper identity, is that of *name*. Naming is different from labelling. Naming is about inner reality, about who we are, rather than about the groups to which we belong. We lend parts of ourselves to our belonging, but we should not confuse that belonging with our being.

If this debate has to do with the personal, it has also to do with the political. The Scottish understanding of sovereignty, as expressed over the last decade or so, is about something which inheres in the people of Scotland and which they can lend in parts to different institutions, so long as those institutions work well on behalf of the people. It makes it easier to cope with parliaments in Edinburgh, London and Strasbourg: each is granted a different part of the sovereignty of the people. The idea that sovereignty belongs to a particular parliament makes life much more difficult.

If, then, we can recognise both a multi-faceted political identity and a many-layered personal belonging, we ought also to be able to find a way to a way of living which does justice both to labels and to names. As a society and as individuals we need to learn from the mistakes of monocultural longings and belongings; we need to know the name which can wear many labels. It is a route to the re-categorisation for which Esler called.

Part Five

All this is in its own way an echo of MacMillan's call for pluralism. His, however, was a very particular call, whereas what is presented here is, I hope, a call for a more general recognition both of underlying and united humanity and of the huge variety of ways humanity has found in which to express itself in belonging and in worshipping. The Scotland of today is not as tolerant of variety as it likes to think of itself as being. James MacMillan has turned our attention to a specific and historic intolerance, but there are others. Those working in the area of race relations continually remind us that those whose difference in ethnic background is made obvious by the colour of their skin face a daily struggle and continual harassment. Anecdotal evidence of the persecution of those who move here from England is too frequently available to be ignored. The abuse of the weak by the strong, whether physical, psychological or economic, is evident from statistics concerning violence against women, bullying at school or at work, common assault or inequalities in wealth and health.

The Leuenberg Church Fellowship (of Lutheran and Reformed Churches in Europe) conducted consultations from 1995 to 1999 on the theme of Church – People – State – Nation. In the text presented for official comments is set out the ambivalence which the modern nation-state produces:

> The reflections thus far have shown that the traditional ties between
> church, people, state and nation, which are still very real in many realms

> today, have many positive aspects. People feel at home in their mother
> tongues, homelands and societies. The relation between people and
> church is especially important to minorities for establishing their own
> identity as persons, as cultural entities and church groups . . . On the
> other hand, we can see negative aspects. Close connections between
> churches and nations can result in small ethnic groups being cut off
> from society as a whole.[5]

The document then goes on to look rather cursorily and unsatisfactorily at
what it calls 'ethics of differences'. What it does say, however, is that 'Europe
does not have an identity which must become a reality, but rather a task which
it must carry out'. Europe is to become a meeting place for cultures and people
where what is best in each can make its contribution. It would not be
impossible to imagine the same on a smaller scale for Scotland. It is an entirely
different vision from the one presented to the Church of Scotland earlier this
century, but one which perhaps is truer to a kingdom where there is neither
Jew nor Greek. It is a vision which calls for repentance on the part of very
many who have presumed to know what Scotland is and what it stands for. It
is a vision which needs to elicit from all Churches a renunciation of
systematised and closed ways of thinking. It is a vision which demands of all
a contribution and from none the dangerous neatness of territoriality. The idea
that to be my neighbour you must think as I think is an idea whose time has
gone.

We have come to recognise the importance of context; what we see depends
on where we stand. Alan McDonald, then vice-convener of the Church and
Nation Committee, spoke at a conference in 1998 which had examined Ireland
and Scotland. Emphasising this obvious truth about seeing, and drawing on
experience in South Africa as well as in Ireland and Scotland, he included these
words from Michael Lapsley:

> Many societies have tried to bury the past. No society in history has
> succeeded. Too often, victims have become victimisers of others . . . Our
> challenge as a nation today is to break that chain. We cannot allow our
> memories to remain gaping wounds which imprison and dehumanise
> us.[6]

We stand today in a different place; we stand with different people at a
different time. All of these things go to make up the context of our existence.
We are people with a future as well as a past and it is a future which is still to
be made. As we look around we see people who are our neighbours who would
not have been our neighbours 80 years ago; all around us re-categorisation is
taking place, and in that we can rejoice. The people around us may wear
different labels from the ones we wear, and all of us will wear different labels
at different times. We do not live in an all-encompassing ideology, and for that
we can be grateful. But we do own a common humanity – a God-given name
of 'beloved'. The ability not to limit the expression of that name in either our
neighbours or ourselves is an ability which needs to be nurtured, but if it can
be nurtured sufficiently well then the Scotland for which James MacMillan
calls can yet be ours together.

Many strides have already been taken towards it, though more could yet be taken. In the work of the Church and Nation Committee, we are joined by observers from the Scottish Episcopal Church, the Salvation Army and the Roman Catholic Justice and Peace Commission. Whenever the Committee visits Northern Ireland, one of the members of the delegation is that Roman Catholic observer. It is a small way of saying that doing things together, acting as neighbours, sharing a common label, is possible and is important. One of the things to come out of these visits is a realisation of how much good work is going on in that part of God's world, work at re-categorisation which would have seemed impossible not very long ago. This work, produced in the midst of sectarianism, is work which speaks not only to the people of that particular situation but to others, including those who visit from Scotland. The Faith and Politics Group from Belfast has recently produced a pamphlet, in the concluding section of which they list four steps which we in Scotland could also take; these are expressed as the need for all: (1) to encourage positive feelings of identity; (2) to have faith; (3) to repent; (4) to welcome the stranger.[7] It is no doubt appropriate, in the context with which we started, that a tentative agenda be provided for us from Ireland – proof, perhaps, that we have indeed moved on in the last 80 years.

Notes

[1] S.J. Brown, '"Outside the Covenant": The Scottish Presbyterian Churches and Irish Immigration', *Innes Review*, 42, 1991, pp.19–45.

[2] D. McCrone, *Catholics in Scotland: A Sociological View* (Edinburgh, 1997).

[3] C. Bryant (ed.), *John Smith: An Appreciation* (London, 1994), p.13.

[4] M. Jacobs, 'Naming and Labelling', address given at Stirling, March 1995, to the Scottish Association for Pastoral Care and Counselling.

[5] Leuenberg Church Fellowship, *Church – People – State – Nation* (unpublished 1999), p.26.

[6] Michael Lapsley at Healing of Memories Workshop, Cape Town, South Africa.

[7] Faith and Politics Group, *Boasting: Self-Righteous Collective Superiority as a Cause of Conflict* (Belfast, 1999), p.32f.

15. PRESBYTERIANISM AND IMAGINATION IN MODERN SCOTLAND

Robert Crawford

Once, when I was a schoolboy sitting on a bench at Maxwell Park station in Glasgow, a teenager came up to me, held the point of a geometry-set compass against my jugular vein and asked me what team I supported. Uncertain what to reply, I hesitated, then opted for the truth. 'I'm not interested in football,' I told him. Oddly, this seemed an effective response. After a little time, he walked away.

I remember this incident from the early 1970s because it scared me, and because I was never sure what team would have been the most dangerous to mention. Was the youth who threatened me Protestant or Catholic? I didn't know. Perhaps he was a disaffected Aberdeen supporter, but I doubt it. As a west of Scotland boy, I was pretty sure that this was Protestant/Catholic, Rangers/Celtic stuff, and that I wanted nothing to do with it.

At home, in suburban Cambuslang, our neighbours were middle-class shopkeepers, on the one side a Protestant chemist, on the other side a Catholic grocer. Even to identify the two as 'a Protestant' and 'a Catholic' sounds slightly false to me now; that wasn't the way I usually thought of them. Long after, when I read Liz Lochhead's autobiographical essay 'A Protestant Girlhood', its title pointed to a degree of denominational self-awareness I thought about comparatively little as a child.[1] True, there were markers of difference visible on my suburb's leafy avenues, school uniforms being the most obvious. Some years I recall there being an Orange parade along Cambuslang Main Street, which disgusted me. In part this revulsion came from my parents, both active members of the Church of Scotland. It would be wrong to airbrush out my memories of their occasionally suggesting that Catholic priests might influence their congregations about which way to vote; equally, though, I remember their distaste at Orange marches and any sort of overt bigotry. They were horrified when Mr Kincaid two doors down was spat at in the street for refusing to endorse the views of the extreme Presbyterian pastor Jack Glass. Mr Kincaid was a Church of Scotland minister.

I remember these things because they were unusual, though, and would be loath to see them added to a cairn marking out sectarianism as the key defining feature of west of Scotland life, or allowing me to claim some spurious glamour of persecution. Every time I have visited Northern Ireland I have been taken aback by the differences in attitude between people there and the people I grew up among. What is most disturbing is the way so many people in Northern Ireland assume that the position in Glasgow, or even Scotland as a whole, is identical to that in Belfast. At one time in my life I was offered a job in Northern Ireland but decided I did not want to live under its psychological weather. In such a climate, I was told, it might be inferred from my attendance at a Protestant church what my politics were. Having grown up in a community where people's surnames were not seen as religious or political markers, I was struck by all the kinds of restrictive cultural coding that people seemed to take for granted. Would it not be possible to be a Protestant republican? Everyone seemed boxed-in, labelled, so warm but also so petrified. When the Catholic woman I stayed with on my first visit joked with some of her Protestant colleagues that 12 July was a holy day of obligation, I knew I would need to have lived in the province for years before I knew to whom I could or could not make such a joke. I have stayed on different occasions in Northern Irish Catholic and Protestant communities. They seemed ironically similar. I liked Scotland, because Scotland was different.

There were plenty of Scottish stereotypes, but as a lower-middle-class boy I did not have to inhabit them. While Scottish sectarianism is surely a gendered phenomenon, far more bound up with Scottish masculinity than with Scottish femininity, neither football nor kilts nor sectarianism nor heavy drinking was an absolutely obligatory concomitant of growing up as a Scottish man. Poetry was my passion from just about as far back as I can remember. Where that came from is hard to say. Neither of my parents was markedly keen on it, though the glass-fronted bookcase in our sitting-room contained various leather-bound editions of Burns, Longfellow, Tennyson, Whittier, the Brownings and other poets. These were the books which my mother's parents had given each other during their long engagement during the earliest years of the twentieth century. I was too young to read them, but they fascinated me like tribal fetishes. If ever I was initiated, it was then.

Growing up as a teenager interested in poetry in the west of Scotland during the 1970s, I inherited a 'critical orthodoxy', though I wouldn't have used that phrase then. This orthodoxy treated my Protestant background as unsympathetic to the arts. I didn't see it that way at the time, because from about the age of 15 I was excited by the acoustic and fire of T.S. Eliot's verse. Perhaps Eliot, coming from his St Louis and New England Protestant and Unitarian background, then converting to the Church of England, expressed in his work a certain imaginative rigour that could appeal to a Protestant imagination. The iconoclasm of the earlier poetry, especially *The Waste Land*, impressed me in the way that works of modernist painting or music did. They seemed a sort of artistic re-formation. Yet the later *Ash Wednesday* and *Four Quartets*, so suffused with Anglo-Catholicism, also excited my imagination with their rhythms and images. Alluring, not altogether foreign, they had the power to talk about spirituality and religion. Developing a taste for modernist painting, music and literature, I identified with these 'Anglo-Catholic' poems, as I would later identify with the poetry of Hugh MacDiarmid. It wasn't a calculated allegiance; it was something deeper than that. As a reader, I didn't feel inhibited by my religious upbringing with its Bible narratives, stained glass and bare walls; a combination of rigour and richness was what art offered in a way that somehow complemented the spiritual presence on offer through the Church of Scotland. I wasn't a member of that Church (I didn't join it until my late twenties) but I was formed by it in many ways, not least as a reader and as a writer. When I read more, though, I realised this ought to be a problem.

The problem is most easily summed up by Edwin Muir, in his celebrated poem 'Scotland 1941'. There he presents the Scottish Reformation, as represented by 'Knox and Melville', as promoting a 'desolation' which will 'crush the poet with an iron text'.[2] As has been pointed out, Muir seemed to take over from T.S. Eliot the highly questionable but once powerful notion of a 'dissociation of sensibility' and transpose it to Scottish culture. The idea of a 'Caledonian antisyzygy' had been developed by Hugh MacDiarmid from the work of the earlier Belfast-based Scottish critic G. Gregory Smith; according to this one-size-fits-all doctrine (which has become rather oppressive for Scottish writers) Scottish literature was characterised and energised by clashes of opposites, splits and doubles. Muir looked at the flipside of the same coin and saw Scottish culture as enfeebled by division. In his book *Scott and Scotland* (1936) he argued that linguistic division damaged Scottish literature, since a national literature required not several languages but one homogeneous language. Similarly, Muir saw the Scottish Reformation and the fissuring tendencies of Protestantism as destroying the wholeness of an earlier Scottish world view. 'Scotland 1941' presents a heraldic, medieval, rural idyll and contrasts it with modern materialism, which Muir denounces through the awkwardly archaic phrase 'pride of pelf'. For Muir that materialism is linked to the Reformation, while Scotland's greatest post-medieval writers appear famously as 'Burns and Scott, sham bards of a sham nation'.

In some ways this imaginative analysis of Scotland is attuned to that of Max Weber. In *The Protestant Ethic and the Spirit of Capitalism* (translated into English in 1930) Weber links the development of Protestantism to the growth of a society preoccupied with individual financial advancement. The iron text of the pelf-proud Reformation is seen by Muir as a deadweight on the imagination, crushing the poet, however courageous or obdurate the Reformation will might have been. On one level, it is hard to argue with this view, which has become something of a commonplace attitude taken by writers and artists towards Protestantism in Scotland and which may sum up a hostility that still exists. This is the Reformation as smashed cathedrals, effigies dinged doon, rose windows gone – iconoclasm. Yet it would be hard to deny that iconoclasm has appealed to aspects of the romantic and modernist imagination, whether in the poetry of Byron or in Mendelssohn's Reformation symphony, just as it was relished by successive generations of modernist artists. My point is not that iconoclasm has been the sole motor of art, but that it can be seen as an important impulse within modern creative processes. The greatest artists of the twentieth century, such as Stravinsky, Picasso, Joyce and Eliot, display an almost hypnotic mixture of iconoclasm and orthodoxy. To argue that either iconoclasm or orthodoxy is what their work is about is to straitjacket the imagination.

So to see iconoclasm as simply anti-art is a misreading, a mistake which can be endangering for Scottish culture, since in a country so smashed up as well as so excited by the forces of Reformation, it might engender a corrosive self-loathing. Cultural self-loathing can be heard in that line, 'Burns and Scott, sham bards of a sham nation'. Burns, one of our many post-Reformation cultural icons, is regarded by most Scots and non-Scots as this country's greatest writer. Yet for Muir, this writer of some of the world's finest love poems is presented as worthless; similarly, Scott, arguably the single most influential figure in the global development of the novel, is scorned. Muir's judgement here seems spectacularly unbalanced, probably because he felt himself to be a victim of the sort of 'bitter wit' which his poem is denouncing. Perhaps when he mentions 'sham bards' he has Ossian in mind, and his anxiety might foreshadow the upset caused by early-1980s arguments like Hugh Trevor-

Roper's about 'The Invention of Tradition: The Highland Tradition of Scotland'.[3] Yet at the start of a new century, and with more than enough experience of post-modernism and virtual reality behind us, we are unlikely simply to denounce the Ossianic as fraudulent or to argue that traditions lose all significance if they are perceived as 'invented'. Particularly for the creative artist, invention is crucial because it is bound up with the power of the imagination. There is a danger that when Muir denounces the 'sham', what he is doing is denouncing some of the greatest Scottish creative imaginations, and even the creative imagination itself.

Muir was one of the most probing twentieth-century Scottish literary critics, perhaps the finest, yet he is recurrently and damagingly wrong. It may be easier to see this now than it was when he and MacDiarmid flyted. A great denouncer of 'the slatternly chaos of Glasgow', industrial Scotland and that mining landscape of which he wrote with regard to painters 'none is likely ever to live in it or be born in it', Muir has been proved wrong by the creative imagination.[4] One of the most exciting art exhibitions of my lifetime in Scotland was surely 'The Vigorous Imagination', that 1987 show which brought together a generation of artists such as Steven Campbell, Calum Colvin, Peter Howson and Kate Whiteford (all from Glasgow's 'slatternly chaos') along with David Mach (from the mining town of Methil in Fife). One can think too of earlier painters, most notably Joan Eardley, who made working-class urban streetlife painterly subject matter. Where Muir's scorn and loathing (understandable in terms of his own upbringing) got the better of his faith in the creative imagination, in invention and reinvention, these artists emerged triumphantly in the very locales Muir contended could bear no art.

Muir's view of the Reformation in Scotland is not straightforwardly wrong, but it is oversimplified and damaging. Accepting it can lead to a sense of pained isolation for the Scottish poet whose formation is Protestant. If poets work with images, runs this argument, then the Scottish Reformation smashed images and so is hostile to poetry. There can be few Protestant Scottish poets who have never felt this sensation and wondered enviously what it might be like to come from a culture filled with hallowed images of Catholicism. For some poets, a commitment to the poetic word leads to an incarnational poetics which demands a viewpoint that is ultimately Catholic. In Australia, the magnificent instance of Les Murray is an example of this – a poet who came from a Free Church background and who converted to Roman Catholicism. It would be hard to argue that the sense of plenitude in Murray's poetry is unconnected with his religious beliefs, though certainly that sense is informed by an interest in Aboriginal spirituality and a vernacular Australian delight in 'sprawl'. At the same time, the example of R.S. Thomas in Wales reminds us that religious poetry can be written out of different traditions, though the preoccupation with absence in Thomas's verse might contrast with the plenitude in Murray's.

What of the Protestant poet who looks with sometimes envious admiration on the imagery of Catholicism, yet who is quite unable to accept some of the basic tenets of the Catholic Church (papal authority, for instance)? One possible feeling can be that of double dispossession, of being an outcast both from a Protestant community characterised as dourly and doucely anti-art and from a Catholic community which seems happy with many aspects of artistic richness, yet remains doctrinally unacceptable. Being an outcast can be

190

empowering, perhaps, for the poet who wants to believe resolutely in his own independence. It can also lead to despair, tough posturing or self-loathing of the sort felt perhaps in some of the finest nineteenth-century Scottish religious poetry which, emerging from sometimes extreme Protestant traditions, turns towards atheism and dark counter-icons of its own. One striking example (valued alike by T.S. Eliot and by Tom Leonard) is James Thomson's remarkable work *The City of Dreadful Night*, a poem determined to come to terms with what characterises it: that despairing self-loathing which some might see as quintessentially Calvinist, the conviction not of the Chosen but of the awful Unchosen remnant.

One way to short-circuit this problem is simply to exterminate the conditions which give rise to it. So we have Tom Nairn's memorable joke about a liberated Scottish future dependent on the last Church of Scotland minister being strangled with the last copy of the *Sunday Post*. Such macho antics may not be necessary, and may themselves smack of class and religious intolerance. Here I want to suggest something different. Scotland has a great and plural linguistic, cultural and religious inheritance. That living body of work includes such masterpieces as Columba's 'Altus Prosator', the aureate religious and bawdily secular poetry of William Dunbar, the masses of Robert Carver and, more recently, Muriel Spark's *The Prime of Miss Jean Brodie*. All these are nourished by a Catholic imagination. They have their origin in a particular community but, like all good works of art, they come to belong to all communities. In a special sense also, and one that leads to much argument, older Catholic Christian artworks may be claimed not only by present-day Catholics but also by modern Protestants, since each group tends to see itself as the heir (reformed in one way or another) of the pre-Reformation Catholic Church.

The power of works of art does not belong exclusively to one community, be it the community of men, of Scots, of Hindus or of university graduates. Individual artworks may have authors, owners or communities whose beliefs mould them, and they may be subject to interpretations in the wider world which their authors, owners or original communities might reject. Nevertheless, in our age of globalisation, art, whether from Catholic Scotland or Classical Greece, is something which carries a charge that increasingly passes across cultural and religious boundaries, however much ownership may be disputed. Awareness of these boundaries gives us a nourishing and important interpretative context for the art, but not its only context in our world. Imaginative perception and complex inter-cultural patterns can lead to a tribal fetish being valued in a Western gallery or a Brazilian poem by a Scottish audience.

In such a world, it is surely easy to admit that a Protestant poet can have a rewarding relationship with a Catholic medieval poem, whether 'The Dream of the Rood' or the verse of William Dunbar. No modern audience, Protestant, Catholic or non-Christian, can react to the work as a medieval audience might. Yet it is a tribute to the imaginative vitality of the poetry that it can communicate across times and varieties of belief. A modern Protestant Scot who did not wish to signal allegiance to the heritage of Catholic Scotland would be mad; equally, a Scot who saw the process of the Reformation in Scotland as stifling all art would be misguided.

There are dangers of ghettoisation as soon as one talks of 'Catholic art' or

'Protestant art'. Clearly, a remarkable Scottish poem such as George Buchanan's Renaissance Latin 'Elegy for Jean Calvin' deploys an energetic anti-Catholic rhetoric, while the later Scots of Jessie Anne Anderson's 'At Sweet Mary's Shrine' shows a hurt devotion to the Virgin Mary.[5] I am aware that the main danger in writing such an essay as this is that it is seen as in some sense sectarian. Ultimately, the finest poetry is not just Scottish poetry, Catholic poetry, Protestant poetry or feminist poetry. It is poetry. At the same time, it is naïve to pretend that the religious attitudes of communities have no bearing on their artistic productions. This is not the same as saying that the crucial thing is whether the artist is a practising Catholic or Protestant. When we consider art from, say, eighteenth-century Scotland, we are considering work that emanates from a predominantly Protestant community; that is a factor which may be at least as important as the official religious affiliation of the artist. So, for instance, just as it might make sense to relate the self-portraits of Rembrandt to that emphasis on self-examination generated by a Dutch Protestant culture anxiously searching for signs of individual grace, so it may be reasonable to relate the remarkable growth in encyclopedias and lexicography in eighteenth- and nineteenth-century Scotland to the Protestant emphasis on direct access to the word, to knowledge and to general education of the sort outlined by Knox and the other reformers.

Certainly, a literature of encyclopedism attracted such figures as Thomas Carlyle and Hugh MacDiarmid, who tended to see literature as a pulpit. MacDiarmid's lexicographical muse could lead to kinds of imagistic as well as verbal richness. 'The Watergaw' is strengthened by its dictionaried opening, 'Ae weet forenicht i' the yow-trummle', and through its being ghosted by George Matheson's hymn 'O Love that wilt not let me go', with its line 'I trace the rainbow through the rain' and its sense of flickering and shining light.[6] Yet throughout MacDiarmid's career there is a fascination with what he would call a 'poetry of fact', something which the historiographically minded imaginative writer Thomas Carlyle might have understood. The Protestant culture of Scotland may have nourished kinds of writing – such as Scott's fiction or Carlyle's prose or the poetries of Hugh MacDiarmid or Edwin Morgan – which find a kind of imaginative poetry within (sometimes recondite) factual, historiographical or scientific material. At its worst, this results in a turning away from lyrical delight, yet at its best it leads to a discovery of kinds of beauty in, say, scientific and informational materials. Sometimes, just as Joyce was formed by a pious Catholicism against which he reacted, so the Calvinism of much of Scotland produced a countering libertinist impulse. This is seen clearly in the work of Burns, or in Byron (whose earliest sexual experiences were bound up with the Calvinism of his nurse), or, more recently, Don Paterson. These are all poets who adopt a witty, libertine stance. Yet it would be wrong to suggest that they are not fascinated by religion and may even wish to use its language, sometimes awkwardly and sometimes with relish, whether in 'The Cotter's Saturday Night' or *A Vision of Judgment* or *God's Gift to Women*.

Like many artists from strictly religious backgrounds, these poets have sought kinds of escape, but also forms of engagement. To take one of the most striking examples of fiction emerging from Scottish Calvinism, Hogg's *Private Memoirs and Confessions of a Justified Sinner* surely depends on the same obsession with self-scrutiny that is manifest in Rembrandt's work. Like Burns in 'Holy Willie's Prayer', Hogg is producing a critique of extreme Calvinist doctrine in a novel with a strikingly experimental structure. At the same time, we might recall that Hogg, poet of 'A Cameronian Ballad' and critic of Protestant extremism, appears to have been a Presbyterian believer. Though some twentieth-century admirers, notably André Gide, wish to reduce the novel to the status of brilliant psychological study, its power resists such epistemological reduction. Hogg's novel refuses to be pigeonholed as either psychology or theology since it occupies a territory that takes in both. It is a work that testifies to the power of religious faith even as it criticises aspects of that belief. Whatever their differences, most modern critics regard it as a masterpiece. The idea that Scottish Presbyterianism has been simply anti-art is misleading, and has been given credence by such arguments as those of Edwin Muir. It is time to move beyond that idea, and to replace it with one that is both more generous and truer to the grain of Scottish cultural history, more attentive to the resonances of Scottish art.

This move may be controversial. What is crucial is that it should not be presented as a Catholic *versus* Protestant issue but as a Catholic *and* Protestant shift. Curiously, if it is Catholics who were literally disenfranchised in Scottish political life, then it is Protestant artists, at least poets, who have been saddled with a cultural mythology which sees them as marginal and irretrievably damaged. Certainly there are aspects of this view which hold true, but it may have been over-internalised by Scottish artists. One need only think of Iain Crichton Smith's reaction to the strictures of Free Church Lewis to see a striking example of a poet tortured by the notion of his community as hostile to the values of his art, so that he found himself crushed between what he called 'The Law and the Grace'.[7] There may be a sense in which Smith's perception of that hostility was a spur to his creative gifts, but I would want to argue that we might reconsider aspects even of what are seen as 'extreme' Protestant movements in Scottish culture, and question perceptions of their relationship to the creative arts.

Outstanding here is that remarkable artwork associated with the Disruption of 1843, Hill and Adamson's project on *Signing the Act of Separation and Deed of Demission*.[8] I use the word 'project' since in retrospect we may wish to consider not just the oil painting which resulted but also the many studies and related works bound up with it, best known of which are the individual and group photographic portraits. This is probably the first instance in the world of the coming together of the new technology of photography and the traditional genre of the oil painter's panoramic group portrait. What is striking about the picture is that, on the one hand, there is a clear focal point on the document being signed – on the word. On the other hand, the myriad surrounding heads of men and women are all painted in similar detail and grouped in such a way that there is not a sense of protagonists and minor figures but of a crowding panoply of equally important figures looking in a variety of directions. As one looks closer, one senses in the work other potential focal points and depictions of texts competing for attention. Visually, this makes the composition distracting, and, though I would call it a work of genius, it is not a painting that has attracted much praise from art critics. The very equality of attention given to all the portraits makes the painting striking. Its many heads and documents – newspapers, manuscripts, Bibles and works of theology – highlight the problems of reconciling words with the Word. It is a democratic picture, in keeping with the daringly democratic nature of its subject matter, and draws on the new technology of photography to present in detailed scrutiny portraits of all the ministers signing the deed. This repeated individual attention carries a focus on individualism so far that it seems to interfere with the corporate nature of the painting, but it is just such tensions which characterise the subject matter. Here is a new Church formed by fissure, and one which will again divide, unite and divide. The tensions between individual self-scrutiny and protested corporate unity, tensions at the heart of much Protestant theology, are brilliantly captured by the form of the painting, a form bound up with the use of new technology. This is an adventurous picture whose apparently self-contradictory nature should be seen as a strength rather than a blemish. It is a painting that is at once accessible and hard to read, one bound up with an effort to stretch the medium of portraiture through its association with the new technology of photography. It is a work both conservative and avant-garde, radical and slightly fousty. This artwork comes out of the milieu of Scottish Protestantism and characterises that milieu. It is also a work linked to a community usually portrayed as hostile to artistic developments.

Imagination tends to fly free of denominations, though it is frequently nurtured by them. Religion is supranational, yet undeniably its local inflections matter to believers. Spirituality needs to work through particular cultural circumstances, though it also involves a belief that there is something beyond those circumstances. In that regard it is similar to the creative imagination. Because religion often operates at the boundaries of human perception, it attracts crazy people of whom the majority is wary; the same can be said about art. Equally undeniably, both religion and art have the ability to communicate with people (often only intermittently) in ways that are more profound than those of what we like to call 'the media'. Matthew Arnold may have been wrong in his suggestion that poetry would come to replace religion; in my experience most poets would be glad to have an average-sized congregation regularly attend their readings. Yet Arnold was right to see poetry and religion as somehow close, not so much, I think, in some supposed opposition to science as in a mutual ability to reach depths in people that normal defensive mechanisms such as embarrassment or fear of the unconventional often seal off.

The combination of art and religion is a potent one. Official bodies in Scotland (including Churches and arts organisations) tend to shy away from it. The Church of Scotland may run a theatre in Edinburgh, but it keeps pretty quiet about the fact, conscious perhaps of Presbyterianism's older hostility towards drama. What is striking about the two best-known Christian spokesmen in contemporary Scotland – Richard Holloway and Thomas Winning – is that neither avoids dangerous issues. I would like to think that there might be more dangerous connections between the Churches in Scotland and Scottish artists. These will come about only if we move beyond the notion that much of Scottish Christianity is of necessity anti-art. Though lots of its energy may have been deflected into now unfashionably polite belles-lettres and the production of a Ben Nevis of published sermons, Presbyterianism in Scotland was very much bound up with literary production and evaluation in the eighteenth century. This was the period when ministers such as Hugh Blair in Edinburgh, Robert Watson in St Andrews and the celebrated homosexual moderator of the Church of Scotland and friend of Robert Burns, William Greenfield, were prominent literati, instrumental in what I have called (in a recent book of the same title) 'the Scottish invention of English literature'.⁹ The involvement of such men was not always beneficial for the arts, yet the way in which they expanded the literary horizons of many students and readers, coupled with their public championing of works such as the poetry of Ossian, so influential on the European and North American romantic imagination, is cause for celebration, criticism and investigation, rather than scornful amusement or neglect.

Our assumptions about the relationship between Presbyterianism and imagination in Scotland need to become more complex and nuanced. The aim is not to deny that the Reformation left a troubling legacy for many imaginative artists in Scotland, but to realise also that it produced impressive and sometimes exciting cultural forms and artefacts. In the field of poetry, I hope that the anthology of Scottish religious poetry which Meg Bateman, James McGonigal and I are co-editing for the Saint Andrew Press will allow readers and writers to see the complicated but strong relationship between religion and verse in Scotland over the last 15 centuries. Curiously, unless you count hymnbooks, there has never been a general anthology of Scottish religious poetry, despite the obvious importance of religion in the formation of Scottish culture and the much-vaunted significance of poetry in this nation's cultural life. Part of the reason for this may be the view that Presbyterianism and the imagination don't mix, and that Scotland was a fundamentally Presbyterian country. At the start of a new millennium, both these assumptions may be open to challenge. New maps of our poetic heritage are emerging. Just as I believe that it is invigorating to see the 'Altus Prosator' of St Columba as the magnificent starting-point for anthologies of Scottish poetry (whether specifically religious poetry or poetry in general), so it would be absurd, surely, not to regard that poem as a product of Catholic Europe, which also forms part of the inheritance of Protestant Europe. However, rather than lining up poets as a Catholic team and a Protestant team, it might be rewarding to see both as part of a rich tradition of poetry shaped by Christian belief. In the territory we now call Scotland such a tradition extends from Columba's 'Altus Prosator' to Don Paterson's *The Eyes*, each of these works being deeply engaged with European sensibility. In Paterson's case the engagement on the part of a poet formed by Protestant fundamentalism with another poet from a deeply Catholic country is surely exemplary, the rigorous bleakness of Paterson's 'Nil Nil' sensibility combining with the lyricism of Antonio Machado to produce work 'about God and love and memory'.¹⁰

These three elements may matter as much to contemporary as to earlier Scottish poetry. In writing some of the poems of my recent collection *Spirit Machines* I wanted to engage with the strains between sensed presence and perceived absence which form part of our experience both of faith and of bereavement. The technologies of communication which we now employ – phones, computers, the Internet – combine the promise of plenitude with the absence of the tangible in a strange 'deincarnation' that may be metaphorically powerful in writing about faith and loss.¹¹ Combining technological materials with religious matter, factual lexis with a lyrical patina, appeals to me as a writer and is something I see happening in the work of some of the Scottish poets of earlier generations whom I most admire. Along with that 'democratic' impulse prized by Scottish Presbyterians (some of whom might value the democratic structures of their Church government and the emphasis on direct access to Word and word more than they might relish inherited Calvinist theology), this appeals to me in the Disruption 'project' of Hill and Adamson.

To argue that any one denomination has a monopoly on spiritual insight is a form of hubris. It corrodes. There is a danger that modern Scottish Protestants may feel they are an embattled minority when compared with the international size of the Catholic Church; similarly, there is a worry that Scottish Catholics may feel they are an embattled minority within a Scotland much of which is still in some sense Protestant by formation, and may even find themselves ill at ease in a global community so shaped by Protestant individualism and free-market capitalism. Each of these 'minority' sensibilities is comprehensible, as is the complementary consciousness of being part of a majority community. A temptation to present oneself as a victim or as a proudly righteous victor is one which Scots often find hard to avoid in politics, religion and other areas. The spiritual pride of the victim and the victor can be sources of self-delusion. What I am arguing for here is not the sense that there is some sort of Protestant sensibility that is superior to a Catholic sensibility. Rather, I contend that there have been and continue to exist in Scotland links between Presbyterianism and imaginative production that are fruitful, that may have produced rewarding cultural patterns and that should be seen as usefully complementing and supplementing the rich image-making faculty traditionally associated with the arts in a Catholic culture. What the Scottish poet needs is access to both of these traditions.

Notes

[1] L. Lochhead, 'A Protestant Girlhood', in Trevor Royle (ed.), *Jock Tamson's Bairns* (London, 1977), pp.112–25.

[2] Edwin Muir, *The Complete Poems*, ed. P. Butter (Aberdeen, 1991), p.100.

[3] H. Trevor-Roper, 'The Invention of Tradition: The Highland Tradition of Scotland', in E. Hobsbawm and T. Ranger (eds.), *The Invention of Tradition* (Cambridge, 1983), pp.15–42.

[4] E. Muir, *Scottish Journey* (1935) repr. (Edinburgh, 1979), p.170.

[5] Along with many of the other Scottish religious poems mentioned in this essay, both these poems (the Latin with a new translation by Edwin Morgan) are contained in M. Bateman, R. Crawford and J. McGonigal (eds.), *Scottish Religious Poems* (Edinburgh, 2000).

[6] Hugh MacDiarmid, *Selected Poems*, ed. A. Riach and M. Grieve (London, 1994), p.9; Matheson's poem is reprinted in Bateman et al., *Scottish Religious Poems*.

[7] I. Crichton Smith, *Collected Poems* (Manchester, 1992), p.54.

[8] David Octavius Hill's painting, *Signing the Act of Separation and Deed of Demission* is reproduced in J. Ward and S. Stevenson, *Printed Light: The Scientific Art of William Henry Fox Talbot and David Octavius Hill with Robert Adamson* (Edinburgh, 1986), p.156; several of the associated calotypes are also reproduced in this book.

[9] See R. Crawford (ed.), *The Scottish Invention of English Literature* (Cambridge, 1998).

[10] D. Paterson, *The Eyes* (London, 1999), p.55.

[11] R. Crawford, *Spirit Machines* (London, 1999), p.65.

PART 5

The Search for Evidence

16. THE PAST IS HISTORY: CATHOLICS IN MODERN SCOTLAND

Michael Rosie and David McCrone

That this book is being published at all will no doubt strike some people as distinctly odd. After all, is not Scotland, and most certainly Britain, one of the most secular societies in the West? Northern Ireland is, of course, the exception, but most people on the British 'mainland' will happily treat the province as thoroughly exceptional. If they think about it at all, it is to treat it as a foreign country; when it comes to religion, they do things differently there.

It came, then, as something of a shock to many when, in 1999, the year of the new Scottish parliament, the debate about sectarianism in Scotland re-emerged, in the title of James MacMillan's Edinburgh Festival lecture, and of this book, as 'Scotland's Shame'. Could it be that despite the official image of Scotland as a progressive, secular and civic-minded society, it harbours a dark secret of religious bigotry and sectarianism? As sociologists, we want to focus in this chapter on the evidence that Scotland is a sectarian society, and particularly the idea that Catholics remain a distinctive group with distinctive attitudes and values which owe much to their historical roots.

The Problem of Conventional Wisdom

The reader will suspect already that we are taking a fairly robust and iconoclastic view of this conventional wisdom. We have entitled our chapter 'The Past Is History' because we want to break away from the view that the position of Catholics in modern Scotland is largely to be accounted for by their history; that their present is largely the outcome of their past. We are, of course, doing this for effect, because no one can deny that history matters. We do, however, take issue with the view that it is the main, indeed, the only thing that matters. In short, we want to argue that as far as Catholics in contemporary Scotland are concerned, the past is indeed history. In other words, they have become virtually indistinguishable from other people living in Scotland.

This, of course, will alarm those, including some of our fellow contributors in this volume, who take the contrary view that anti-Catholicism is endemic and insidious in modern Scotland: 'sleep-walking bigotry', to use James MacMillan's term. We have a problem with this characterisation because, as sociologists, we deal in empirical evidence and social categories. It may, then, seem a tall order to define sectarianism and bigotry, especially of an implicit, 'sleep-walking' kind. In a collection of essays to which we contributed in 1998, the editors wrote in their concluding chapter, 'To some, sectarianism, or discrimination against Catholics, does not exist because it cannot be statistically or materially proven.'[1] One is tempted to ask, 'Do they mean us?'

It would be foolish to assert that a phenomenon only exists if it has statistical or material provenance. Nevertheless, if sectarianism arises in Scotland, social scientists would expect it to have some measurable manifestations which were systematic and structured.

The second observation to make about the comment is that it elides two phenomena: sectarianism and discrimination. Put simply, while we may have trouble measuring the former, as social scientists we would certainly expect to find systematic evidence for the latter. If Catholics are discriminated against when it comes to jobs, housing and educational and other social opportunities, then we would surely be able to prove it.

The problem we have with the view that Catholics in Scotland are discriminated against is that, as Steve Bruce and Lindsay Paterson show in this volume, one is hard pushed to find systematic and endemic discrimination of this sort. That is where 'sectarianism' comes in. After all, 'discrimination' is behavioural; it's what people do, or don't do, to each other on a systematic basis. 'Sectarianism', on the other hand, occupies a much more shadowy corner: it's about attitudes and prejudices. It's what people encounter on the streets, in the pubs, behind the hand. It is, in a word, street-level bigotry.

Let us explore this a little by looking at other social groups. Women and black people are well used to street-level sexism and street-level racism respectively. It's what they have to put up with in their daily lives, and, one might argue, no amount of anti-discriminatory legislation can put a stop to it. Well no, not entirely, but one has to say that it is much harder to harbour racist and sexist thoughts if you are liable to be fined or imprisoned for acting them out. Lest we appear entirely naïve, let us agree that there is evidence of continuing and serious discrimination against women and black people when it comes to social opportunity. It is, in effect, institutionalised, and not simply dependent on the personal behaviour of individuals.

Apply this analysis to Catholics in Scotland. Whatever the dark feelings some non-Catholics may harbour about them, it is very difficult to find systematic discrimination against Catholics. To be sure, it did happen in the past, but, as we say, that is history. We are left instead with accusations of prejudice, not discrimination, of attitudes rather than systematic and institutionalised behaviour.

We have another problem. It is not at all clear what we mean by the terms we are using. Think a little about what we mean by 'Catholic'. It can refer to someone who accepts the doctrinal beliefs in transubstantiation, the immaculate conception, papal infallibility and so on. Alternatively, it can be defined in terms of religious practice, what sociologists refer to as 'religiosity' or church attendance. Thirdly, it can be a matter of simple self-definition: 'I think of myself as a Catholic'. Relatedly, it can refer to one's origins and upbringing, possibly being educated at a Catholic school, although one is lapsed. Fifthly, being a Catholic may be a matter of cultural practices such as learning Irish dancing, or supporting Celtic FC. There is nothing inherently 'Catholic' about these, but they are firmly associated in Scotland with the ethnic and social origins of most Catholics. Finally, and possibly even more attenuated, claiming to be a 'Catholic' may be a matter of politics – supporting a united Ireland, and/or republicanism.

The point we are making here is that the term 'Catholic' is used in all these ways and more, and we can never be sure exactly which is in operation during debate. ('Protestant' too carries a varied and complex baggage, but that is beyond the scope of this chapter.) It is our view that too much of the debate about sectarianism has simply threaded many of these meanings together, run them through history and treated 'Catholic' as a self-evident – but thoroughly confused – social category. Some, indeed, may be treated as 'more Catholic' than others. For instance, we have heard the argument that 'real Catholics' are those who live where most Catholics live, west-central Scotland, and that somehow those living in the east and the north don't share the experience of 'most Catholics'. Undoubtedly, those outwith west-central Scotland are far less 'cultural' Catholics, and there is undoubtedly tension between them. The small numbers in the north-east, for example, take considerable pride in the indigenously Scottish, and pre-Reformation, origins of their faith.

The Northern Irish Model

There is another, much more significant model of anti-Catholicism which is being trailed across much of the contemporary debate in the form of the statement that Scotland is 'Northern Ireland without the guns'. This is altogether a serious and worrying accusation, and it deserves some scrutiny before we focus on Catholics in Scotland. In an important contribution to these matters, two sociologists at Queen's University, Belfast, John Brewer and Gareth Higgins,[2] have recently explored anti-Catholicism in Northern Ireland. They argue that anti-Catholicism is critical to the self-defining identity of most Protestants in the province, that it is for them a master-status which permeates the political and everyday discourse and culture of the place. They comment:

> Anti-Catholicism can thus be conceptualised as a sociological process for the production of different rights, opportunities and material rewards between people in a society where religious labels are used to define group boundaries.

In other words, anti-Catholicism in Northern Ireland is used as a resource to defend the socio-economic and political position of Protestants, and as a means of legitimating that position when it is under attack. It operates at three levels: at the level of ideas and theological beliefs (the Catholic faith as at best misguided and at worst dangerous); at the level of individual behaviour (in day-to-day social interaction); and at the level of social structure (institutional discrimination against Catholics). The authors also point out that compared with anti-Protestantism in the province, anti-Catholicism is more systematic, sustained and culturally embedded. It is the key, defining resource for stratifying the society and maintaining social closure, whereas anti-Irish racism as such is largely absent, as, much to the chagrin of generations of socialists, is social class as a means of organising identity.

How does this play in Scotland? One has to conclude: hardly at all. There is little evidence of institutional discrimination against Catholics in Scotland. In terms of religious beliefs, it is very hard to find the kind of self-righteously hostile Protestantism, except in some far, reactionary corners of Free Presbyterianism. One might pause a little at the level of individual behaviour, but that is difficult to sustain without the institutional and theological support systems which operate still in Northern Ireland. Above all, the rate and progress of secularisation have been much more thorough in Scotland. In Scotland, there simply is no Protestant hegemony, and no defining political-constitutional position around which to gather the wagons.

There is some irony that anti-Catholicism in Scotland is a construct of some Catholic apologists themselves, so that 'anti-Catholicism' is construed out of Donald Findlay's rendition of 'The Sash', attacks on individual Celtic fans, the high-profile defence by Cardinal Winning of traditional Catholic teaching on abortion and sexuality and of Catholic schools, whether or not Pope Pius XII was soft on the Nazis and whether Article II of the Treaty of Union should be repealed to allow the monarch to be or to marry a Catholic. Important though these issues are, it is difficult to assemble them into a case for full-blown sectarianism itself.

In all this debate, little attention is being paid to the views of Catholics themselves, or perhaps one should say those who identify themselves as such – in the manner of these things at the moment, the latter seems the more appropriate definition to use. Let us then examine the evidence by drawing upon the series of election studies in Scotland which have asked people about their religious practices and attitudes, as well as their views on social and political issues. These studies have the added value of allowing comparison with those affiliating with the Church of Scotland as well as those who describe themselves as having no religion.

How 'Religious' Are We? – Church Attendance, Affiliation and Upbringing

On the basis of the 1997 Scottish Election Study, 14 per cent of Scots claim to be Catholic, 41 per cent Protestant (here limited to those with a Church of Scotland affiliation[3]), and 31 per cent claim no religious affiliation. The most cursory comparison of reported upbringing and present affiliation suggests a striking 'leakage' from all the denominational groups to the 'no religion' category.

Table 1: Affiliation and Upbringing

% by column	UPBRINGING	CURRENT AFFILIATION
Church of Scotland	55	41
Roman Catholic	18	14
Episcopalian	5	3
Other Christian	11	8
Other	1	1
No religion	10	31
N	*882*	*882*

This pattern is repeated in earlier election surveys: in 1992 the 'no religion' category accounted for 7 per cent of family background and 25 per cent of current affiliation. Both the 1992 and the 1997 surveys suggest that, amongst the large denominations, the Church of Scotland is losing adherents at the highest rate. Put crudely, around a quarter of those in both surveys who had been brought up 'within' the Church of Scotland no longer regarded themselves as affiliated to that Church. Amongst Catholics, the rate of 'leakage' in the 1992 survey was around 5 per cent, and in 1997 22 per cent. As yet unpublished data from the 1999 Scottish election study indicate that by the new millennium the largest group would be those with no religious affiliation whatsoever. The key point is that across all the denominations, leakage tends towards the 'no religion' group; movement between the religious denominations is rare. Very few Catholics become Protestants, or vice versa. Less than 3 per cent of Catholics have Church of Scotland backgrounds, and less than 1 per cent of Church of Scotland identifiers have been brought up as Catholics.

Church Attendance

In Scotland, Catholics are more frequent church attenders than Protestants, with 41 per cent of Catholics claiming weekly attendance compared to 17 per cent of Church of Scotland identifiers. In 1992 the relevant figures were 51 per cent compared to 14 per cent. This pattern matches that of self-described 'religiosity', where respondents were asked how religious they were. A similar question was asked in 1974, allowing a comparison over 25 years.

Table 2: 1974: Are You Religious?

% by column	RC	CoS
Very much so	52	18
To some extent	26	36
Not really	23	46
N	137	530

Table 3: 1997: How Religious Are You?

% by column	RC	CoS
Very	10	8
Somewhat	54	43
Not very	25	36
Not religious	10	13
N	126	365

These figures suggest two interesting things: that Catholics are more likely to be religious than Protestants, and that religiosity was more widely reported in 1974 than in 1997. Related to this, it would appear that the gap between the two denominations is considerably smaller in 1997 than it was in 1974. In other words, in terms of religiosity, Catholics and Protestants appear to have become more like each other.

To some extent, responses to the question of religiosity are influenced by the age and gender of the respondent as well as by their denominational background. If we combine the two 'positive' responses to the question of religiosity in the 1997 survey (i.e. those who answer 'very religious' and those who answer 'somewhat religious'), a clear religion-gender-age pattern can be discerned, with older people, women and Catholics more likely to be positively

203

religious than young people, men and – to a far less marked degree – Church of Scotland identifiers. Thus, 86 per cent of Catholics over the age of 55 say they are very or somewhat religious, compared with 66 per cent of Catholic women, 62 per cent of Catholic men, and 64 per cent of women over 55. At the other end of the spectrum, the least 'religious' are men aged 18–24 (a mere 19 per cent), men aged 35–54 (27 per cent), and women aged 18–24 (29 per cent).

There are significant differences, therefore, between young and old, men and women, and Catholic and Protestant in terms of self-described religiosity. In general, the gender ratio among those affiliated to the Church of Scotland in our sample is 2:1 female to male; the split among Catholics is roughly 60/40, while men are more likely than women to be non-religious (by 52/48). In terms of age, a majority of Protestants are over 55, while Catholics are evenly distributed between age groups 18–34, 35–54 and over 55. The non-religious, on the other hand, are mainly younger people, with only 14 per cent over 55. There are, then, important demographic differences at play here; Catholics, for example, contain a higher proportion of women than the non-religious group, although not as many as the Church of Scotland sample. The Church of Scotland affiliates are older and female, while the non-religious are younger and male.

In terms of regional distribution, Catholics are overwhelmingly urban dwellers (only 2 per cent live in rural districts), and three-quarters of Catholics live in west-central Scotland. Despite this concentration, Catholics make up only a quarter of the population of the west. Protestants are a majority in the small (and geographically diverse) rural sample, which includes the north as well as the south. Not only are there fewer Catholics in the north-east and east-central Scotland, but these regions are much more secular than the west-central region, in which a majority of the population is Protestant. In broad terms, then, west-central Scotland, around which much of the current debate about sectarianism hangs, has a majority which is Protestant, with Catholics and the non-religious each making up around a quarter. In the east, on the other hand, Catholics comprise less than one in ten, with 43 per cent Protestant and 37 per cent with no religious affiliation.

Perceptions of 'Sectarian' Conflict

How concerned are the Scots about the nature of the relationship between Catholics and Protestants in the late twentieth century? When asked 'how serious' they felt 'conflict' was between Scottish Protestants and Scottish Catholics around 60–65 per cent in the 1979, 1992 and 1997 surveys answered either that the 'conflict' was 'not very serious', or that there was 'no conflict'.

Table 4: Conflict between Protestants and Catholics

% by column	1979	1992	1997
Very serious	15	9	12
Fairly serious	20	25	27
Not very serious	43	49	49
There is no conflict	22	14	11
N	637	957	871

One can, of course, read these figures the other way and note that over a third of Scots believe the conflict to be, to some degree, 'serious', either 'very' or 'fairly'. There is also a problem of interpretation: in large-scale surveys such as these we cannot tell whether or not each respondent defines the terms 'conflict' and 'serious' in the same way. There is also the problem of knowing the basis on which people respond. In a rapidly secularising society such as Scotland, most people are unlikely to have much personal experience on which to draw, and therefore may tend to rely much more on media reports. When there is particular media attention on the issue such as that which surrounded James MacMillan's lecture, Donald Findlay's sing-song or the stabbing of a Celtic supporter, it is quite possible that people will generally translate heightened awareness into a perception of greater conflict.

There are differences between the three religious groups in how they answer this question. Catholics are more likely than Protestants to answer 'very serious' or 'fairly serious'. To some degree, however, this seems to be a product of age, and to a lesser degree gender, rather than a straightforward by-product of religious affiliation.

Table 5: Conflict between Protestant and Catholic

% by column	RC	CoS	NONE	M	F	18–34	35–54	55+
Very serious	15	9	14	11	12	17	11	9
Fairly serious	32	26	27	31	23	36	25	21
Not very serious	45	50	49	47	49	39	56	50
No conflict	6	15	7	9	13	6	8	18
N	126	365	270	376	506	255	301	317

Younger people are far more likely to think conflict is serious than older people (53 per cent compared with 30 per cent). Not all the variation between the religious groups on this question can be explained by age, however. Although partitioning the data into religion and age together produces fairly small numbers (for Catholics the sub-groups contain only 40 or so) and, at best, we can only make some fairly cautious claims, there do seem to be grounds for arguing that Catholics are more likely to perceive serious conflict than the other groups in all three age categories. Again, however, it seems the greatest variation is across age group rather than across denomination:

Table 6: % Believing Protestant/Catholic Conflict Is 'Very Serious' or 'Fairly Serious'

% by column	18–34	35–54	55+
Roman Catholic	61	39	41
Church of Scotland	56	39	26
No religion	48	34	38

We also find that there is considerable variation according to region, with west-central Scotland having a higher perception of 'serious' conflict than the other areas:

Table 7: Protestant/Catholic 'Conflict' by Region

% by column	WCS	ECS	NES	RURAL
Very serious	16	9	8	7
Fairly serious	33	21	27	17
Not very serious	43	55	45	54
No conflict	6	12	15	20
N	*371*	*260*	*108*	*126*

These variations should hardly surprise us, given that most symbolic manifestations of modern Scottish sectarianism (the marching season and the Old Firm, for example) are centred in the west, and that sectarianism has been very much a feature of urban, rather than rural, Scotland. We might cautiously infer from these results that those most likely to have a perception of 'serious' conflict would be young people living in the west of Scotland, probably male and claiming a religious affiliation:

Table 8: Perceptions of Religious Conflict among Young Scots (18–34)

% by column	ALL		WCS	
	MALE	FEMALE	MALE	FEMALE
Very/fairly serious	55	51	61	66
None/not serious	43	47	36	33
N	*105*	*142*	*44*	*55*

Broadly similar results were achieved through analysis of the 1992 survey, and taken together the data seem to lend credence to Steve Bruce's claim that sectarianism in Scotland is, in essence, a boy's game.[4]

Attitudes to Separate Schooling

One of the key issues in the debate over sectarianism in Scotland has been the existence of state-provided Catholic schools since the Munro Education Act of 1918. The Act granted to minorities – Catholics and Episcopalians – guarantees on religious instruction which were denied to the majority Presbyterian Churches (who had gifted their schools to the state in 1872) and removed an onerous financial burden from the minority communities. The seeming imbalance of privileges – Catholic religious instruction was guaranteed by statute whereas Presbyterian instruction relied on the goodwill of local educational authorities – led many Protestants in the inter-war period to complain of 'Rome on the Rates' and to demand at least parity of treatment.

Opposition to Catholic schools need not, however, be motivated by sectarian jealousy. Indeed, possibly the greatest motivator of those opposed to separate schools is a concern that the present segregated system itself contributes to social division. In other words, opposition to segregated education can spring from 'anti-sectarian' motives. Across age, gender and region there is a widespread belief – between 73 per cent and 82 per cent – that education should be integrated, and even amongst Catholics themselves there is a strong desire for reform.

Table 9: Attitude towards Separate Catholic Schools

% by column	ALL	CoS	RC	NONE
Retain separate schools	20	18	52	12
Phase out	78	80	45	86
N	871	365	126	270

These figures are very similar to those in the 1992 survey, where Catholics split 51–47 in favour of retaining separate schools, and are broadly in line with unpublished figures for 1999. In 1979, 45 per cent of Catholics felt that the government should maintain separate Catholic schools whilst 42 per cent felt it should not. A Church-commissioned Gallup poll in 1978 found that 77 per cent of Catholics agreed that 'Catholic schools are an important element in Catholic life', although this figure was markedly lower amongst Catholics who had not themselves attended Catholic schools, who were infrequent church attenders or who had a non-Catholic spouse. Overall the survey revealed strong Catholic support for the schools with 'a sizeable minority [who] thought that Catholic schools should not continue'.[5]

Attitudes to Northern Ireland

The symbolism of sectarianism in Scotland has an overwhelming obsession with the politics of the Northern Ireland conflict. The songs sung at Ibrox and Parkhead and the tunes drummed out during the marching season relate only rarely to Scotland's religious past. The election surveys, however, do not suggest that opinions on Northern Ireland break down simplistically on religious lines. Where the long-term solution of the Northern Ireland conflict is concerned, there is a marked preference for a united Ireland over the maintenance of the Union, although it should be noted that (in both the 1992 and the 1997 surveys) there was a high proportion of 'don't know's. There was majority support for a united Ireland amongst Catholics and the non-religious (both 60 per cent) and amongst those in the youngest and middle age groups (57 per cent and 51 per cent). The oldest age group split evenly (38–38) between reunification and retaining Northern Ireland in the United Kingdom. Only amongst the Church of Scotland sample was there more support for the Union than for a united Ireland (42–33), although this reflects a stronger backing for the Union amongst the oldest section of the Church of Scotland group (45–28). Younger Protestants are evenly balanced between the two options.

Table 10: Long-Term Policy for Northern Ireland should be to:

% BY COLUMN	ALL	RC	CoS	NONE
Remain within UK	31	18	42	23
Unify with Republic	48	60	33	60
Other	7	6	8	5
Don't know	15	17	16	12
N	882	126	365	270

It might seem reasonable to assume that if Scots understood the Troubles from a sectarian perspective, then Catholics would favour a united Ireland and Protestants the Union (mirroring the Northern Ireland situation itself). Whilst the Catholic sample does seem to fit this hypothesis in the main, it is much more difficult to see evidence of it amongst the Church of Scotland sample, thereby reinforcing the point we made earlier about the lack of a sustained anti-Catholicism in Scotland. The non-religious – who do not fit easily with our rather crude 'Ulster hypothesis' – display a preference for Irish unification at least as strongly as the Catholic sample.

On this evidence there is little to suggest a sectarian conception of Northern Ireland amongst Scots. Indeed, the very high incidence of, 'don't knows' suggests that Scots are reluctant to be drawn on a painful and complex problem. Although there are differences between the denominations regarding the weight they give to the various constitutional options for the province, it is striking that there is no polarisation on the issue which forms the cornerstone of sectarian symbolism in Scotland.

Catholics and Scotland

How do Catholics – given the immigrant experience of much of their community's recent ancestors – relate to notions of 'Scotland' and of 'Scottishness'? Writing of the 1920s, Stewart Brown[6] argues that for Catholics in Scotland 'there was not much encouragement for them to feel Scottish whilst maintaining their Faith and their "Irish heritage"'. For a number of influential Presbyterians in the first half of the twentieth century, 'religious and cultural pluralism was an evil, and to be Scottish was to be Protestant'. In political terms, it has been argued, by Tom Gallagher[7] amongst others, that the 'Protestant' and 'Imperial' aspects of Scotland/Scottishness have made Catholics reluctant to support either constitutional change or the SNP, or indeed to identify themselves with Scotland. For similar reasons, it has been argued, Catholics – especially of an Irish background – find it difficult to embrace 'Britishness'. The election surveys allow us to test such claims and examine whether Scots Catholics struggle with 'Scottishness' and whether the nationalist vote is disproportionately *non*-Catholic.

(a) Catholics and National Identity

Although 'national identity' is a deceptively slippery term, the election surveys reveal that whatever Catholics felt in the past, in the late twentieth century they are just as likely as any other group to express feelings of Scottishness.

We can begin with the question 'Which nationality best describes you?', asked in 1997:

Table 11: Denomination and Nationality

% by column	ALL	COS	RC	NONE
Scottish	74	79	74	72
British	20	18	21	20
Other	6	3	5	8
N	871	365	126	270

It is clear that similarities between the denominational groups far outweigh differences. It should also be noted that the majority of those Catholics who answered 'other' gave their nationality as 'European' or 'English' rather than 'Irish' or 'Northern Irish' (in 1992, 5 per cent of Catholics described themselves as 'Irish'). The 1997 figures match closely the 1992 figures, where 71 per cent of Catholics said 'Scottish' compared with 72 per cent of the population as a whole. Historically there does seem to have been a shift in the way that Scots describe themselves when surveyed, with an increasing number of Scots answering 'Scottish' and a declining number answering 'British'. Indeed, between 1979 and 1997 the proportion of Scots answering 'British' has halved.

Table 12: Nationality

% by column	1979	1992	1997
Scottish	56	72	74
British	38	25	20
Other	6	3	6
N	658	957	871

Catholics have mirrored this process exactly: the proportion of Catholics describing themselves as Scottish has risen from 50 per cent in 1979 to 74 per cent in 1997, whilst the proportion describing themselves as British has dropped from 39 per cent to 21 per cent. In other words, the responses on this question over all three surveys throw into considerable doubt the claim that Catholics feel less Scottish than non-Catholics.

The 1997 survey also asked respondents whether or not they thought of themselves as belonging to a range of possible nationalities, allowing them to claim as many, or as few, as they wished. Again the denominational similarities are striking, and the differences negligible: 81 per cent of Catholics thought of themselves as Scottish, compared to 83 per cent overall, whilst 51 per cent of Catholics thought of themselves as British, compared to 52 per cent overall. Interestingly, twice as many Catholics thought of themselves as 'European' (10 per cent) as thought of themselves as Irish (3 per cent) and Northern Irish (2 per cent).

Responses to the 'Moreno' question – where respondents are invited to 'balance' their Scottish and British identities – also undermine the notion that Catholics have particular difficulties with Scottishness.

Table 13: Religious Denomination and National Identity

% by column	ALL	CoS	RC	NONE
Scottish not British	23	21	24	30
More Scottish than British	39	43	39	36
Equally Scottish and British	26	30	25	22
More British than Scottish	4	4	4	3
British not Scottish	4	1	4	5
N	871	365	126	270

Around two-thirds, regardless of religious denomination, prioritise their sense of Scottishness. Again the most striking aspects of the data are the similarities rather than the differences. Those differences which do exist are probably a reflection of the different age structures in the denominational samples. If we collapse the responses into only three groups – those who gave priority to being Scottish, those who gave equal weight to being Scottish and being British, and those who gave priority to being British – and compare the Catholic responses to the overall response over different ages, the similarities in terms of Scottishness become even more striking (again, however, the small size of the Catholic sub-samples should be stressed).

Table 14: Catholicism, National Identity and Age

% by column	18–34		35–54		55+	
	ALL	RC	ALL	RC	ALL	RC
Scottish	63	63	61	61	56	55
Equally Scottish and British	18	20	25	20	33	34
British	5	2	11	17	6	5
N	254	41	300	41	315	44

Further evidence that Catholics are just as Scottish as everyone else can be found when respondents are asked to choose between a 'national' and a 'class' identity (the question is phrased: 'Do you feel you have more in common with an English person of your own class or a Scottish person of a different class?'). Once again there is no significant difference in denominational answer.

Table 15: Religious Denomination and Class/National Identity

% by column	ALL	CoS	RC	NONE
Same class, English	24	24	21	23
Different class, Scottish	45	46	47	46
Neither/depends	24	25	22	23
N	871	365	126	270

The issue of class, of course, raises the question as to how similar our three denominational samples are in terms of their class profile. The broader question – that of the underlying class structure of religious groups in Scotland – will only be satisfactorily addressed if and when the census contains a religious question. Our purposes here are simply to demonstrate that there are class differences within the data; on the more general debate on class and social mobility, see the contribution by Lindsay Paterson in this volume.

Table 16: Denomination and (Registrar-General) Social Class:

% by column	ALL	CoS	RC	NONE
I. Professional	4	4	2	3
II. Intermediate	21	22	17	22
IIIn. Skilled, non-manual	23	26	21	20
IIIm. Skilled, manual	19	17	21	21
IV. Part-skilled	16	13	22	18
V. Unskilled	10	11	10	12
Never had job	5	5	3	5
N	882	365	126	270

From the 1997 survey we can see that while Catholics broadly share the same social-class profile as other denominations, there are slightly fewer Catholics in classes II and IIIn, and more in classes IIIm and IV. This may, in part, be a reflection of the particular sample and the influences of gender and age noted above rather than of underlying social differences.

In terms of class identity – that is, how people define themselves – there is some evidence that Catholics have a very strong conception of their own working-class identity.

Table 17: Denomination and Class Identity

% by column	ALL	CoS	RC	NONE
Middle-class identity	12	12	6	14
Working-class identity	40	42	56	32
No class identity	47	46	36	52
N	871	365	126	270

A similar result was also found in the 1992 survey, although Catholic identification with the working class was less strong: 49 per cent of Catholics in 1992 described themselves as working class, compared with 37 per cent overall. Over half (52 per cent) of all respondents in 1992 and just under half in 1997, it should be noted, did not find class a useful concept for self-identification.

(b) Catholics and the Constitutional Question

Alongside the claim that, historically, Catholics have been unable to feel Scottish has been the claim that Catholics have declined to involve themselves in the movement and mood for constitutional change. Tom Gallagher[8], for example, has consistently argued that there has been a Catholic suspicion that a self-governing Scotland would increase the power and confidence of Protestantism (as happened under the Northern Ireland parliament at Stormont). According to this view, this suspicion separated Scottish Catholics from early Home Rule agitations, and as a consequence their support for nationalism was likely to be relatively weak. Once more, the evidence of the election surveys runs firmly to the contrary.

Table 18: Religious Denomination and Constitutional Change

% by column	ALL	CoS	RC	NONE
Independence from UK and EU	8	7	5	11
Independence in Europe	18	12	15	26
Parliament, with tax powers	42	43	49	41
Parliament, no tax power	9	9	12	6
No elected body	18	25	10	12
N	871	365	126	270

In terms of the devolutionary proposals for a parliament with or without tax-varying powers, Catholic support seems disproportionately high, at 61 per cent compared to 51 per cent overall. In terms of the independence options, 20 per cent of Catholics are in favour compared to 26 per cent overall. It should be noted that in the 1997 Referendum Survey, Catholic support for independence matches that of the sample as a whole, at just over one-third. Put simply, although there may have been some differences in the end objective, Catholics, Protestants and the non-religious were united in 1997 in their desire for constitutional reform. The result of the subsequent Constitutional referendum in September 1997 seems to bear this out; it seems inconceivable that such a resounding 'Yes-Yes' vote could have been possible if the Catholic community had been hostile or even lukewarm to the prospect of change.

Neither does Catholic support for constitutional change seem particularly new, and it would certainly seem to predate the 'Thatcher factor'.

Table 19: Constitutional Option: 1979, 1992 and 1997

% by column	1979		1992		1997	
	ALL	RC	ALL	RC	ALL	RC
Independence	8	8	23	28	28	20
Devolution*	62	66	50	50	51	61
No elected body	30	26	24	18	18	10
N	630	84	957	148	871	126

* The precise meaning of 'devolution' has, of course, changed over time.

In many ways what is surprising is that commentators have been willing to give credence to the counterview for so long despite evidence to the contrary. There is further evidence that Catholics in the 1970s were as likely to support constitutional change as non-Catholics: two-thirds of both Catholics and Protestants favoured a Scottish assembly in 1974, and in 1979, 48 per cent of Catholics claimed to have voted 'Yes' in the devolution referendum, compared with 44 per cent of all respondents. Again in 1979, 70 per cent of Catholics favoured a devolved assembly with considerable scope over Scottish affairs, compared with 59 per cent overall. In short, then, there is strong evidence over the last two decades suggesting that the conventional wisdom that Catholics are hostile to constitutional change requires substantial revision. The will for change – including an increased desire for the dissolution of the 1707 Union – has embraced Scotland's Catholics as much as – indeed, if not more than – non-Catholics.

(c) The 'Catholic Vote'

Where the literature on modern Scottish politics touches upon issues of religion it is usually to stress the alliance between Scotland's Catholics and the Labour Party. Some commentators have also claimed that a large degree of antipathy exists amongst Catholics towards the SNP, for broadly similar reasons to those set out in the debate about 'Scottishness'. Writing in the late 1970s, Jack Brand[9] claimed:

If we are to identify support for the SNP we would not expect to find it in strength among Catholics. We would expect Scottish sentiment to exist in the Church of Scotland since this institution bears much of the tradition of Scotland.

Catholic reticence towards the nationalist movement has also been ascribed to the virulent strain of anti-Irish and anti-Catholic sentiment which can be found in the early history of the National Party. To some sections of the party during the inter-war period, the 'Irish' in Scotland were nothing less than a 'menace' to Scotland's economy and culture:

> Taken along with the similar outbursts emanating from the Scottish Protestant Churches [in the 1920s and 1930s], this amounted in Catholic eyes to the equation of Scottish nationalism with anti-Catholic bigotry.[10]

Is there evidence of Catholic antipathy to the SNP in the 1990s? If we examine the survey evidence for the last three Westminster general elections, there are two aspects which are immediately noticeable. Firstly, the voting habits of Catholics are very evident over all three elections, with Labour claiming an outright majority of Catholics on all three occasions. Secondly, Catholic antipathy towards the Conservatives seems very marked; in each election Catholics were only one-third as likely as the overall sample to have voted Conservative. On the other hand, however, the evidence for Catholic reluctance to support the SNP is less convincing.

Table 20: Religious Denomination and Vote: 1987[11], 1992 and 1997

% by column	1987		1992		1997	
	ALL	RC	ALL	RC	ALL	RC
Conservative	23	8	22	6	11	4
Labour	35	59	32	53	41	59
SNP	12	9	20	16	15	10
Lib-Dem/Alliance	8	5	9	7	10	3
N	957	148	957	148	871	126

It is also interesting to note that the Conservatives are very reliant on Church of Scotland voters, although this may well be a function of age. In 1997, 60 per cent of Conservative voters belonged to the Church of Scotland, although only 16 per cent of Church of Scotland voters supported the Conservatives. Whilst, therefore, it can still be said in the late 1990s that Scottish Conservatives are mainly Protestant, it is no longer the case that Scottish Protestants are mainly Conservative.

Table 21: Denominational Composition of Party Votes (1997 election)

% by column	ALL	LAB.	SNP	CONS.
Roman Catholic	15	21	9	5
Church of Scotland	42	40	46	60
No religion	31	30	34	19
Other	13	10	11	16
N	871	358	132	99

One might speculate that the lower incidence of Catholics voting for the SNP has far more to do with the continuing support for Labour than any widespread distrust of the SNP. There is certainly little evidence in the surveys to suggest the latter; in both 1992 and 1997 Catholics were more likely to name the SNP as their 'second-choice party' than the non-Catholic groups (in 1992, 28 per cent of Catholics named the SNP as their second choice, compared to 22 per cent overall; in 1997 the figures were 32 per cent Catholic and 27 per cent overall).

Where the surveys asked respondents how they felt about the Nationalist party there was little difference between religions. Catholics have shared in and contributed to the emergence of the SNP as Scotland's main rival to the Labour Party.

Table 22: How Do You Feel about the SNP?

% by column	1979		1997	
	ALL	RC	ALL	RC
Favour	40	39	49	46
Neutral	7	5	29	33
Against	53	57	21	19
N	729	88	871	126

Finally, it is clear that on a number of questions relating to the major political parties, there is far greater similarity between Catholics and non-Catholics than difference. Catholics are more pro-Labour and anti-Conservative than the population as a whole, a trend which puts them at the forefront rather than the margins of the contemporary political mood. In terms of how they view the Nationalist party, however, Catholics are quite unexceptional.

Table 23: Denominational Attitudes to the Political Parties

% BY COLUMN	SNP		CONS.		LABOUR	
	ALL	RC	ALL	RC	ALL	RC
'X' are						
Good for one class	21	23	79	84	15	10
Good for all classes	57	56	15	10	74	81
Keep promises	42	42	10	4	51	57
Break promises	15	14	79	84	16	7
Capable, strong govt	35	32	21	18	83	84
Not capable govt	40	41	74	76	6	6
Extreme	42	43	48	55	16	17
Moderate	41	43	36	25	73	72

All this suggests that there is considerable scope for the SNP to increase their share of the Catholic vote. In the debate over 'Scottishness' there has been a re-imagining, a re-inventing, of Scotland since the 1960s, and to a large degree the SNP has emerged as a major political beneficiary of the new mood of national sentiment. Scotland's Catholics have not in any way been immune to, or marginalised from, these changes. It may well be that a spell of Labour government – in both London and Edinburgh – with all the pitfalls of responsibility will lead to further erosion of Catholic support for Labour.

Can we conclude from these data that religious affiliation plays a prominent role in determining voting behaviour? On the face of it, the answer seems obvious: after all, we have shown that Catholics are strongly pro-Labour and anti-Conservative. Voting, however, is related to a number of social factors – class, gender and age, for example – of which religion is merely one. That Catholics have a greater propensity to vote Labour does not prove that being a Catholic 'causes' people to vote Labour. It is possible that religion is only spuriously connected to political behaviour; for example, it may be that being working class rather than being Catholic explains the propensity to vote Labour. Discovering whether this is the case or not would involve the building of a complex statistical model of voting in which a number of possible factors – separately and in conjunction – are tested to see how much they cause voting patterns to vary.

The most important factor distinguishing supporters of the two parties in the 1992 election was their preference for constitutional change; supporting independence decreased the odds of being a Labour voter as opposed to an SNP one.[12] The second most influential factor, however, was whether or not one was a Catholic. In other words, there was still a strong association between voting Labour and being a Catholic, over and above social class. Hence, though Catholics are, by and large, working class, their class alone does not explain their greater propensity to vote Labour rather than SNP. Religion also proved a significant discriminator of vote when it came to Conservative versus Labour/SNP voting. One of the most striking findings in the analysis of the 1992 election data was that the best predictor of non-Tory voting was being a Catholic, even taking into account constitutional preference, social class and national identity.

We can conclude, then, that while Scottish Catholics remain strong supporters of the Labour Party, they are increasingly susceptible to the appeals of the SNP. It remains true, however, that they are much more resistant than either non-Catholic Scots or British Catholics as a whole to voting for the Conservative Party, an ongoing feature reflected in the first elections for the Scottish parliament in 1999.

The Catholic Attitude: Politics and Society

In line with their voting habits and party predilections, Scottish Catholics are consistently more left wing in their political attitudes than the Scottish population as a whole. The differences, however, are not marked, the similarities between Catholics and non-Catholics again being considerably more striking than the differences. On ten questions relating to how economic resources should be allocated, Catholics consistently emerge on the left of the political spectrum.

Table 24: Political Attitudes

% AGREEING WITH STATEMENT THAT . . .	ALL	RC
Government should increase tax and spend more	72	74
Government responsible for full employment	67	72
Increase tax and spend on education	69	76
Increase taxes to provide better pensions	57	63
More aid to Africa and Asia	36	43
Public services/industry should be state-owned	43	50
Income and wealth should be redistributed	70	76
Spend more money to abolish poverty	94	94
Law should set a minimum wage	73	77
Government should get rid of private education	31	30

The data suggest that Scottish Catholics not only vote for parties of the left but take a clear leftist stance on an array of political values, notably on educational spending, overseas aid, public ownership and redistribution of income and wealth. Indeed, where the 1997 survey asked respondents to place themselves on a left-right scale, 38 per cent of Catholics located themselves left of centre compared with 29 per cent of the population as a whole. In other words, the propensity of Catholics to vote for the left is not simply the result of political habit and convenience; it is also a matter of political principle.

While there may be relatively little difficulty in accepting that Scottish Catholics are left of centre politically, given their history (working class, Labour-voting), it may come as something of a surprise that a community marked by its religiosity should be no more conservative in its views than other Scots.

Table 25: Social Attitudes

% AGREEING . . .	ALL	RC
Bring back the death penalty	45	37
Prison should reform not punish	77	79
Life sentences should mean life	86	84
More opportunities for women	43	36
More opportunities for blacks and Asians	29	26
More opportunities for gays and lesbians	19	14
Availability of abortion gone too far	33	52
Censorship necessary to uphold morals	68	70

Although there are some differences in the data, the results, taken together with those for 1992, suggest that on most of the moral issues surveyed there is little significant difference between Catholics and Scots overall – apart, unsurprisingly, from attitudes to abortion. Whilst one-third of the 1997 survey felt that the availability of NHS abortions had gone too far, just over half of the Catholic sample felt so, reflecting too a substantial minority who do not agree.

Again, therefore, with the (expected) exception of abortion, the data very strongly suggest that Scottish Catholics are by no means divided from non-Catholics in their general moral outlook.

Conclusion

This overview of attitudes and values among Scottish Catholics, compared with those of people belonging to the main Protestant Church, as well as those of the non-religious, suggests that they differ little from the population as a whole. In this context, it is difficult to sustain a thesis that Catholics in Scotland see themselves as aliens in an alien land. Whatever may have been the case in the past, the evidence from studies in the 1990s indicates an acculturation and assimilation into mainstream Scottish society. While others in this book are exploring directly the thesis that Catholics are systematically discriminated against in Scotland, our evidence here makes that a very difficult argument to sustain. Scottish Catholics at the start of the new millennium are not the people they were. Their past is indeed history.

Notes

[1] R. Boyle and P. Lynch (eds.), *Out of the Ghetto? The Catholic Community in Modern Scotland* (Edinburgh, 1998), p.197.

[2] J. Brewer and G. Higgins, 'Understanding Anti-Catholicism in Northern Ireland', *Sociology*, 33, May 1999.

[3] As a convenient shorthand, we will refer to such people as 'Protestants', while recognising that this term covers members of other Churches in the reformed tradition.

[4] S. Bruce, *No Pope of Rome: Anti-Catholicism in Modern Scotland* (Edinburgh, 1985).

[5] *Flourish*, 29 April 1979.

[6] S.J. Brown, '"Outside the Covenant": The Scottish Presbyterian Churches and Irish Immigration, 1922–1938', *Innes Review*, 42, no.1, 1991, p.42.

[7] T. Gallagher, *Glasgow, The Uneasy Peace: Religious Tension in Modern Scotland* (Manchester, 1987).

[8] Ibid.

[9] J. Brand, *The National Movement in Scotland* (London, 1978), p.130.

[10] G. Walker, *Intimate Strangers: Political and Cultural Interaction between Scotland and Ulster in Modern Times* (Edinburgh, 1995), p.105.

[11] 1987 data are remembered vote of respondents in the 1992 sample.

[12] J. Brand, J. Mitchell and P. Surridge, 'Identity and the Vote: Class and Nationality in Scotland', in D. Denver et al. (eds.), *British Elections and Parties Yearbook 1993* (London, 1994).

17. THE PULPIT AND THE BALLOT BOX: CATHOLIC ASSIMILATION AND THE DECLINE OF CHURCH INFLUENCE

Iain R. Paterson

The Catholic community is thoroughly integrated in Scottish society. As described elsewhere, there are no longer any significant differences in social status or educational attainment between Catholics and other Scots. The post-war expansion of the public sector coupled with the growth of externally owned private manufacturing, severely limited the local Protestant's ability to favour his own in the labour market. Thereafter, the reorganisation of secondary schooling in 1965 dramatically enhanced the prospects of entry into higher education for many Catholic school-leavers, allowing them to compete for professional and technical positions without the real threat of discrimination.

Given that Catholics are now equal participants in Scotland's economic life, it is important to consider how social mobility has affected a communal Catholic identity, particularly in terms of adherence to Church teaching. This chapter offers the most recent data on Mass attendance, fertility rates, attitudes to abortion and denominational education, and the level of mixed marriages, all combining to outline the modern relationship between Church and laity. There is also an evaluation of the clergy's ability to influence the political direction of the Catholic vote and an assessment of how both Labour and the SNP have fared in targeting it. The increase in Catholic support for the latter over recent years is given particular attention, as it is strong evidence of a growing attraction to national identity derived from the assimilation process.

A Parochial Life? Catholic Religious Vitality in Modern Scotland

Church attendance is an important measure of the social significance of religion for any individual with denominational affiliation. While overall attendance at Christian services always tended to be higher in districts with a strong Catholic population, the levels recorded at Catholic Mass itself have declined in the post-war era, particularly since the 1970s. In 1959 it was estimated that an average of 63 per cent of Catholic adults turned out at Sunday Mass.[1] The table below presents the Catholic Church's own estimates of current attendance throughout Scotland.

Table 1: Attendance at Catholic Mass, 1 November 1997

DIOCESE	POPULATION	MASS ATTENDANCE	% ATTENDING MASS
St Andrews and Edinburgh	111,400	39,091	35
Aberdeen	17,650	7,450	42

Argyll and the Isles	11,200	5,372	48
Dunkeld	38,100	13,141	35
Galloway	47,200	14,315	30
Glasgow	233,800	69,197	30
Motherwell	165,900	60,110	36
Paisley	80,500	26,937	33
Scotland	**705,650**	**235,613**	**33**

Source: data complied from *The Catholic Directory for Scotland 1998/9*, Glasgow: Burns

Although this information simply constitutes a snapshot of church attendance and is only suggestive of recent trends, it is interesting to note that it was recorded on All Saints' Day, a Holy Day of Obligation in the Liturgical Calendar. It is plausible that attendance on this particular day is higher than the yearly average, as many Catholics who attend Mass irregularly or hardly ever may well be present. Despite this, it is clear that two-thirds of the Catholic population was not present at church. It is also evident that attendance at Mass is now proportionally higher in the parts of Scotland with the smallest Catholic populations: Aberdeen and Argyll and the Isles. Glasgow, hosting the largest number of Catholics, records the lowest figure. This may well mean that overall, Christian practice is now more popular in outlying areas.

The decline in public worship has often been attributed to the younger generation's failure to practise the faith adequately, the backbone of the congregation being overwhelmingly formed by the older population. But the information in table 2, while showing a poor level of church attendance amongst young Catholics, by no means adds weight to such a popular assertion.

Table 2: Frequency of Church Attendance: 23-year-olds in the West of Scotland

	NON-CATHOLIC	CATHOLIC	TOTAL
Weekly	8%	30%	15%
Once a month	6%	9%	7%
Several a year	12%	14%	12%
Less than once a year	5%	1%	4%
Only on special occasions	61%	42%	55%
Never	9%	4%	7%
Total	68% (458)	32% (214)	100% (672)

Source: West of Scotland 20-07 Health Study, MRC Medical Sociology Unit, University of Glasgow (1995)

The proportion of young Catholics living in the west of Scotland who attend church on a weekly basis is identical to that recorded for attendance on All Saints' Day within the Archdiocese of Glasgow, and only slightly less than those for Paisley and Motherwell. While direct comparisons between tables 1 and 2 are hazardous because of differing methods of data collection and overlapping sample areas, it is still possible to suggest that there is in fact no age-effect in operation; the decline in church attendance may cut across all age groups in the Catholic population, at least in the part of the country where the vast majority resides.

Table 2 alone indicates that while young Catholics are more likely than young non-Catholics to attend church on a regular basis, a very large proportion attend 'only on special occasions' such as weddings, funerals and commemorative services. In general, over half of the total sample of young people do not attend church for spiritual purposes.

So by the 1990s, Catholics were not unlike other Scots in dismissing churchgoing as an unimportant part of their lives, with projected trends showing that religious activity will decline even further.[2] While leaders of the established Churches in Scotland have not been too reluctant in accepting this, Catholic authorities may ponder to what extent this may be symptomatic of a wider leakage from the faith which will impact upon their ability to influence the laity on issues such as abortion and the use of contraception.

The way in which the Catholic community now treats the latter may be determined by studying its changing fertility rates. In 1957, the six highly Catholic areas of Scotland had a combined fertility rate which was 21 per cent higher than the Scottish average. In 1964 the difference had been reduced to 13 per cent and by 1977 it was only 5 per cent. The researchers conclude that 'lay Catholics at least have developed much more tolerant and pragmatic attitudes towards contraception'.[3]

Although the question of abortion is not the exclusive concern of the Catholic Church and laity, it is something which is overwhelmingly attributed to them because of strict Church doctrine framed by the *Humanae Vitae*. Cardinal Winning, the leader of the Catholic Church in Scotland, publicly criticised the Labour Party for banning the anti-abortion 'Labour Life' group in 1991 and raised the matter again with Tony Blair on the eve of the 1997 general election. Prior to the Scottish elections in May 1999, he urged prospective MSPs to 'recognise the inherent dignity of every human being, born or unborn under the law'.[4] Such pressure will not trouble those who will sit at Holyrood, however, as the matter of abortion will be reserved with the Westminster parliament. Perhaps it is regarded as too controversial and divisive an issue to form a remit north of the border, yet a decision based on such reasoning may in fact be unwarranted. The Scottish Election Survey indicated that while Catholics remain more opposed to abortion than Protestants or those of no religious identity, their opposition is now significantly weaker than before. In 1979, 46 per cent of Catholics felt that the availability of abortion on the NHS had gone too far, yet by 1992 this figure had dropped to 16 per cent. Furthermore, when asked if the availability of abortion was about right, 41 per cent agreed in 1992, whereas only 22 per cent had done so 13 years earlier. More recently, the majority of a 400-strong Catholic opinion poll stated that they would favour abortion under certain circumstances.[5] Catholics, or anyone else for that matter, with particularly strong feelings on this specific social issue had the opportunity to engage politically by placing their vote with the Pro-Life Alliance at the Scottish elections. Single-issue parties battled out the lower-order places in the party lists (second vote), with the Alliance polling around 1 per cent of the vote in the regions they contested.[6]

Evidence presented so far suggests that Catholics now prefer to make their own decisions relating to immediate family size and the options available to limit it. While the decline of church attendance provides an indicator of weakening communal Catholic activity, attitudes towards the existence of separate Catholic schools can also provide a measure of the relationship that the community has with its own institutions. Since the introduction of the 1918 Education (Scotland) Act, the presence of state-funded Catholic schools in Scotland has provoked enduring and occasionally vibrant controversy. The Catholic Church regards it as a fundamental right that Catholic parents can send their children to Catholic schools, while all the major political parties recognise their legitimacy so long as the parents do exactly that. However, falling school rolls, resulting from both the decline and shift of population and financial cutbacks, have not only meant that Catholic schools have been forced to close, but have also heightened the calls for school integration.[7]

Economic rationalisation is only a small part of the issue. While the Orange Order and the Free Church of Scotland are unsurprisingly dedicated in their opposition to separate Catholic education, it also comes under attack from secular or humanist viewpoints. In his address at the 1999 Edinburgh Festival, James MacMillan attacked *The Herald* as being one of the main players in the 'anti-Catholic-schools industry'. The paper's editorial vigorously defended itself, while its letters page became the focus of a debate which lasted for over a week. Although the wider issue of sectarianism prevailed, the question of Catholic schools was raised regularly. In summary, their existence was largely maligned by non-Catholics claiming divisiveness and backed by Catholics claiming prejudice. It is always the task of social analysis to get beyond such anecdote, with table 3 providing a more appropriate gauge of opinion.

Table 3: The Future of Catholic Schools

	CATHOLIC	PROTESTANT	OTHER	NONE	TOTAL
Retain RC schools	52%	15%	17%	12%	19%
Phase out RC schools	48%	85%	83%	88%	81%
Total	100% (119)	100% (380)	100% (66)	100% (259)	100% (824)

Source: Scottish Election Survey 1997

The Catholic response is most interesting. It is not known how many in the Catholic sample are parents, nor is it clear what the timescale in phasing out the schools could be. Despite this, almost half of Catholics surveyed did not support their own schools. Back in 1990, the Strathclyde Education Committee defended their decision to close or amalgamate some Catholic schools by claiming that they were enjoying a lessening support from their own community. These figures may well vindicate that decision.

Perhaps some Catholics do not regard their schools as the academic peers of the non-denominational schools, at least in their immediate vicinity. Perhaps some agree with the many non-Catholics who think that separate schools promote bigotry and division in Scotland. Or perhaps Catholics no longer feel that they require a distinct educational system in a society in which they are elsewhere fully absorbed. Whatever the reasons, the Church can no longer expect to receive the backing from even the clear majority of the Catholic community for the schools provided for it.

What we are beginning to see is a process of 'normalisation', where the bonds of attachment to the religious pillars which define membership of the Catholic community are being weakened and many individuals instead display characteristics more commonly associated with membership of wider

Scottish society. One of the clearest indications of such Catholic assimilation in Scotland has been the increase of marriages to non-Catholics. For many years after settling in Scotland, the vast majority of Irish Catholic immigrants resisted marriage into the wider community. In 1851, 80 per cent of Irish men and women in Greenock married amongst their own faith, and by 1891 this figure had dropped by less than 10 per cent.[8] The Vatican's *Ne Temere* decree of 1908 made the conditions for marriage to a non-Catholic even more stringent and served to maintain a distinct Irish Catholic community in Scotland for quite a while.

The position has changed dramatically over the last 30 years. In 1966, 36 per cent of all Catholic marriages involved a non-Catholic, rising to 48 per cent in 1977. There are diocesan variations: inter-marriage is higher in areas where there are fewer Catholics and therefore less chance of meeting co-religionists, whereas it is lower in and around the Clyde Valley.[9] Yet although the Diocese of Motherwell recorded the lowest number of mixed marriages during that period, the figure also grew significantly from 24 per cent to 37 per cent. In 1998, the figure stood at 43 per cent.[10] Although similar updated records are not available, it is very likely that, based on previous trends, mixed marriages now form over half of total Catholic marriages in Glasgow, Paisley and Galloway, and the vast majority in Dunkeld, Aberdeen, Argyll and St Andrews and Edinburgh. We must also bear in mind that there has been a major increase in the number of civil marriages and couples choosing co-habitation over marriage, both processes that will involve Catholics as well as non-Catholics.

The level of Catholic inter-marriage in Scotland also provides strong evidence of the absence of a polarised society based on ethno-religious division. By way of comparison, it is worth noting the rate of mixed marriages in Ulster. In 1991, the Diocese of Down and Connor (incorporating Belfast) recorded marriage with non-Catholics at 20 per cent. While way below the Scottish figures, this was by far the highest in the province: in Derry the figure was 9 per cent, while the Diocese of Armagh recorded a mere 4 per cent.[11] While both Catholics and Protestants in Northern Ireland are under considerable internal pressure to maintain homogenous communities in the face of external threat, interaction has also been limited by deliberately orchestrated physical constraints. In order to maintain predictable electoral outcomes, the Unionist-controlled government allocated municipal housing from 1921 onwards in a way that would prevent the development of mixed communities and threaten voting trends.[12] The scale of residential segregation was also exacerbated by the outbreak of the Troubles in the late 1960s, which forced many families to flee back into traditional Catholic and Protestant strongholds of villages, towns or particular housing estates.

In the nineteenth century, Catholic and Protestant immigrants from Ireland settled in particular locations in and around Glasgow so that the Garngad became 'Green' and Bridgeton 'Orange'. In fact, all such districts were partially mixed; ethnic Irish neighbourhoods did not develop in Glasgow as acutely as in Boston or even Liverpool. In any case, the massive rehousing programmes applied between the 1930s and the 1970s broke up the inner-city Victorian districts, dispersing Catholics and Protestants alike into peripheral housing schemes. Unlike in Northern Ireland, there was no political basis for segregation so no sectarian quota was used in housing allocation. The result was the creation of mixed communities, greater interaction and the dilution of communal activity and hence communal identities. Post-war occupational mobility also allowed many Catholics to gravitate to the upper-working-class new towns of East Kilbride and Cumbernauld, while the burgeoning white-collar workforce headed for the expanding suburbs. In all cases, the strong ties with the old inner-city Catholic parishes were never going to be replicated. There do remain towns and villages in Lanarkshire with predominant Catholic or Protestant overtones, a legacy of the segregation enforced by coalmasters to keep Irish Catholic and Ulster Protestant mineworkers apart during the latter part of the nineteenth century.[13] However, Lanarkshire is historically unique for playing host to large-scale sectarian friction, with the recent 'Monklandsgate' affair demonstrating its continuing potency in that part of the country. In any case, the population distribution in its various localities is a weak comparison with the sheer scale of segregation in Ulster.

Courting the Catholic Vote: Socialism, Nationalism and the Church

The redevelopment of Glasgow mentioned above has largely been presided over by a Labour administration which first took control of the Corporation in 1933. The party's rise to power was built on cross-community support, and although the bulk of its votes at both local and national level has always been delivered by Protestants, its backbone is reinforced by overwhelming and continuous support from the Catholic community. Prior to the resolution of the Irish Home Rule question, the majority of immigrant Catholics who were eligible to vote were far more interested in events back home and placed their vote with the Liberal Party through the United Irish League. It was only after the creation of the Irish Free State that they turned to the party that would best serve their everyday material needs. Catholics transferred their allegiance to their 'class' party, contributing to a modest but strategic increase in Labour's electoral support which proved decisive in the party's breakthrough of 1922.[14] Thereafter, the political map of urban Scotland turned red.

Catholic attachment to Labour was not only a tangible sign of integration into mainstream society but further evidence of weakening Church influence. The community chose not to form its own political party but instead to back a secular British-wide organisation. Had a Catholic party been formed before or in response to the militant Protestant parties of the 1930s, then distinct battle-lines would have been drawn and the political system would have become notably sectarian.[15] Furthermore, the Church was fiercely opposed to socialism, with Pope Leo XII's *Rerum Novarum* condemning the vivid anti-clerical threat of the European movements. The clergy in Scotland had previously been successful in convincing most of the laity that socialism was inextricably linked with atheism, but, helped in no small part by John Wheatley's *Catholic Socialist Society*, many were encouraged to recognise their compatibility.[16] Eventually the clergy endorsed the laity's support for the Labour Party, possibly aware that continued opposition would turn many adherents away from the faith. On occasion, it urged Catholics to join the movement in order to sabotage any radicalism emanating from the Independent Labour Party.[17]

While the Catholic community has solidly backed Labour ever since, recent trends indicate a growing support for the SNP. The party did not become a force in Scottish politics until the 1960s, when it broke through in the west by winning Hamilton in 1967 and then Govan in 1973. In the early years of the nationalist movement, founder members such as Andrew Dewar Gibb and George Malcolm Thomson regularly disparaged people of Irish descent as racially inferior to Scotsmen. Dewar Gibb described the Irish as 'riff raff . . . responsible for the most crime committed in Scotland which otherwise would be the most law-abiding country in the world'.[18] His colleague wrote, 'The Scots are a dying people. They are being replaced in their own country by a people alien in race, temperament and religion, at a speed which is without parallel in history outside the era of barbarian invasions.'[19] Another figurehead, John MacCormick, argued that Section 18 of the Education Act ought to be abolished and that no benefit should be paid to unemployed Irish labourers who had not been resident in Scotland for a certain number of years.[20] But their outlook had to change if they were ever to make a serious challenge in the Labour heartlands. There was clear frustration at the SNP's inability to gain seats in the west precisely because of the strength of the Catholic–Labour alliance. Speaking in 1967, the son of John MacCormick stated,

> Politically, many of these Scots fail to appreciate that they are now as Scottish as anyone else, and fail to see that Scotland's future is now their future. It is more the pity that so many working-class Catholics regard it as an article of faith to vote Labour come what may. Such a vote is meaningless and only matched in futility by the ritual Conservative vote of working-class Orangemen. Catholics could make a great contribution to the Scotland of the future were they to cast aside the 'ghetto' approach to Scottish politics now.[21]

Iain MacCormick was a Catholic convert who later was the MP for Argyllshire, a position he held between 1974 and 1979. Although the SNP fielded several Catholic candidates during the 1970s, the Catholic vote was not forthcoming. The traditional Catholic support for Labour obviously restricted the party's success; only 12 per cent of Catholics voted for the party in 1974 when it recorded its greatest electoral success (see table 4). Perhaps the lack of Catholic support was also due to the thought of an independent Scotland evoking the fear of a 'Protestant Scotland' and too close a parallel to Northern Ireland. The experience of Ulster Catholics from 1921 onwards, coupled with the fact that their Scottish counterparts were a smaller minority, may also have given rise to anti-nationalist resistance. The SNP never publicly involved itself in the Northern Ireland conflict during the 1970s, and never publicly refuted suggestions that a separate Scotland would affect Catholic status. On the other hand, it has regularly denied accusations of playing the Orange card in order to challenge Labour in key constituencies. The Hamilton success of 1967 was met with allegations that the party had pandered to the Orange vote (its placards being that colour), and the party was also accused of mobilising anti-Catholic feeling in the Monklands East by-election in 1994. *The Herald* singled out SNP leader Alex Salmond for particular criticism, but printed an apology following his angry response. Salmond himself writes for the Catholic newspaper *Flourish*.[22]

Table 4: The Catholic Vote in Scotland 1974–1997

	1974 (OCT)	1979	1992	1997
Labour	75%	78%	65%	81%
SNP	12%	8%	20%	10%
Conservative	11%	12%	7%	5%
Liberal	2%	3%	8%	4%
Total	100% (121)	100% (76)	100% (122)	100% (98)

Source: Scottish Election Surveys of 1974 (Oct), 1979, 1992 and 1997

The jibe of 'Tartan Tories' levelled at the SNP during the 1970s had a ring of truth to it, given that the party's support was almost as distinctly Protestant as that of the Conservatives. However, the party has made significant gains amongst Catholics since, particularly in the 1990s. Table 4 indicates that 20 per cent of Catholics voted for the SNP in 1992 (almost as much as the Protestant support, at 23 per cent). Perhaps the lower support recorded for the party in 1997 indicates that Catholics only flirted with the idea of Scottish nationalism for a brief period. On the other hand, it could be the case that many SNP supporters, of all confessional groups and none, tactically backed Labour to ensure the end of Tory control in Scotland. Following the referendum and the creation of the Scottish parliament, they could now realign themselves with the nationalists. Catholics, of course, have always been the most hostile to Conservative rule and possibly took this approach more than most to ensure change. Such speculation is given credibility by the results of a pre-election opinion poll in 1998, which indicated that Catholic support for the SNP matched that of Protestants at 30 per cent. Of greater significance, 58 per cent of Catholics claimed that they would vote for independence in a referendum, compared with 51 per cent of Protestants. The poll also demonstrated that SNP support among Catholics had trebled since 1974, while there has been a dramatic decline in support for Labour over the same period.[23] Commenting on these results, Monsignor Tom Connelly, the spokesman for the Catholic Church, warned Labour that it could no longer take the Catholic vote for granted.

The SNP received a further boost two months later, when Cardinal Winning appeared strongly supportive of Scottish nationalism in an address to a multi-denominational conference in Brussels. He described it as 'mature, respectful of democracy and international in outlook', and when asked if he thought devolution would lead to independence, he stated, 'I certainly think things are heading in that direction. There is a loosening of ties and the next decade will show if we're better off as an independent country or not.'[24] The content of Winning's address spoke volumes about his opinion of New Labour. As mentioned earlier, its relationship with the Catholic Church has been uneasy in recent years, partly because of the issue of abortion but also because of the school closures. The SNP has used the schools issue in an attempt to win Catholic votes from Labour, giving assurances about their future first in the 1992 Govan by-election and more recently in its 1999 manifesto.[25] It is thus interesting to note that the party could well be accused of pandering to both Catholics and Protestants in different constituencies in the space of a few years. We can only anticipate the results of the next election survey to discover the strength of Catholic support for Labour and the SNP. In 1999 Labour became the largest party but failed to win an overall majority and formed a coalition government with the Liberal Democrats. The SNP won 35 seats and 30 per cent of the vote, which was their best performance since 1974. Back then, few Catholics rallied to the nationalist cause, but given recent voting shifts this is most unlikely now.

Political support for denominational education, coupled with the less than subtle backing from the most senior Catholic figure, could be the reason why Catholics are now just as likely as Protestants to vote for the SNP. Yet we need to remind ourselves of the current relationship that the community has with its schools and church. With almost half a Catholic sample no longer supporting the former, the political currency of state-funded Catholic schools is disputable. Should legislation be introduced that affects the existence of the denominational system, it may well cause further fragmentation of the Catholic vote, rather than its entrenchment. Also, given the decline in Mass attendance and relaxing attitudes towards abortion and contraception, the influence that Cardinal Winning has over the Catholic community and hence its voters is clearly also limited. It is more appropriate to view his speech as a response to, rather than a catalyst for, growing SNP support. No political party can hope to manipulate a Catholic social issue effectively for the simple reason that there is no longer a staunchly Catholic bloc vote available for deployment. There are now few Catholics who are Catholic enough to base their vote purely on specific Catholic issues.

Growing Catholic support for the SNP is more likely to rest with socio-economic equality. With Catholics now fully integrated across the class spectrum, there is a far greater Catholic confidence with Scottish nationhood. Catholics are no longer overconcentrated in unskilled work but are well represented in the professional, commercial and technical ranks, and are even over-represented as local and national politicians. They are far removed from the disadvantaged and differentiated immigrant minority who feared and mistrusted wider society and its institutions, responding to hostility by retreating into its own sub-society centred on the parish church. Table 5 indicates that the vast majority of Catholics are happy to cite a Scottish identity.

Table 5: National Identity by Religion

	CATHOLIC	PROTESTANT	OTHER	ALL
Scottish not British	26%	16%	21%	19%
Scottish > British	37%	40%	43%	40%
Scottish = British	30%	35%	31%	33%
British > Scottish	1%	4%	3%	3%
British not Scottish	1%	3%	2%	4%
None of these	5%	1%	1%	1%
Total	100% (148)	100% (511)	100% (298)	100% (957)

Source: Scottish Election Survey 1992

According to these results, Catholics are more likely to profess a purely Scottish identity than non-Catholics. While two-thirds also accept a British identity in part, this may well be a practical identification with the wider state rather than a celebration of it. Although it would have been useful to better test the extent of Irish identity among the Catholic sample, the respondents were nevertheless given the opportunity to cite such an alternative and very few actually did. There was very little expression of the relationship between Irishness and Catholicism, whether as 'Irish' or 'Irish-Scots'.

It has been realistically calculated that around 80 per cent of Scottish Catholics are of Irish descent.[26] Most of them are now third, fourth or even fifth generation, and the emotional ties to Ireland become ever distant as the bloodline becomes ever diluted. Those seeking to reaffirm an Irish Catholic identity, or to construct one, can do so in the orchestrated and ritualised football environment of Celtic Park. Yet the very support given to the development of Celtic FC over a century ago signalled the Irish community's willingness to participate in Scottish sport. Had they sought a uniquely Irish social identity they would have followed the example set by the Gaelic Athletic Association in Ireland and refused to participate in 'English-style' games.[27] Instead, Celtic, Hibernian and Dundee Harp (the forerunner of United) stimulated cross-community interaction through an extremely popular game. Few Catholics today will even be aware of the GAA's tiny Scottish wing, which has struggled to recruit members in the shadow of football.[28] Celtic fans offer up a whole repertoire of songs relating to the Ulster conflict, some young men scrawl IRA slogans on city walls and some join the Republican Band Alliance or James Connolly societies. For most Scottish Catholics though, the future of Northern Ireland is only a passive concern, best omitted from their own country's functioning political arena and peaceful public life.

Through declining fertility rates and a huge slump in the number of Catholic marriages and baptisms, the Catholic population is now at its lowest for 50 years, forming less than 14 per cent of Scotland's total population.[29] While this does not yet cast a major shadow over the very future of Catholicism in Scotland, it has been brought about by Catholics themselves as a response to the social and economic forces that evolved during the twentieth century. Adherence to Church teaching is now a matter of individual spirituality. All the evidence presented here suggests that Catholics are assimilated into Scottish society to the extent that the very phrase 'Catholic community' has lost much of its salience.

Acknowledgements

My thanks to Paula Surridge at the University of Salford for supplying the Scottish Election Survey material and Patrick West at the MRC Medical Sociology Unit, University of Glasgow, for the West of Scotland 20-07 Health Study data. Thanks also to Frank Cassidy at the Diocese of Motherwell for supplying marriage and baptism figures, and Bill Horton at the Archdiocese of Glasgow for providing a revised list of Catholic secondary schools in Scotland.

Notes

[1] C. Brown, *Religion and Society in Scotland since 1707* (Edinburgh, 1997), p.61. Also chapter 2 of J. Highet, *The Scottish Churches: A Review of their State 400 Years after the Reformation* (London, 1960). Estimated adult membership of the Catholic Church in 1959 was 530,550, while the estimated attendance at Sunday service was 334,300.

[2] P. Brierly and F. MacDonald, *Prospects for Scotland 2000: Trends and Tables from the 1994 Scottish Church Census* (The National Bible Society of Scotland, 1995). Trends are projected to 2005.

[3] S. Kendrick, F. Bechhofer and D. McCrone, 'Recent Trends in Fertility Differentials in Scotland', in H. Jones (ed.), *Population Change in Contemporary Scotland* (Norwich, 1984), pp.35–52. The six 'highly Catholic areas' were identified as those where 30 per cent of all marriages in 1973 were performed in a Roman Catholic church.

[4] *The Scotsman*, 6 October 1998.

[5] *The Herald*, 18 February 1997.

[6] See 'Scotland decides' in *The Herald*, 8 May 1999.

[7] Catholic schools that have closed since the mid-1980s are as follows: St Columba of Iona, St Gerard's, St Gregory's, St Leonard's, St Pius, John Bosco and St Augustine's; Our Lady and St Francis has amalgamated with St Mungo's (all Glasgow); St Aelred's in Paisley, Sacred Heart in Girvan, Our Lady's in Broxburn. The Dumbarton schools of St Patrick's and Notre Dame were amalgamated to form Our Lady and St Patrick's. Information supplied by Bill Horton, RE advisor at the Archdiocese of Glasgow.

[8] See T. Gallagher, *Glasgow, The Uneasy Peace: Religious Tension in Modern Scotland* (Manchester, 1987), p.49.

[9] J. Darragh, 'The Catholic Population of Scotland 1878–1978', in D. McRoberts (ed.), *Modern Scottish Catholicism* (Glasgow, 1979), pp.211–47.

[10] Figure supplied by Frank Cassidy at the Diocese of Motherwell.

[11] V. Morgan, M. Smyth, G. Robinson and G. Fraser, *Mixed Marriages in Northern Ireland: Institutional Responses,* Paper for the Centre for the Study of Conflict, University of Ulster, 1996.

[12] See B. O'Leary and J. McGarry, *The Politics of Antagonism: Understanding Northern Ireland* (London, 1993), p.120.

[13] For a discussion of sectarian friction in the mining industy, see A.B. Campbell, *The Lanarkshire Miners: A Social History of their Trade Unions, 1775–1874* (Edinburgh, 1979).

[14] I. Hutchison, *A Political History of Scotland 1832–1924* (Edinburgh, 1986), p.287.

[15] For details of the rise and fall of the Scottish Protestant League and Protestant Action, see S. Bruce, *No Pope of Rome: Anti-Catholicism in Modern Scotland* (Edinburgh, 1985).

[16] S. Gilley, 'Catholics and Socialists in Glasgow, 1906–1912', in K. Lunn (ed.), *Hosts, Immigrants and Minorities* (London, 1980), pp.160–200.

[17] T. Gallagher, 'Catholics in Scottish Politics', *Bulletin of Scottish Politics*, 1981, pp.21–43.

[18] A. Dewar Gibb, *Scotland in Eclipse* (London, 1930), p.54.

[19] G.M. Thomson, *Caledonia or the Future of the Scots* (London, 1927), p.10.

[20] R.J. Finlay, *Independent and Free* (Edinburgh, 1994), p.193.

[21] Quoted in Gallagher, *Uneasy Peace*, p.276.

[22] See G. Walker, *Intimate Strangers: Political and Cultural Interaction between Scotland and Ulster in Modern Times* (Edinburgh, 1995), pp.180–4. In 1992, the Catholic-dominated Labour-controlled Monklands District Council were accused of employing co-religionists and relatives. They were also accused of favouring 'Catholic' Coatbridge over 'Protestant' Airdrie by spending £600 per head in the former and only £50 per head in the latter. Following three independent commissions and an internal investigation into the running of the local party, no evidence of sectarianism was provided, although charges of nepotism were upheld. The scandal became politicised at national level following the death of local MP and party leader John Smith in 1994. The Monklands East by-election was bitterly fought by parties accusing each other of sectarianism. The Conservatives ran a poster campaign depicting the local Labour Party as a 'Catholic Mafia', the SNP were accused of pandering to similar prejudice, while Labour canvassers had told Catholic

voters that the SNP would close Catholic schools and 'create a Northern Ireland'. Although the Catholic Helen Liddell was returned, Labour's majority was slashed from 16,000 to just 1,640 from the SNP.

[23] *The Scotsman*, 28 August 1998.

[24] Ibid., 6 October 1998.

[25] *Scotland on Sunday*, 20 August 1998.

[26] R. Williams, 'Can Data on Scottish Catholics Tell Us about Descendants of the Irish in Scotland?', *New Community* 19 (2), 1993, pp.296–309.

[27] See G. Finn, 'Racism, Religion and Social Prejudice: Irish Catholic Clubs, Soccer and Scottish Society, I', *The International Journal of the History of Sport*, 8, 1, 1991, pp.72–95.

[28] For details, see J. Bradley, 'Heritage, Culture and Identity: The Gaelic Athletic Association in Scotland', in G. Jarvie (ed.), *Sport in the Making of Celtic Cultures* (Leicester, 1999), pp.100–11.

[29] Darragh, 'Catholic Population', p.230. The Catholic population doubled from 332,600 in 1878 to 662,300 in 1931. It rose further to 750,000 in 1951 and peaked at 823,500 in 1977. The 1997 figure listed in table 1 in this article is 705,650. See also Brown, *Religion and Society*, p.55. Between 1975 and 1995, the number of Catholic marriages solemnised by the Church has more than halved from 6,003 to 2,948. The Catholic proportion of all marriages has returned to the level of 1855.

18. GOING BUT NOT GONE: CATHOLIC DISADVANTAGE IN SCOTLAND

Rory Williams and Patricia Walls

Introduction

Over the last two years, a number of respected academics have assured us that Catholic disadvantage in Scotland is no more. The present chapter argues not only that this is not true, but also that it is refuted by the data sources to which these same commentators appeal.

Assuming that the case made in this chapter is supported, how can such a disagreement have arisen? It will be helpful for readers to be aware from the start of issues in interpreting the evidence which make disagreement possible.

The first interpretive issue of importance is the weakness of the data available. If we were starting from scratch with enough money to pick a sample to resolve the question of whether there is Catholic disadvantage in Scotland, we would be unlikely to choose anything smaller than a sample of 40,000, of which 7,500 would be Catholics. The reason for this is that we would ideally want to look at men and women separately, to break down the picture by age group to see whether there might have been change over time, and to look at regional differences in these trends as well – particularly any differences between west-central Scotland, where most Catholics live, and the rest of the country. Within these subdivisions, we would also want to be reasonably sure that we could detect a specified difference between the percentages of Catholics and others having the opportunity of good jobs or housing, or whatever other advantage was of interest. We might accept, for example, that a difference of 1 or 2 per cent was not worth bothering about but decide that a difference of 5 per cent or more was significant enough to begin to matter. With these considerations in mind, most researchers would reckon on a sample of around 7,000 to 8,000 Catholics and would know that if they had to settle for less, they would be unable to detect some differences which really exist. With a smaller sample they would also get some spurious positive differences by chance, but even in a small sample procedures are available for screening out chance differences. Thus the main effect of taking too small a sample is that we cannot trust a finding of no difference very far, especially if there is a history which suggests that differences can be expected.

In the data for Scotland analysed here, the Scottish Election Surveys on which previous reports have largely relied, the sample sizes are 957 for 1992 and 882 for 1997. The sample of the west of Scotland survey is larger (2,618) and has the advantage that it was collected for three indicative age groups, 15, 35 and 55, so that the numbers in each age group are higher than they would have been if they had been spread across all ages. But clearly none of these data will enable us to be very confident about findings that there is no difference between Catholics and others.

The second interpretive issue which readers will need to bear in mind is that one may get different answers according to the question one asks. In the title of this book, the question tacitly asked is whether Scotland is a sectarian country. Sectarianism is an ideology of conflict rooted in religious differences, in this case differences between Catholics and Protestants, and it is tempting to suppose that if fewer and fewer people in Scotland manifest the attitudes of a sectarian ideology, and if those that do are swiftly marginalised by those who speak for and to the public, then Scotland has ceased to be sectarian in any significant degree, and Catholics have in effect become accepted and fully integrated. Such, in essence, is the position taken by Steve Bruce in his book *No Pope of Rome.*[1] 'Anti-Catholicism in Scotland,' he concludes, 'is no longer a force . . . In some urban areas, young Protestants and Catholics still fight but even this violence is considerably less than it was in the days of the "Billy Boys" and the "Norman Conks". It is just a boys' game. Most Scots . . . see the young bloods of the Scottish Loyalist movement as unprincipled thugs; they see the Highland Calvinists as quaint oddities. Most Scots live in a secular society.' This view was repeated, and given further prominence, in the *Scottish Government Yearbook* for 1982.[2] Similarly, David McCrone and Michael Rosie,[3] whose interests are in the political implications of sectarianism, use data from the 1992 Scottish Election Survey to examine perceptions of religious conflict by region, age and gender and, finding that in most groups those who think it serious are in a minority, note that 'religious conflict is perceived as "serious" only among a majority of young males in the west of Scotland. This would seem to lend support to Steve Bruce's assessment.' And after reviewing a number of other attitudinal measures they conclude, 'There is considerable evidence that, for the majority of Scots, political sectarianism is an irrelevance which belongs firmly in the past.'

Bearing this evidence on the question of manifest sectarianism in mind, it is perhaps not surprising that these and other scholars approach evidence on Catholic disadvantage with the hypothesis that difference no longer exists. 'In Scotland,' says Steve Bruce, 'all the social surveys of the last two decades show no discernible difference in the socio-economic status of Catholics and non-Catholics.'[4] McCrone and Rosie too, despite noting what they evidently feel are minor qualifications, are happy to declare that 'the social-class profile of Catholics has mirrored that of the population as a whole since the 1970s'. Even Lindsay Paterson, whose interest is more specifically in the role of education and whose comments are usually carefully defined, has summed up the Catholic situation in Scotland as revealed by the 1997 Scottish Election Study[5] by saying, 'There is no point in claiming that Catholic schools are needed because Catholics are discriminated against. By and large they are not.' If this is a general claim about discrimination, with the implication that there are no longer any socio-economic differences between Catholics and others in Scotland, as readers might infer, then Paterson too joins the recent consensus that inequality is a thing of the past.

In this chapter, however, the evidence is surveyed with a different set of questions in mind, questions which arise firstly from the study of religious and ethnic minorities around the world, and secondly from the implications of their social situation for health. The Scottish Catholic community has in the past included large numbers of people who have suffered from the way in which both their religious and their ethnic identities have been perceived by the majority population.

Most of the recent British work that has been done on minorities has focused on groups which have largely arrived in Britain since the war. This is unfortunate because it has bolstered a naïve supposition that religious stereotyping is different from ethnic stereotyping and racism, and that racism is only perpetrated on black groups. This is very far from being the case, as the Holocaust should have taught us. Not only were the Jews, a white group, subjected to the most thoroughgoing racist assault by a Western country in the twentieth century, but their religion was tied up in this assault as well as their ethnic origin. This alerts us to the fact that sectarianism may not be a simple matter of religious difference. We need to consider whether a religious minority is also an ethnic minority, and whether it is, or ever has been, racialised – that is, whether behavioural differences between the minority and the majority have ever been constructed as biological differences.[6] In asking the last part of the question in this way, and specifically in using the word 'constructed', we are explicitly rejecting the idea that the notion of racial differences in behaviour has any scientific validity. Scientists have long repudiated any such idea.[7] We are, however facing the fact that many people have fallen into such invalid patterns of thought in the past, and are still capable of doing so.

In the case of Scottish Catholics these questions are soon answered. It has been estimated that in Scotland as a whole around 65 per cent of Catholics – and in Clydeside in particular 80 per cent or more – are of Irish descent.[8] And in nineteenth-century Scotland, the Irish – that is, the indigenous or Catholic Irish – were unequivocally constructed as an alien race. For example, the Scottish Registrar-General, in the Report on the Census of 1871,[9] commented at length on the deleterious results, lowered moral tone and increased need for sanitary and police precautions which he ascribed to the presence of 'the Irish race', and as late as 1923 the Church of Scotland published a report on the Scottish Education Act, which incorporated Catholic schools into the state system, with the title 'The menace of the Irish race to our Scottish nationality.'[10] Leaders of the Scottish Protestant League and Protestant Action, active with anti-Catholic propaganda in the 1920s and 1930s, had German fascist connections and racist sympathies.[11] Racialised constructions of Irish identity were also common in England.[12]

Such characterisations largely disappeared from public discussion after the Second World War, although in private life it remained commonplace for Irish and blacks to be lumped together in discriminatory advertisements for jobs and housing until the Race Relations Act of 1965.[13] At the public level, the 1948 British Nationality Act and the 1962 Commonwealth Immigrants Act both treated the Irish – even when they were citizens of the Republic – as if they were British subjects. This reconstruction of Irish identity by the British government has long been cited by British authors as evidence that the Irish were now regarded as assimilated, and their inclusion in a homogeneous white category certainly underlined the way the government's ethnic classifications had come to coincide with skin colour. Access to Cabinet papers has, however, made clear that the Irish were treated as if they were British subjects for rather more complicated reasons, which were to do with policy towards Northern Ireland. The military and strategic importance of Northern Ireland was still felt to be paramount at this period, though it has since been disavowed by the Downing Street Declaration of 1993. Placing a British immigration control on

233

migrants from Northern Ireland risked offending the Unionists, whose co-operation was essential, yet to place a control on the border between Northern Ireland and the Republic was impossible. Reluctantly, the conclusion was reached that 'the only way out of the dilemma would appear to be to argue boldly along the lines that the population of the whole British Isles is for historical and geographical reasons essentially one'.[14, 15]

Thus the period since the war has, at the governmental level, been characterised by a carefully fostered myth of the homogeneity of the Irish and British populations, quite the opposite of the racialised myth of the decades which preceded the war. Awkward evidence of religious discrimination has been kept in the background: when the Race Relations Act of 1965 was formulated, the Stormont government successfully requested that Northern Ireland be excluded from the operation of the Act, and questions in the House of Commons revealed that religious discrimination was therefore not to be covered by the Act; later, in 1970, religious discrimination was dealt with separately by the Stormont government as if this was something peculiar to Northern Ireland.[16, 17] The myth of the homogeneity of the British and Irish populations is thus evidently as much a subject for prudent scepticism as the myth that they are different races. Clearly the myth of homogeneity is often less harmful to a minority than the myth that they are an inferior race, but it can be harmful nonetheless, by rendering the minority invisible at the governmental level, and by making the question of their welfare and their equal access to jobs, housing and schools correspondingly difficult to address and to research.

On this evidence, it will immediately be apparent to anyone who has studied the situation of minorities that the present circumstances of Scottish Catholics should be reviewed with some well-known cautions in mind. Research on world minorities has revealed the importance of several key issues.

Firstly, unequal results, disadvantageous to minorities, can be produced by institutional practices which have no discernible discriminatory intention at all. Clarification of how this happens has only followed a long debate over the term 'institutional racism', a term first used to describe the plight of American blacks by Stokely Carmichael and Charles Hamilton in *Black Power*.[18] There they describe institutional racism as 'the operation of established and respected forces in the society'. They explain, 'When white terrorists bomb a black church and kill five black children, that is an act of individual racism, widely deplored by most segments of the society. But when in that same city – Birmingham, Alabama – 500 black babies die each year because of the lack of proper food, shelter and medical facilities, and thousands more are destroyed and maimed physically, emotionally and intellectually because of conditions of poverty and discrimination in the black community, that is a function of institutional racism.' The trenchant vigour and realism of this book's analysis struck chords on both sides of the Atlantic and 'institutional racism' soon became a popular term, being used in an increasing variety of contexts.

But as time went on, the term's meaning became more and more ambiguous, and this ambiguity caused Lord Scarman to reject the term in his report on Brixton in 1981, though he sought to substitute the notion of practices which were 'unwittingly discriminatory' instead. Most of those acquainted with the reality of these situations found this too crude a solution, and two careful studies tried to disentangle the components of the varying outcomes and explanations for which 'institutional racism' had served as a portmanteau term.[19, 20] They pointed out amongst other things that disadvantage might be intended or not intended in varying degrees; that if foreseen it might be justified by an ideology or merely by what is regarded as common sense; that it was the product of an interaction between both parties to a relationship; and that a number of different institutions might work together to produce the disadvantageous effect. Finally, Robert Miles[21] drew the emerging conclusion: that it is unwise to combine an outcome with an explanation in the same term – for example to assume that observed discrimination is always caused by racism – and also that it is unwise to use the same term to cover too many different explanations. He proposed that observation of exclusionary practices – of disadvantage – should be the starting-point for enquiry, and that a wide range of possible explanations, intentional or unintentional, ideological, commonsensical or merely founded in routine behaviour, be considered. 'Institutional racism' should refer only to explanatory findings which show that these particular exclusionary practices originally arose from a racist discourse but are no longer explicitly justified by such a discourse, though other words may continue to carry the original meaning. This same empirical method is the one proposed here.

Secondly, a related problem, already hinted at in Miles's definition of 'institutional racism' above, is the persistence of inequality in spite of the disappearance of racist language from public discussion since the Second World War. Although the arrival of migrants in large numbers in the UK in the 1950s certainly evoked racist responses, it became apparent that at the governmental level race theories like those of the Nazis were not a feature of justification for public decisions, even those decisions which were as adverse to minorities as policy before the war, and something else was needed to account for such decisions. Even Enoch Powell confined himself to asserting the incompatibility of different cultures and the disruptive consequences of forcing them to mix, and the same theme has often been taken up by other Conservatives, including Margaret Thatcher.[22] This led to arguments of this kind being dubbed 'the new racism',[23] and to attitudes of cultural superiority, even with no biological implications, being defined as further forms of racism.[24] At the same time, other researchers protested at these expansions in the use of the word 'racism',[25, 26] and advocated preserving distinctions by using separate terms like 'ethnocentrism' for attitudes of cultural superiority. (The restricted sense of racism advocated by these last two writers is adopted for clarity here.) These debates indicate that if sectarian language and manifestations have diminished since the Second World War, we should be wary of concluding that inequality has therefore diminished.

Finally, if open sectarianism is dying, there are other ideas now in the ascendant which may become closely connected with racial or cultural ideologies in a given context. One of these ideas, which is often connected with attitudes of racial or cultural superiority, is nationalism. This is of importance here for two reasons. First, the contest between unionists (many of whom are of Scottish descent) and nationalists in Northern Ireland is a contest about nationality; and second, there has been a resurgence of the sense of Scottish nationality. At the moment there is evidence that many Scottish Catholics see potential benefits for themselves in Scottish nationalism,[27] but it is not clear whether these benefits are also related to Irish nationalism, and how the relationship between Scottish and Irish nationalism will evolve remains an open question.

The upshot of this review of research on minorities is that the current reduction in overt sectarianism in Scotland is not a trustworthy indication of whether Scottish Catholics suffer exclusion and disadvantage, and we would be wise to begin by measuring disadvantage directly. If we find any, we should consider whether ideological biases are involved in its genesis, or persisting institutional practices, and, if the latter, whether these practices are inherited from a period when overt racist and sectarian attitudes undoubtedly prevailed, or whether they arise from other institutional pressures such as those generated by the evolution of the economic system.

In addition to these reasons for starting with measures of disadvantage, derived from studies of minorities in many situations, health is of interest in this chapter because social disadvantage is closely associated with ill health. Which causes which? This question has long been the subject of debate, resolved in recent years by demonstrations that ill health acts as a cause of social disadvantage only in rather limited and specific contexts, while social disadvantage regularly precedes ill health.[28, 29] The intervening factors in this relationship are many and complex, and it is unlikely that all of them can be identified. But the situation is clear enough for the government to have named social inequality as a root cause of ill health in their White Papers on health.[30, 31] They have stated a need to monitor inequalities and to prepare health improvement plans with targets to be measured by the monitoring. This does not, of course, mean that every disease is due to inequality; liability to specific diseases may be due to specific physiological or genetic causes. Nevertheless, heightened morbidity and mortality across a wide range of causes should be investigated as possible indicators of general handicaps in the environment and are often associated with reduced standard of living, which in turn is largely determined by the level of jobs to which a group has access.[32]

Measures of disadvantage have traditionally focused on jobs, housing, qualifications, wealth and income, but these measures are not interchangeable. Jobs are generally regarded as the key indicator, as jobs create the income for housing and other goods, and qualifications are mainly of interest as a predictor of future job levels and as a test of whether minorities are actually getting the jobs they are qualified for, without the intervention of bias against them. Such bias has been demonstrated for some minorities,[33] and we should beware of conclusions which are based on educational qualifications alone. Similarly, we should beware of conclusions based on equal percentages of Catholics and others moving from the job level held by their father to a higher job level. If Catholic fathers were disadvantaged, an equal rate of upward progress is not enough – it will simply reproduce the disadvantage. Current job levels are the test. The respondent's own job level is the indicator used in the present chapter.

Measures to indicate whether people see themselves – or, perhaps more to the present point, whether they are seen by others – as being part of the group which we have loosely called Scottish Catholics need to be sensitive to past patterns of discrimination for which we are testing. Catholics undoubtedly suffered discrimination in the past, especially in Clydeside, where Catholics are, as noted above, overwhelmingly of Irish descent. The chief discriminatory practices involved identifying people either by Catholic schooling or by Irish name. These ways of classifying remind us that we are not dealing here primarily with attitudes to religious practice as an adult, nor are we dealing primarily with descent from just anyone born in Ireland. Rather, the attitudes we are concerned with here have to do with origins among the people of Ireland who were traditionally Catholic and whose names existed in Ireland before the main influx of Scottish and English settlers from the seventeenth century. This distinction is part of the baggage of British rule over Ireland from that time. If other Catholics, or Protestant Irish, accidentally get caught up in these ways of identifying, that is part of the crudity of these popular stereotypes. Thus if a religious indicator is used to get an accurate picture of how people of Irish Catholic background are faring in Scotland today – and such indicators are all that is available here – it is preferable to use an indicator not of current religion but of background religion, of affiliation in childhood. Moreover, we need to be aware that in regions outside west-central Scotland this measure will be less sensitive to the ethnic overtones of possible exclusionary practices, since it will include a larger proportion of incomers to Scotland who come from, for example, Catholic countries in Europe and who are likely, as is usually the case with migrants within the European Community, to be in good jobs.

With these cautions in mind, we can now turn to the data which are available.

Data

Readers who are not interested in technical details can skip straight to the next section headed 'Results'. For the technically minded, very briefly, three data sets are presented here. Together they represent the total body of data to which appeal has previously been made on the question of Catholic job disadvantage. The 1992 Scottish Election Survey had a random sample of 957 respondents, representing 74 per cent of those sought, of which 166 (17.3 per cent) said they had been brought up as Catholic. The 1997 Scottish Election Survey had a random sample of 882 respondents, representing 62 per cent of those sought, of which 156 (17.7 per cent) said they had been brought up as Catholic. Further information can be obtained at http://dawww.essex.ac.uk, using the 'searching for data' facility for study numbers 3171 and 3889. The west of Scotland survey had a random sample of 1,009 15-year-olds, 985 35-year-olds and 983 55-year-olds in 1987/8. They were drawn from an enhanced electoral register with age available, requiring permission for age to be passed on to the samplers; 70 per cent, 65 per cent and 55 per cent agreed at ages 15, 35 and 55, and 85 per cent, 90 per cent and 87 per cent of these completed interviews. For speed in meeting the deadline of this book, the present data are mostly taken from the follow-up in 1990, when 908, 852 and 858 respondents were re-interviewed (2,618 in all) and their 1987/8 data, including job and religious details, were united with the 1990 data into one set.[34] At ages 15 and 55, 280 (31 per cent) and 284 (33 per cent) said they had had a Catholic parent. At age 35, 262 (31 per cent) said they had been born into the Catholic faith. These groups were classified as Catholic for present purposes. In addition, job details are also presented from the 1995 follow-up of the youngest cohort, when they were 23.

Two measures of job level were made in the election surveys; the Registrar-General's social class measure is used here as it provides comparability with the west of Scotland survey. This lists six job levels in descending order from professional and kindred occupations in social class I to unskilled occupations in social class VI, with a division between non-manual and manual jobs halfway. Because of small numbers, the emphasis here is on the percentage in non-manual jobs, the simplest, though certainly a crude, way of assessing access to high-status jobs. The respondent's own job level is assessed unless otherwise stated.

As a check, the second measure of job level available, the Goldthorpe-Hope scale, was also tested for the tables of this chapter. The results are similar except that the religious differences for west-central Scotland in table 2, though present, are not statistically significant. In the light of the more substantial figures for central Clydeside in table 3, this is of little consequence.

Age needs careful and detailed classification to identify possible points of change. The small numbers in five-year age groups lead to rather abrupt chance fluctuations, so we used a moving average of the percentage in non-manual jobs by age. This was computed in ten-year age groups over the span of life from age 25 to 55 where we expected change to show up, starting each successive ten-year age group five years on from the previous one. So, for example, the percentage of Catholics in non-manual jobs at age 25–34 is followed by the percentage at age 30–39, and that is followed by the percentage at age 35–44, and so on. This produces a smoother and clearer pattern. Each age group is represented by the age at its midpoint, rounded to the nearest whole number; for example, the age group 25–34 is marked as age 30 (rounded up from 29.5) on the graphs. The initial age group starts from age 18 and goes up to 29, so its midpoint is 24, and the final age group is open-ended, including everyone aged 55 and over.

The 1997 Scottish Election Survey made provision for weighting the data to correct for a different way of sampling using one person per household as well as for variations in non-response. However, for statistical tests it is better to use unweighted data in the absence of a correction for the increase in the standard error from weighting.[35] The 1992 survey did not weight for non-response within Scotland, and the west of Scotland data set is also unweighted for non-response. Weighted results for 1997 have been checked and are similar to unweighted.

Statistics are computed for the one-tailed hypothesis that Catholics are still disadvantaged.

Results

Considering results for all Scotland first, table 1 shows that 43 per cent of Catholics in 1992 and 42 per cent in 1997 were in non-manual jobs, compared to 51 per cent and 54 per cent of non-Catholics – an 8 per cent gap in 1992 and a 12 per cent gap in 1997. The religious difference across all six job levels for 1992 could be down to chance, using conventional ways of reckoning chance results, but the difference in percentage of those in non-manual jobs is unlikely to be due to chance. The 1997 result is also unlikely to be due to chance, both for percentage in non-manual jobs and for all six levels, and this

Table 1: All Scotland – 1992 and 1997: job level of those with Catholic and other background

OCCUPATIONAL CLASS	1992 CATHOLIC	OTHER	1997 CATHOLIC	OTHER
I	2.5%	2.4%	2.7%	4.3%
II	22.9%	22.0%	17.7%	24.1%
III (non-manual)	17.8%	26.5%	21.1%	25.7%
All non-manual	43.2%	50.9%	41.5%	54.1%
Catholic deficit	-7.7%		-12.6%	
III (manual)	24.8%	20.7%	22.4%	19.8%
IV	21.7%	19.9%	22.4%	16.0%
V	10.2%	8.4%	13.6%	10.1%
Total	*157*	*758*	*147*	*676*
	100.0%	100.0%	100.0%	100.0%

Source: Scottish Election Surveys.

highlights the discrepancy between the two surveys in estimates of the percentage of Catholics in social class II. These crucial estimates seem to fluctuate in this size of survey, unless some change for the worse has occurred in occupations at this level.

Numbers are not big enough to get a reliable picture for either gender separately, but the pattern of disadvantage appears more consistent for men in both 1992 and 1997. It is noticeable that Catholic women are well represented in social class II, the group into which teachers and nurses are put. Classifying women who are not in work by their husband's job makes no difference to the results.

The importance of checking the overall picture for Scotland by looking at west-central Scotland was stressed at the end of the introduction. Most Catholics live in this area, and it is particularly here that the linked connotations of Irish and Catholic background led to discrimination in the past. Table 2 gives the job levels of Catholics and others in west-central Scotland compared with the rest of Scotland. In west-central Scotland, 40 per cent of Catholics in 1992 and 38 per cent in 1997 were in non-manual jobs, compared to 51 per cent and 50 per cent of non-Catholics – an 11 per cent gap in 1992 and a 12 per cent gap in 1997. Neither of these results is likely to be due to chance. It is noticeable that there is now more consistency between the 1992 and 1997 surveys. Where the difference between the surveys occurs is in the picture for the rest of Scotland, where 1992 shows Catholics on equal terms with the rest, while 1997 shows a 9–10 per cent gap. These fluctuations may be due to small numbers; for example, the more rosy picture in 1992 could be due to chance variations in the migration of small groups of professionals from Catholic countries in Europe and elsewhere to centres like Edinburgh.

It is clear from these results that the optimistic assessments previously given of these socio-economic data for Catholics in Scotland, suggesting that no

Table 2: West-Central Scotland 1992 and 1997: job level of those with Catholic and other background

| | 1992 | | 1997 | |
OCCUPATIONAL CLASS	CATHOLIC	OTHER	CATHOLIC	OTHER
Non-manual	40.4%	51.3%	37.6%	50.0%
Catholic deficit	-10.9%		-12.4%	
Total	*109*	*298*	*85*	*230*

Source: Scottish Election Surveys.

differences remain, have been wide of the mark. It is easy to see what one hopes to see and not to look in enough detail at the evidence. But hopes about the position of Catholics have been based on real changes – a real decline in open sectarian behaviour, and a real and rapid advance in the qualifications achieved by Scottish Catholic schools.[36, 37] Therefore we need to look particularly carefully at the pattern of disadvantage by age, and to consider the possibility that the younger generation is finding its way out of the old pattern. This is not as straightforward as it sounds. Age differences can occur for several reasons, and only one is a change in experience of young people compared with, say, ten or twenty years ago. This generational difference is called a cohort effect. But an age difference can also merely mean that young people always start towards the bottom of the job market and gradually work their way up, and therefore there might be little to choose between religious groups as regards the jobs they start with, though there might be considerable differences in the job level they have reached by middle age. Again, if religious discrimination primarily affects promotion prospects in middle age, it may be that stress, blocked promotion, resignation, job loss and downward mobility are more pronounced among Catholics only after this point in their lives (there is some evidence for this among the Irish in England).[38] In these two examples, age tells us something about a life-cycle effect. Finally, a difference between now and 20 years ago would probably show up in everyone's experience, no matter what their age. This is a period effect. So we need to look carefully at earlier data to see exactly what has changed, and for what age groups. Then at the same time as these results are considered, we can begin to bring in the more substantial sample of the west of Scotland survey, where all the figures are age-specific.

Let us begin with the good news. In 1975 the Scottish Social Mobility Study produced, amongst other things, data on the job levels of those from Catholic schools and others, broken down by a very simple division into two working age groups, 20–42 and 43–64.[39] Thus by using the same age groups, we can compare the situation in 1975 with that in 1992 and 1997, using a graph which shows disadvantage by age.

Figure 1 is a graph of this kind, and this figure and those following all have broadly the same format. On the left, on the vertical axis, is the percentage of

Figure 1: A new wave of young Catholics on equal terms? What we should see in 1992 and 1997 vs 1975

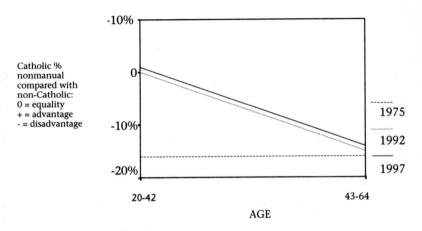

Catholic %
nonmanual
compared with
non-Catholic:
0 = equality
+ = advantage
- = disadvantage

Catholics in non-manual jobs in each age group *minus* the percentage of non-Catholics, thus showing the size of the Catholic disadvantage (minus figures) or advantage (plus figures) in that age group as a single figure. So, for example, if 30 per cent of Catholics and 40 per cent of non-Catholics are in non-manual jobs, the figure plotted on the graph is minus 10 per cent. The figure 0 thus represents equality. The horizontal axis, meanwhile, shows age groups running from the youngest on the left to the oldest on the right.

If there has been a change for the better in Catholic disadvantage in this period of around 20 years, a change focused on the new generation (a cohort effect in the terms just discussed), we would expect on the left an incoming wave of younger Catholics in 1992 and 1997 (the dotted and unbroken lines respectively) who are about equal in access to non-manual jobs (0 on the vertical axis), well above their age group in 1975 (the broken line). Meanwhile the age group 43–64 (on the right) would remain much the same in all three years. Please note that the broken, dotted and unbroken lines are not really necessary to understand this rather simple graph with only two age groups and could be replaced with points, but we use the same lines in later graphs with more age groups, where the lines are a useful visual aid.

Figure 2 now shows us the Scottish figures for 1975, 1992 and 1997 as they actually are. It is clear that there is indeed a new wave of younger Catholics who are close to equality in access to non-manual jobs. The change is dramatic, and the figures for both 1992 and 1997 confirm it with only small differences. At the same time, the change does not appear in the older age group, where strong differences from the experience of the younger group, unlikely to be due to chance, are still apparent. So there is indeed a cohort effect.

However there also seem to have been some other things going on which need watching. The slightly worse showing in 1997 compared with 1992 might be due to small numbers and to chance, but it is consistent at both younger and older ages. With an incoming cohort of young Catholics doing

Figure 2: Catholic job level compared with non-Catholic. 1992 and 1997 vs 1975: actual results

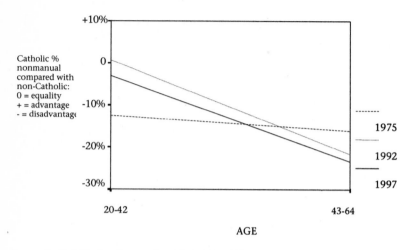

Source: Scottish Election Surveys. Scottish Social Mobility Survey, 1975

better, we would actually expect 1997 to show slightly less disadvantage than 1992, especially in the younger age group, yet we find it showing slightly more. This is considered in more detail in the next paragraphs.

In addition, there is a serious down side to the change since 1975, though it does not outweigh the achievement of the younger generation. Catholics in the older age group actually look to be at a greater disadvantage in 1992 and 1997 than in 1975 – the deficit in non-manual jobs has increased substantially from 16 per cent to 22–23 per cent. Whatever has happened over the last 20 years or more has made life better for young Catholics but worse for older Catholics at working ages.

Let us now consider the comparison between 1992 and 1997 by more detailed age groups to see whether the incoming wave of young Catholics with equality of access to jobs is still advancing. We cannot place too much reliance on the figures because of the problem of small numbers already referred to, but if the advance is still occurring we would expect to see something like figure 3. Here seven age groups are represented on the horizontal axis by the age at their midpoint, except for the oldest group on the right which includes everyone aged 55 and over. For the technically minded, the details are explained in the section entitled 'Data'. On the left, we would expect the incoming wave of young Catholics who have achieved equality, as pictured in 1992 (the dotted line), to fall towards a trough from around age 35, as we come to the older groups who have experienced disadvantage all their lives; but by 1997 (the unbroken line) we might expect the wave to have advanced by five years, the fall towards the trough beginning at around age 40.

Figure 4 shows what was actually found in 1992 and 1997. In 1992 (the dotted line), the wave of younger Catholics who have achieved equality is clearly visible on the left and bears a close resemblance to the expected picture

Figure 3: A new wave of young Catholics on equal terms? What we should see by age in 1992 and 1997

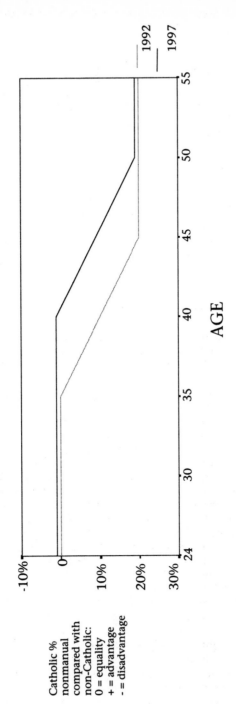

Source: Scottish Election Surveys.

Figure 4: Catholic job level compared with non-Catholic by age. 1992 and 1997: actual results

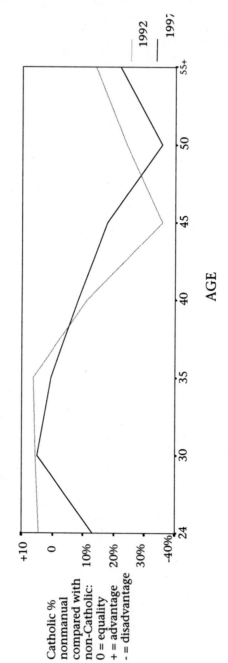

Source: Scottish Election Surveys.

for 1992 (the dotted line in figure 3). In this sample, equality is maintained up to age 35, though disadvantage increases from age 40. However, by 1997 (the unbroken line) the wave seems to have slumped and flattened, showing a number of differences from the unbroken line in figure 3. It is true that the unbroken line (1997) does at least seem to show less disadvantage at age 45, but it does not carry forward the levels achieved by the dotted line (1992) five years before; in particular, the unbroken line at age 40 does not carry forward the high level achieved by the dotted line at age 35. Moreover, further examination has shown that this impression is an average of different experiences for men and women. The level of the dotted line at age 35 is carried forward in the unbroken line for women five years later, but for men the unbroken line plunges sharply, though this is not shown because of small numbers. These results provide reason for caution about whether the younger generation of Catholics did sustain a position of equality as they got older during the 1990s. In addition, the youngest age group of Catholics has gone back to a deficit in 1997 where there was no deficit in 1992.

As an example of the numbers we are dealing with here, note that the crucial age group 35–44 contains only 28 Catholics in the 1992 sample and 37 in 1997. In spite of such small numbers, most of the religious differences in age groups between 40 and 54 in the two samples are unlikely to be due to chance. But there is no clear answer as yet on whether the exact pattern of change required by the hypothesis of figure 3 has occurred. Rather, we can see what sort of evidence and analysis is needed, and future studies of the maintenance of equality by age group should prepare to get adequate numbers especially for those aged around 35–44 in 1992 and 1997.

Meanwhile, the much larger west of Scotland survey can tell us whether these age-related patterns are repeated in the key area of the Clydeside conurbation, where Catholics are overwhelmingly of Irish descent. Table 3 gives results for men and women aged 15, 35 and 55 in 1987–8, with the addition of the most recent figures for the 15-year-olds when they had reached age 23 in 1995 (the sample has been followed up over time). The change in the 15-year-olds is important because they were categorised by the job level of whichever parent was head of their household when they were aged 15, but by their own job level at age 23. At the other ages, the job level assessed is that of the head of the household.

Beginning on the right-hand side of table 3 amongst the oldest age group, the 55-year-olds, we see the expected disadvantage for Catholics in both men and women, in neither case likely to be due to chance, with the difference between Catholics and others running at the level of 11.6 per cent for men and 18.6 per cent for women. Moving next to the left we find the figures for 35-year-olds, where the gap is still clear in both men and women and is still unlikely to be due to chance, running at the level of 12.4 per cent for men and 10.7 per cent for women. Finally we come to the 15-year-olds, who were 23 in 1995. Here we see that when classified by their parents' jobs in 1987/8 there was the same clear gap between Catholics and others, yet when they come to be classified by their own jobs at age 23 the gap has disappeared (the 6.6 per cent deficit for women is likely to be due to chance, and Catholic men actually have a slight advantage, probably also a chance result).

These larger-scale comparisons confirm that Catholic disadvantage persists in Clydeside for both men and women in a way that is unlikely to be due to

Table 3: Central Clydeside Conurbation, three age groups: job level of those with Catholic and other background

YEAR	1987/8	1995	1987/8	1987/8
AGE	15	23	35	55
Men	% of Catholics or others in nonmanual jobs			
a) Catholics	36.6%	54.7%	47.6%	28.9%
b) others	49.3%	49.4%	60.0%	40.5%
Difference (a-b)	-12.7%	+5.3%	-12.4%	-11.6%
Totals – Catholics	*131*	*86*	*126*	*128*
Others	*288*	*170*	*245*	*269*
Women				
a) Catholics	31.0%	78.8%	43.5%	34.6%
b) others	47.2%	85.4%	54.2%	53.2%
Difference (a-b)	-16.2%	-6.6%	-10.7%	-18.6%
Totals – Catholics	*142*	*85*	*131*	*156*
Others	*322*	*192*	*325*	*301*

Source: west of Scotland survey.

chance, except for the youngest group, aged 15 in 1987/8, who by 1995 were on equal terms with non-Catholics. This youngest group confirms that in Clydeside too equality has been established in the new wave of young Catholics. The west of Scotland survey is likely to be of enormous value in the future because of its unique ability to follow personal careers over time and to reveal patterns of job gain and job loss at later ages.

Conclusions and Questions for the Future

Catholic disadvantage in Scotland is indeed going but is not yet gone. Claims for its demise are not only premature but have ignored worrying trends in the data which suggest that the progress of some of the new generation of Catholics who achieved equality may have stalled in early middle age, in their late thirties or early forties. Catholics over 40 cannot simply be forgotten, nor can unequal experiences of promotion or job loss, if they have occurred, be regarded as history simply because job entry by school-leavers is equal. Nor can we ignore the fact that past discrimination was tied to the link between Catholicism and Irish descent which is most prominent in west-central Scotland, nor blink the fact that indicators of inequality in west-central Scotland are sharper than in the rest of the country. There can be no excuse for complacency, and a public information strategy is needed which, in accordance with the government's commitment in its White Papers on health, will monitor the progress of social inequalities between Catholics and other Scots over the next 20 years at least, and the progress of Catholic health, about which we comment below, over a still longer period.

Explanations of the great change for the better in the generation which entered the job market between 1975 and the 1990s are not far to seek. Lindsay Paterson[40] has argued that this was the signal achievement of Catholic schools in Scotland, and we have little to add to that interpretation other than the hope that this will be tested rigorously along the lines already developed by Heath and McMahon for other minorities,[41] to see whether any residual deviation exists from the pattern of subsequent job levels predicted by educational qualifications, which might indicate the presence of other more questionable factors which are helping or hindering young people in their search for jobs. We would also add that any argument that Catholic schools are no longer needed because equality has arrived has to be set aside until we have cleared up the question of whether the progress of some young Catholics has stalled in middle age. If, for example, Catholics face greater obstacles in their working life and only get as far as they do because of their educational head start, it would be foolish to abolish that head start until the later obstacles are researched and abolished.

What, then, could be happening in middle age? A revisit of the trends in figure 2 and figure 4 suggests that the period of the life cycle in which Catholics currently have equal job chances runs at best from about age 24 to about age 40. Some may still find it more difficult to get non-manual jobs after leaving school – that needs testing – and it is definitely more difficult for the age groups from 40 onwards to get or keep good jobs – indeed, it may be more difficult after this age than it was in 1975. The change since 1975 suggests that there may be an element of a period effect among both younger and older Catholics – one which goes opposite ways depending on age. New technology and the growth of services favour the young against the old, and it seems that this transformation has been felt more acutely among Catholics. We need to ask whether shake-outs, business failure, downsizing and other symptoms of increasing pressure on labour costs have been managed in a way which acts selectively against Catholics and blocks some promotions or increases downward mobility. At the same time, replacement by younger people at lower salaries may have favoured Catholics, whether because of their educational qualifications or because low salaries were still an improvement on what they would previously have got. Have average incomes for young Catholics been lower than for others at each job level?

Another issue is suggested by the figures for west-central Scotland. If inequality is still sharper in the Irish Catholic heartland, where discrimination was a known problem in the past, is that because of differences in the type of job market in west-central Scotland, or because of discriminatory ideologies, or what? McCrone[42] has argued that when locally owned businesses, run by a unionist and Protestant élite, collapsed after the 1960s, large national or international firms or governmental organisations took over, using bureaucratic methods of selection. Was this phenomenon less thoroughgoing in west-central Scotland than elsewhere? Future study of these questions will need to have enough numbers to look at types of industry and types of job market as well as at religious background at different ages.

In addition, a more complete picture is needed which includes those who have failed to get into the job market altogether. A review of the figures on this which are available in the present data sets would take too much space for this chapter, and it is enough to say that just as there is a gap in attainment of non-manual jobs, so there is a greater tendency, often attributable for the moment to chance, for Catholics to be unemployed or otherwise outside the job market. The variations are not great enough to compel serious qualifications of the more optimistic results in this chapter, but this is another subject which should be reconsidered with more adequate numbers.

The groundwork for this research requires not only big numbers, though, but also a more intimate understanding of people's experience which can elicit how people in west-central Scotland identify one another, in terms of religion or ethnicity or related concepts, and how they construct those identities in terms of the experience and behaviour likely to be associated, at work, in life at home and in the community. These ideological constructions may be linked to production of inequalities, whether wittingly or unwittingly, and small, sensitive qualitative studies are needed to elicit such patterns of thinking. A start has been made on this line of research,[43] which will be indispensable in reaching a well-grounded picture of possible ways in which inequality is being sustained.

What is at stake is not merely economic well-being, but also health. Research carried out in the west of Scotland has shown a health disadvantage among those of Catholic background[44, 45] and among those of Irish heritage,[46] and socio-economic disadvantage at an earlier date is related to the subsequent excess mortality among those of Irish heritage.[47] Historical data from Ireland, where mortality was low until well into the twentieth century, suggest that the causes of disadvantage lie not in Ireland but in Britain.[48] These findings in Scotland of an Irish Catholic health disadvantage mirror evidence from England and Wales that people born in Ireland, or with a parent born in Ireland, have higher mortality, greater morbidity and greater overall social and material disadvantage than the general population.[49-61] This kind of health disadvantage has a long lead-in time. The social disadvantages which produce it begin to interact with increasing wear and tear in the body around middle age, and some years are needed before problems begin to become chronic and to increase the risk of early death. Thus even if all social inequality among Scottish Catholics were abolished tomorrow, there would still be a need to continue monitoring until health equality is achieved.

Meanwhile, even by the end of 1999, the machinery for monitoring and achieving this had not yet been set up, though to do so would be a simple matter. The information strategy being developed by the Scottish Executive for the new Scottish parliament, which includes government surveys of a size and sophistication not seen in Scotland before, has so far failed to include information about religion. The Scottish Household Survey, for example, has begun a four-year programme to interview 62,000 households. Information about smaller ethnic minorities is quite rightly being included, yet Scottish Catholics, who comprised 18 per cent of the population in 1997, remain invisible. Preparations are also now being made for the Scottish census of 2001, which offers a unique opportunity to include such information, and representations have been made on the importance of doing so. It is the census above all which has the responsibility for monitoring inequalities, in accordance with the government's stated intention, and most of the important discoveries of health inequalities have been made by linking the census with other sources of data like death certificates. We have said that a Scottish survey which has a general sample of at least 40,000, or a special sample of at least 7,000 to 8,000 Catholics, would enable us to tell decisively which age groups and genders are still suffering from disadvantage, and if repeated at intervals it could tell us much about whether the improvement since 1975 is still sustained. But we could not show authoritatively which industries or job markets are involved, and in which regions, without the census; nor, without the census, could we follow up the pattern of deaths within a time period which would enable health services to respond to the information provided, since death is a rare event which requires large numbers in vulnerable age groups to reveal its patterns.

In January 2000, the Deputy First Minister, following a line long prepared by the Scottish Executive, announced that the 2001 census would not have a question on religion; but a strong reaction from the Scottish parliament, and in particular its Equal Opportunities Committee, caused the Executive to retreat, and a question on religion will now be included. The significance of this moment, both for Scotland's religious minorities and for the accountability of the Executive of Parliament, is apparent. From this decision on the census, monitoring of inequality by religion can begin to inform policy. The indications have never been more propitious for achieving a rapid end to Scotland's oldest story of social exclusion.

Acknowledgements

We are grateful to our colleagues Patrick West, Kate Hunt, Graeme Ford and Joanne Abbotts for assistance with the data for the west of Scotland survey; to Geoff Der for advice on statistical matters; and to Sally Macintyre, Joanne Abbotts and Hannah Bradby for comments on earlier drafts. Lindsay Paterson discussed the findings with notable patience and critical attention, and contributed to a number of improvements. We acknowledge the Data Archive, which supplied the Election Surveys, and those responsible for funding and collecting these data. The copyright holder, the original data producer, the relevant funding agencies and the Data Archive bear no responsibility for the further analysis or interpretation of these data.

Notes

[1] S. Bruce, *No Pope of Rome: Anti-Catholicism in Modern Scotland* (Edinburgh, 1985).

[2] S. Bruce, 'Sectarianism in Scotland: A Contemporary Assessment and Explanation', *Scottish Government Yearbook*, 1988, pp.150–65.

[3] D. McCrone and M. Rosie, 'Left and Liberal: Catholics in Modern Scotland', in R. Boyle and P. Lynch (eds.), *Out of the Ghetto? The Catholic Community in Modern Scotland* (Edinburgh, 1998), pp.67–94.

[4] S. Bruce, 'Inspection of the facts points to a ready assimilation', *The Herald*, 10 August 1999.

[5] L. Paterson, 'Catholic Education and Scottish Democracy', *Journal of Education and Christian Belief* (in press).

[6] R. Miles, *Racism* (London, 1989).

[7] H. Bradby, 'Ethnicity: Not a Black and White Issue', *Sociology of Health and Illness* 17, 1995, pp.405–17.

[8] R. Williams, 'Can Data on Scottish Catholics Tell Us about Descendants of the Irish in Scotland?', *New Community* 19, no.2, 1993, pp.296–309.

[9] Census, 'Report' (Edinburgh, 1871).

[10] R. Miles and A. Dunlop, 'Racism in Britain: The Scottish Dimension', in P. Jackson (ed.), *Race and Racism: Essays in Social Geography* (London, 1987).

[11] Ibid.

[12] L.P. Curtis, *Anglo-Saxons and Celts* (Connecticut, 1968).

[13] C. Bennett, 'The Housing of the Irish in London', PNL Irish Studies Centre Occasional Papers no.3 (London, 1991).

[14] M.J. Hickman, 'Reconstructing Deconstructing "Race": British Political Discourses about the Irish in Britain', *Ethnic and Racial Studies* 21, no.2, 1998, pp.288–307.

[15] T. Connor, *The London Irish* (London, 1987).

[16] R. McVeigh, 'Is Sectarianism Racism? Theorising the Racism/Sectarianism Interface', in D. Miller (ed.), *Rethinking Northern Ireland* (London, 1998).

[17] A. Dickie, 'Anti-incitement Legislation in Britain and Northern Ireland', *New Community* 2, 1972, pp.133–8.

[18] S. Carmichael and C.V. Hamilton, *Black Power: The Politics of Liberation in America* (London, 1967).

[19] D. Mason, 'After Scarman: A Note on the Concept of "Institutional Racism"', *New Community* 10, 1982, pp.38–45.

[20] J. Williams, 'Redefining Institutional Racism', *Ethnic and Racial Studies* 8, 1985, pp.323–48.

[21] Miles, 'Racism'.

[22] R. Miles, *Racism after Race Relations* (London, 1993).

[23] J. Solomos and L. Back, 'Conceptualising Racisms: Social Theory, Politics and Research', *Sociology* 28, no.1, 1994, pp.143–61.

[24] F. Anthias, 'Connecting "Race" and Ethnic Phenomena', *Sociology* 26, no.3, 1992, pp.421–38.

[25] Miles, 'Racism'.

[26] D. Mason, 'On the Dangers of Disconnecting Race and Racism', *Sociology* 28, no.4, 1994, pp.845–58.

[27] McCrone, 'Left and Liberal'.

[28] E. Dahl, 'Social Mobility and Health: Cause or Effect?', *British Medical Journal* 313, 1996, pp.435–36.

[29] C. Power, S. Matthews and O. Manor, 'Inequalities in Self-rated Health in the 1958 Birth Cohort: Lifetime Social Circumstances or Social Mobility?', *British Medical Journal* 313, 1996, pp.449–53.

[30] Secretary of State for Health, 'Saving Lives: Our Healthier Nation' (London, 1999).

[31] Secretary of State for Scotland, 'Towards a Healthier Scotland – a White Paper on Health' (Edinburgh, 1999).

[32] G. Davey Smith and others, 'Lifetime Socio-economic Position and Mortality: Prospective Observational Study', *British Medical Journal* 314, 1997, pp.547–52.

[33] A. Heath and D. McMahon, 'Education and Occupational Attainments: The Impact of Ethnic Origins', in V. Karn (ed.), *Ethnicity in the 1991 Census, vol.4: Employment, Education and Housing among the Ethnic Minority Populations of Britain* (London, 1997).

[34] J. Abbotts and others, 'Morbidity and Irish Catholic Descent in Britain: An Ethnic and Religious Minority 150 Years on', *Social Science and Medicine* 45, no.1, 1997, pp.3–14.

[35] R. Ecob and R. Williams, 'Sampling Asian minorities to assess health and welfare', Journal of Epidemiology and Community Health 45, 1991, pp.93–101.

[36] Paterson, 'Catholic Education'.

[37] J.D. Willms, 'Pride or Prejudice? Opportunity Structure and the Effects of Catholic Schools in Scotland', *International Perspectives on Education and Society* 2, 1992, pp.189–213.

[38] M. Hickman and B. Walter, *Discrimination and the Irish Community in Britain* (London, 1997).

[39] G. Payne and G. Ford, 'Religion, Class and Educational Policy', *Scottish Educational Studies* 9, no.2, 1977, pp.83–99.

[40] Paterson, 'Catholic Education'.

[41] Heath, 'Education'.

[42] D. McCrone, *Understanding Scotland: The Sociology of a Stateless Nation* (London, 1992).

[43] P. Walls and R.G.A Williams, 'Irish and Catholic – Double Disadvantage? Linking Minority Religious and Ethnic Identity to Health Inequality', in BSA Medical Sociology Group Conference (York, 1998).

[44] Abbotts, 'Morbidity', 1997.

[45] J. Abbotts and others, 'Morbidity and Irish Catholic Descent in Britain: Relating Health Disadvantage to Behaviour', *Ethnicity and Health* (in press).

[46] J. Abbotts, R. Williams and G. Davey Smith, 'Mortality in Men of Irish Heritage in West Scotland', *Public Health* 112, no.4, 1998, pp.229–32.

[47] J. Abbotts, R. Williams and G. Davey Smith, 'Association of Medical, Physiological, Behavioural and Socio-economic Factors with Elevated Mortality in Men of Irish Heritage in West Scotland', *Journal of Public Health Medicine* 21, no.1, 1999, pp.46–54.

[48] R. Williams, 'Medical, Economic and Population Factors in Areas of High Mortality in Britain: The Case of Glasgow', *Sociology of Health and Illness* 16, 1994, pp.143–81.

[49] M.G. Marmot, A.M. Adelstein and L. Bulusu, *Immigrant Mortality in England and Wales 1970–78* (London, 1984).

[50] R. Cochrane and S.S. Bal, 'Mental Hospital Admission Rates of Immigrants to England: A Comparison of 1971 and 1981', *Social Psychiatry and Psychiatric Epidemiology* 24, 1989, pp.2–11.

[51] R. Balarajan and L. Bulusu, 'Mortality among Immigrants in England and Wales, 1979–1983', in M. Britton (ed.), *Mortality and Geography: A Review in the Mid-'80s* (London, 1990).

[52] J. Raftery, D.R. Jones and M. Rosato, 'The Mortality of First and Second Generation Irish Immigrants in the UK', *Social Science and Medicine* 24, no.3, 1990, pp.91–4.

[53] V.S. Raleigh and R. Balarajan, 'Suicide Levels and Trends among Immigrants in England and Wales', *Health Trends* 24, no.3, 1992, pp.91–4.

[54] Department of Employment, *Labour Force Survey* (London, 1993).

[55] R. Williams, 'Britain's Regional Mortality', *Social Science and Medicine* 39, 1994, pp.189–99.

[56] R. Balarajan, 'Ethnicity and Variations in the Nation's Health', *Health Trends* 27, no.4, 1995, pp.114–19.

[57] D. Owen, 'Irish-born People in Great Britain: Social and Economic Circumstances' (Centre for Research in Ethnic Relations, University of Warwick, 1995).

[58] S. Harding and R. Balarajan, 'Patterns of Mortality in Second Generation Irish Living in England and Wales: Longitudinal Study', *British Medical Journal* 312, 1996, pp.1389–92.

[59] S. Harding and R. Maxwell, 'Differences in Mortality of Migrants', in F. Drever and M.

Whitehead (eds.), *Health Inequalities: Decennial Supplement* (London, 1997).

[60] S. Wild and P. McKeigue, 'Cross-sectional Analysis of Mortality by Country of Birth in England and Wales, 1970–92', *British Medical Journal* 314, 1997, pp.705–9.

[61] R. Williams and R. Ecob, 'Regional Mortality and the Irish in Britain: Findings from the ONS Longitudinal Study', *Sociology of Health and Illness* 21, no.3, 1999, pp.344–67.

19. THE SCOTTISH PARLIAMENT AND SECTARIANISM: EXPLORING THE UNEXPLORED, DOCUMENTING THE UNDOCUMENTED, INFORMING THE UNINFORMED

Peter Lynch

> I hope that the work of the Commission, by opening wounds to cleanse them, will thereby stop them from festering. We cannot be facile and say bygones will be bygones, because they will not be bygones and will return to haunt us. True reconciliation is never cheap, for it is based on forgiveness which is costly. Forgiveness in turn depends on repentance, which has to be based on an acknowledgement of what was done wrong, and therefore on disclosure of the truth. You cannot forgive what you do not know.
>
> Archbishop Desmond Tutu, Chair of the Truth and Reconciliation Commission.[1]

A Hidden Past and Present

The main problem with sectarianism in Scotland is that what we know is vastly overshadowed by what we don't. As an issue, it has been shoved to the side, perhaps out of embarrassment, perhaps out of a belief that it has gone away. What is clear, though, is how little we know about sectarianism, whether it is a small, declining phenomenon or something that remains widespread in Scottish society. Key questions lack clear answers. How much sectarianism is there, when and where does it occur, who is involved in the discrimination, what effect does it have? Is it institutionalised or individualised, is it violent or merely low-level banter? These are all questions for which we have very few answers. Instead, we have lingering suspicions, stories our parents tell us and lots of speculation.

The absence of definite information about sectarianism clouds the present as much as the past. There remains a dearth of even the most simple statistical information about the prevalence and extent of sectarianism, despite the preponderance of social surveys, opinion polling, election surveys and health, unemployment and educational statistics. There are large numbers of pollsters and social researchers examining social change in Scotland, often government-funded, but they seldom focus on century-old questions about sectarianism, religious identity or social change amongst Scottish Catholics and Protestants, particularly in their attitudes to each other.

Such limited information has clearly affected the output of academics seeking to address questions of religion and identity in Scotland. Steve Bruce's discussion of the changing position of the Catholic community could find no better statistical source than the Scottish Social Mobility Survey from the mid-1970s.[2] David McCrone and Michael Rosie's 1998 survey of Catholic political and social attitudes was based on a sample of only 148 Catholics out of a total of 957 interviewees from the Scottish Election Survey of 1992.[3] Both pieces of work generated interesting conclusions, but such researchers would benefit from a wider variety of detailed statistical sources in order for them to draw a more accurate picture of Catholicism and the problem of sectarianism.

The dearth of information is perhaps most surprising given that the government has become interested in issues of social inclusion/exclusion and has produced a Scottish Household Survey to provide much more detailed information than that included in the national census or the various social trends surveys produced for the whole of the United Kingdom. The Scottish Household Survey is a major new continuous survey funded by the Scottish Executive covering some 62,000 households over its first four years. It has produced a number of statistical reports assessing current levels of housing tenure, employment, household incomes, assets and savings, health and disabilities, and so on.[4] Such statistical information has been seen as a key part of the Scottish Executive's strategy for social inclusion. However, it leaves the issue of sectarianism and discrimination and the position of minorities to one side.

Of course, it is arguable that surveys are a rather blunt instrument for assessing the level of religious discrimination in Scotland. McCrone and Rosie's survey analysis found that concern about the seriousness of sectarianism was mostly limited to young males in the west of Scotland and such election surveys seem to indicate the limited concerns of voters about religious discrimination. However, mass surveys are not particularly suitable for dealing with rather sensitive questions about sectarianism. They may determine that sectarianism is not a major issue, but they do not gauge how much of an issue or a problem it is. Surveys haven't mapped people's attitudes or behaviours in relation to religious discrimination, or why they have changed. They have also failed to examine what can be termed 'actually existing discrimination', how people experience religious discrimination and how they respond to it. One of the major problems with exploring such issues is that they are so often related to two cliché-ridden areas: football and Catholic schools. These might be the only arenas for perceived discrimination in Scotland, but we don't know that for sure. Once again we lack the information to make judgements about the existence of discrimination.

It is useful to compare the treatment of sectarianism with that of other issues of discrimination, especially the areas of racism and gender inequality. The subject of racism and the problems of ethnic minorities within Scotland have received some attention by governmental organisations.[5] Local authorities, police forces and central government have sought to design strategies to combat racism and forge links with ethnic-minority communities. The success of such efforts is variable, but they have generated a degree of information and scrutiny that has pushed the problems of ethnic minorities up the political agenda. For example, we are able to monitor the changing employment and unemployment patterns of ethnic minorities, reports of attacks and discrimination, and more. The situation is far from perfect, but it is possible to document the issue of discrimination towards ethnic minorities in ways that assist the policy process rather than avoid it, as in the case of sectarianism. For example, police forces have been able to monitor and categorise the level of racial attacks in their area,[6] which has illustrated the nature and extent of racial incidents. This is a far cry from the information available about sectarian incidents.

Similarly, the women's movement in Scotland has been effective in getting some gender issues addressed by government and the public sector.[7] Think of the zero-tolerance campaign and the campaign for fairer representation for women in the Scottish parliament and you can see two clear campaigning successes which changed public policy. Groups such as Engender compiled annual audits of women's employment patterns, providing some of the statistical raw material for campaigns for fair representation with figures on the numbers of women judges, solicitors and councillors, housing patterns of women, levels of violence against women and so on.[8] In effect, it was a fairly complete statistical account of the changing/unchanging position of women in Scottish society. Again contrast that with what we know about religious discrimination and it is easy to see the knowledge gap that requires to be filled if we are to make a serious effort to assess the level of sectarianism in Scotland.

Putting the Past Behind Us

We live in an age in which some of the wrongs of the past have been addressed retrospectively, either through public demand or through governmental action. The need for reconciliation has been a major theme of the peace process in Northern Ireland; South Africa has been subject to the extensive probing of the Truth and Reconciliation Commission; many democratising East European states established bodies to restore property to citizens which had been confiscated under the old system; and President Clinton came very close to apologising for America's participation in the slave trade on his visit to Africa in 1998. All these developments are linked by the need to give recognition to the sins of the past and to put them on the public record. As discussed above, that is exactly what we do not have in relation to sectarianism in Scotland. There is no public record, merely a fragmented history of anecdotes and beliefs about discrimination, and no investigation or apology by the state, local authorities or businesses for any religious or ethnic discrimination that has taken place. There are memories and suspicions of bigotry and sectarianism but we lack the evidence, and, as Archbishop Tutu pointed out above, without examining the wounds caused by discrimination, we will be left with a festering sore.

It doesn't have to be this way. We don't have to accept the past as a series of festering sores, complaints and suspicions about religious discrimination and who did what to whom. Rather we should find mechanisms to research the past – and, indeed, the present – to construct a realistic view of sectarianism in Scotland. Post-apartheid South Africa offers one example of an extensive attempt to examine past discrimination, and to do so through a state-sponsored mechanism imbued with democratic legitimacy. South Africa chose to do so through the Truth and Reconciliation Commission, a special investigative body charged with examining the subject of human-rights abuses under the apartheid regime. The Promotion of National Unity and Reconciliation Act in 1995 created the Truth and Reconciliation Commission (TRC) to investigate and establish:

... as complete a picture as possible of the nature, causes and extent of gross violations of human rights committed during the period from 1 March 1960 to the cut-off date contemplated in the Constitution (1994), and the fate or whereabouts of the victims of such violations . . . affording victims an opportunity to relate the violations they suffered; the taking of measures aimed at the granting of reparation to, and the rehabilitation and the restoration of the human and civil dignity of, victims of violations of human rights; reporting to the Nation about such violations . . .[9]

The Commission established three separate bodies to undertake its investigation into the human-rights situation under apartheid: a Committee on Human Rights Violations, a Committee on Amnesty and a Committee on Reparation and Rehabilitation. The Committee on Human Rights Violations investigated allegations of human-rights violations based on statements made to the TRC itself. Individuals would appear before the committee to provide evidence of abuse, with the committee charged with establishing the details of the abuse. Once identified, such abuse would be referred to the Committee on Reparation and Rehabilitation, which would provide victim support and make proposals for the rehabilitation of victims, which could involve financial compensation. Finally, the Amnesty Committee was responsible for considering requests for amnesties from perpetrators of human-rights abuses in South Africa, mostly in exchange for testifying to such abuses before the TRC.

The TRC operated from 1995 onwards and published a five-volume report on its findings on 29 October 1998. The report dealt with the basis and rationale for the work of the Commission and the manner in which it functioned; gross violations of human rights on all sides of the conflict; gross violations of human rights from the perspective of the victim; the nature of the society in which gross violations of human rights took place, through reporting on a series of 'institutional hearings' which sought to explore the broader institutional and social environment of apartheid; and the Commission's final conclusions and recommendations. However, despite the publication of the TRC's report, its work was not complete. The Amnesty Committee continued to meet in 1999 to discuss requests from individuals for amnesty for violent actions during the apartheid years.

The value of the Truth and Reconciliation Commission was that it succeeded in providing a conclusive investigation of discrimination in the apartheid years. Its hearings, testimonies and inquiries placed a large number of previously secret events on the public record, such as political murders, bombings, torture, police and military activity, terrorist actions by the ANC and inter-community violence between ANC and Inkatha supporters. The victims and the perpetrators of violence and discrimination had their say. Confessions were made, victims were able to speak up without fear of intimidation and some of the past was put to rest.

Clearly, Scotland has not experienced anything like the degree of discrimination in South Africa under apartheid. However, it is not being suggested here that we copy the South African example, merely that we learn from it and recognise that there are dangers in allowing 'Scotland's shame' to continue unchallenged, either in the past or currently. We cannot just sweep sectarianism under the carpet and pretend it doesn't exist or that it is something that has been consigned to the past. We might have attempted this so far in Scotland, but the current debate shows how unsuccessful this approach has been. States such as South Africa responded to this type of problem by designing wide-ranging institutions and processes to provide a definitive public record of past discrimination in order to draw a line under the past and allow South African society to move on from the apartheid years. Would that we could do the same in Scotland with the issue of sectarianism and religious discrimination, past and present. Instead, we seem determined either to point to the decline of sectarianism as justification for inaction or to simply deny the issue is a problem at all.

The Scottish Parliament and Sectarianism

With devolution, Scotland has entered a new political era. The establishment of the Scottish parliament has meant that we now have an institution capable of addressing major social issues in Scotland. Debates that would have been unthinkable at Westminster are now becoming entirely commonplace on the Mound. Through a variety of activities such as legislation, motions for debate, committee investigations, question times and public petitions, the parliament has the opportunity to discuss issues such as sectarianism. The parliament also has a variety of committees which have an interest in the area of sectarianism and religious discrimination, such as the Justice and Home Affairs Committee and the Equal Opportunities Committee. Since July 1999, the Equal Opportunities Committee has spent its time examining issues such as the Macpherson report on policing and ethnic minorities, police complaints procedures and the Improvement in Education bill. The committee also agreed to examine the issue of sectarianism in its race reporters' group, following brief discussion of the Act of Settlement.[10]

However, whilst parliamentary investigations into sectarianism would be useful, they would not examine the backlog of actual and suspected discrimination from the past. Parliament could examine the current state of religious discrimination – and this would certainly be valuable – but not look backwards to the 1920s, 1930s or 1950s. What the Scottish parliament should do is establish a Special Commission to examine the issue of sectarianism in Scotland from an historical and contemporary perspective. Similar to the Truth and Reconciliation Commission, it could take evidence from individuals, both victims and alleged perpetrators, about religious discrimination; it could examine government documents and policy towards religious discrimination in Scotland; and it could create a definitive public record of discrimination so that we can establish some facts about the issue. Such a venture might demonstrate that Scotland was and remains a heavily sectarian society, with fundamental divisions between its main religious groups. Alternatively, the process might reveal that there actually wasn't as much discrimination as people thought. Its findings would enable open discussion and could lead to policy changes to address the issue of religious discrimination, much in the same way as research into racism and sexism has aided anti-discrimination and equal-opportunities policies in a range of public institutions.

Of course, one argument against such a Commission is that it would open up a can of worms. Public and private institutions, from central government to local authorities, banks and even football teams, would find themselves under investigation. It would prove embarrassing. Major institutions would find themselves under attack; some might face claims for compensation. It would also see a repetition of the ritualised exchanges between Catholics and Protestants about schools, inter-marriage and football. But the argument here is that we would be better off getting to grips with religious discrimination and facing up to the past than seeking to ignore or deny it. There has been enough fudging and festering about sectarianism and far too much hot air expounded about the topic for too long. Rather than be burdened by an actual or perceived sectarian past (and present), the Scottish parliament must take steps to address the issue in order to draw a line under the past and prevent us from dragging last century's quarrels into the next.

Notes

[1] Statement upon appointment as chair of the Truth and Reconciliation Commission, 30 November 1995.

[2] S. Bruce, 'Out of the Ghetto: The Ironies of Acceptance', *Innes Review*, no.2, 1992, pp.145–54.

[3] D. McCrone and M. Rosie, 'Left and Liberal: Catholics in Modern Scotland', in R. Boyle and P. Lynch (eds.), *Out of the Ghetto? The Catholic Community in Modern Scotland* (Edinburgh, 1998).

[4] Scottish Executive, *The Scottish Household Survey Bulletin No.2* (1999).

[5] M. Burman, L. Mann and N. Bourque, *Feasibility Study of Legal Representation Among White and Ethnic Minority Criminal Accused*, Crime and Criminal Justice Research Finding No.22 (Scottish Office, 1998); and Crime and Criminal Justice Research Findings No.28; and Jason Ditton, *Attitudes Towards Crime, Victimisation and the Police in Scotland: A Comparison of White and Ethnic Minority Views*, Crime and Criminal Justice Research Findings No.28 (Scottish Office, 1999).

[6] Strathclyde Police, *Chief Constable's Annual Report 1998–99*, Glasgow – which recorded 501 racial crimes in the police authority area.

[7] Fiona Myers, *Women in Decision-Making in Scotland: A Review of Research*, Women's Issues Research Findings No.2 (Scottish Office, 1999); Sheila Henderson, *Service Provision to Women Experiencing Domestic Violence in Scotland*, Crime and Criminal Justice Research Findings No.20 (Scottish Office, 1998).

[8] See engender WWW site at http://www.engender.org.uk for details.

[9] Promotion of National Unity and Reconciliation Act, 1995, No.34, 26 July 1995.

[10] Scottish Parliament, Equal Opportunities Committee, Official Record, 2 November 1999.

Part 6

Commentaries

20. THEN AND NOW: CATHOLICS IN SCOTTISH SOCIETY, 1950–2000

T.M. Devine

One of the most remarkable features of this collection of essays is the absence of any clear consensus on the central issue under debate. This lack of consensus does not come from any simple ideological division among the contributors. Catholic writers like Patrick Reilly ('To ask if there is anti-Catholicism in Scotland is like asking if there are Frenchmen in Paris') and Bishop Joseph Devine, who would argue that James MacMillan's lecture is 20 years out of date, take up radically different positions. To some extent this disagreement must stem from different personal experiences as so many of the issues in the debate come down to subjective judgements.

In addition, however, there are probably two other important reasons why no final agreed position is yet possible on the question of anti-Catholicism in modern Scottish society. First, the protagonists are often arguing about two different areas. Some of the contributors in part one of this book are concerned with social attitudes, the territory of the mind, the heart and the spirit, where 'a culture of prejudice', in the words of Gerry Finn, is still rampant. Other essayists, especially those from a background in academic social science, are more interested in plotting the objective experience of Catholics, their position in the class structure, the labour market and related matters, topics which are central to the issue of continuing discrimination. The questions are obviously intimately linked but may still produce radically different answers. As Steve Bruce points out, any improvement in the material position of Catholics in Scotland (which he and others contend has been very significant in recent decades) came about not because of 'personal virtue' in Scottish society but because of changing economic and social circumstances which made it impossible to practise discrimination as overtly as in the past. Anti-Catholic employers, in other words, may still harbour their prejudices but of necessity now maintain a much lower profile than before.

Secondly, there is the vital problem of incomplete and ambiguous evidence which inevitably produces contrasting and often conflicting results. Quite simply, we do not yet have enough hard data on key aspects of the debate to be entirely certain about our conclusions. This is particularly so in relation to attitudes, the most difficult and complex area of all. Here competing anecdotes and repeated rhetoric fill the void. Patrick Reilly, for instance, eloquently asserts that 'there is a Himalayas of anecdotal evidence from almost every Catholic family in the west of Scotland as to alleged injustices suffered'. Quite so, but is he talking of the past (where the point is incontrovertible) or the present and whether there has been a perception of change over time?

The problem of evidence even dogs the social-science investigators who place their faith in statistical tabulation and analysis. The chapters by Rosie and McCrone and by Paterson paint an optimistic picture of Catholic social mobility and successful integration into Scottish society which contradicts any model of continuing discrimination. Their data and the conclusions they derive from them cannot be discounted, but as Rory Williams and Patricia Walls point out, their base in evidence is still slim and fragile. The latter pair assert that 'more of these data will enable us to be very confident about findings that there is no difference between Catholics and others'. In their view, a sample of 40,000 Scots, of which 7,500 should be Catholics, would be required to determine in a rigorous fashion whether there was any Catholic disadvantage in Scotland today. The Scottish Election Surveys of 1992 and 1997 seem pitifully small by comparison, with samples of 957 and 882 respectively, although the west of Scotland survey at 2,618 is substantially larger. Nevertheless, is there really enough hard evidence here to justify McCrone and Rosie's claims that 'the past is history'? 'Big numbers' are essential and they are not yet available to answer some of the key outstanding questions. As Peter Lynch concedes, 'The main problem with sectarianism in Scotland is that what we know is vastly overshadowed by what we don't . . . we have lingering suspicions, stories our parents tell us and lots of speculation.'

At the time of writing it does not appear that these gaps in academic knowledge will be easily or quickly filled. The subjects of racism and gender inequality in Scotland have commanded much attention from government agencies. Not so sectarianism. Racial attacks are monitored and recorded by police forces but sectarian attacks are not. In the Scottish Household Survey, information is collated on 62,000 households. Smaller ethnic minorities are included but Scottish Catholics, who made up 18 per cent of the Scottish population in 1997, are not. Even more crucially, the Scottish census has not contained information on religion. Since the next census in 2001 will now do so, many of the central questions will in due course be answered more reliably and with more statistical authority. As Rory Williams and Patricia Walls concluded, before this decision was taken:

> If subsequent debate in the Scottish parliament does not ensure that the census gathers information about religion, the monitoring of evidence on the health and social disadvantage of Scottish Catholics will be set back for more than a decade, till the issue returns at the next census. On the other hand, if the new Scottish parliament grasps the nettle and sets up the machinery to monitor the position, the indications have never been more propitious for achieving a rapid end to Scotland's oldest story of social exclusion. In one stroke, the Scottish parliament would have inaugurated a new Scotland.

Undoubtedly, if this were to occur, James MacMillan's intervention would have been more than amply justified by ushering in a vigorous debate leading to serious scrutiny of a subject traditionally under-studied in Scotland.

To say, however, that our knowledge is sparse is not to say that we currently have no alternative but to remain agnostic about sectarianism. There is already enough evidence to demonstrate that even if anti-Catholic attitudes still flourish in modern Scotland, their effect on the life changes of young Catholics has significantly receded in the last two decades. Indeed, a silent revolution has taken place. Overt discrimination of the kind endemic in the older industries disintegrated with their speedy demise. Studies reported in this volume show no significant social-class differences between Catholics and non-Catholics, a remarkable transformation compared to previous generations. In addition, Catholics, partly because of their traditional loyalty to Labour, have an impact on national and local politics out of all proportion to their numbers. The past nine provosts of Glasgow, Scotland's largest city, have been Catholic, while in the 1997 general election 31 per cent of candidates elected to Scottish seats were of the same persuasion, although Catholics comprised only 13 per cent of the electorate.

And Scottish Catholics seem to be achieving a new *rapprochement* with nationalism, feared as recently as the 1970s as a political force, which in the view of many older Catholics, threatened to restore Protestant hegemony in Scotland. Indeed, the most recent surveys suggest that Scots from a Catholic background are marginally more likely to favour independence than Protestants and that Catholics identify at least as strongly with 'Scottishness' as non-Catholics. Such a sea-change in political attitudes could hardly have been possible if Catholics still regularly experienced discrimination on account of their religion in the workplaces and professional offices of Scotland. Crucially, in the 1980s the nation came through the most serious economic crisis since the 1920s but, unlike the inter-war period, there was no escalation of sectarian tensions.

The media have also become much less tolerant of sectarian behaviour. Witness the eerie silence emanating from most Scottish newspapers in the very recent past about the blatant anti-Catholic recruitment policies of Glasgow Rangers, the country's leading soccer team, and contrast it with the very public humiliation that same press visited upon the hapless Donald Findlay, QC, in 1998 when he was caught on camera singing sectarian songs at a private function. Who also would have guessed that the leader of Scotland's Catholics, Cardinal Thomas J. Winning, would have become the darling of the media and by far the most high-profile churchman in the land?

In the light of all this, it might appear that James MacMillan's Edinburgh Festival speech is out of date, perhaps an accurate vision of the Catholic experience in the 1950s and 1960s but no longer a realistic picture. The criticism is convincing in part. MacMillan's analysis pays scant attention to the remarkable shift in the status of Catholic people in Scotland over the period of his own lifetime. But in another sense he touches a nerve when he states that there remains 'a desire to narrow and restrict the definition of what it means to be Scottish'. For Catholics like him, the historic identification of Scot and Presbyterian will no longer suffice. A mature, modern Scotland with its reconvened parliament should seek to be inclusive, or, as Patrick Reilly puts it, 'we must all become Jock Tamson's bairns, regardless of creed or colour'. The message from James MacMillan is that such an aspiration should allow Scottish Catholics to maintain and celebrate their identity without any pressure to surrender it and allow all Scots to search for 'an enriching multi-cultural pluralism' which remembers the Catholic Christian heritage which for many centuries before the Reformation formed the cultural and religious backbone of this ancient nation. A mature democracy should have little difficulty in accepting both of these precepts.

21. 'I HAD NOT THOUGHT ABOUT IT LIKE THAT BEFORE'

James MacMillan

People have asked me, in the aftermath of my speech 'Scotland's Shame', why I felt motivated to speak out about religious prejudice in Scotland. I suppose I felt, with the excitement at the establishment of the Scottish parliament, that it was important, in the new spirit of inclusiveness, that no part of Scottish society should feel less than fully involved in the 'new Scotland'. It seemed to me that there was no better time for the Scottish people to begin to acknowledge one of the more uncomfortable aspects of our national condition, and to open the debate about what to do about it.

One of the strongest taboos in Scottish society is the discussion of religion. They say that 'religion and politics should never be discussed' at polite dinner parties, yet our nation is openly obsessed with politics and covertly obsessed with religion. In the last few months, the religious taboo has been broken. The reaction in the Scottish media and in the letters pages of our newspapers has testified to the complex and sometimes painful experience of this. Many reactions were supportive of my thesis, others were not. But there seems to have been a gradual acknowledgement that the bout of national soul-searching might have been good for us. It allowed us to clear the air and perhaps now we can move forward to tackle the mean-spiritedness which denies us a true pluralism in this issue and in others.

Some commentators were embarrassed that the subject had been raised in such a public forum as the Edinburgh International Festival, with the world looking on as we washed our dirty linen in public. The prickliness of this response higlighted to observers that public Scotland protested too much. Many other reactions were obviously and unfortunately ill informed.

That is why Tom Devine's initiative in commissioning this book is such a welcome contrast. Here is the proliferation of ideas and debate instead of their stifling obfuscation. His efforts should be universally applauded. Professor Devine observes an 'absence of any clear consensus on the central issue under debate'. This too should be celebrated. Scotland needs more consensus and conformity like it needs a hole in the head. What Scotland needs is the sharing of conflicting ideas, the airing of hidden perspectives and the ability of one to say to another with respect and gratitude, 'I may not agree with you, but the free expression of your ideas allows me to see how things may not be as clear-cut as I had previously thought. *I had not thought about it like that before.*' It was within this spirit that I had hoped my speech would be received, and I am delighted now to see, belatedly, that this is the case.

The positive reactions to my speech confirmed my belief that there was a potentially huge range of broad alliances to be built in tackling the problem of prejudice in Scotland. Once a taboo is broken and long-frustrated conversations are facilitated, the thought-numbing, talk-numbing dead hand of polite conversation looks increasingly unattractive.

This was brought home to me in any number of letters from fellow Christians who were clergy and lay people in the Church of Scotland, Episcopal and Catholic Churches, friends in the Iona community and so on, who communicated their enthusiasm at the broad ecumenical thrust behind my speech which was clouded by garish newspaper headlines at the time. But this is an issue which has implications beyond religious belief. I wrote as a socialist, with a radical criticism of conservative elements in society (and within my own Church) and of the excesses of free-market capitalism. I called for common cause to be made with countless others in Scotland to build a just and fair society. It was gratifying to see positive responses from the secular left, and from bodies outside the immediate maelstrom of the debate such as the Scottish Commission for Racial Equality, which recognised the broader implications of what I had said. It was, after all, a speech which called for a celebration of pluralism and diversity.

In the autumn after my speech there were reports of outrage in the local community in Bearsden about the prospect of a new mosque being built in this leafy suburb of Glasgow. The local Muslim community had submitted a planning application to East Dunbartonshire Council and the local white neighbourhood was up in arms. A petition to the council had been organised. Claims of Islamophobia were emphatically denied. The local Muslim community, continually referred to as 'Mohammedans' by the people organising the campaign against them, have maintained a dignified and conciliatory patience throughout. This desire to blend in, not to speak out or draw attention to the differences of a minority community, has been mentioned before in this book, notably by Professor Gallagher and Dr Finn. In his article, Dr Gerry Finn discusses the inter-relationship of 'sectarianism' and 'racism'. He identifies obstacles that hinder the identification of racism in Scotland and the need to move against it.

> . . . racism is often denied by the powerful chorus that there is 'No problem here'. Or, if the problem of racism is accepted, the problem is localised and racism becomes equated with an identifiable presence of the racialised ethnic minority. Identification of racism with specific localities occurs because the presence of a target community makes the overt display of racism so much more probable there. However, this identification of racism with areas where the minority is to be found leads to the belief that the emergence of racism is itself the responsibility of the minority. So the target community whose presence becomes the rallying point for the racist 'cause' is now transformed into the cause of racism. That process also serves to deny majority ethnic responsibility for the racism.

Attacks on the Muslim community represent another admixture of religious and racist prejudice. Already the Muslim community in Glasgow has been subjected to accusations that their 'displays of difference' (i.e. mosque attendance, public piety, the first Islamic school on the Southside) are 'root causes of social division'. The Catholic community is, of course, used to this and it should be a source of great distress to all Scottish pluralists to see history begin to repeat itself.

Hand in hand with the call for the celebration of diversity is a recognition of how dire the alternative could be. This is echoed in David Sinclair's essay: 'The Scotland of today is not as tolerant of variety as it likes to think of itself as being . . . Those working in the area of race relations continually remind us that those whose difference in ethnic background is made obvious by the colour of their skin face a daily struggle and continual harassment. Anecdotal evidence of the persecution of those who move here from England is too frequently available to be ignored.' Sinclair is the secretary of the Church and Nation Committee of the General Assembly of the Church of Scotland. In recognising the validity of the accusation of sleep-walking bigotry, he also sees a bigger picture, citing what the Macpherson report on the Stephen Lawrence case called 'institutionalised racism'. 'It is the kind of deep-seated prejudice which becomes as natural as the air we breathe, neither noticed nor in need of justification, just the way things are.' This demonstrates a common desire to deliver a wake-up call – 'a call to pluralism and toleration, even to a rejoicing in difference and variety'.

Another contribution that made an equally profound impression was Robert Crawford's essay, 'Presbyterianism and Imagination in Modern Scotland'. Reading this was both a moving and a humbling experience in the gradual realisation of how painfully and onerously a negative cultural assessment of the Reformation sits on the shoulders of a contemporary Presbyterian artist. I began to regret my clumsy and lame attempt at humour in comparing Knox with Mao. I still hold, nevertheless, that 1560 represents a cultural revolution which involved a violent repudiation of art and music, from which, it could be argued, we have not fully recovered. This view chimes with Andrew O'Hagan's assertion that 'the depredations of Calvinism on Scottish art are evident to this very hour'. But Crawford provides the necessary balance – 'Our assumptions about the relationship between Presbyterianism and imagination in Scotland need to become more complex and nuanced. The aim is not to deny that the Reformation left a troubling legacy for many imaginative artists in Scotland, but to realise also that it produced impressive and sometimes exciting cultural forms and artefacts.' As I read his essay, the ground shifted a little beneath me, and an earlier point made here comes back to illuminate the ongoing discussion: 'I may not agree with you, but the free expression of your ideas allows me to see how things may not be as clear-cut as I had previously thought. *I had not thought about it like that before.*'

As I write these words in the first weeks of a new year, a new millennium, the mood of optimism inspires me to say something positive about how the debate has moved forward in the last few months. One of the motivations for speaking as I did last August was a desire for inclusion, for an acceptance that, as Scotland embraces the new situation created by the establishment of the first Scottish parliament for 300 years, all citizens should feel that their contribution will be recognised and valued.

The most tangible evidence so far that the Catholic community is included in this new Scotland is the motion tabled by the Scottish Nationalist MSP Mike Russell which was signed by almost 80 out of the 129 members of the Scottish parliament. The motion, which called for the repeal of those parts of the Act of Settlement which prohibit the heir to the throne from marrying a Catholic or a Catholic from becoming monarch, also expressed the Scottish parliament's view that 'Scottish society must not disbar participation in any aspect of our national life on the grounds of religion'. It was passed after amendment by the Scottish Executive to acknowledge that it concerned a matter reserved to the Westminster parliament, but, in the absence of an opposing amendment, it was passed unanimously.

During a sometimes eloquent debate on the motion on 16 December 1999, Lord James Douglas-Hamilton (Conservative, Lothians) emphasised the true symbolic importance of the debate: 'Our vote today should serve as a signal that blatant and hurtful legislation discriminating against a Christian religion is not acceptable, just as discrimination against a race or ethnic community is not acceptable. Today we have the opportunity to give an example to Britain, by recommending that such discrimination is an offensive anachronism that should be swept away.' Michael Matheson (SNP, Central Scotland) said, 'No community or individual should be treated as a second-class citizen by virtue of religion, race or other standing in society. The Act of Settlement serves as nothing other than a form of institutional bigotry. I sincerely hope that Westminster will take the views of this parliament seriously and will see this debate as a catalyst for a change that should take place.'

Although welcome, I would be concerned if the passing of this motion meant that the opposition parties in the Scottish parliament thought that no further action from them was necessary; that by this act alone the parliament had proved that there is no problem to be addressed concerning religious prejudice in Scotland. Some within the Catholic community actually consider that the offensive parts of the Act of Settlement are merely symbolic compared to the much more insidious prejudice that continues in Scotland.

The reaction of the UK government has been disappointing. In a response to a letter written by Lord James Douglas-Hamilton, the Prime Minister, Tony Blair, indicated that the repeal of the Act of Settlement was extremely complicated and would require the repeal and amendment of many other pieces of legislation as well as the constitutions of Commonwealth nations. Secretary of State John Reid tried to make light of the matter during a television debate on the subject but was seen to be seriously out of step with public opinion. In January 2000, Justice Minister and Deputy First Minister Jim Wallace indicated that the following year's census questionnaire in Scotland would not include a question about religious observance, despite such a question being included for the English census. Through pressure exerted by the parliament's Equal Opportunities Committee and academics he was forced into a U-turn. An important opportunity to quantify and track the religious diversity of Scotland was almost lost. This would have denied the baseline for those who would wish to conduct in-depth empirical research into the subject of religious intolerance in Scotland. Surely one of the most important factors in looking for ways of dealing with the problems of religious intolerance in Scotland is to have up-to-date information about how many people would claim a religious affiliation and how many would consider themselves Catholics, Jews, Protestants, Muslims and of other faiths or none in Scotland today.

The Scottish Executive claims not to be complacent about the subject, but the fact remains that their pronouncements so far have been lacking in specificity and clarity of purpose. When Tom McCabe (the Minister for Parliament) spoke in the Act of Settlement debate at the end of 1999, he said, 'We are focusing the work of this parliament on the scourge of domestic violence. We are focusing our work on ending child poverty. We want this parliament to commit money to the areas of greatest need. We hope that the whole parliament is determined to continue that work through the unprecedented power that we now have. We should pursue an end to discrimination with vigour but we should do it in a way that will not deny social progress across the country. In moving the amendment we condemn discrimination and acknowledge it has no place in a multi-faith, multi-cultural society.'[1]

I await with interest the various initiatives which have been anticipated at various stages by the Scottish Executive, and I am encouraged that they appear to have taken seriously the comments I made in August 1999. But in all their responses there is a reference to 'discrimination', which was only referred to tangentially in my speech. I was really talking about prejudice, which has been the focus of many contributions to this book. It is much more difficult to tackle prejudice, which is a cancer in the hearts of men and women and something felt subjectively by those against whom it is directed. It is more difficult to research empirically, and more difficult to eradicate it from society. Let us hope that the Scottish Executive does not ignore it as 'too difficult'. For, as Gerry Finn comments, various forms of low-level prejudice make the more virulent expressions of prejudice much more probable.

Whatever problems are tackled by official and unofficial initiatives, it is worth remembering that this is a time when, all over the world, there is exciting evidence of a universal desire for reconciliation. Some might feel uncomfortable about Peter Lynch's citation of the Northern Irish peace process, the South African Truth and Reconciliation Commission, the democratisation of East European states and the move for America to apologise for the slave trade as positive models from which we could learn here in Scotland. In all these instances, there is an opportunity to give recognition to past sins, to put them on public record, to say sorry, to forgive and to emerge into a better shared future with the slates of guilt and grudge wiped clean. Archbishop Desmond Tutu talks of 'opening wounds to cleanse them . . . [to] stop them from festering'. He says, 'You cannot forgive what you do not know.'

Lynch is careful to emphasise that Scotland's negative experiences with ethnic tension are nowhere near as bad as those in apartheid-ridden South Africa:

> However, it is not being suggested here that we copy the South African example, merely that we learn from it and recognise that there are dangers in allowing 'Scotland's shame' to continue unchallenged, either in the past or currently. We cannot just sweep sectarianism under the carpet and pretend it doesn't exist or that it is something that has been consigned to the past. We might have attempted this so far in Scotland, but the current debate shows how unsuccessful this approach has been.

His suggestion that the Scottish parliament establish a Special Commission to examine the issue of sectarianism in Scotland is a challenging and provocative one. Whatever forum emerges in the future, we need to be able to use it to come together as a diverse community, to forgive and receive absolution for the sins and prejudices of the past on all sides, to experience the healing embrace of reconciliation, and to say to one another, again with respect and gratitude but also with compassion and even love, 'I may not agree with you, but the free expression of your ideas allows me to see how things may not be as clear-cut as I had previously thought. *I had not thought about it like that before.'*

Notes

[1] Official Report, column 1629, Thursday, 16 December 1999.

INDEX